MODERN INSURANCE LAW

AUSTRALIA AND NEW ZEALAND
The Law Book Company Ltd.
Sydney : Melbourne : Perth

CANADA AND U.S.A.
The Carswell Company Ltd.
Agincourt, Ontario

INDIA
N. M. Tripathi Private Ltd.
Bombay
and
Eastern Law House Private Ltd.
Calcutta and Delhi
M.P.P. House
Bangalore

ISRAEL
Steimatzky's Agency Ltd.
Jerusalem : Tel Aviv : Haifa

MALAYSIA : SINGAPORE : BRUNEI
Malayan Law Journal (Pte.) Ltd.
Singapore and Kuala Lumpur

MODERN INSURANCE LAW

SECOND EDITION

By

JOHN BIRDS, LL.M.
Reader in Law, University of Sheffield

LONDON
SWEET & MAXWELL
1988

First Edition 1982
Second Edition 1988

Published by
Sweet & Maxwell Limited of
11, New Fetter Lane, London
Computerset by Promenade Graphics Limited, Cheltenham
Printed by Butler and Tanner Limited,
Frome, Somerset

British Library Cataloguing in Publication Data
Birds, John
  Modern insurance law.—2nd ed.
  1. Insurance Law—England
  I. Title
  344,206'86   KD1859

  ISBN 0–421–37140–4
  ISBN 0–421–37150–1 Pbk

All rights reserved.
No part of this publication may be
reproduced or transmitted, in any form
or by any means, electronic; mechanical, photocopying,
recording or otherwise, or stored in any retrieval
system of any nature, without the written permission
of the copyright holder and the publisher, application
for which shall be made to the publisher.

©
John Birds
1988

TO MY FAMILY

TO MY FAMILY

PREFACE

The courts have been fairly busy with insurance cases in the six years since the first edition of this book was published. Some of the decisions are of limited importance but a number are of great significance and the appropriate parts of the text have been rewritten to incorporate them. In particular, there have been several important cases on the doctrine of *uberrima fides* and a number concerning issues of insurable interest and subrogation. Perhaps the most significant case of all is *Banque Keyser Ullman* v. *Skandia Insurance* which is due to go to the Court of Appeal; the decision of that court is eagerly awaited. For the present all that I have been able to do is point out its potential significance if the first instance decision is upheld, at appropriate points. A broad duty on an insurer to display the utmost good faith could lead to a significant body of case-law over the next few years.

In contrast the legislature has, regrettably, not been very active in the area of insurance contract law. Certain aspects of insurance law are touched on by the Financial Services Act 1986, although the length of this book has not enabled me to do more than hint at the general scheme of investor protection established thereby for, *inter alia*, long-term insurance policyholders. In addition I have been able to deal with the draft regulations which will extend compulsory motor insurance as required by the EEC. However, there has been no implementation of the Law Commission's important Report No. 104 on Non-Disclosure and Breach of Warranty. Instead revised self-regulation has been adopted. As is stated at several points in the text, this may be regarded as unfortunate. Because the Report appears to have been shelved at least for the foreseeable future, I thought it right to cut down the consideration given to it, so that readers will have to refer elsewhere, not least of course to the Report itself, for the detail.

I hope that this second edition will continue to prove a useful guide to students of law and of insurance and, indeed, to practitioners in those fields. The cross-references to *MacGillivray and Parkington on Insurance Law*, which remains the best source of detailed reference, are to the paragraphs of the 8th edition of that book which should appear at more or less the same time as this appears.

My thanks are due to the staff at Sweet & Maxwell for their

encouragement and for preparing the Tables. I have tried to state the law as at June 1987, with some additional references inserted at proof stage.

John Birds
Faculty of Law
University of Sheffield
November 1987

CONTENTS

Preface	vii
Table of Cases	xiii
Table of Statutes	xxxv

1. **Introduction: The Nature and Definition of Insurance and Insurance Law**   1
   - Some classifications of insurance   5
   - The legal definition of insurance   7

2. **The Parties to the Contract of Insurance**   15
   - The regulation of insurers   15

3. **Insurable Interest**   24
   - Insurable interest in life insurance   26
   - Insurable interest in property insurance   36
   - Insurance of third parties' interests   46

4. **Formalities and Formation of the Insurance Contract**   53
   - Formation of the insurance contract   53
   - Formalities   58
   - Forming the contract at Lloyd's   60
   - Temporary cover and cover notes   61
   - Duration and renewal of insurance policies   67

5. **Void, Voidable and Illegal Policies**   72
   - Void contracts of insurance   72
   - Voidable contracts of insurance   74
   - Avoiding liability under a valid contract   75
   - Loss of the right to avoid the contracts or to avoid liability   76

6. **Fraud, Non-Disclosure and Misrepresentation**   78
   - Fraud   78
   - Misrepresentation   78
   - Non-Disclosure   80
   - Disclosure during the contract   94
   - Practice in and reform of non-disclosure and misrepresentation   96

Contents

7. **Warranties and Conditions**   99
   - Warranties   99
   - Clauses descriptive of the risk   109
   - Agents and the Proposal Form   111
   - Conditions   116
   - Practice in and reform of the Law of Warranties and Condition   119

8. **Premiums**   121
   - Return of premium   123

9. **Assignment**   128
   - Assignment of the subject-matter of insurance   128
   - Assignment of the benefit of an insurance policy   132
   - Assignment of the policy   135

10. **Intermediaries**   137
    - Agent of insurer or insured   138
    - Relevant agency principles   141
    - The regulation of intermediaries   151

11. **Construction and Causation: Risks Covered and Risks Excepted**   157
    - Introduction   157
    - General   158
    - Risk   161
    - Principles of construction   163
    - Specific descriptions and specific words   168
    - Cover provided—consequential points   182
    - Causation   185

12. **Claims under the Policy**   190
    - Public policy   190
    - The claims procedure   198
    - Fraudulent claims   209
    - Settlement claims   211

13. **The Measurement of Loss**   215
    - Total loss in the case of goods   217
    - Total loss in the case of land   219
    - Partial loss under an indemnity policy   221
    - The insured with a limited interest   224
    - Loss under a valued policy   225
    - Under-insurance   226

Excess and franchise clauses 227
Payment of interest 228

14. Reinstatement 229
Contractual reinstatement 229
Statutory reinstatement 232

15. Subrogation 236
The two aspects of subrogation 238
The insured cannot make a profit 239
The insurer's right to take action 243
The future of subrogation 257

16. Contribution and Double Insurance 259
The ratio of contribution 262
Conditions regarding double insurance 265

17. Life Insurance 270
Assignment of life policies 270
Trusts of life policies 273

18. Liability Insurance in General 280
Bankruptcy of the insured 280
Contractual provisions 284
Sums insured and costs 289
Insurer's duty to the victim 291

19. Motor Insurance 292
The scope of compulsory cover 293
Common terms and exceptions 298
Third parties' rights under the Road Traffic Act 306
Third parties' rights against the Motor Insurers' Bureau 311
Extension of compulsory requirements 318

20. Employer's Liability and other Compulsory Insurances 321
Employer's liability insurance 321
Other compulsory insurances 327

Index 329

TABLE OF CASES

Ackbar v. Green (C.F.) & Co. [1975] Q.B. 582; [1975] 2 W.L.R. 773; 119 S.J.
219; [1975] 2 All E.R. 65; [1975] 1 Lloyd's Rep. 673 146
Adams v. Andrews [1964] 2 Lloyd's Rep. 347; [235 L.T. 692] 313
Adams v. Dunne [1978] R.T.R. 281; [1978] Crim.L.R. 365, D.C. 296
Adamson (T.H.) & Sons v. Liverpool & London & Globe Insurance Co.
[1953] 2 Lloyd's Rep. 355; [104 L.J. 133] 200
Adie v. The Insurance Corporation (1898) 14 T.L.R. 544 .... 53, 57
Agnew Surpass Shoe Stores Ltd. v. Cummer-Yonge Investments Ltd.
(1973) 55 D.L.R. (3d) 248 252
Albert v. M.I.B. [1972] A.C. 301; [1971] 3 W.L.R. 291; 115 S.J. 588; [1971] 2
All E.R. 1345; [1972] R.T.R. 230; [1971] Lloyd's Rep. 229, H.L. 317
Albion Insurance Co. v. Government Insurance Office of New South Wales
(1969) 121 C.L.R. 342 .... 260, 261
Alchorne v. Favill (1825) 4 L.J.O.S.Ch. 47 230
Alder v. Moore [1961] 2 Q.B. 57; [1961] 2 W.L.R. 426; 105 S.J. 208; [1961] 1
All E.R. 1; [1960] 2 Lloyd's Rep. 325; [77 L.Q.R. 300; 24 M.L.R. 637],
C.A.; reversing [1959] 2 Lloyd's Rep. 487; [1959] C.L.Y. 388 167
Allen v. Robles. Compagnie Parisienne de Garantie, Third Party [1969] 1
W.L.R. 1193; [1969] 3 All E.R. 154; [1969] 2 Lloyd's Rep. 61; sub nom.
Allen v. Robles (1969) 113 S.J. 484, C.A. 209
Alliss-Chalmers Co. v. Fidelity & Deposit Co. of Maryland (1916) 114 L.T.
433; 32 T.L.R. 263, H.L. 54
Allobrogia Steamship Corporation, Re [1978] 3 All E.R. 423 281
Aluminium Wire and Cable Co. Ltd. v. Allstate Insurance Co. Ltd. [1985] 2
Lloyd's Rep. 280 289
American Surety Co. of New York v. Wrightson (1910) 103 L.T. 663; 27
T.L.R. 91; 16 Com.Cas. 37 264
Anctil v. Manufacturers' Life Insurance Co. [1899] A.C. 604; 68 L.J.C.P.
123; 81 L.T. 279, P.C. 31, 77
Anderson v. Commercial Union Assurance Co. 34 W.R. 189; 1 T.L.R. 511,
D.C.; affirming (1885) 55 L.J.Q.B. 146, C.A. 231, 232
—— v. Fitzgerald (1853) 4 H.L.Cas. 484; 21 L.T.O.S. 245; 17 Jur. 995; 10
E.R. 551, H.L. 106, 124
—— v. Norwich Union Fire Insurance Society [1977] 1 Lloyd's Rep. 253,
C.A. 166
—— v. Pacific Fire & Marine Insurance Society (1872) L.R. 7 C.P. 65; 26
L.T. 130; 20 W.R. 280; 1 Asp.M.L.C. 220 83
Andrews v. Patriotic Assurance Co. (1886) 18 L.R.Ir. 355 233
Anglo-African Merchants v. Bayley [1970] 1 Q.B. 311; [1969] 2 W.L.R. 686;
113 S.J. 281; [1969] 2 All E.R. 421; sub nom. Anglo-African Merchants
and Exmouth Clothing Co. v. Bayley [1969] 1 Lloyd's Rep. 268 138,
140, 146
Anstey v. British Natural Premium Life Association Ltd. (1908) 99 L.T. 765;
24 T.L.R. 871, C.A.; affirming 99 L.T. 16; 24 T.L.R. 594 76
Arterial Caravans Ltd. v. Yorkshire Insurance Co. [1973] 1 Lloyd's Rep. 169 91
Aubrey (Richard) Film Productions Ltd. v. Graham [1960] 2 Lloyd's Rep.
101 217

xiii

Table of Cases

Austin v. Drewe (1816) 6 Taint. 436; 2 Marsh. 130; 128 E.R. 1104 .... 170, 184
—— v. Zurich General Accident & Liability Insurance Co. [1945] K.B. 250;
   [1945] 1 All E.R. 316; 114 L.J.K.B. 340; 172 L.T. 174; 61 T.L.R. 214; 78
   Ll.L.Rep. 185, C.A. 259, 267
Australian Agricultural Co. v. Saunders (1875) L.R. 10 C.P. 668; 44 L.J.C.P.
   391; 33 L.T. 447; 3 Asp.M.L.C. 63, Ex.Ch.; affirming (1872) 28 L.T.
   844 267
Australia and New Zealand Bank v. Colonial and Eagle Wharves Ltd., Boag
   (Third Party) [1960] 2 Lloyd's Rep. 241 84
Ayrey v. British Legal & United Provident Assurance Co. [1918] 1 K.B. 136;
   87 L.J.K.B. 513; 118 L.T. 255; 34 T.L.R. 111 .... 85, 145
B. (A Minor) v. Knight [1981] R.T.R. 136 295
Babatsikos v. Car Owners' Mutual Insurance Co. [1970] 2 Lloyd's Rep. 314 . 89
Banque Keyser Ullman S.A. v. Skandia Insurance Co. [1987] Lloyd's Rep.
   69 80
Barnes v. London, Edinburgh & Glasgow Life Assurance Co. Ltd. [1892] 1
   Q.B. 864; 8 T.L.R. 143; 36 S.J. 125, D.C. 31
Barnett, (Arthur) Ltd. v. National Insurance Co. of New Zealand [1965]
   N.Z.L.R. 874 246
Barrett v. London General Insurance Co. [1935] 1 K.B. 238; 104 L.J.K.B. 15;
   152 L.T. 256; 51 T.L.R. 97; 78 S.J. 898; 40 Com.Cas. 125; 50 Ll.L.Rep.
   99 303
Barrett Bros. (Taxis) v. Davies (Lickiss and Milestone Motor Policies at
   Lloyd's, Third Parties) [1966] 1 W.L.R. 1334; 110 S.J. 600; sub nom.
   Lickiss v. Milestone Motor Policies at Lloyd's [1966] 2 All E.R. 972;
   [1966] 2 Lloyd's Rep. 1, C.A. 116, 201, 202, 207, 284
Bauman v. Royal Indemnity Co. (1961) 36 N.J. 12 160
Bawden v. London, Edinburgh & Glasgow Assurance Co. [1892] 2 Q.B.
   534; 61 L.J.Q.B. 792; 57 J.P. 116; 8 T.L.R. 566; 36 S.J. 502, C.A. 112, 113
Bazeley v. Forder (1868) L.R. 3 Q.B. 559; 9 B. & S. 599; sub nom. Baseley v.
   Forder 37 L.J.Q.B. 237; 18 L.T. 756; 32 J.P. 550 29
Beach v. Pearl Assurance Co. Ltd. [1938] 1 A.C.Rep. 3 54
Beacon Carpets Ltd. v. Kirby [1985] Q.B. 755; [1984] 3 W.L.R. 489; (1984)
   128 S.J. 549; [1984] 2 All E.R. 726; (1984) 48 P. & C.R. 445; (1984) 81
   L.S.Gaz. 1603, C.A. 51, 52
Beacon Insurance Co. v. Langdale [1939] 4 All E.R. 209; 83 S.J. 908; 65
   Ll.L.Rep. 57, C.A. 285
Beauchamp v. National Mutual Indemnity Insurance Co. [1937] 3 All E.R.
   19 102
Becker, Gray & Co. v. London Assurance Corporation [1918] A.C. 101;
   [1916–1917] All E.R. Rep. 146; 87 L.J.K.B. 69; 117 L.T. 609; 34 T.L.R.
   36; 62 S.J. 35; 14 Asp.M.L.C. 156; 23 Com.Cas. 205, H.L.; affirming
   [1915] 3 K.B. 410; [1916] 2 K.B. 156, C.A. 184, 185, 187
Bedford Insurance Co. v. Instituto de Ressaguros do Brazil [1985] Q.B. 966;
   [1984] 3 W.L.R. 726; (1984) 128 S.J. 701; [1984] 3 All E.R. 766; [1984] 1
   Lloyd's Rep. 210; [1985] F.L.R. 49; [1984] L.M.C.L.Q. 386; (1984) 134
   New L.J. 34; (1985) 82 L.S.Gaz. 37 15
Bell v. Lever Bros. [1932] A.C. 161; [1931] All E.R.Rep. 1; 101 L.J.K.B. 129;
   146 L.T. 258; 48 T.L.R. 133; 76 S.J. 50; 37 Com.Cas. 98, H.L.;
   reversing S.C. sub nom. Lever Bros. Ltd. v. Bell [1931] 1 K.B. 574,
   C.A. 213
Beller, (Marcel) Ltd. v. Haydon [1978] Q.B. 694; [1978] 2 W.L.R. 845; (1977)
   122 S.J. 279; [1978] 3 All E.R. 111; [1978] R.T.R. 344; [1978] 1 Lloyd's
   Rep. 472 .... 32, 172, 173, 175, 179

Table of Cases

Beresford v. Royal Insurance Co. [1938] A.C. 586 .... 161, 190, 191, 192
Berger v. Pollock [1973] 2 Lloyd's Rep. 442 89
Beswick v. Beswick [1968] A.C. 58; [1967] 3 W.L.R. 932; 111 S.J. 540; [1967] 2
   All E.R. 1197; [83 L.Q.R. 687; 31 M.L.R. 342], H.L.; affirming [1966]
   Ch. 538; [1966] 3 W.L.R. 396; 110 S.J. 507; [1966] 3 All E.R. 1; [1966]
   C.L.Y. 1915; [27 M.L.R. 657], C.A.; reversing [1965] 3 All E.R. 858;
   [1965] C.L.Y. 632; [110 S.J. 641] 275, 276
Biddle v. Johnston 109 S.J. 395; [1965] 2 Lloyd's Rep. 121 297
Biggar v. Rock Life Assurance Co. [1902] 1 K.B. 516; 71 L.J.K.B. 79; 85 L.T.
   636; 18 T.L.R. 119; 46 S.J. 105 .... 112, 116
Black King Shipping Corp. v. Massie Litsion Pride, The [1985] 1 Lloyd's
   Rep. 437; (1984) 134 New L.J. 887 .... 80, 210
Blackley v. National Mutual Life Association of Australasia [1972] N.Z.L.R.
   1038 .... 86, 145
Blanchette v. C.I.S. Ltd. (1973) 36 D.L.R. (3d) 561 .... 114, 115, 116
Boardman v. Phipps [1967] 2 A.C. 46; [1966] 3 W.L.R. 1009; 110 S.J. 853;
   [1966] 3 All E.R. 721; [31 Conv. 63] H.L.; affirming sub nom. Phipps v.
   Boardman [1965] Ch. 992; [1965] 2 W.L.R. 839; 109 S.J. 197; [1965] 1
   All E.R. 849; [29 Conv. 233; 28 M.L.R. 587], C.A.; affirming [1964] 1
   W.L.R. 993; 108 S.J. 619; [1964] 2 All E.R. 187, [114 L.J. 813, 20 Conv.
   310; 98 I.L.T. 275]; [1964] C.L.Y. 3345; [1965] C.L.Y. 3575 145
Boehm v. Bell (1799) 8 T.R. 154; 101 E.R. 1318 42
Bolton Partners v. Lambert (1888) 41 Ch.D. 295; 58 L.J.Ch. 425; 60 L.T. 687;
   on appeal (1889) 41 Ch.D. 302, C.A. 143
Bond Air Services Ltd. v. Hill [1955] 2 Q.B. 417; [1955] 2 W.L.R. 1194; 99 S.J.
   370; [1955] 2 All E.R. 476; [1955] 1 Lloyd's Rep. 498 119
Boss v. Kingston [1963] 1 W.L.R. 99; 106 S.J. 1053; [1963] 1 All E.R. 177; 61
   L.G.R. 109; sub nom. Boss and Hansford v. Kingston [1962] 2 Lloyd's
   Rep. 431, D.C. 131
Bowskill v. Dawson (No. 2) [1955] 1 Q.B. 13; [1954] 3 W.L.R. 275; 98 S.J. 523;
   [1954] 2 All E.R. 649; [21 Sol. 255], C.A. 278
Bradley and Essex and Suffolk Accident Indemnity Society, Re [1912] 1 K.B.
   415; [1911–1913] All E.R.Rep. 444; 81 L.J.K.B. 523; 105 L.T. 919; 28
   T.L.R. 175, C.A. 80, 118, 160, 326
Braunstein v. Accidental Death Insurance Co. (1861) 1 B. & S. 782; 31
   L.J.Q.B. 17; 5 L.T. 550; 8 Jur.N.S. 506; 121 E.R. 904 201
British and Foreign Marine Insurance Co. v. Gaunt [1921] 2 A.C. 41; [1921]
   All E.R.Rep. 447; 90 L.J.K.B. 801; 125 L.T. 491; 37 T.L.R. 632; 65 S.J.
   551; 15 Asp.M.L.C. 305; 26 Com.Cas. 247; 7 Ll.L.Rep. 62, H.L.;
   affirming S.C. sub nom. Gaunt v. British and Foreign Insurance
   Co. Ltd. & Standard Marine Insurance Co. Ltd. [1920] 1 K.B. 903,
   C.A. 169
British Bank of the Middle East v. Sun Life Assurance Co. of Canada (U.K.)
   Ltd. [1983] 2 Lloyd's Rep. 9; [1983] Com.L.R. 187; (1983) 133 New
   L.J. 575, H.L. 143
British Traders' Insurance Co. v. Monson (1964) 38 A.L.J.R. 20; 111 C.L.R.
   86 .... 36, 46, 51, 224, 234
British Workmen's & General Assurance Co. v. Cunliffe (1902) 18 T.L.R.
   502, C.A. 126, 127
Britton v. Royal Insurance Co. (1866) 4 F. & F. 905; 15 L.T. 72, N.P. .. 161, 209
Brook v. Trafalgar Insurance Co. (1946) 79 Ll.L.Rep. 365 .... 142, 201, 209
Brown v. Roberts [1965] 1 Q.B. 1; [1963] 3 W.L.R. 75; 107 S.J. 666; [1963] 2
   All E.R. 263; sub nom. Brown v. Roberts and Nicholls [1963] 1 Lloyd's
   Rep. 314 295

Table of Cases

Brown v. Royal Insurance Co. (1859) 1 El. & El. 853; 28 L.J.Q.B. 275; 33 L.T.O.S. 134; 5 Jur.N.S. 1255; 7 W.R. 479; 120 E.R. 1131 .... 230, 231, 232
—— v. Zurich General Accident & Liability Insurance Co. [1954] 2 Lloyd's Rep. 243; [99 S.J. 19] 304
Browning v. Phoenix Assurance Co. Ltd. [1960] 2 Lloyd's Rep. 360 302
Buchanan v. Motor Insurers' Bureau [1955] 1 W.L.R. 488; 119 J.P. 227; 99 S.J. 319; [1955] 1 All E.R. 607; [1954] 2 Lloyd's Rep. 519 313
Buckland v. Palmer [1984] 1 W.L.R. 1109; (1984) 128 S.J. 565; [1984] 3 All E.R. 554; [1985] R.T.R. 5; (1984) 81 L.S.Gaz. 2300, C.A. 248
Bugge v. Taylor [1941] 1 K.B. 198 294
Burnand v. Rodocanachi (1882) 7 App.Cas. 333; 51 L.J.Q.B. 548; 47 L.T. 277; 31 W.R. 65; 4 Asp.M.L.C. 576 .... 27, 225, 237, 242
Burridge v. Haines (1918) 87 L.J.K.B. 641; 118 L.T. 681; 62 S.J. 521 208
Burts & Harvey Ltd. v. Vulcan Boiler & General Insurance Co. [1966] 1 Lloyd's Rep. 354 228
C.T.I. International Inc. v. The Oceanus Mutual Underwriting Association (Bermuda). *See* Container Transport International Inc. v. Oceanus Mutual Underwriting Association.
Canadian General Electric Co. v. Liverpool & London & Globe Insurance Co. (1980) 106 D.L.R. (3d) 750 184
Canadian Indemnity Co. v. Walken Machinery & Equipment Ltd. (1975) 52 D.L.R. (3d) 1 .... 176, 178
Candler v. London & Lancashire Guarantee & Accident Co. of Canada (1963) 40 D.L.R. (2d) 408 172
Canning v. Farquhar (1886) 16 Q.B.D. 727; 55 L.J.Q.B. 225; 54 L.T. 350; 34 W.R. 423; 2 T.L.R. 386, C.A. 55, 56, 70
Carr and Sun Ins., Re (1897) 13 T.L.R. 186, C.A. 211
Carreras Ltd. v. Cunard Steamship Co. [1918] 1 K.B. 118; 87 L.J.K.B. 824; 118 L.T. 106; 34 T.L.R. 41 227
Carter v. Boehm (1766) 3 Burr. 1905; 1 Wm.Bl. 593; 97 E.R. 1162 ...... 80, 82, 85, 89
Carter Bros. v. Renouf (1962) 36 A.L.J.R. 67 35
Cassel v. Lancashire & Yorkshire Accident Insurance Co. (1885) 1 T.L.R. 495 200
Castellain v. Preston (1883) 11 Q.B.D. 380; 52 L.J.Q.B. 366; 49 L.J. 29; 31 W.R. 557, C.A. 129, 224, 236, 238, 239, 252
Central Bank of India v. Guardian Assurance Co. (1936) 54 Ll.L.R. 247 .... 210, 211
Chadwick v. Gibraltar General Insurance Co. (1981) 34 O.R. (2d) 488 42
Chandris v. Argo Insurance Co. [1963] 2 Lloyd's Rep. 65; 107 S.J. 575 282
Cherry Ltd. v. Allied Insurance Brokers Ltd. [1978] 1 Lloyd's Rep. 274 147
Church and General Insurance Co. v. Connolly (1983) unreported, noted (1983) 5 D.U.L.J.(N.S.) 291 52
Cipriani v. Barnett [1933] A.C. 83 316
City Tailors Ltd. v. Evans (1921) 91 L.J.K.B. 379; 126 L.T. 439; [1921] All E.R.Rep. 399; 38 T.L.R. 230; 9 Ll.L.Rep. 46, C.A. 44
Clark & Sons v. Finnamore (1973) 32 D.L.R. (3d) 236 248
Clarke v. National Insurance and Guarantee Corporation [1964] 1 Q.B. 199; [1963] 3 W.L.R. 710; 107 S.J. 573; [1963] 3 All E.R. 375; [1963] 2 Lloyd's Rep. 35, C.A.; reversing [1963] 2 Q.B. 790; [1963] 2 W.L.R. 1396; 107 S.J. 317; [1963] 2 All E.R. 470; [1963] 1 Lloyd's Rep. 322 304
—— v. Clarke v. Vedel [1979] R.T.R. 26, C.A. 318

Table of Cases   xvii

Cleaver v. Mutual Reserve Fund Life Assurance [1892] 1 Q.B. 147; 61 L.J.Q.B. 128; 66 L.T. 220; 56 J.P. 180; 40 W.R. 230; 8 T.L.R. 139; 36 S.J. 106, C.A. 276
Clidero v. Scottish Accident Insurance Co. (1892) 19 R. 355; 29 Sc.L.R. 303 .. 173
Clough v. County Livestock Insurance Association (1916) 85 L.J.K.B. 1185; 32 T.L.R. 526; 60 S.J. 642; W.C. & Ms.Rep. 373 205
Clover, Clayton & Co. Ltd. v. Hughes [1910] A.C. 242; [1908–1910] All E.R.Rep. 220; 79 L.J.K.B. 470; 102 L.T. 340; 26 T.L.R. 359; 3 B.W.C.C. 275; sub nom. Hughes v. Clover, Clayton & Co. 54 S.J. 374, H.L. 176
Cobb v. Williams [1973] R.T.R. 113 295
Coleman's Depositories Ltd. & Life & Health Assurance Association, Re [1907] 2 K.B. 798; [1904–1907] All E.R.Rep. 383; 76 L.J.K.B. 865; 97 L.T. 420; 23 T.L.R. 638, C.A. 65, 66, 67
Collingridge v. Royal Exchange Assurance Corporation (1877) 3 Q.B.D. 173; 47 L.J.Q.B. 32; 37 L.T. 525; 42 J.P. 118; 26 W.R. 112 129
Commercial Union Assurance Co. v. Hayden [1977] Q.B. 804; [1977] 2 W.L.R. 272; [1977] 1 All E.R. 441; [1977] 1 Lloyd's Rep. 1, C.A. 263
—— v. Lister (1874) L.R. 9 Ch. 483; 43 L.J.Ch. 601. L.JJ. 245
Commonwealth Construction Co. v. Imperial Oil (1976) 69 D.L.R. (3d) 558 .... 51, 253, 256
Commonwealth Smelting v. Guardian Royal Exchange Assurance [1986] 1 Lloyd's Rep. 121, C.A.; affirming [1984] 2 Lloyd's Rep. 608; (1984) 134 New L.J. 1018 170
Compania Columbiana de Seguros v. Pacific Steam Navigation Co.; Empresa de Telefono de Bogota v. Same [1965] 1 Q.B. 101; [1964] 2 W.L.R. 484; 108 S.J. 75; [1964] 1 All E.R. 216; [1963] 2 Lloyd's Rep. 479; [28 Conv. 176] 249
Conn v. Westminster Motor Insurance Association [1966] 1 Lloyd's Rep. 407; 116 New L.J. 894, C.A.; reversing [1966] 1 Lloyd's Rep. 123; 116 New L.J. 554 .... 105, 305
Constitution Insurance Co. of Canada v. Kosmopoulos (1987) 34 D.L.R. (4th) 208 .... 40, 41
Container Transport International Inc. v. Oceanus Mutual Underwriting Association (Bermuda) [1984] 1 Lloyd's Rep. 476, C.A.; reversing [1982] 2 Lloyd's Rep. 178; [1982] Com.L.R. 68 88
Cooper v. Motor Insurers' Bureau [1985] Q.B. 575; [1985] 2 W.L.R. 248; (1985) 129 S.J. 32; [1985] 1 All E.R. 449; [1985] R.T.R. 273; [1985] F.L.R. 175; (1985) 82 L.S.Gaz. 202, C.A.; affirming [1983] 1 W.L.R. 592 294
Co-operative Fire & Casualty Co. v. Saindon (1975) 56 D.L.R. (3d) 556 196
Corfield v. Groves [1950] W.N. 116; 66 T.L.R. (Pt. 1) 627; 94 S.J. 225; [1950] 1 All E.R. 488 297
Cornish v. Accident Insurance Co. (1889) 23 Q.B.D. 453; 58 L.J.Q.B. 591; 54 J.P. 262; 38 W.R. 139; 5 T.L.R. 733, C.A. 172
Cousins v. Sun Life Assurance Society [1933] Ch. 126 274
Cousins, H. & Co. Ltd. v. D. & C. Carriers Ltd. [1971] 2 Q.B. 230; [1971] 2 W.L.R. 85; (1970) 114 S.J. 882; [1971] 1 All E.R. 55; [1970] 2 Lloyd's Rep. 397, C.A. 243, 248
Coward v. Motor Insurers' Bureau [1963] 1 Q.B. 259; [1962] 2 W.L.R. 663; 106 S.J. 34; [1962] 1 All E.R. 531; [1962] 1 Lloyd's Rep. 1; [25 M.L.R. 458], C.A.; affirming [1961] 1 Lloyd's Rep. 583; [1961] C.L.Y. 7879 317
Cox v. Orion Insurance Co. Ltd. [1982] R.T.R. 1, C.A. 76, 104
Craine v. Colonial Mutual Fire Insurance Co. Ltd. sub nom. Yorkshire Insurance v. Craine (1920) 28 C.L.R. 305; [1922] 2 A.C. 541 207

Table of Cases

Crisci v. Security Co. (1967) 66 Cal. (2d) 425; 426 P. (2d) 173 285
Cross v. British Oak Insurance Co. [1938] 2 K.B. 167; [1938] 1 All E.R. 383;
    107 L.J.K.B. 577; 159 L.T. 286; 60 Ll.L.Rep. 46 .... 291, 309
Dalby v. India and London Life Assurance Co. (1854) 15 C.B. 365; 3 C.L.R.
    61; 24 L.J.C.P. 2; 24 L.T.O.S. 182; 18 Jur. 1024; 3 W.R. 116; 139 E.R.
    465, Ex.Ch. 27
Darrell v. Tibbitts (1880) 5 Q.B.D. 560; 50 L.J.Q.B. 33; 42 L.T. 797; 44 J.P.
    695; 29 W.R. 66, C.A. 238, 239, 251
Davjoyda Estates v. National Insurance Co. of New Zealand Ltd. (1967) 65
    S.R. (N.S.W.) 381 .... 38, 43, 51, 52
Dawson v. Bankers' & Traders' Insurance Co. [1957] V.R. 491 260
—— v. Monarch Insurance Co. of New Zealand [1977] 1 N.Z.L.R. 372 64
Dawsons Ltd. v. Bonnin [1922] 2 A.C. 413; [1922] All E.R.Rep. 88; 91
    L.J.P.C. 210; 128 L.T. 1; 38 T.L.R. 836; 11 Ll.L.Rep. 57; 12 Ll.L.Rep.
    237, H.L. 102, 106
De Hahn v. Hartley (1786) 1 T.R. 343; 99 E.R. 1130 100
De Maurier (Jewels) Ltd. v. Bastion Insurance and Coronet Insurance Co.
    [1967] 2 Lloyd's Rep. 550; sub nom. De Maurier Jewels v. Bastion
    Insurance Co. (1967) 117 New L.J. 1112 .... 104, 109
Department of Trade and Industry v. St. Christopher Motorists' Association Ltd. [1974] 1 W.L.R. 99; (1973) 117 S.J. 873; [1974] 1 All E.R. 395;
    [1974] 1 Lloyd's Rep. 17 .... 7, 10, 11
Derry v. Peek (1889) 14 App.Cas. 337; 58 L.J.Ch. 864; 61 L.T. 265; 54 J.P. 148;
    38 W.R. 33; 5 T.L.R. 625; 1 Heg. 292, H.L.; reversing sub nom. Peek v.
    Derry (1887) 37 Ch.D. 541, C.A. 78
Dicks v. S.A. Mutual Fire & General Insurance Co. [1963] (4) S.A. 501 62
Digby v. General Accident Fire and Life Assurance Corporation [1942] 2 All
    E.R. 319; [1943] A.C. 121; 111 L.J.K.B. 628; 167 L.T. 222; 58 T.L.R.
    375; 87 S.J. 29; 73 Ll.L.Rep. 175, H.L. 300
Distillers Co. v. Ajax Insurance Co. (1974) 48 A.L.J.R. 136, High Ct. of
    Australia 286, 287
Duckett v. Williams (1834) 2 C. & M. 348; 4 Tyr. 240; 3 L.J.Ex. 141; 149 E.R.
    794 .... 106, 124
Dunbar (A.J.) v. A. & B. Painters and Economic Insurance Co. and
    Whitehouse Co. [1986] 2 Lloyd's Rep. 38, C.A.; [1985] 2 Lloyd's Rep.
    616 .... 111, 150, 151
Eagle Star Insurance Co. v. Spratt [1971] 2 Lloyd's Rep. 116, C.A.; reversing
    [1971] 1 Lloyd's Rep. 295 .... 61, 142
Eaton, (T.) Co. Ltd. v. Smith (1977) 92 D.L.R. (3d) 425 252
Ecclesiastical Commissioners v. Royal Exchange Assurance Corporation
    (1895) 11 T.L.R. 476; 39 S.J. 623 129
Edmunds v. Lloyds Italico & l'Ancora Compagnia di Assicurazioni &
    Riassicurazione SpA [1986] 1 W.L.R. 492; (1986) 130 S.J. 242; [1986] 2
    All E.R. 249; [1986] 1 Lloyd's Rep. 326; (1986) 83 L.S.Gaz. 876, C.A. ... 216
Edwards (John) & Co. v. Motor Union Insurance Co. Ltd. [1922] 2 K.B. 249;
    91 L.J.K.B. 921; 128 L.T. 276; 38 T.L.R. 690; 16 Asp.M.L.C. 89; 27
    Com.Cas. 367; 11 Ll.L.Rep. 122, 170 .... 25, 239
Eisinger v. General Accident Fire and Life Assurance Corporation [1955] 1
    W.L.R. 869; 99 S.J. 511; [1953] 2 All E.R. 897; [1955] 2 Lloyd's Rep. 95;
    [18 M.L.R. 613] 181
Elcock v. Thomson [1949] 2 K.B. 755; 65 T.L.R. 566; 93 S.J. 562; [1949] 2 All
    E.R. 381; 82 Ll.L.Rep. 892; [13 M.L.R. 97] 225
Elizabeth v. Motor Insurers' Bureau, The Times, March 3, 1981 316

Table of Cases

Elliot v. Grey [1960] 1 Q.B. 367; [1959] 3 W.L.R. 956; 124 J.P. 58; 103 S.J. 921; [1959] 3 All E.R. 733; *sub nom.* Elliot v. Gray, 57 L.G.R. 357, D.C. 294
Engelbach, *Re*; Tibbetts v. Engelbach [1924] 2 Ch. 348; [1923] All E.R.Rep. 93; L.J.Ch. 616; 130 L.T. 401; 68 S.J. 208 .... 274, 276
English v. Western [1940] 2 K.B. 156; [1940] 2 All E.R. 515; 109 L.J.K.B. 728; 162 L.T. 370; 56 T.L.R. 680; 84 S.J. 465; 67 Ll.L.Rep. 45, C.A. .. 166, 167
Equitable Fire & Accident Insurance Co. v. Ching Wo Hong [1907] A.C. 96; 76 L.J.P.C. 31; 96 L.T. 1; 23 T.L.R. 200, P.C. 268
Euro-Diam Ltd. v. Bathurst [1987] 1 Lloyd's Rep. 178 191
Evans v. Bignold (1869) L.R. 4 Q.B. 622; 10 B. & S. 621; 38 L.J.Q.B. 293; 20 L.T. 659; 17 W.R. 882 33
—— v. Employers' Mutual Insurance Association [1936] 1 K.B. 505; 105 L.J.K.B. 141; 154 L.T. 137; [1935] All E.R.Rep. 659 286
Everett v. Desborough (1829) 5 Bing. 503; 3 Moo. & P. 190; 7 L.J.O.S.C.P. 223; 130 E.R. 1155 79
—— v. Hogg, Robinson & Gardner Mountain (Insurance) [1973] 2 Lloyd's Rep. 217 151
—— v. London Assurance Co. (1865) 19 C.B.N.S. 126; 6 New Rep. 234; 34 L.J.C.P. 299; 11 Jur.N.S. 546; 13 W.R. 862; 144 E.R. 734 170
Ewer v. National Employers' Mutual General Insurance Association [1937] 2 All E.R. 193; (1937) 157 L.T. 16; 53 T.L.R. 485; 57 Ll.L.Rep. 172 .... 91, 210, 217
Exchange Theatre Ltd. v. Iron Trades Mutual Ins. Co. Ltd. [1984] 1 Lloyd's Rep. 149, C.A.; affirming [1983] 1 Lloyd's Rep. 674 95
Facer v. Vehicle & General Insurance Co. [1965] 1 Lloyd's Rep. 113 113
Farmers' Mutual Insurance Co. v. New Holland Turnpike Road Co. (1888) 122 Pa. 37 41
Farnham v. Royal Insurance Co. [1976] 2 Lloyd's Rep. 437 95
Farr v. Motor Traders' Mutual Insurance Society [1920] 3 K.B. 669; 90 L.J.K.B. 215; 123 L.T. 765; 36 T.L.R. 711, C.A. 109
Farrell v. Federated Employers' Insurance Association Ltd. [1970] 1 W.L.R. 1400; 114 S.J. 719; [1970] 3 All E.R. 632; [1970] 2 Lloyd's Rep. 170; affirming [1970] 1 W.L.R. 498 .... 207, 283, 325
Fenton v. Thorley & Co. Ltd. [1903] A.C. 443 176
Field v. Receiver of Metropolitan Police [1907] 2 K.B. 853 165
Fire, Auto & Marine Insurance Co. v. Greene [1964] 2 Q.B. 687; [1964] 3 W.L.R. 319; 108 S.J. 603; [1964] 2 All E.R. 761; [1964] 2 Lloyd's Rep. 72 317
Fire & All Risks Co. Ltd. v. Powell [1966] V.R. 513 194
Fleetwood's Policy, *Re* [1926] Ch. 48; [1925] All E.R.Rep. 262; 95 L.J.Ch. 195; 133 L.T. 374 274
Forney v. Dominion Insurance Co. Ltd. [1969] 1 W.L.R. 928; 113 S.J. 326; [1969] 3 All E.R. 831; [1969] 1 Lloyd's Rep. 502 290
Foster, *Re* [1938] 3 All E.R. 357 276
——, *Re* [1966] 1 W.L.R. 222; 110 S.J. 151; [1966] 1 All E.R. 432 .... 276, 277
Fraser v. Furman (B.N.) (Productions), Miller Smith & Co. (A Firm) Third Party [1967] 1 W.L.R. 898; [1967] 3 All E.R. 57; 2 K.I.R. 483; [1967] 2 Lloyd's Rep. 1; *sub nom.* Fraser v. Furman (B.N.) (Productions), Miller Smith & Co. (A Firm) Third Party (1967) 111 S.J. 471; [84 L.Q.R. 11], C.A. 151, 289
Freeman & Lockyer v. Buckhurst Park Properties [1964] 2 Q.B. 480; [1964] 2 W.L.R. 618; 108 S.J. 96; [1964] 1 All E.R. 630; [114 L.J. 367; 108 S.J. 722], C.A. 142
Freshwater v. Western Australian Assurance Co. [1933] 1 K.B. 515; 102 L.J.K.B. 75; 148 L.T. 275; 49 T.L.R. 131; 76 S.J. 888, C.A. 283

Table of Cases

Gale v. Motor Union Insurance Co.; Loyst v. General Accident Fire & Life Assurance Corporation Ltd. [1928] 1 K.B. 359; [1926] All E.R.Rep. 170; 96 L.J.K.B. 199; 138 L.T. 712; 43 T.L.R. 15; 70 S.J. 1140; 26 Ll.L.Rep. 65 .... 264, 266
Gardner v. Moore [1984] A.C. 548; [1984] 2 W.L.R. 714; (1984) 128 S.J. 282; [1984] 1 All E.R. 1100; [1984] R.T.R. 209; [1984] 2 Lloyd's Rep. 135; (1984) 81 L.S.Gaz. 1444, H.L. 194
Gedge v. Royal Exchange Assurance Corporation [1900] 2 Q.B. 214; 69 L.J.Q.B. 506; 82 L.T. 463; 16 T.L.R. 344; 9 Asp.M.L.C. 57; 5 Com.Cas. 229 35
Geismar v. Sun Alliance & London Insurance [1978] Q.B. 383; [1978] 2 W.L.R. 38; (1977) 121 S.J. 201; [1977] 3 All E.R. 570; [1977] 2 Lloyd's Rep. 62; [1977] Crim.L.R. 475 191
General Accident Insurance Corporation v. Cronk (1901) 17 T.L.R. 233; 45 S.J. 261, D.C. 54, 57, 65
General Accident, Fire and Life Assurance Corporation Ltd. and Drysdale v. Midland Bank Ltd., Scoffin & Willmott Ltd. and Plant Bros. Ltd. (In Liquidation) [1940] 2 K.B. 388; [1940] 3 All E.R. 252; 110 L.J.K.B. 177; 164 L.T. 33; 56 T.L.R. 905; 84 S.J. 548; 45 Com.Cas. 309; 67 Ll.L.Rep. 218, C.A. 211
General Assurance Society v. Chandermull Jain A.I.R. (1966) S.C. 1644 68
General Omnibus Co. Ltd. v. London General Insurance Co. Ltd. [1936] I.R. 596 288
General Reinsurance Corp. v. Forsakringsaktiebolaget Fennia Patria [1983] Q.B. 856; [1983] 3 W.L.R. 318; (1983) 127 S.J. 389; [1983] 2 Lloyd's Rep. 287, C.A.; [1982] Q.B. 1022; [1982] 2 W.L.R. 528; (1982) 126 S.J. 32; [1982] 1 Lloyd's Rep. 87; [1981] Com.L.R. 280 61
Gerhardt v. Continental Insurance Companies and Firemen's Insurance Co. of Newark [1967] 1 Lloyd's Rep. 380 .... 160, 169
Gibson v. Sun Life Assurance Co. of Canada (1985) 7 C.C.L.I. 65 237
Gladitz, Re, Guaranty Executor & Trustee Co. Ltd. v. Gladitz [1937] Ch. 588; [1937] 3 All E.R. 173; 106 L.J.Ch. 254; 157 L.T. 163; 53 T.L.R. 857; 81 S.J. 527 274
Glasgow Assurance Corporation v. Symondson (1911) 16 Com.Cas. 109 81
Glen v. Lewis (1853) 8 Ex. 607; 1 C.L.R. 187; 22 L.J.Ex. 228; 21 L.T.O.S. 115; 17 Jur. 842; 155 E.R. 1494 95
Glen Falls Insurance v. Spencer (1956) 3 D.L.R. (2d) 745 183
Glenlight Shipping Ltd. v. Excess Insurance Ltd. 1983 S.L.T. 241 173
Glicksman v. Lancashire & General Assurance Co. [1927] A.C. 139; 136 L.T. 263; 43 T.L.R. 46; 70 S.J. 1111; 32 Com.Cas. 62; [1926] All E.R.Rep. 161; affirming [1925] 2 K.B. 593 .... 86, 90, 91
Globe & Rutgers Fire Insurance Co. v. Truedell [1927] 2 D.L.R. 659; 60 O.L.R. 227 245
Glyn v. Scottish Union & National Insurance Co. (1963) 40 D.L.R. (2d) 929 .... 48, 237
Godfrey v. Britannic Assurance Co. Ltd. [1963] 107 S.J. 536; [1963] 2 Lloyd's Rep. 515; [114 L.J. 436] 83
Godsall v. Boldero (1807) 9 East 72; 103 E.R. 500 .... 26, 27
Goodbarne v. Buck [1940] 1 K.B. 771; [1940] 1 All E.R. 613; 109 L.J.K.B. 837; 162 L.T. 259; 56 T.L.R. 433; 84 S.J. 380; 31 Cox, C.C. 380; 60 Ll.L.Rep. 129, C.A. 296
Gorely, ex p. Re Barker (1864) 4 De G.J. & Sm. 477; 5 New Rep. 22; 34 L.J.Bcy. 1; 11 L.T. 319; 10 Jur.(N.S.) 1085; 13 W.R. 60; 46 E.R. 1003, L.C. 233

Gould v. Curtis [1913] 3 K.B. 84; 82 L.J.K.B. 802; 108 L.T. 779; 29 T.L.R. 469;
  57 S.J. 461; 6 Tax Cas. 302, C.A. 8, 9
Goulstone v. Royal Insurance Co. (1858) 1 F. & F. 276 42
Grant v. Co-operative Insurance Society (1984) 134 N.L.J. 81 216
Gray v. Barr, Prudential Assurance Co. (Third Party) [1971] 2 Q.B. 554;
  [1971] 2 W.L.R. 1334; 115 S.J. 364; [1971] 2 All E.R. 949; [1971] 2
  Lloyd's Rep. 1, C.A.; affirming [1970] 2 Q.B. 626; [1970] 3 W.L.R.
  108; [1970] 2 All E.R. 702; sub nom. Gray v. Barr (1970) 114 S.J. 413; sub
  nom. Gray & Gray v. Barr, Prudential Assurance Co. (Third Party)
  [1970] 2 Lloyd's Rep. 69 .... 172, 176, 189, 192, 196, 197, 198
Green v. Russell, McCarthy (Third Party) [1959] 2 Q.B. 226; [1959] 3 W.L.R.
  17; 103 S.J. 489; [1959] 2 All E.R. 525; [1959] C.L.J. 153; 103 S.J. 497; 22
  M.L.R. 519; [23 Conv. 310], C.A.; affirming [1959] 1 Q.B. 28; [1958] 3
  W.L.R. 371; 102 S.J. 684; [22 M.L.R. 97]; [1958] C.L.Y. 884 .... 32, 278
Green & Silley Weir Ltd. v. British Railways Board [1985] 1 All E.R. 237;
  (1980) 17 Build.L.R. 94 282
Greenwood Shopping Plaza v. Beattie (1980) 111 D.L.R. (3d) 257 252
Griffin v. Squires [1958] 1 W.L.R. 1106; 123 J.P. 40; 102 S.J. 828; [1958] 3 All
  E.R. 468; 56 L.G.R. 442; 103 S.J. 5, D.C. 294
Griffiths v. Fleming [1909] 1 K.B. 805; [1908–1910] All E.R.Rep. 760; 78
  L.J.K.B. 567; 100 L.T. 765; 25 T.L.R. 377; 53 S.J. 340, C.A. 29
Groom v. Crocker [1938] 2 All E.R. 394; [1939] 1 K.B. 194; 108 L.J.K.B. 296;
  158 L.T. 477; 54 T.L.R. 861; 82 S.J. 374; 60 Ll.L.Rep. 393, C.A. 284, 285,
  286, 288
Grover & Grover Ltd. v. Mathews [1910] 2 K.B. 401; 79 L.J.K.B. 1025; 102
  L.T. 650; 26 T.L.R. 411; 15 Com.Cas. 249 .... 50, 143
Guardian Assurance v. Sutherland [1939] 2 All E.R. 246; 55 T.L.R. 576; 83
  S.J. 398; 63 Ll.L.Rep. 220 299
Gurtner v. Circuit [1968] 2 Q.B. 587; [1968] 2 W.L.R. 668; (1967) 112 S.J. 73;
  [1968] 1 All E.R. 328; sub nom. Gurtner v. Circuit and Motor Insurers'
  Bureau [1968] 2 Lloyd's Rep. 171, C.A. 317
Haigh v. Lawford (1964) 114 L.J. 208 247
Hair v. Prudential Assurance Co. Ltd. [1983] 2 Lloyd's Rep. 667; (1983) 133
  New L.J. 282 .... 87, 103
Hales v. Reliance Fire and Accident Insurance Co. [1960] 2 Lloyd's Rep.
  391 .... 102, 103
Halford v. Kymer (1830) 10 B. & C. 724; 8 L.J.O.S.K.B. 311; 109 E.R. 619 .... 30, 275
Hall D'Ath v. British Provident Association for Hospital & Additional
  Services (1932) 48 L.T.R. 240; 76 S.J. 111 .... 11, 12
Hamlyn v. Crown Accidental Insurance Co. Ltd. [1893] 1 Q.B. 750; 62
  L.J.Q.B. 409; 68 L.T. 701; 57 J.P. 663; 41 W.R. 531; 9 T.L.R. 427; 4 R.
  407, C.A. 172, 173
Hampton v. Toxteth Co-operative Society [1915] 1 Ch. 721; 84 L.J.Ch. 633;
  113 L.T. 62; 31 T.L.R. 314; 59 S.J. 397, C.A. 10, 11, 12
Hansen v. Marco Engineering (Aust.) Pty. Ltd. [1948] V.L.R. 198; 2 A.L.R.
  17 286
Harbutt's "Plasticine" Ltd. v. Wayne Tank and Pump Co. Ltd. [1970] 1
  Q.B. 447; [1970] 2 W.L.R. 198; 114 S.J. 29; [1970] 1 All E.R. 225; [1970]
  1 Lloyd's Rep. 15; [33 M.L.R. 441; 86 L.Q.R. 513], C.A. 188, 249
Hardy v. Motor Insurers' Bureau [1964] 2 Q.B. 745; [1964] 3 W.L.R. 433; 108
  S.J. 422; [1964] 2 All E.R. 742; [1964] 1 Lloyd's Rep. 397; [27 M.L.R.
  717; 81 L.Q.R. 7; 1965 S.L.T. 25; 99 I.L.T. 319], C.A.; Petition for
  leave to appeal to House of Lords dismissed sub nom. Motor
  Insurers' Bureau v. Hardy [1964] 1 W.L.R. 1155, H.L. 193, 194,
  195, 197, 198

Harr v. Allstate Insurance Co. (1969) 54 N.J. 287 143
Harrington v. Pearl Life Assurance Co. (1914) 30 T.L.R. 613, C.A. 55
Harrington Motor Co., Re [1928] Ch. 105 280
Harris v. Poland [1941] 1 K.B. 462; [1941] 1 All E.R. 204; 110 L.J.K.B. 712; 164
    L.T. 283; 57 T.L.R. 252; 85 S.J. 290; 46 Com.Cas. 162; 69 Ll.L.Rep. 35 . 170
Harse v. Pearl Life Assurance Co. [1903] 2 K.B. 92; 72 L.J.K.B. 638; 89 L.T.
    94; 19 T.L.R. 474, D.C.; reversed on other grounds [1904] 1 K.B. 558,
    C.A. 31, 126
—— v. Pearl Life Assurance Co. Ltd. [1904] 1 K.B. 558; 73 L.J.K.B. 373; 90
    L.T. 245; 52 W.R. 457; 20 T.L.R. 264; 48 S.J. 275, C.A. 25, 30, 35, 127
Haseldine v. Hosken [1933] 1 K.B. 822; [1933] All E.R.Rep. 1; 102 L.J.K.B.
    441; 148 L.T. 510; 49 T.L.R. 254; 44 Ll.L.Rep. 127, C.A. 195
Hebdon v. West (1863) 3 B. & S. 579; 1 New Rep. 431; 32 L.J.Q.B. 85; 7 L.T.
    854; 9 Jur.(N.S.) 747; 11 W.R. 422; 122 E.R. 218 .... 31, 32
Henson v. Blackwell (1845) 4 Hare 434; 14 L.J.Ch. 329; 5 L.T.O.S. 191; 9 Jur.
    390; 67 E.R. 718 26
Hepburn v. Tomlinson (Hauliers). See Tomlinson (Hauliers) v. Hepburn.
Herbert v. Railway Passengers Assurance Co. [1938] 1 All E.R. 650; 158 L.T.
    417; 60 Ll.L.Rep. 143 309
Heyman v. Darwins [1942] A.C. 356; [1942] 1 All E.R. 337; 111 L.J.K.B. 241;
    166 L.T. 306; 58 T.L.R. 169, H.L. 100, 205, 206, 209
Heywood v. Wellers [1976] Q.B. 446; [1976] 2 W.L.R. 101; (1975) 120 S.J. 9;
    [1976] 1 All E.R. 300; [1976] 2 Lloyd's Rep. 88, C.A. 285
Highland Insurance Co. v. Continental Insurance Co. [1987] 1 Lloyd's Rep.
    109 .... 80, 84, 88
Hobbs v. Marlowe [1978] A.C. 16; [1977] 2 W.L.R. 777; 121 S.J. 272; [1977]
    2 All E.R. 241; [1977] R.T.R. 253, H.L.; affirming 120 S.J. 838,
    C.A. 227, 237, 241, 246, 254
Holmes v. Payne [1930] 2 K.B. 301; [1930] All E.R.Rep. 322; 99 L.J.K.B. 441;
    143 L.T. 349; 46 T.L.R. 413; 74 S.J. 64; 35 Com.Cas. 289; 37 Ll.L.Rep.
    41 .... 180, 212
Home District Mutual Insurance Co. v. Thompson (1847) 1 E. & A. 247 231
Hooley Rubber & Chemical Man. Co., Re [1920] 1 K.B. 257; 88 L.J.K.B. 1120;
    121 L.T. 270; 35 T.L.R. 483; affirmed [1920] 1 K.B. 264; 89 L.J.K.B.
    179; 122 L.T. 173; 36 T.L.R. 81; 25 Com.Cas. 23; 1 Ll.L.Rep. 3, 25,
    C.A. 143
Horry v. Tate & Lyle Refineries Ltd. [1982] 2 Lloyd's Rep. 416 .... 212, 291
Horne v. Poland [1922] 2 K.B. 364; [1922] All E.R.Rep. 551; 91 L.J.K.B. 718;
    127 L.T. 242; 38 T.L.R. 357; 66 S.J. 368; 10 Ll.L.Rep. 175, 275 89
Horse, Carriage & General Insurance Co. v. Petch (1916) 33 T.L.R. 131 247
Houghton v. Trafalgar Insurance Co. [1954] 1 Q.B. 247; [1953] 3 W.L.R. 985;
    97 S.J. 831; [1953] 2 All E.R. 1049; [1953] 2 Lloyd's Rep. 503; [103 L.J.
    808], C.A.; affirming [1953] 2 Lloyd's Rep. 18 .... 64, 167
Huddleston v. R.A.C.V. Insurance Pty. Ltd. [1975] V.R. 683 103
Hughes v. Liverpool Victoria Legal Friendly Society [1916] 2 K.B. 482;
    [1916–1917] All E.R.Rep. 18; 85 L.J.K.B. 1643; 115 L.T. 40; 32 T.L.R.
    525, C.A. 127
Husak v. Imperial Life Assurance Co. of Canada (1970) 9 D.L.R. (3d) 602 191
Inglis v. Stock (1885) 10 App.Cas. 263; 54 L.J.Q.B. 582; 52 L.T. 821; 33 W.R.
    877; 5 Asp.M.L.C. 422, H.L.; affirming sub nom. Stock v. Inglis (1884)
    12 Q.B.D. 564, C.A. 42
Inn. Cor. International Ltd. v. American Home Assurance Co. (1974) 42
    D.L.R. (3d) 46 65

Table of Cases xxiii

Integrated Container Service v. British Traders Insurance Co. [1984] 1
Lloyd's Rep. 154; (1984) 81 L.S.Gaz. 353, C.A.; [1981] Com.L.R. 212;
[1981] 2 Lloyd's Rep. 460; [1980] C.L.R. 212 184
Ioakimidis Policy Trusts, Re, Ioakimidis v. Hartcup [1925] Ch. 403; [1925]
All E.R.Rep. 164; 95 L.J.Ch. 24; 133 L.T. 796; 41 T.L.R. 486; 69 S.J.
662 274
Jabbour v. Custodian of Israeli Absentee Property [1954] 1 W.L.R. 139; 98
S.J. 45; [1954] 1 All E.R. 145; [1953] 2 Lloyd's Rep. 760 216
Jaglom v. Excess Insurance Co. [1972] 2 Q.B. 250; [1971] 3 W.L.R. 594; 115
S.J. 639; [1972] 1 All E.R. 267; [1971] 2 Lloyd's Rep. 171 61
James v. British General Insurance Co. [1927] 1 K.B. 311 .... 193, 196
―― v. Insurance Brokers Registration Council, The Times, February 16,
1984 155
Jason v. Batten; Jason v. British Traders' Insurance Co. [1969] 1 Lloyd's
Rep. 281; sub nom. Jason v. British Traders' Insurance Co., 119 New
L.J. 697 187
Joel v. Law Union & Crown Insurance Co. [1908] 2 K.B. 863; 77 L.J.K.B.
1108; 99 L.T. 712; 24 T.L.R. 898; 52 S.J. 740, C.A. 83, 84, 88, 106
Jones v. Birch Bros. Ltd. [1933] 2 K.B. 597; 102 L.J.K.B. 746; 149 L.T. 507; 49
T.L.R. 586, C.A. 283, 308
―― v. Lock (1865) 1 Ch.App. 25; 35 L.J.Ch. 117; 13 L.T. 514; 11 Jur.(N.S.)
913; 14 W.R. 149, L.C. 275
―― v. Welsh Insurance Corporation [1937] 4 All E.R. 149; (1937) 54 T.L.R.
22; 157 L.T. 483; 81 S.J. 886; 59 Ll.L.Rep. 13 .... 301, 307
Jones Construction v. Alliance Assurance Co. [1961] 1 Lloyd's Rep. 121,
C.A.; affirming [1960] 1 Lloyd's Rep. 264; [1960] C.L.Y. 1563 70
Jureidini v. National British and Irish Millers' Insurance Co. [1915]
A.C. 499; 84 L.J.K.B. 640; 112 L.T. 531; 31 T.L.R. 132; 59 S.J. 205,
H.L. 206, 209
Keeling v. Pearl Assurance Co. (1923) 129 L.T. 573; [1923] All E.R.Rep. 307 . 112
Kelly v. Cornhill Insurance Co. [1964] 1 W.L.R. 158; 108 S.J. 94; [1964] 1 All
E.R. 321; [1964] 1 Lloyd's Rep. 1; 1964 S.C. (H.L.) 46; 1964 S.L.T. 81;
[80 L.Q.R. 306], H.L.; reversing 1963 S.C. 113; 1963 S.L.T. 13; [1963]
C.L.Y 3072 300
Kelly v. London and Staffs Fire Insurance Co. (1883) Cab. & E. 47 142
―― v. Solari (1841) G.M. & W. 54; 11 L.J.Ex. 10; 6 Jur. 107; 152 E.R. 24 212
Kelsall v. Allstate Insurance Co. Ltd., The Times, March 20, 1987 88
Kennedy v. Smith (1976) S.L.T. 110 102
Kettlewell v. Refuge Assurance Co. See Refuge Assurance Co. v. Kettlewell.
King, Re, Robinson v. Gray [1963] Ch. 459; [1963] 2 W.L.R. 629; 107 S.J. 134;
[1963] 1 All E.R. 781; [1963] R.V.R. 245; [27 Conv. 223; 234 L.T. 200,
589; [1963] R.V.R. 707], C.A.; reversing [1962] 1 W.L.R. 632; 106 S.J.
509; [1962] 2 All E.R. 66; [1962] R.V.R. 621; [112 L.J. 470; 106 S.J. 683,
717; 26 Conv. 319]; [1962] C.L.Y. 1690 .... 25, 36, 38, 51, 52, 252
King v. Victoria Insurance Co. Ltd. [1896] A.C. 250; 65 L.J.P.C. 38; 74 L.T.
206; 44 W.R. 592; 12 T.L.R. 285, P.C. 239, 247
Kirby v. Cosindit Società per Azioni [1969] 1 Lloyd's Rep. 75 70
Kirkbridge v. Donner [1974] 1 Lloyd's Rep. 549 102
Knight of St. Michael, The [1898] P. 30; 67 L.J.P. 19; 78 L.T. 90; 46 W.R. 396;
14 T.L.R. 191; 8 Asp.M.L.C. 360; 3 Com.Cas. 62 184
Koskas v. Standard Marine Insurance Co. Ltd. (1926) 25 Ll.L.R. 363; (1927)
137 L.T. 165; 43 T.L.R. 169; 17 Asp.M.L.C. 240; 32 Com.Cas. 160;
reversed (1927) 27 Ll.L.R. 61, C.A. 159

Kumar v. Life Insurance Corporation of India (1973) 117 S.J. 833; [1974] 1 Lloyd's Rep. 147 124
Lambert v. Co-operative Insurance Society [1975] 2 Lloyd's Rep. 485; (1976) 39 M.L.R. 478, C.A. 87, 92
Landress v. Phoenix Insurance Co. (1933) 291 U.S. 491 173
Lane (W.J.) v. Spratt [1970] 2 Q.B. 480; [1969] 3 W.L.R. 950; 113 S.J. 920; [1970] 1 All E.R. 162; [1969] 2 Lloyd's Rep. 229 .... 105, 163
Langford v. Legal & General Assurance Soc. Ltd. [1986] 2 Lloyd's Rep.103 164
Lawrence v. Accidental Insurance Co. (1881) 7 Q.B.D. 216; 50 L.J.Q.B. 522; 45 L.T. 29; 45 J.P. 781; 29 W.R. 802, D.C. 186, 187
Ledingham v. Ontario Hospital Services Commission (1974) 46 D.L.R. (3d) 699 241
Leebov v. United States Fidelity & Guaranty Co. (1960) 401 Pa. 477 184
Lees v. Whitley (1866) L.R. 2 Eq. 143; 35 L.J.Ch. 412; 14 L.T. 472; 14 W.R. 534 235
Leggate v. Brown [1950] W.N. 384; 66 T.L.R. (Pt. 2) 281; 114 J.P. 454; 94 S.J. 567; [1950] 2 All E.R. 564; 49 L.G.R. 27; 84 Ll.L.Rep. 395, D.C. 73
Leppard v. Excess Insurance Co. [1979] 1 W.L.R. 512; (1979) 122 S.J. 182; [1979] 2 All E.R. 668; [1979] 2 Lloyd's Rep.91; (1979) 250 E.G. 751, C.A. 220, 223, 226
Lewis v. Norwich Union Fire Insurance Co. [1916] A.C. 509 121
Leyland Shipping Co. v. Norwich Union Fire Insurance Society [1918] A.C. 350; [1918–19] All E.R.Rep. 443; 87 L.J.K.B. 395; 118 L.T. 120; 34 T.L.R. 221; 62 S.J. 307; 14 Asp.M.L.C. 258, H.L.; affirming [1917] 1 K.B. 873; 86 L.J.K.B. 905; 116 L.T. 327; 33 T.L.R. 228; 14 Asp.M.L.C. 4, C.A. 185, 187, 188
Lickiss v. Milestone Motor Policies at Lloyd's. *See* Barrett Bros. (Taxis) v. Davies (Lickiss and Milestone Motor Policies at Lloyd's, Third Parties).
Life Association of Scotland v. Foster (1873) 11 Macph. 351; 45 Sc.Jur. 240 ... 83
Lister v. Romford Ice & Cold Storage Ltd. [1957] A.C. 555; [1957] 2 W.L.R. 158; 121 J.P. 98; 101 S.J. 106; [1957] 1 All E.R. 125 *sub nom.* Romford Ice & Cold Storage Co. v. Lister [1956] 2 Lloyd's Rep. 505; [73 L.Q.R. 283; 20 M.L.R. 220, 437; 22 M.L.R. 652; 121 J.P.J. 128; 24 Sol. 177; 101 S.J. 217; 103 S.J. 161; 227 L.T. 67; [1957] C.L.J. 25; 94 I.L.T.R. 85], H.L. affirming *sub nom.* Romford Ice & Cold Storage Co. v. Lister [1956] 2 Q.B. 180; [1955] 3 W.L.R. 631; 99 S.J. 794; [1955] 3 All E.R., 460; [1955] 2 Lloyd's Rep. 325; [221 L.T. 31; 106 L.J. 4, 68, 342; 1956 S.L.T. 1; [1956] C.L.J. 101; 72 L.Q.R. 7]; [1955] C.L.Y. 984, C.A. 243, 247, 253, 255, 256
Liverpool & London & Globe Insurance Ltd. v. Canadian General Electric Co. Ltd. (1981) 123 D.L.R. (3d) 513 184
Lloyd v. Grace, Smith & Co. [1911] 2 K.B. 489; 80 L.J.K.B. 959; 104 L.T. 789; 27 T.L.R. 409, C.A.; reversed on another point [1912] A.C. 716, H.L. 142
Lloyd, (J.J.) (Instruments Ltd.) v. Northern Star Insurance Co. Ltd. [1987] 1 Lloyd's Rep. 32; [1985] 1 Lloyd's Rep. 264 .... 185, 186, 189
Lloyd's Bank Ltd. v. Bundy [1975] Q.B. 326; [1974] 3 W.L.R. 501; 118 S.J. 714; [1974] 3 All E.R. 757; [1974] 2 Lloyd's Rep. 366, C.A. 291
Locker v. Law Union & Rock Insurance Co. Ltd. [1928] 1 K.B. 554 55
Locker & Wolf Ltd. v. Western Australian Insurance Co. [1936] 1 K.B. 408; 105 L.J.K.B. 444; 154 L.T. 667; 52 T.L.R. 293; 80 S.J. 185; 41 Com.Cas. 342; 54 Ll.L.Rep. 211, C.A. 91

Table of Cases xxv

Lombard Australia Ltd. v. N.R.M.A. Insurance Ltd. [1969] 1 Lloyd's Rep. 575 173
London & Lancashire Fire Insurance Co. v. Bolands [1924] A.C. 836; [1924] All E.R.Rep. 642; 93 L.J.P.C. 230; 131 L.T. 354; 40 T.L.R. 603; 68 S.J. 629, H.L. 165
London & Manchester Plate Glass Co. v. Heath [1913] 3 K.B. 411; 82 L.J.K.B. 1183; 108 L.T. 1009; 29 T.L.R. 581; 6 B.W.C.C.N. 107, C.A. ... 214
London & North Western Railway Co. v. Glyn (1859) 1 E. & E. 652; 28 L.J.Q.B. 188; 33 L.T.O.S. 199; 5 Jur(N.s.) 1004; 7 W.R. 238; 120 E.R. 1054 46
London & Provincial Leather Processes Ltd. v. Hudson [1939] 2 K.B. 724; 109 L.J.K.B. 100; 162 L.T. 140; 55 T.L.R. 1047; 83 S.J. 733; 3 All E.R. 857; 64 Ll.L.Rep. 352; [1938–1939] B. & C.R. 183 180
London Assurance v. Clare, Adair v. Clare, British Equitable Assurance Co. Ltd. (Consolidated) v. Clare [1937] 81 S.J. 258; 51 Ll.L.Rep. 254 .. 211
——— v. Mansel (1879) 11 Ch.D. 363; 48 L.J.Ch. 331; 41 L.T. 225; 43 J.P. 604; 27 W.R. 444 90
London Guarantee Co. v. Fearnley (1880) 5 App.Cas. 911; 43 L.T. 390; 45 J.P. 4; 28 W.R. 893, H.L. 117, 118, 203
Lucas v. Export Credits Guarantee Department [1974] 1 W.L.R. 909; 118 S.J. 461; [1974] 2 All E.R. 889; [1974] 2 Lloyd's Rep. 69, H.L.; reversing [1973] 1 W.L.R. 914; 117 S.J. 506; [1973] 2 All E.R. 984; sub nom. Lucas (L.) and Lamet Trading v. Export Credits Guarantee Department [1973] 1 Lloyd's Rep. 549, C.A. 243, 250
Lucena v. Craufurd (1806) 2 B. & P.N.R. 269; (1808) 1 Taunt. 325; 127 E.R. 858, H.L. 39, 41
Lynch v. Dalzell (1729) 4 Bro.P.C. 431; 2 E.R. 292, H.L. 25
McCall v. Brooks [1984] R.T.R. 99 73
Macaura v. Northern Assurance Co. [1925] A.C. 619; 94 L.J.P.C. 154; 133 L.T. 152; 41 T.L.R. 447; 69 S.J. 777; [1925] All E.R.Rep. 51; 31 Com.Cas. 10, H.L. 36, 39, 40, 41, 42, 44, 205
McCormick v. National Motor & Accident Insurance Union Ltd. (1934) 50 T.L.R. 528; 78 S.J. 633; 40 Com.Cas. 76; 49 Ll.L.Rep. 361, C.A. . 89, 303
M'Farlane v. Royal London Friendly Society (1886) 2 T.L.R. 755, D.C. 34
McKay v. London General Insurance Co. (1935) 51 Ll.L. 201 107
Mackender v. Feldia A.G. [1967] 2 Q.B. 590; [1967] 2 W.L.R. 119; [1966] 2 All E.R. 847; sub nom. Mackenda v. Feldia, 110 S.J. 811; sub nom. Mackender, Hill and White v. Feldia A.G., C.H. Brachfield and Sons S.A. and Diamil S.R.L. [1966] 2 Lloyd's Rep. 449; [1966] C.L.Y. 9908, C.A. 82
Mackie v. European Assurance Society (1869) 21 L.T. 102; 17 W.R. 987 .... 61, 62, 141
McLeod v. Buchanan 1940 84 S.J. 452; [1940] 2 All E.R. 179, H.L. 295
McNealy v. Pennine Insurance Co. (1978) 122 S.J. 229; [1978] 2 Lloyd's Rep. 18; [1978] R.T.R. 285, C.A. 138, 148, 149
Macphee v. Royal Insurance Co. (1979) S.L.T. 54 103
Magee v. Penine Insurance Co. [1969] 2 Q.B. 507; [1969] 2 W.L.R. 1278; 113 S.J. 303; [1969] 2 All E.R. 891; [1969] 2 Lloyd's Rep. 378, C.A. 100
Mammone v. R.A.C.V. Insurance Pty. Ltd. [1976] V.R. 617 103
March v. Piggott (1771) 2 Burr. 2862 24
March Cabaret Club & Casino Ltd. v. London Assurance; March Cabaret Club & Casino v. Thompson & Bryan [1975] 1 Lloyd's Rep. 169 92
Marene Knitting Mills v. Greater Pacific General Insurance Ltd. [1976] 2 Lloyd's Rep. 631 63

Table of Cases

Marlborough Properties Ltd. *v.* Malborough Fibreglass Ltd. [1981] 1
N.Z.L.R. 464 252
Mark Rowlands Ltd. *v.* Berni Inns Ltd. [1985] Q.B. 211 .... 36, 40, 51, 251, 252
Marsden *v.* City & County Insurance (1865) L.R.I.C.P. 232; Har. & Ruth.
53; 35 L.J.C.P. 60; 13 L.T. 465; 12 Jur.(N.s.) 76; 14 W.R. 106 185
Marzouca *v.* Atlantic and British Commercial Insurance Co. Ltd. [1971] 1
Lloyd's Rep. 449, P.C. 96
Mason *v.* Harvey (1853) 8 Ex.Ch. 819; 22 L.J.Ex. 336; 21 L.T.O.S. 158; 155
E.R. 1585 201
—— *v.* Sainsbury (1782) 3 Doug.K.B. 61; 99 E.R. 538 243
Maurice *v.* Goldsborough Mort & Co. [1939] A.C. 452; 108 L.J.P.C. 75; 161
L.T. 146; 55 T.L.R. 714; 83 S.J. 563; [1939] 3 All E.R. 63; 64 Ll.L.Rep. 1,
P.C. 182
Mayne Nickless *v.* Pegler (1974) 1 N.S.W.L.R. 228 .... 63, 66
Meah *v.* McCreamer (No. 2) [1986] 1 All E.R. 943; (1986) 136 New L.J. 235 196
Medical Defence Union *v.* Department of Trade and Industry [1979] 2 All
E.R. 421, 428 .... 7, 8, 9, 10, 11, 13
Merchants' & Manufacturers' Insurance Co. *v.* Hunt [1941] 1 K.B. 295; 110
L.J.K.B. 375; 165 L.T. 49; 57 T.L.R. 208; [1941] 1 All E.R. 123; 68
Ll.L.Rep. 117, C.A. 309, 310
Metropolitan Life Insurance Co. *v.* Conway (1930) 252 N.Y. 449, 169 N.E.
642 77
Michigan Hospital Services *v.* Sharpe (1954) 339 Mich. 375, 63 N.W. (2d)
638 237
Michigan Medical Services *v.* Sharpe (1954) 54 N.W. (2d) 713; 339 Mich.
574 237
Midland Insurance Co. *v.* Smith (1881) 6 Q.B.D. 561; 50 L.J.Q.B. 329; 45
L.T. 411; 45 J.P. 699; 29 W.R. 850 162
Miller, Gibb & Co. *Re* [1957] 1 W.L.R. 703; 101 S.J. 392; [1957] 2 All E.R. 266;
[1957] 1 Lloyd's Rep. 258 238
Mills *v.* Smith (No. 2) [1964] 1 Q.B. 30; [1963] 3 W.L.R. 367; 107 S.J.
175; [1963] 2 All E.R. 1078; [1963] 1 Lloyd's Rep. 168; [79 L.Q.R.
472] 177, 178, 189
Minister of Transport *v.* Canadian General Insurance (1971) 18 D.L.R. (3d)
617 299
Mint Security Ltd. *v.* Blair [1982] 1 Lloyd's Rep. 188 .... 101, 146, 147
Monk *v.* Warbey [1935] 1 K.B. 75; 104 L.J.K.B. 153; 152 L.T. 194; 51 T.L.R.
77; 78 S.J. 783; [1934] All E.R. Rep. 373; 50 Ll.L.Rep. 33, C.A. 297
Moore, *Re, ex p.* Ibbetson (1878) 8 Ch.D. 519; 39 L.T. 1; 26 W.R. 843, C.A. 272
Moore *v.* Evans [1918] A.C. 185; 87 L.J.K.B. 207; 117 L.T. 761; 34 T.L.R. 51;
62 S.J. 69; 23 Com.Cas. 124, H.L. 179, 180
—— *v.* Manchester Liners Ltd. [1910] A.C. 498; 79 L.J.K.B. 1175; 103 L.T.
226; 26 T.L.R. 618; 54 S.J. 703; 3 B.W.C.C. 527, H.L.; reversing [1909]
1 K.B. 417, C.A. 322
Moore, (J.H.) *v.* Crowe [1972] 2 Lloyd's Rep. 563 69
Morley *v.* Moore [1936] 2 K.B. 359 .... 238, 245
Moran, Galloway & Co. *v.* Uzielli [1905] 2 K.B. 555; 74 L.J.K.B. 494; 54 W.R.
250; 21 T.L.R. 378; 10 Com.Cas. 203 41
Morawietz *v.* Morawietz (1984) 5 C.C.L.I. 11 255
Morgans *v.* Launchberry [1973] A.C. 127; [1972] 2 W.L.R. 1217; 116 S.J. 396;
[1972] R.T.R. 406; [1972] 1 Lloyd's Rep. 483; [122 New L.J. 488], H.L.;
reversing *sub nom.* Launchberry *v.* Morgans [1971] 2 Q.B. 245; [1971]
2 W.L.R. 602; (1970) 115 S.J. 96; [1971] 1 All E.R. 642; [1971] 1 Lloyd's
Rep. 197; [1971] R.T.R. 97; [115 S.J. 801], C.A. 299

Morris v. Ford Motor Co.; Cameron Industrial Services (Third Party); Roberts (Fourth Party) [1973] 1 Q.B. 792; [1973] 2 W.L.R. 843; 117 S.J. 393; [1973] 2 All E.R. 1084; [1973] 2 Lloyd's Rep. 27, C.A. 237, 238, 244, 255, 257
Mumford Hotels Ltd. v. Wheler [1964] Ch. 117; [1963] 3 W.L.R. 735; 107 S.J. 810; [1963] 3 All E.R. 250; [[1963] R.V.R. 707; 107 S.J. 1016; 28 Conv. 78; 114 L.J. 854] 37, 51, 235
Murfitt v. Royal Insurance Co. (1922) 38 T.L.R. 334; 10 Ll.L.Rep. 191 .... 54, 62, 141
Murphy v. Taylor (1850) 1 Ir.Ch.R. 92; 3 Ir.Jur. 85 .... 223, 271
Murray v. Legal & General Assurance Society [1970] 2 Q.B. 495; [1970] 2 W.L.R. 465; 113 S.J. 720; [1969] 3 All E.R. 794; [1969] 2 Lloyd's Rep. 405 .... 283, 325
Mutual Life Insurance Co. of New York v. Ontario Metal Products Co. Ltd. [1925] A.C. 344 88
Nancollas v. Insurance Officer [1985] 1 All E.R. 833, C.A. 322
National Employers' Mutual v. Hayden [1980] 2 Lloyd's Rep. 149, C.A.; reversing [1979] 2 Lloyd's Rep. 235 267
National Farmers' Union Mutual Insurance Society v. Dawson [1941] 2 K.B. 424; 111 L.J.K.B. 38; 166 L.T. 245; 70 Ll.L.Rep. 167 .... 305, 307
Nelson v. Board of Trade (1901) 84 L.T. 565 12
Newsholme Bros. v. Road Transport & General Insurance Co. [1929] 2 K.B. 356; 98 L.J.K.B. 751; 141 L.T. 570; 45 T.L.R. 573; 73 S.J. 465; [1929] All E.R.Rep. 442; 34 Com.Cas. 330; 24 Ll.L.Rep. 247, C.A. 112, 113, 114, 115, 138, 143, 144, 150, 155
North British & Mercantile Insurance Co. v. London Liverpool & Globe Insurance Co. (1877) 5 Ch.D. 569; 46 L.J.Ch. 537; 36 L.T. 629, C.A. 251, 260, 261
North British & Mercantile Insurance Co. v. Moffatt (1871) L.R. 7 C.P. 25; 41 L.J.C.P. 1; 25 L.T. 662; 20 W.R. 114 .... 46, 48
North of England Oil Cake Co. v. Archangel Marine Insurance Co. (1875) L.R. 10 Q.B. 249; 44 L.J.Q.B. 121; 32 L.T. 561; 24 W.R. 162; 2 Asp.M.L.C. 571, D.C. 136
North & South Trust v. Berkeley [1971] 1 W.L.R. 470 .... 138, 140, 146
Norton v. Royal Life Assurance Co. (1885) The Times, August 12; (1885) 1 T.L.R. 460 210
O'Connor v. Kirby [1972] 1 Q.B. 90 .... 111, 150, 151
Oei v. Foster [1982] 2 Lloyd's Rep. 170 185
Ogden (Claude R.) & Co. Pty. v. Reliance Fire Sprinkler Co. Pty.; Davies (First Third Party); Stenhouse (N.S.W.) (Second Third Party) [1975] 1 Lloyd's Rep. 52; 65 (Aus. High Ct.) 148
Orapko v. Manson Investments [1978] A.C. 95; [1977] 3 W.L.R. 229; (1977) 121 S.J. 632; (1977) 36 P. & C.R. 1, H.L.; affirming [1977] 1 W.L.R. 347; (1977) 121 S.J. 256; [1977] 1 All E.R. 666, C.A. 238
Osman v. Moss (J. Ralph) [1970] 1 Lloyd's Rep. 313, C.A. 146
Page v. Scottish Insurance Corporation, Forster v. Page (1929) 98 L.J.K.B. 308; 140 L.T. 571; 45 T.L.R. 250; 73 S.J. 157; 34 Com.Cas. 236; 33 Ll.L.Rep. 134, C.A. 244, 245
Pan American World Airways Inc. v. Aetna Casualty and Surety Co. [1975] 1 Lloyd's Rep. 77, U.S.C.A.; affirming [1974] 1 Lloyd's Rep. 207, U.S.D.C. 164
Paterson v. Costain & Press (Overseas) Ltd. 123 S.J. 142; [1979] 2 Lloyd's Rep. 204, C.A.; affirming [1978] 1 Lloyd's Rep. 86 323

Paterson v. Harris (1861) 1 B. & S. 336; 30 L.J.Q.B. 354; 5 L.T. 53; 7 Jur.(N.S.)
1276; 9 W.R. 743; 1 Mar.L.C. 124; 121 E.R. 740 228
Pawson v. Watson (1778) 2 Cowp. 785; 98 E.R. 1361; *sub nom*. Pawson v.
Ewer, Pawson v. Snell, Pawson v. Watson 1 Doug.K.B. 12n 100
Persson v. London Country Buses [1974] 1 W.L.R. 569; (1973) 118 S.J. 134;
[1974] 1 All E.R. 1251; [1974] R.T.R. 346; [1974] 1 Lloyd's Rep. 415,
C.A. 315, 316
Peters v. General Accident Fire and Life Assurance Corporation Ltd. (1938)
158 L.T. 476; 54 T.L.R. 663; 82 S.J. 294; [1938] 2 All E.R. 267; 36 L.G.R.
583; 60 Ll.L. 311; [1937] 4 All E.R. 628 .... 132, 135, 301
Petrofina (U.K.) v. Magnaload [1984] Q.B. 127; [1983] 3 W.L.R. 805; (1983)
127 S.J. 729; [1983] 3 All E.R. 35; [1983] 2 Lloyd's Rep. 91; (1984) 25
Build.L.R. 37; (1983) 80 L.S.Gaz. 2677 .... 47, 252
Phoenix Assurance Co. v. Spooner [1905] 2 K.B. 753; 74 L.J.K.B. 792; 93 L.T.
306; 54 W.R. 313; 21 T.L.R. 577; 49 S.J. 553; 10 Com.Cas. 282; on
appeal (1906) 22 T.L.R. 695, C.A. 247
Phoenix General Insurance Co. of Greece S.A. v. Administratia Asiguraliror de Stat [1986] 2 Lloyd's Rep. 552 73
Photo Production Ltd. v. Securicor Transport Ltd. [1980] 2 W.L.R. 283;
(1980) 124 S.J. 147; [1980] 1 All E.R. 556; [1980] 1 Lloyd's Rep. 545,
H.L.; reversing [1978] 1 W.L.R. 856; (1978) 122 S.J. 315; [1978] 3 All
E.R. 146; [1978] 2 Lloyd's Rep. 172, C.A. [130 New L.J. 307] 188
Pickles v. Insurance Brokers Registration Council [1984] 1 W.L.R. 748; (1984) 128
S.J. 365; [1984] 1 All E.R. 1073; (1984) 81 L.S.Gaz. 1205, D.C. 155
Pim v. Reid (1843) 6 M. & G. 1; 6 Scott N.R. 982; 12 L.J.C.P. 299; 1 L.T.O.S.
230; 134 E.R. 784 .... 94, 218
Pioneer Concrete (U.K.) v. National Employers Mutual General Insurance
Association [1985] 2 All E.R. 395; [1985] 1 Lloyd's Rep. 274; (1985)
F.L.R. 251 283
Pleasurama Ltd. v. Sun Alliance & London Insurance Ltd. [1979] 1 Lloyd's
Rep. 289 222
Port-Rose v. Phoenix Assurance (1986) 136 New L.J. 333 .... 105, 162
Portavon Cinema Co. v. Price & Century Insurance Co. [1939] 161 L.T.
417; 84 S.J. 152; [1939] 4 All E.R. 601; 45 Com.Cas. 93; 65 Ll.L.Rep.
161 .... 232, 262
Porter v. Motor Insurers' Bureau [1978] 2 Lloyd's Rep. 463; [1978] R.T.R.
503; (1978) 122 S.J. 592 313
Post Office v. Norwich Union Fire Insurance [1967] 2 Q.B. 363; [1967] 2
W.L.R. 709; 111 S.J. 71; [1967] 1 All E.R. 577; [1967] 1 Lloyd's Rep.
216, C.A.; reversing 110 S.J. 867; [1966] 2 Lloyd's Rep. 499; 116 New
L.J. 1544; [1966] C.L.Y. 6351; Petition for leave to appeal to the
House of Lords dismissed 282
Praet v. Poland [1960] 1 Lloyd's Rep. 416; [1960] C.L.Y. 1582 60
Pritchard v. Merchants' and Tradesmen's Mutual Life Assurance Co.
(1858) 3 C.B.(N.S.) 622; 27 L.J.C.P. 169; 30 L.T.O.S. 318; 4 Jur.(N.S.)
307; 6 W.R. 340; 140 E.R. 885 .... 67, 71
Provincial Insurance Co. Ltd. v. Morgan [1933] A.C. 240; [1932] All
E.R.Rep. 899; 102 L.J.K.B. 164; 49 T.L.R. 179; 38 Com.Cas. 92; *sub
nom*. Morgan v. Provincial Insurance Co. 148 L.T. 385, H.L.;
affirming *sub nom*. Re Morgan & Provincial Insurance Co. Ltd. [1932]
2 K.B. 70, C.A. 107, 108, 110, 159
Prudential Insurance Co. v. Inland Revenue Commissioners [1904] 2 K.B.
658; 73 L.J.K.B. 734; 91 L.T. 520; 53 W.R. 108; 20 T.L.R. 621; 48 S.J.
605 8

Table of Cases

Prudential Staff Union v. Hall [1947] K.B. 685; [1948] L.J.R. 619; 63 T.L.R. 392; 80 Ll.L.Rep. 410 .... 45, 48
Pyman Steamship Co. v. Admiralty Commissioners [1919] 1 K.B. 49; 88 L.J.K.B. 277; 119 L.T. 735; 36 T.L.R. 79; 14 Asp.M.L.C. 364, C.A. 184
Queensland Government Railways and Electric Power Transmission Pty. Ltd. v. Manufacturers' Mutual Life Insurance Ltd. (1968) 118 C.L.R. 314; [1969] 1 Lloyd's Rep. 214 169
R. v. Delmayne [1970] 2 Q.B. 170; [1969] 3 W.L.R. 300; 133 J.P. 458; 113 S.J. 605; [1969] 2 All E.R. 980; sub nom. R. v. Delmayne (Anthony), 53 Cr.App.R. 392, C.A. 58
—— v. National Insurance Commissioners, ex p. East [1976] I.C.R. 206, C.A. 323
—— v. ——, ex p. Michael [1977] 1 W.L.R. 109; (1976) 120 S.J. 856, C.A.; affirming [1976] I.C.R. 90; [1976] 1 All E.R. 566, D.C. 323
Randall v. Motor Insurers' Bureau [1968] 1 W.L.R. 1900; 112 S.J. 883; [1969] 1 All E.R. 21; [1968] 2 Lloyd's Rep. 553 .... 294, 313
Rapp (Leo) Ltd. v. McClure [1955] 1 Lloyd's Rep. 292 164
Rayner v. Preston (1881) 18 Ch.D. 1; 50 L.J.Ch. 472; 44 L.T. 787; 45 J.P. 829; 29 W.R. 547, C.A. 52, 129, 130, 132, 134, 229, 234, 239
Refuge Assurance Co. Ltd. v. Kettlewell [1909] A.C. 243; 78 L.J.K.B. 519; 100 L.T. 306; 25 T.L.R. 395; sub nom. Kettlewell v. Refuge Assurance Co. Ltd. 53 S.J. 339, H.L.; affirming [1908] 1 K.B. 545 125
Regina Fur v. Bossom [1958] 2 Lloyd's Rep. 425, C.A.; affirming [1957] 2 Lloyd's Rep. 466; [1957] C.L.Y. 1760 92
Reid v. Traders' General Insurance Co., Dares Motors and Myers (1963) 41 D.L.R. (2d) 148 150
Reynolds v. Phoenix Assurance Co. (1978) 122 S.J. 161; [1978] 2 Lloyd's Rep. 22, 440; (1978) 247 E.G. 995, C.A. 89, 92, 93, 94, 221, 222, 231
Rice v. Baxendale (1861) 7 H. & N. 96; 30 L.J.Ex. 371; 158 E.R. 407 217
Richardson v. Mellish (1824) 2 Bing. 229; 9 Moore, C.P. 435 190
Roberts v. Avon Insurance [1956] 2 Lloyd's Rep. 240 86
—— v. Security Co. Ltd. [1897] 1 Q.B. 111; 66 L.J.Q.B. 119; 75 L.T. 531; 45 W.R. 214; 13 T.L.R. 79; 41 S.J. 95, C.A. 56, 57
—— v. State General Insurance Manager [1974] 2 N.Z.L.R. 312 162
—— v. Warne [1973] R.T.R. 217; [1973] Crim.L.R. 244, D.C. 296
Robinson v. Evans Bros. [1969] V.R. 885 .... 173, 175, 178, 179
Rogerson v. Scottish Automobile & General Insurance Co. Ltd. (1931) 146 L.T. 26; 48 T.L.R. 17; 75 S.J. 724; [1931] All E.R.Rep. 606; 37 Com.Cas. 23; 41 Ll.L.Rep. 1, H.L. 130
Roselodge Ltd. v. Castle 110 S.J. 705; [1966] 2 Lloyd's Rep. 105, C.A.; reversing [1966] 2 Lloyd's Rep. 113; 116 New L.J. 1378 .... 84, 89, 91, 92
Ross Southwood Tire Ltd. v. Pyrotech Products Ltd. (1975) 57 D.L.R. (3d) 248 252
Roumeli Food Stores v. New India Assurnce Co. [1972] 1 N.S.W.L.R. 227 ... 233
Rozanes v. Bowen (1928) 32 Ll.L.Rep. 98, C.A. 138
Rust v. Abbey Life Assurance Co. [1979] 2 Lloyd's Rep. 334, C.A.; affirming [1978] 2 Lloyd's Rep. 386 .... 53, 54, 57
S. & M. Carpets (London) Ltd. v. Cornhill Insurance Ltd. [1982] 1 Lloyd's Rep. 423; affirming [1981] 1 Lloyd's Rep. 667 210
Sadler's Co. v. Badcock (1743) 2 Atk. 554; 1 Wils. 10; 26 E.R. 733, L.C. 25, 37, 50, 229
Salt v. Marquess of Northampton [1892] A.C. 1; 61 L.J.Ch. 49; 65 L.T. 765; 40 W.R. 529; 8 T.L.R. 104; 36 S.J. 150, H.L. 271

Samuel (P.) & Co. v. Dumas [1924] A.C. 431; 93 L.J.K.B. 415; 130 L.T. 771;
40 T.L.R. 375; 68 S.J. 439; [1924] All E.R.Rep. 66; 16 Asp.M.L.C. 305;
29 Com.Cas. 239, H.L.; affirming *sub nom.* Samuel (P.) & Co. v.
Merchants Marine Insurance Co. Ltd. (No. 2) [1923] 1 K.B. 592,
C.A. 253
Samuelson v. National Insurance and Guarantee Corp. [1985] 2 Lloyd's
Rep. 541, C.A.; [1984] 3 All E.R. 107; (1984) 128 S.J. 855; [1984] 2
Lloyd's Rep. 416; (1985) 82 L.S.Gaz. 444 302
Sands v. O'Connell [1981] R.T.R. 42, D.C. 299
Saunders v. Ford Motor Co. Ltd. [1970] 1 Lloyd's Rep. 379 291
—— v. Vautier (1841) Cr. & Ph. 240; 10 L.J.Ch. 354; 41 E.R. 482, L.C. 278
Schebsman, Re, ex p. Official Receiver, Trustee v. Cargo Superintendents
(London) Ltd. & Schebsman [1944] 1 Ch. 83; 113 L.J.Ch. 33; 170 L.T.
9; 60 T.L.R. 128; 88 S.J. 17; [1943] 2 All E.R. 768, C.A. 276
Schoolman v. Hall [1951] 1 Lloyd's Rep. 139, C.A.; affirming *The Times,* July
5, 1950 .... 86, 92
Schuler, (L.) A.G. v. Wickman Machine Tool Sales [1974] A.C. 235; [1973] 2
W.L.R. 683; 117 S.J. 340; [1973] 2 All E.R. 39; [1973] 2 Lloyd's Rep. 53,
H.L.; affirming *sub nom.* Wickman Machine Tool Sales v. Schuler (L.)
A.G.) [1972] 1 W.L.R. 840; 116 S.J. 352; [1972] 2 All E.R. 1173, C.A. ... 76
Scott v. Avery (1856) 5 H.L.C. 810; 25 L.J.Ex. 308; 28 L.T.O.S. 207; 2
Jur.(N.S.) 815; 4 W.R. 746; 10 E.R. 1121, H.L. 204, 308
Scottish Amicable Heritable Securities Association v. Northern Assurance
Co. (1883) 11 R. (Ct. of Sess.) 287; 21 Sc.L.R. 189 .... 221, 230
Scottish Union & National Insurance Co. v. Davis [1970] 1 Lloyd's Rep. 1,
C.A. 240
Sebring v. Fidelity Phoenix Insurance Co. (1931) 255 N.Y. 382 82
Seddon v. Binions; Zurich Insurance Co. (Third Party); Stork v. Binions,
Zurich Insurance Co. (Third Party) (1977) 122 S.J. 34; [1978] R.T.R.
163; [1978] 1 Lloyd's Rep. 381, C.A. 301, 302, 303
Shaw v. Robberds (1837) 6 Ad. & El. 75; 1 Nev. & P.K.B. 279; Will., Woll. &
Dav. 94; 6 L.J.K.B. 106; 1 Jur. 6; 112 E.R. 29 .... 95, 162
Shilling v. Accidental Death Insurance Co. (1857) 2 H. & N. 42; 26 L.J.Ex.
266; 29 L.T.O.S. 98; 5 W.R. 567; 157 E.R. 18; subsequent proceed-
ings, 27 L.J.Ex. 16; (1858) 1 F. & F. 116, N.P. 30, 34
Sillem v. Thornton (1854) 3 E. & B. 868; 2 C.L.R. 1710; 23 L.J.Q.B. 362; 23
L.T.O.S. 187; 18 Jur. 748; 2 W.R. 524; 118 E.R. 1367 227
Simcock v. Scottish Imperial Insurance Co. (1902) 10 S.L.T. 286 32
Simpson v. Accidental Death Insurance Co. (1857) 2 C.B.(N.S.) 257; 26
L.J.C.P. 289; 30 L.T.O.S. 31; 3 Jur.(N.S.) 1079; 5 W.R. 307; 104 E.R.
413 .... 70, 71
Simpson v. Scottish Union Insurance Co. (1863) 1 H. & M. 618; 1 New Rep.
537; 32 L.J.Ch. 329; 8 L.T. 112; 9 Jur.(N.S.) 711; 11 W.R. 459; 71 E.R.
270 233
—— v. Thomson (1877) 3 App.Cas. 279; 38 L.T. 1; 3 Asp.M.L.C. 567,
H.L. 248
Sinclair v. Maritime Passengers' Assurance (1861) 3 E. & E. 478; 30 L.J.Q.B.
77; 4 L.T. 15; 7 Jur.(N.S.) 367; 9 W.R. 342; 121 E.R. 521 172
Sinnot v. Bowden [1912] 2 Ch. 414; [1911–1913] All E.R.Rep. 752; 81 L.J.Ch.
832; 107 L.T. 609; 28 T.L.R. 594; 6 B.W.C.C.N. 157 234
Smith v. Colonial Mutual Fire Insurance Co. Ltd. (1880) 6 Vict.L.R. 200 231
—— v. National Mutual Fire Insurance Co. Ltd. [1974] 1 N.Z.L.R. 278 67
—— v. Pearl Assurance Co. [1939] 1 All E.R. 95 .... 205, 283
Smith (M.H.) (Plant Hire) Ltd. v. D.L. Mainwaring [1986] BCLC 342 243

Table of Cases   xxxi

Smith, (W.H.) *v.* Clinton & Harris (1908) 99 L.T. 840; 25 T.L.R. 34 191
Socony Mobil Oil Co. Inc. *v.* West of England Ship Owners Mutual Ins.
    Ass. [1984] 2 Lloyd's Rep. 408 283
Solicitors & General Life Assurance Society *v.* Lamb (1864) 2 De G.J. & S.
    251; 4 New Rep. 313; 33 L.J.Ch. 426; 10 L.T. 702; 10 Jur.(N.s.) 739; 12
    W.R. 941; 46 E.R. 372, L.JJ. 236
Solle *v.* Butcher [1950] 1 K.B. 671; 66 T.L.R. (Pt. 1) 448; [1949] 2 All E.R. 1107;
    [94 S.J. 465, 482, 514; 209 L.T. 66, 167; 15 M.L.R. 297; 66 L.Q.R. 169;
    14 Conv. 93], C.A. 213, 214
Soole *v.* Royal Insurance Co. [1971] 2 Lloyd's Rep. 332 286
South Staffordshire Tramways Co. *v.* Sickness & Accident Assurance
    Association [1891] 1 Q.B. 402; 60 L.J.Q.B. 260; 64 L.T. 279; 55 J.P. 372;
    39 W.R. 292; 7 T.L.R. 267, C.A. 290
Southern Cross Assurance Co. Ltd. *v.* Australian Provincial Assurance
    Association Ltd. (1935) 53 C.L.R. 618 27
—— *v.* —— (1939) 39 S.R. (N.S.W.) 174 56
Sparenborg *v.* Edinburgh Life Assurance Co. [1912] 1 K.B. 195; 81 L.J.K.B.
    299; 106 L.T. 567; 28 T.L.R. 51 124
Stanley *v.* Western Insurance Co. (1868) L.R. 3 Ex. 71; 37 L.J.Ex. 73; 17 L.T.
    513; 16 W.R. 369 177
State ex rel. Duffy *v.* Western Auto Supply Co., 134 Ohio St. 163 (1938) 10
Steadfast Insurance Co. *v.* F. & B. Trading Co. (1972) 46 A.L.J.R.
    10 .... 268, 269
Stearns *v.* Village Main Reef Gold Mining Co. (1905) 10 Com.Cas. 89; (1905)
    21 T.L.R. 236, C.A. 241
Stebbing *v.* Liverpool & London & Globe Insurance Co. [1917] 2 K.B. 433;
    [1916–1917] All E.R.Rep. 248; 86 L.J.K.B. 1155; 117 L.T. 247; 33
    T.L.R. 395, D.C. 205, 206
Stewart *v.* Merchants' Marine Insurance Co. (1885) 16 Q.B.D. 619; 55
    L.J.Q.B. 81; 53 L.T. 892; 34 W.R. 208; 2 T.L.R. 156; 5 Asp.M.L.C. 506,
    C.A. 228
—— *v.* Oriental Fire & Marine Insurance Co. [1985] Q.B. 988; [1984] 3
    W.L.R. 741; (1984) 128 S.J. 645; [1984] 3 All E.R. 777; [1984] 2 Lloyd's
    Rep. 109; [1985] F.L.R. 64; [1984] E.C.C. 564; (1984) 134 New L.J. 584;
    (1984) 81 L.S.Gaz. 1915 15
Stirling *v.* Vaughan (1809) 11 East 619; 2 Camp. 225; 103 E.R. 1145 42
Stockton *v.* Mason [1979] R.T.R. 130; [1978] 2 Lloyd's Rep. 430, C.A. ... 62, 63,
    138, 141, 143
Stokell *v.* Heywood [1897] 1 Ch. 459; 65 L.J.Ch. 721; 74 L.T. 781; 12 T.L.R.
    463 68
Stone *v.* Reliance Mutual Insurance Society [1972] 1 Lloyd's Rep. 469,
    C.A. 114, 115, 142
Stoneham *v.* Ocean Railway and General Accident Insurance Co. (1887) 19
    Q.B.D. 237 117
Stuart *v.* Freeman [1903] 1 K.B. 47; 72 L.J.K.B. 1; 87 L.T. 516; 51 W.R. 211; 19
    T.L.R. 24, C.A. 67, 71
Sun Fire Office *v.* Hart (1889) 14 App.Cas. 98; 58 L.J.P.C. 69; 60 L.T. 337; 53
    J.P. 548; 37 W.R. 561; 5 T.L.R. 289 68
Sutherland *v.* Sun Fire Office (1852) 14 D. (Ct. of Sess.) 775 229
Sweeney *v.* Kennedy [1950] Ir.R. 85 102
Sydney Turf Club *v.* Crowley (1972) 126 C.L.R. 420 259
Symington *v.* Union Insurance Society of Canton (1928) 97 L.J.K.B. 546;
    (1927) 164 L.T.Jo. 390 .... 170, 183, 185

Tailby v. Official Receiver (1888) 13 App.Cas. 523; 58 L.J.Q.B. 75; 60 L.T. 162; 37 W.R. 513; 4 T.L.R. 726, H.L.; reversing *sub nom.* Official Receiver v. Tailby (1886) 18 Q.B.D. 25, C.A. 132
Tattersall v. Drysdale [1935] 2 K.B. 174; 104 L.J.K.B. 511; 153 L.T. 75; 51 T.L.R. 405; 79 S.J. 418; [1935] All E.R.Rep. 112; 52 Ll.L.Rep. 21 .131, 299
Taunton v. Royal Insurance Co. (1864) 2 H. & M. 135; 33 L.J.Ch. 406; 10 L.T. 156; 28 J.P. 374; 10 Jur.(N.s.) 291; 12 W.R. 549; 71 E.R. 413 214
Taylor v. Allon [1966] 1 Q.B. 304; [1965] 2 W.L.R. 598; 109 S.J. 78; [1965] 1 All E.R. 557; [1965] 1 Lloyd's Rep. 155, D.C. 57, 64, 296
—— v. Caldwell (1863) 3 B. & S. 826; 2 New Rep. 198; 32 L.J.Q.B. 164; 8 L.T. 356; 27 J.P. 710; 11 W.R. 726; 122 E.R. 309 231
Terry v. Trafalgar Insurance Co. [1970] 1 Lloyd's Rep. 524 287
Theobald v. Railway Passengers' Assurance Co. (1854) 10 Exch. 45; 2 C.L.R. 1034; 23 L.J.Ex. 249; 23 L.T.O.S. 222; 18 Jur. 583; 2 W.R. 528; 156 E.R. 349 .... 182, 236
Thomas v. Dando [1951] 2 K.B. 620; [1951] 1 T.L.R. 1067; 115 J.P. 344; [1951] 1 All E.R. 1010; 49 L.G.R. 793, D.C. 294
—— v. National Farmers' Union Mutual Insurance Society [1961] 1 W.L.R. 386; 105 S.J. 233; [1961] 1 All E.R. 363; [1960] 2 Lloyd's Rep. 444; [25 Conv. 244; 105 S.J. 317] 45, 48
Thomas Cheshire & Co. v. Vaughan Bros. & Co. [1920] 3 K.B. 240; 89 L.J.K.B. 1168; 123 L.T. 487; 84 J.P. 233; 15 Asp.M.L.C. 69; 25 Com.Cas. 242; 3 Ll.L.Rep. 213, C.A. 151
Thompson v. Equity Fire Insurance Co. [1910] A.C. 592; 80 L.J.P.C. 13; 103 L.T. 153; 26 T.L.R. 616, P.C. 164
—— v. Madill (1986) 13 C.C.L.I. 242 42
Thomson v. Weems (1884) 9 App.Cas. 671, H.L. 106, 124
Tinline v. White Cross Insurance Association [1921] 3 K.B. 327; 90 L.J.K.B. 1118; 125 L.T. 632; 37 T.L.R. 733; 26 Com.Cas. 347 .... 193, 196
Toller v. Law Accident Insurance Society [1936] 80 S.J. 633; [1936] 2 All E.R. 952, C.A. 205
Tomlinson (Hauliers) v. Hepburn [1966] A.C. 451; [1966] 2 W.L.R. 453; 110 S.J. 86; [1966] 1 All E.R. 418; [1966] 1 Lloyd's Rep. 309, H.L.; affirming [1966] 1 Q.B. 21; [1965] 2 W.L.R. 634; 109 S.J. 10; [1965] 1 All E.R. 284; [1965] 1 Lloyd's Rep. 1; [1965] C.L.Y. 2017, C.A.; affirming [1964] 1 Lloyd's Rep. 416 .... 46, 47, 48, 51, 52, 261
Trickett v. Queensland Insurance Co. [1936] A.C. 159; 105 L.J.P.C. 38; 154 L.T. 228; 52 T.L.R. 164; 80 S.J. 74; [1935] All E.R.Rep. 729; 41 Com.Cas. 143; 53 Ll.L.Rep. 225, P.C. 304
Trident General Insurance Co. Ltd. v. McNiece Bros. Pty. Ltd. March 31, 1987 (unreported) 49, 50
Trim Joint District School Board of Management v. Kelly [1914] A.C. 667; 83 L.J.P.C. 220; 111 L.T. 305; 30 T.L.R. 452; 58 S.J. 493; 7 B.W.C.C. 274, H.L.; affirming *sub nom.* Kelly v. Trim Joint District School Board of Management 6 B.W.C.C. 921, C.A. 171
Trollope & Colls Ltd. v. Haydon [1977] 1 Lloyd's Rep. 244, C.A. 291
Turcan, *Re* (1888) 40 Ch.D. 5; 58 L.J.Ch. 101; 59 L.T. 712; 37 W.R. 70, C.A. 132, 273
Tyrie v. Fletcher (1777) 2 Cowp. 666; cited in 2 Doug.K.B. 784; 98 E.R. 1297 . 123
United Motor Services v. Hutson [1937] 1 D.L.R. 737; S.C.R. 294; 7 F.L.J. (Can.) 115 251
Vandepitte v. Preferred Accident Insurance Corporation of New York [1933] A.C. 70; 76 S.J. 798; [1932] All E.R.Rep. 527; 102 L.J.P.C. 21; 148 L.T. 169; 49 T.L.R, 90 .... 48, 49, 298

Table of Cases

Vandyke v. Fender (Sun Insurance Office, Third Party) [1970] 2 Q.B. 292; [1970] 2 W.L.R. 929; 114 S.J. 205; [1970] 2 All E.R. 335; 8 K.I.R. 854; [1970] R.T.R. 236; sub nom. Vandyke v. Fender and Reddington Foundries; Sun Insurance Office (Third party) [1970] 1 Lloyd's Rep. 320, C.A.; reversing [1969] 3 W.L.R. 217; 113 S.J. 467; 7 K.I.R. 14; [1969] 2 Lloyd's Rep. 164; sub nom. Vandyke v. Fender (Sun Insurance Office, Third Party) [1969] 3 All E.R. 1291 322
Verelst's Administratrix v. Motor Union Insurance Co. [1925] 2 K.B. 137; 94 L.J.K.B. 659; 133 L.T. 364; 41 T.L.R. 343; 69 S.J. 412; 30 Com.Cas. 256 199
Vernon v. Smith (1821) 5 B. & Ald. 1; 106 E.R. 1094 234
Wainewright v. Bland (1835) 1 Moo. & R. 481; subsequent proceedings (1836) 1 M. & W. 32 29
Walker v. Pennine Insurance Co. [1980] 2 Lloyd's Rep. 156, C.A.; affirming [1979] 2 Lloyd's Rep. 139 203
Warren v. Sutton (Henry) & Co. [1976] 2 Lloyd's Rep. 276, C.A. 149, 150
Waterkeyn v. Eagle Star Insurance Co. (1920) 5 Ll.L.R. 42 41
Waters v. Monarch Fire and Life Assurance Co. (1856) 5 E. & B. 870; 25 L.J.Q.B. 102; 26 L.T.O.S. 217; 2 Jur.(N.S.) 375; 4 W.R. 245; 119 E.R. 705 .... 46, 47, 48, 50, 51
Watkins v. O'Shaughnessy (1939) 83 S.J. 215; [1939] 1 All E.R. 384, C.A. 317
Watts v. Simmons (1924) 18 Ll.L.R. 177 203
Wayne Tank Co. v. Employers' Liability Assurance Corporation [1974] 1 Q.B. 57; [1973] 3 W.L.R. 483; 117 S.J. 564; [1973] All E.R. 825; [1973] 2 Lloyd's Rep. 237, C.A.; reversing [1972] 2 Lloyd's Rep. 141 ...... 187, 188
Webb, Re [1941] Ch. 225 277
Webb v. Bracey (1964) 108 S.J. 445; sub nom. Webb and Hughes (trading together as Wright and Webb) v. Bracey [1964] 1 Lloyd's Rep. 465 70
Webster v. British Empire Mutual Life (1880) 15 Ch.D. 169; 49 L.J.Ch. 769; 43 L.T. 229; 28 W.R. 818, C.A. 228
—— v. General Accident Fire and Life Assurance Corporation Ltd. [1953] 1 Q.B. 520; [1953] 2 W.L.R. 491; 97 S.J. 155; [1953] 1 All E.R. 663; [1953] 1 Lloyd's Rep. 123; [Sec.Jo., May 1953, p. 425; 22 Sol. 95; 69 L.Q.R. 163] 181
Weddell v. Road Transport & General Insurance Co. [1932] 2 K.B. 563; 75 S.J. 852; [1931] All E.R.Rep. 609; 101 L.J.K.B. 620; 146 L.T. 162; 48 T.L.R. 59; 41 Ll.L.Rep. 69 266
Weir v. Northern Counties Insurance (1879) 4 L.R.Ir. 689 202
Welch v. Royal Exchange Assurance [1939] 1 K.B. 294; 82 S.J. 969; [1938] 4 All E.R. 289; 108 L.J.K.B. 83; 159 L.T. 580; 55 T.L.R. 96; 44 Com.Cas. 27; 62 Ll.L.Rep. 83, C.A. 119, 201
West v. National Motor and Accident Insurance Union [1955] 1 W.L.R. 343; 99 S.J. 235; [1955] 1 All E.R. 800; [1955] 1 Lloyd's Rep. 207, C.A.; affirming [1954] 2 Lloyd's Rep. 461 100
West Wake Price & Co. v. Ching [1957] 1 W.L.R. 45; 101 S.J. 64; [1956] 3 All E.R. 821; [1956] 2 Lloyd's Rep. 618; [24 Sol. 87; 107 L.J. 437] 284
West of England Fire Insurance v. Isaacs [1897] 1 Q.B. 226; 66 L.J.Q.B. 36; 75 L.T. 564, C.A. 247
Western Australian Insurance Co. v. Dayton (1924) 35 C.L.R. 355; V.L.R. 533; 31 Argus L.R. 170 116
Westminster Fire Office v. Glasgow Provident Investment Society (1888) 13 App.Cas. 699; 59 L.T. 641; 4 T.L.R. 779, H.L. 44, 221, 224, 233

Table of Cases

White v. London Transport [1971] 2 Q.B. 721; [1971] 3 W.L.R. 169; [1971] R.T.R. 326; *sub nom.* White v. London Tranport Executive, 115 S.J. 368; [1971] 3 All E.R. 1; *sub nom.* White v. London Transport Executive and Motor Insurance Bureau [1971] 2 Lloyd's Rep. 256, C.A. 318

Williams v. Baltic Insurance Association of London [1924] 2 K.B. 282; 68 S.J. 814; [1924] All E.R.Rep. 368; 93 L.J.K.B. 819; 131 L.T. 671; 40 T.L.R. 668; 29 Com.Cas. 305; 19 Ll.L.Rep. 126 .... 45, 48, 49, 50, 298

Williams v. North China Insurance Co. (1876) 1 C.P.D. 757; 35 L.T. 884; 3 Asp.M.L.C. 342, C.A. 50

—— v. Thorp (1828) 2 Sim. 257; 57 E.R. 785 273

Wilkinson v. General Accident Fire and Life Assurance Corporation Ltd. [1967] 2 Lloyd's Rep. 182 142

Wilson v. Jones (1867) L.R. 2 Ex. 139; 36 L.J.Ex. 78; 15 L.J. 669; 15 W.R. 435; 2 Mar.L.C. 452 41

Wilson and Scottish Insurance Corporation, *Re* [1920] 2 Ch. 28; 64 S.J. 514; [1920] All E.R.Rep. 185; 89 L.J.Ch. 329; 123 L.T. 404; 36 T.L.R. 545 . 217, 218, 219, 226

Wimbledon Golf Club v. Imperial Insurance Co. (1902) 18 T.L.R. 815 234

Wing v. Harvey (1854) 5 De G.M. & G. 265; 2 Eq.Rep. 533; 23 L.J.Ch. 511; 23 L.T.O.S. 120; 18 Jur. 394; 2 W.R. 370; 43 E.R. 872, L.JJ. 143, 144

Winicofsky v. Army and Navy General Insurance Co. (1919) 88 L.J.K.B. 111; 35 T.L.R. 28 .... 96, 186

Winspear v. Accident Insurance Association (1880) 6 Q.B.D. 42; 50 L.J.Q.B. 292; 43 L.T. 459; 45 J.P. 110; 29 W.R. 116, C.A. 186

Wolenberg v. Royal Co-operative Collecting Society (1915) 83 L.J.K.B. 1316; 112 L.T. 1036, D.C. 123

Wood v. General Accident (1948) 65 T.L.R. 53; W.N. 430; 92 S.J. 720; 82 Ll.L.Rep. 77 301

Woolcott v. Excess Insurance Co. and Miles, Smith Anderson and Game [1979] 1 Lloyd's Rep. 231, C.A.; reversing [1978] 1 Lloyd's Rep. 633; [1979] 2 Lloyd's Rep. 210 .... 86, 138, 139, 144, 145, 148, 149

—— v. Sun Alliance & London Insurance [1978] 1 W.L.R. 493; (1977) 121 S.J. 744; [1978] 1 All E.R. 1253; [1978] 1 Lloyd's Rep. 629 92

Woolfall & Rimmer v. Moyle [1942] 1 K.B. 66 .... 102, 103, 289

Worthington v. Curtis [1975] 1 Ch.D. 419 .... 28, 35

Wright and Pole, *Re* (1834) 1 A. & E. 621; 110 E.R. 1344; *sub nom. Re* Sun Fire Office & Wright 3 Nev. & M.K.B. 819 182

Wyndham Rather Ltd. v. Eagle Star & British Dominions Insurance Co. Ltd. (1925) 21 Ll.L.Rep. 214 65

Yorkshire Insurance Co. v. Nisbet Shipping Co. [1962] 2 Q.B. 330; [1961] 2 W.L.R. 1043; 105 S.J. 367; [1961] 2 All E.R. 487; [1961] 1 Lloyd's Rep. 479; [231 L.T. 258] 106, 237, 242, 249, 250

Young v. Sun Alliance & London Insurance [1977] 1 W.L.R. 104 166

Ziel Nominees Pty. Ltd. v. V.A.C.C. Insurance Co. Ltd. (1976) 50 A.L.J.R. . 130

Zurich General Accident v. Morrison [1942] 2 K.B. 53; 111 L.J.K.B. 601; 86 S.J. 267; [1942] 1 All E.R. 529; 167 L.T. 183; 58 T.L.R. 217, C.A. 310

Zurich General Accident & Liability Insurance Co. Ltd. v. Rowberry [1954] 2 Lloyd's Rep. 55, C.A. 141, 260

TABLE OF STATUTES

1677	Statute of Frauds (c. 3)—	
	s. 4	58
1745	Marine Insurance Act (c. 37)	25
1774	Life Assurance Act (14 Geo. 3, c. 48)	24, 25, 28, 29, 36, 37, 38, 39, 44, 45, 50, 51, 52, 126, 261
	s. 1	26, 27, 33, 34, 35, 37, 38, 39, 50, 275
	s. 2	26, 33, 34, 35, 36, 37, 38, 39, 51, 52, 275
	s. 3	26, 27, 28, 29, 30, 32, 38, 39, 51, 225, 237
	s. 4	25, 37, 45
	Fires Prevention (Metropolis) Act (14 Geo. 3, c. 78)	51, 129, 235
	s. 83	38, 232, 233, 234, 261
1788	Marine Insurance Act (28 Geo. 3, c. 56)	25
1845	Gaming Act (8 & 9 Vict. c. 109)	25, 39, 225
	s. 18	25, 36
1867	Policies of Assurance Act (30 & 31 Vict. c. 144)	272
	s. 3	272
	s. 5	272
1870	Life Assurance Companies Act (33 & 34 Vict. c. 61)	12, 16
1871	Lloyds Act (c.xxi)	2
1882	Married Women's Property Act (45 & 46 Vict. c. 75)—	
	s. 11	29, 274, 275, 278
1896	Life Assurance Companies (Payment into Court) Act (59 & 60 Vict. c. 8)	273
1906	Marine Insurance Act (6 Edw. 7, c. 41)	2, 3, 74
	s. 4	25
	s. 17	210
	s. 18	84, 88
	s. 20	79
	s. 22	58
1906	Marine Insurance Act —cont.	
	s. 50	135
	ss. 60–63	179
	s. 79	242
	Sched. 2	25
1909	Assurance Companies Act (9 Edw. 7, c. 49)	12
	s. 1	12
	s. 30	12
1925	Trustee Act (15 & 16 Geo. 5, c. 19)—	
	s. 20 (4)	235
	Law of Property Act (15 & 16 Geo. 5, c. 20)—	
	s. 47	132, 133, 134
	(1)	133, 134
	(2)	133, 135
	s. 108 (2)	235
	s. 136	132, 249, 272
1930	Third Parties (Rights Against Insurers) Act (20 & 21 Geo. 5, c. 25)	281, 282, 309, 310, 327
	s. 1 (1)	281
	(2)	281
	(3)	281
	(6)	281
	s. 2	281
	s. 3	281
1934	Law Reform (Miscellaneous Provisions) Act (24 & 25 Geo. 5, c. 41)—	
	s. 3 (1)	228, 248
	Road Traffic Act (24 & 25 Geo. 5, c. 50)	304, 307
1939	New York Insurance Law (s. 41)	10
1943	Law Reform (Frustrated Contracts) Act (6 & 7 Geo. 6, c. 40)—	
	s. 1 (1)	232
	(3)	232
	s. 2 (5) (b)	232

1945	Australian Life Insurance Act—		1969	Employers' Liability (Compulsory Insurance) Act—*cont.*	
	s. 84	77		s. 2—*cont.*	
	ss. 95–99	69		(2)	324
	Sched. 6	69		s. 3	326
1948	Industrial Assurance and Friendly Societies Act (11 & 12 Geo. 6, c. 39)—			s. 4 (1)	326
				(2)	326
				s. 5	326
	s. 2	29	1972	Road Traffic Act (c. 20)	63, 73, 149, 194, 195, 306, 313, 319, 322, 327
	Agricultural Holdings Act (11 & 12 Geo. 6, c. 63)	45			
				s. 143	293, 294, 296, 297
1950	Arbitration Act (14 Geo. 6, c. 27)—			(2)	292, 297
				s. 144	293, 312
	s. 4	205		s. 145	64, 131, 292, 294, 298, 299
	s. 24	206			
1952	Defamation Act (15 & 16 Geo. 6 & 1 Eliz. 2, c. 66)—			(4)	294, 319
				(*b*)	319
				s. 146	294
	s. 11	191		s. 147	296
1958	Insurance Companies Act (6 & 7 Eliz. 2, c. 72)	15		(2)	296
				s. 148	304, 309, 311, 319
				(1)	305, 306, 307, 308, 320
1960	Civil Aviation (Licensing) Act (8 & 9 Eliz. 2, c. 38)—				
				(2)	283, 306, 325
				(4)	37, 45, 49, 298, 299
	s. 2	328		s. 149	135, 139, 194, 308, 310, 311
1961	Factories Act (c. 34)	195			
	Suicide Act (9 & 10 Eliz. 2, c. 60)	192		(1)	319
				(1A) (*b*)	320
1964	Riding Establishments Act (c. 70)—			(1C)	320
				(1E)	319
	s. 1	328		(2) (*a*)	309
1965	Nuclear Installations Act (c. 57)	328		(*b*)	309
				(*c*)	309
1967	Misrepresentation Act (c. 7)—			(3)	309, 310
				(4)	310
	s. 2 (2)	80		(4A)	320
	Companies Act (c. 81)—			(4B)	320
	Pt. II	15		(5) (*b*)	88
1969	Nuclear Installations Act (c. 18)	328		s. 150	310
				s. 153	297
	Family Law Reform Act (c. 46)—			ss. 155–156	294
				s. 158	296
	s. 19	274		s. 162	297
	Employers' Liability (Compulsory Insurance) Act (c. 57)	321, 327		s. 196 (1)	294
				Pt. VI	293
	s. 1	322, 324	1973	Matrimonial Causes Act (c. 18)—	
	(1)	321, 324			
	(2)	326		s. 24	275
	(3)	324		Insurance Companies Amendment Act (c. 58)	15, 157
	s. 2	324			

1973	Insurance Companies Amendment Act—*cont.*		1977	Protection from Eviction Act (c. 43)—	
	s. 50	33, 35		s. 5	43
	Australian Life Insurance Act—			Insurance Brokers (Registration) Act (c. 46)	137, 154, 327
	ss. 95–99	69		s. 2	154
	Sched. 6	69		s. 10	155
1974	Consumer Credit Act (c. 39)	42, 122, 157		s. 11	155
				s. 12	155
	s. 8	122		(2)	155
	s. 9	122		ss. 13–20	155
	s. 11 (1) (*a*)	122		s. 22	154
	s. 12 (*a*)	122		Unfair Contract Terms Act (c. 50)	4, 13, 14, 157, 159
	s. 16 (5)	122			
	s. 189	122		Sched. 1, para. 1 (*a*)	8
	Pt. VIII	271	1979	Estate Agents Act (c. 38)	328
	Insurance Companies Act (c. 49)	16		Sale of Goods Act (c. 54)	157
				s. 18, rule 1	130
	Road Traffic Act (c. 50)—			rule 5	131
	s. 20	311		s. 20	132
	Rehabilitation of Offenders Act (c. 53)	92		s. 39	130
				s. 61 (1)	45
	s. 4 (3) (*a*)	93	1981	Insurance Companies Act (c. 31)	16
	s. 7 (3)	94	1982	Forfeiture Act (c. 34)—	
1975	Social Security Act (c. 14)—			s. 1	192
	s. 53	322		s. 2	192
	Sex Discrimination Act (c. 65)—			(4)	192
				s. 5	192
	s. 29	91		Insurance Companies Act (c. 50)	13, 17, 18, 21, 60, 153, 270
	s. 45	91			
	Policyholders Protection Act (c. 75)	17, 22		s. 1	18
				s. 2	15, 17, 73
	ss. 5–12	22		(5)	11, 17
	s. 6	312		s. 3	17, 18
	s. 7	312		s. 4	17
	s. 11	22		s. 6	18
	s. 16	22		s. 7	18
	s. 17	22		(3)	18
	ss. 18–22	22		s. 8 (2)	18
1976	Adoption Act (c. 36)—			ss. 8 and 9	18
	s. 39	274		s. 9	18
	Supplementary Benefits Act (c. 71)—			(5)	18
				s. 11	18
	s. 17	29		s. 12	19
	s. 18	29		s. 15 (*b*)	17
	Race Relations Act (c. 74)—			s. 16	10, 19
				ss. 17–24	19
	s. 1	91		ss. 27–29	20
	s. 3	91		s. 32	19
	s. 20	91		s. 35	19

1982 Insurance Companies Act—*cont.*
ss. 37–48 20
s. 45 21
s. 46 21
ss. 53–59 21
s. 62 20
s. 72 58
　(5) 58
　(6) 58
s. 73 58
s. 74 152
ss. 75–77 59
s. 75 (4) 59
s. 83 22
s. 84 .... 18, 19
s. 86 22
Sched. 1 .... 12, 15, 18
Sched. 2 .... 12, 15, 18
　Pt. II 17
Lloyds Act (c. xiv) 2
1984 Australian Insurance Contracts Act (No. 80)—
s. 17 40

1984 Australian Insurance Contracts Act—*cont.*
s. 18 35
s. 19 35
1985 Companies Act (c. 6) 153
Insolvency Act (c. 65) 281, 310
1986 Insolvency Act (c. 45) 281, 310
ss. 423–425 274
Financial Services Act (c. 60) 2, 6, 152, 327
s. 51 59
s. 62 (1) 59
　(4) 59
s. 132 73
　(1) 73, 125
　(3) 73
　(6) 73
s. 133 58
s. 138 154
Sched. 1 59
　Pt. I, para. 10 270
　para. 5 (3) 59

Chapter 1

INTRODUCTION: THE NATURE AND DEFINITION OF INSURANCE AND INSURANCE LAW

The contract of insurance is basically governed by the rules which form part of the general law of contract, but there is equally no doubt that over the years it has attracted many principles of its own to such an extent that it is perfectly proper to speak of a law of insurance. Some of these principles owe their existence to the fact that the documents of the standard insurance contract, principally the proposal form and the policy, have long been drafted in a fairly uniform way. The effect of this will be seen throughout this book. In addition, the reasons for many of the principles of insurance can be found by looking at the history of insurance and of the insurance contract. A detailed examination of this history would be inappropriate in a book of this size,[1] but a brief excursus is useful to set the scene.

History

The origins of the modern insurance contract are to be found in the practices adopted by Italian merchants from the fourteenth century onwards, although there is little doubt that the concept of insuring was known long before then. Maritime risks, the risk of losing ships and cargoes at sea, instigated the practice of medieval insurance and dominated insurance for many years. The habit spread to London merchants but not, it appears, until the sixteenth century. At first, there were no separate insurers. A group of merchants would agree to bear the risks by each other among themselves.

For a long time, the common law played little or no part in the regulation of disputes concerning insurance. For this purpose merchants in 1601 secured the establishment by statute of a chamber of assurance which was outside the normal legal system. However, with the appointment of Lord Mansfield as Lord Chief Justice in the mid-eighteenth century, the common law courts took an interest in insurance contracts. Lord Mansfield

---

[1] See for more detail, Holdsworth, "The Early History of the Contract of Insurance" (1917) 17 Col.L.R. 85; Clayton, *British Insurance* (1970).

applied principles derived from the law merchant as well as more traditional common law concepts to the solution of disputes over insurance, and by the time of his retirement in 1788, the jurisdiction of the courts over insurance matters had been established.

Marine insurance retained its prominent position for some considerable time, and from the late seventeenth century onwards was increasingly transacted at a coffee-house in the City of London owned by a man called Lloyd. There developed the practice that the merchant wishing insurance would pass round to the people willing to provide it, who were gathered there, a slip of paper on which he had written the details of the ship, voyage and cargo etc. The slip was initialled by those willing to accept a proportion of the risk. When the total amount of insurance required was underwritten, the contract was complete.[2] From this practice comes the term "underwriter" which, of course, is still in use today and the name of the owner of the coffee-house attached itself to the institution. Lloyd's of London is now itself a Corporation formed with statutory authority,[3] and it has long since ceased to operate from a coffee-house, but the notable thing is that its members still underwrite the risks personally, putting at risk their entire personal fortunes, and they conduct their business in much the same way as it was done in the coffee-house.[4] The influence of Lloyd's on insurance and insurance law has been very significant; for example, the standard Lloyd's marine insurance policy was adopted as the statutory form in the Marine Insurance Act 1906. This is not to deny, however, that there have long been numer-

---

[2] For a more detailed legal analysis of this, see Chapter 4 at pp. 60–61.

[3] Lloyd's Acts 1871–1982. For a detailed description of this legislation, see Ellis and Wiltshire, *The Regulation of Insurance Business*. See also Ferguson, "Self-regulation at Lloyd's: The Lloyd's Act 1982" (1983) 46 M.L.R. 56.

[4] Despite the revised regime established by the Lloyd's Act 1982, recent years have witnessed a number of scandals there. These occurred at least partly because of the fact that the organisation of business at Lloyd's leaves large sums of money paid by insureds, nominally to the underwriters, in fact in the hands of the underwriting agents who manage the syndicates in which the actual insurers, the "names," are organised. There were also conflicts of interest arising from the same people having interests in both underwriting agencies and in firms of Lloyd's brokers, through whose hands all insurance placed at Lloyd's must go. The scandals led to calls for Lloyd's to be brought within the framework of the Financial Services Act 1986, in so far as its working members hold and deal in money for the benefit of the names, but these calls were successfully resisted. Some amendment of the present regime seems, however, likely in the near future.

Introduction 3

ous other companies and associations transacting the business of insurance.[5]

The principles developed in regard to marine insurance have by and large been applied to the other types of insurance subsequently developed.[6] The first of these was fire insurance, its birth stimulated by the Great Fire of London in 1666. This was followed by life and personal accident insurance, the latter growing rapidly as the railways and industrialisation spread rapidly in the nineteenth century. The present century has seen such development that it is now possible to insure almost every conceivable event or thing against the risk of loss or damage. Nevertheless, the law governing all these insurances is basically the same. Marine insurance law was codified in the Marine Insurance Act 1906 and is generally regarded as *sui generis*. This book is not directly concerned with marine insurance, but on occasion reference will be made to sections of the 1906 Act and to marine cases, especially where they establish a principle of general applicability or provide authority for a principle which is also valid for non-marine insurance. In general, non-marine insurance contracts are still based on case-law, but there have been some statutory inroads.[7]

Reform and practice

More wide-ranging statutory reform of non-marine insurance contract law appears unlikely for the foreseeable future, despite the fact that important reforms were recommended by the Law

---

[5] See Chapter 2 for a brief description of those bodies allowed to act as insurers. For a readable description and critique of the British insurance market, see McCrae and Cairncross, *Capital City* (2nd ed., 1985), Chapter 7.

[6] This is perhaps the major reason for the unsatisfactory nature of some of the principles of insurance law, at least as they apply to consumer contracts. There is obviously a vast difference between the circumstances surrounding a marine policy in the early days of insurance and those surrounding the modern mass-produced motor, household etc policies. An explanation for the courts' (and indeed the legislature's) failure to intervene and correct these unsatisfactory rules may lie in the fact that Britain has long had a comprehensive social security insurance system. In contrast, in the United States, where such a system is of a more recent origin and much less extensive, and where therefore private insurance was and is much more important in providing basic protection, the courts have been very active in intervening to protect the position of insureds: see Hasson, "The special nature of the insurance contract: a comparison of the American and English law of insurance" (1984) 47 M.L.R. 505.

[7] In particular, in respect of life insurance contracts; see Chapter 4 below.

Commission in 1980.[8] Further, although there is considerable protection afforded to insureds against an insurer's insolvency, as will be seen in Chapter 2, there is no existing or indeed potential control of policy terms and conditions, in contrast with the position in many other countries, especially those with a civil law system. It may well be that a general freedom from state control has led to benefits for insurance consumers in terms of both the cover provided and its costs.[9]

However, there are aspects of insurance contract law whose potential unfairness, particularly as far as individual consumers are concerned, has often been recognised and some of these were the subject of the Law Commission Report mentioned above. In respect of these aspects, reform by "self-regulation" has become the vogue.[10] First there are *Statements of Insurance Practice*, first introduced in 1977[11] and revised in 1986,[12] under which most insurers undertake not to exercise some of their legal rights against their individual policyholders. The *Statements of Practice* are not legally binding, although no doubt a large majority of insurers observes their terms.[13] Second, there are codes of practice regulating the activities of insurance intermediaries.[14] Third, there are useful complaints mechanisms for individual consumer insureds outside the traditional court structure. The more widely used of these, the Insurance Ombudsman Bureau,[15] provides for an independent ombuds-

---

[8] Report No. 104, Cmnd. 8064. Brief accounts of the Law Commission's recommendations can be found at pp. 96–98 and 119–120, below. See also, Birds, "The Reform of Insurance Law" [1982] J.B.L. 449.

[9] For a useful study, comparing the British system with the much more regulatory German system, see the Institute for Fiscal Studies, *Insurance: Competition or Regulation?*, Report Series No. 19, 1985.

[10] For a more detailed account, see Birds, "Self-regulation and insurance contracts," *New Foundations for Insurance Law*," (1987) Chapter 1. For an interesting study of the many agreements, many of them modifying the legal rules, under which the insurance industry operates, see Lewis, "Insurers' agreements not to enforce strict legal rights: bargaining with government and in the shadow of the law" (1985) 48 M.L.R. 275.

[11] This was in return for the exemption of insurance contracts from the Unfair Contract Terms Act 1977. See Birds (1977) 40 M.L.R. 677.

[12] The text can be found in Part 7 of the *Encyclopedia of Insurance Law*.

[13] Note, though, that in respect of the original 1977 *Statements*, it took some considerable time for some insurers to comply; see the report of the Scottish Consumer Council, *Forms without Fuss*, 1981.

[14] See Chapter 10, below, at p. 152.

[15] The other mechanism, Personal Insurances Arbitration Service, was formed as a rival to the Insurance Ombudsman Bureau by a number of insurers who feared, groundlessly as it turned out, that the ombudsman would become a

man supported by a council a majority of whose members are independent of the insurance company members of the Bureau. The ombudsman conciliates and arbitrates upon disputes between member companies and policyholders under terms of reference which provide that the companies, but not the policyholders, are bound by his adjudications. The ombudsman decides cases in accordance with good practice as much as in accordance with the law, but he is not simply a consumer champion. His decisions and the advice he has given to both insurers and insureds provide an interesting picture of the operation of the modern insurance industry.[16]

Despite the existence of these self-regulatory devices, it is thought that the case for reform of aspects of insurance contract law has not disappeared, principally because a minority of insurers remains outside the regulatory framework.[17] Suggestions for reform as well as descriptions of the content of these devices will be made at appropriate places throughout this book.

Some Classifications of Insurance

The insurance industry today transacts vast amounts of business, not just in Britain but overseas. The risks which it covers can be classified in several different ways. It is worthwhile explaining two of these classifications because they relate to some important legal distinctions.

First and third party insurance

First, one can distinguish first party insurance, under which one insures one's own life, house, factory or car etc. from third party or liability insurance, that is, insuring against one's potential liability in law to pay damages to another. Of course, first and third party aspects may well be combined in the same policy. The law reflects this difference, first by demanding that

---

consumer champion. It still exists but very little is known about its workings, as, unlike the I.O.B., there are no regular reports published.

[16] See the Annual Reports of the Bureau.

[17] That is principally those insurers who are not members of the Association of British Insurers or of Lloyd's. Although the Department of Trade and Industry expects these insurers to comply, there does not seem to be any really effective means of monitoring how they deal with their insureds. Another argument for legal reform is that the liquidator of a failed insurance company would be bound to apply the law, not the practice, in dealing with the company's policyholders' claims.

some third party insurances should be compulsory[18] and secondly by recognising that in practice, third party insurance involves the third party as much as the insured person. Often in practice, for example, the victim of a car accident may talk in terms of claiming from the negligent driver's insurer rather than from the driver, which in law is the correct way of expressing the position. The law has deemed that in certain cases the third party should be protected from the strict contractual rights and liabilities between insured and insurer.[19] Although we are not generally concerned with the economics of insurance nor with how efficient it is, it is worth pointing out that in general third party insurance is much more expensive and less efficient than first party insurance, a factor, among others, which has led many people to conclude that in certain areas, especially road and work accidents involving personal injury or death, the present system of third party insurance backing up a system of liability in tort should be replaced by first party insurance. The latter could be run by private insurers, but more logically should be taken over by the state as part of the social security system.[20] It must be admitted that such a development at present appears highly unlikely.

Life and other insurances

A second classification, which is well recognised in law and meaningful in insurance circles, distinguishes between life insurance on the one hand and all other forms of insurance on the other. There is a great variety of forms of life insurance,[21] ranging from pure whole life insurance, an undertaking to pay a certain sum on the death of the life insured whenever this occurs, to endowment policies whereby the insured receives a sum if he survives beyond a certain age, to modern devices which combine an element of life insurance with the more substantial element of investment in securities or property.[22] Whatever the type of life policy, the uncertainty which, as will be

---

[18] See Chapters 19 and 20.
[19] *Ibid.*
[20] See generally, *e.g.* Atiyah, *Accident Compensation and the Law* (3rd. ed., 1980); Report of the Royal Commission on Civil Liability and Compensation for Personal Injury (The Pearson Report), 1978 Cmnd. 7054.
[21] See further Chapter 17.
[22] That in practice many life insurance policies are in reality investments has been recognised by the incorporation of many forms of life insurance within the investor protection framework established by the Financial Services Act 1986. The detailed consideration of this framework is outside the scope of this book, but aspects of it are considered; see especially pp. 59–60 and 154, below.

seen shortly, is a necessary feature of all insurances is of a different nature from the uncertainty in other insurances. Death is certain; the uncertainty is as to when it will occur. On the other hand, the property insured against loss by fire may never burn down, the motor insured may never be involved in an accident. Accordingly, contracts of life insurance and related ones such as personal accident insurances, are regarded simply as contracts for contingency insurance, in other words, contracts to pay an agreed sum of money when the event insured against occurs. Non-life insurance contracts are, in general, contracts to indemnify the insured only in respect of the loss suffered if it is actually suffered and only to the amount of the loss suffered.[23] We shall return to this distinction at the relevant points throughout this book.

Terminology

There are one or two related points as to the terminology of insurance. It is sometimes said that the proper description of the contract which insures a life is life *assurance* and this is indeed a common, though not universal, usage. The reason is simply that death is assured of happening, the risks covered by other insurances are not. But because the usage is not universal, we shall in general use the terms "insurance" and "insured" in all cases. It is also not uncommon, both in policies and in statute, to refer to the "policyholder" rather than the insured, but this book will tend to use the latter term.

The Legal Definition of Insurance

An essential task at this stage is to attempt to formulate a legal definition or at least an explanation of the meaning of the contract of insurance. As has been pointed out judicially,[24] this is not an easy matter. The statutes dealing with the regulation of insurance business, of which the Insurance Companies Act 1982 is the current one, have never contained a definition, no doubt because of the risk of inadvertantly excluding contracts which should be within their scope.[25] One effect of this,

---

[23] Valued policies, where the insured is entitled to a stated sum regardless of the exact measure of his loss, are rare but possible in non-marine insurance; see Chapter 13 at pp. 225–226.
[24] *Department of Trade and Industry* v. *St. Christopher Motorists' Association Ltd.* [1974] 1 All E.R. 395; *Medical Defence Union* v. *Dept. of Trade* [1979] 2 All E.R. 421 at 429.
[25] See the *St. Christopher* case, at 396–7.

though, must be that it gives the regulatory authority, the Department of Trade and Industry, a considerable discretion which can be challenged effectively only by a body going to court in order to seek a declaration that it is not carrying on insurance business or having to defend an application by the Department for a declaration that it is. Apart from the desirability of defining the scope of what the law of insurance applies to, clearly the fundamental reason for any attempt to define the meaning of insurance contract is because the business of providing insurance under contracts of insurance is closely regulated. We shall briefly consider the nature of this regulation in the next chapter.

However, there are other reasons. Insurance law has its peculiar principles, for example the doctrine of *uberrima fides*,[26] and it may be necessary to know whether a contract is one of insurance in order to know whether this doctrine applies. Furthermore, a statute may include within or exempt from its operation "contracts of insurance" without defining these. The obvious case is the exemption of such contracts from the Unfair Contract Terms Act 1977.[27]

As it happens, almost all the decided cases which have considered this problem have been concerned to discover whether or not a business was subject to regulation as insurance. Others have been concerned with tax statutes and one or two only with principles peculiar to the insurance contract.[28] It will be assumed for the present that a definition can be found which works for all purposes, and only afterwards considered whether, in fact, it might not be useful to have different definitions for different purposes.

A suggested definition for regulatory purposes

It is suggested that a contract of insurance is any contract whereby one party assumes the risk of an uncertain event,[29] which is not within his control, happening at a future time, in which event the other party has an interest, and under which

[26] See Chapter 6.
[27] Sched. 1, para. 1(*a*): see the text above at footnote 11.
[28] One area which has given rise to litigation and to difficulties is that of distinguishing contracts of insurance from contracts of guarantee. See Blair, "The Conversion of Guarantee Contracts" (1966) 39 M.L.R. 522.
[29] It is clear that the uncertain event need not be adverse to the other party, though in cases other than certain endowment and annuity policies, it will be. See *Gould* v. *Curtis* [1913] 3 K.B. 84, qualifying the definition given in the leading case of *Prudential Insurance Co.* v. *I.R.C.* [1904] 2 K.B. 658, and the discussion by Megarry V.C. in the *Medical Defence Union* case, above at 427–428.

contract the first party is bound to pay money or provide its equivalent if the uncertain event occurs. It would follow that anyone who regularly enters into such contracts as the party bearing the risks is carrying on insurance business for the purposes of the statute regulating insurance business. Several aspects of this definition merit closer attention.

Legal entitlement
First, there must clearly be a binding contract, and the insurer must be legally bound to compensate the other party. A right to be considered for a benefit which is truly only discretionary is not enough. In *Medical Defence Union* v. *Department of Trade*,[30] the plaintiff was a company whose members were practising doctors and dentists. Its business consisted primarily of conducting legal proceedings on behalf of members and indemnifying them against claims made against them in respect of damages and costs. However, under its constitution, its members had no right to such benefits, merely the right to request that they be given assistance or an indemnity. It was held that the company was not carrying on insurance business. The contracts between it and its members were not contracts of insurance because to be that a contract must provide for the right of the insured to money or money's worth on the happening of the uncertain event. The right to request assistance was not such a right.

Uncertainty
Second, the uncertainty which is a necessary feature of insurance, as we have already seen, is in most cases as to whether or not the event insured against will occur. In life insurance, it is as to the time when it will occur.[31]

Insurable interest
Third, the other party, the insured, must have an insurable interest in the property or life or liability which is the subject of the insurance. This will be examined in detail in Chapter 3.

Control
Fourth, it seems essential that the event insured against be outside the control of the party assuming the risk. No English

---
[30] See note 24, above.
[31] See *Gould* v. *Curtis*, above.

case has directly considered this point, but it has been raised in two cases when it was not necessary for decision.[32] The potential problem can be illustrated by considering the case of a manufacturer who contractually guarantees his products to his consumers. The example may be taken of a washing machine manufacturer who undertakes to repair any fault arising from defective manufacture within a year of purchase. He has clearly undertaken to provide a service in money's worth in assuming the risk of an uncertain event in which the consumer clearly has an interest. Yet surely he has not entered into a contract of insurance as most people would understand it. It is suggested that the answer is to introduce the element of control.[33] In the example, all that the manufacturer has done is to guarantee to put things right which he has put wrong in the first place, *i.e.* defects in manufacture. Therefore, his guarantee is not a contract of insurance.[34] On the other hand, however, someone who in return for a consideration guarantees a product against certain risks which are not within his control because they are not his products, nor has he sold them, is arguably entering into contracts of insurance. The same would be true if a manufacturer did more than simply guarantee his products against manufacturing defects, for example, if he undertook to replace them if they were damaged from specified causes.[35] Associations which provide a repair or recovery service for car owners upon breakdown might also be regarded as providing insur-

---

[32] The *St. Christopher* case, above, at 401; the *Medical Defence Union* case, above at 424.

[33] Perhaps "control" is a misleading term, as in practice a manufacturer may have very little actual control over his warranted products. An alternative formulation might be whether the alleged insurer is in fact responsible for producing the event giving rise to the claim for indemnity.

[34] See the American cases cited in Hellner, "The Scope of Insurance Regulation: What is Insurance for the Purposes of Regulation?' (1963) 12 Am. J. Comp. L. 494 at 505.

[35] *Ibid.* at 505–506. The leading U.S. case is perhaps *State ex rel. Duffy* v. *Western Auto Supply Co.* 134 Ohio St. 163 (1938). The New York Insurance Law, s.41, among others, incorporates the control test into its definition of insurance contracts. However, the use of this test has been criticised; see, *e.g.* Hellner *op. cit.*, especially at 500–502. If such a manufacturer were held to be entering into contracts of insurance, that does not necessarily imply that he is carrying on the business of insurance for the purposes of the 1982 Act; see Megarry V.C. in the *Medical Defence Union* case at 431–432. It should be noted that were this the result, the manufacturer is not strictly entitled to carry on any other commercial business (Insurance Companies Act 1982, s.16) which would obviously be ridiculous. See also Parkash, [1985] *Law Society's Gazette* 3547.

ance, assuming that their members have a right to their services and not just a right to be considered.[36]

Provision of money's worth
Fifth, there seems no reason in principle why it should be necessary for the insurer to have to undertake to pay money on the occurrence of the uncertain event, although this was the view taken by some of the leading books.[37] In any event, there is now clear authority that the provision of something other than money is enough, provided that it is of money's worth. In *Department of Trade and Industry* v. *St. Christopher's Motorists' Association Ltd.*,[38] the defendant undertook to provide its members with chauffeur services should they be disqualified from driving due to being convicted of having more than the permitted level of alcohol in the blood. It was held that this constituted insurance. The fact that the benefits were not in money was irrelevant. As was pointed out in the subsequent case of *Medical Defence Union* v. *Dept. of Trade*, which has already been examined, it is not sufficient nor accurate to say that the provision of services is enough.[39] It is better to say that it must be the provision of something that is clearly worth money, whether that be a right to valuable services, a right to advice[40] or a right to have an item of property repaired or replaced.

Other requirements?
Certain authorities suggest, however, that the above definition may not be sufficiently comprehensive. *Hampton* v. *Toxteth Co-operative Society*[41] and *Hall D'Ath* v. *British Provident*

---

[36] This is implicitly recognised by the fact that the activities of such associations are exempt from the control of the Insurance Companies Act 1982; see reg. 23 of the Insurance Companies Regs. 1981 S.I. No. 1654, made under s.2(5) of the 1982 Act.
[37] *e.g. Chitty on Contracts* (23rd ed.), para. 991, a view revised in the 24th ed., para. 3901, following the *St. Christopher* case.
[38] Note 24, above. It should be noted that by the time the case was heard, the defendant had in fact made arrangements for insurance which were satisfactory to the Department of Trade, so that they did not appear in court.
[39] [1979] 2 All E.R. at 428.
[40] It was also said in the *Medical Defence Union* case, above, at 430, that a right to advice and assistance conferred on members of a club should involve the "insurer" in additional expenses, rather than being merely part of the general costs of running the club for the benefit of members generally. Megarry V.C. would therefore add "or the provision of services to be paid for by the insurer" to "money or money's worth."
[41] [1915] 1 Ch. 721.

Association[42] both appear to suggest that there can be no insurance business carried on in the absence of a clearly stipulated premium and policy. In the *Hampton* case, membership of a local co-operative society was expressed to confer the right to a sum of money on the death of a member's spouse, the sum to be calculated by reference to the member's purchases from the society over a certain period. This was held not to constitute the provision of life insurance, so that the society was not required to deposit the sum of £20,000 under the relevant regulating statute, the Assurance Companies Act 1909. It is clear that the majority of the Court of Appeal[43] did regard the absence of a policy as crucial; the decision may also have turned upon the fact that under the rules of the society as the court read them, there was no enforceable contractual right to the sums concerned. It has already been seen how this is essential.

The absence of a policy was probably crucial because the 1909 Act, in sections 1 and 30, expressly referred to the carrying on of insurance business under *policies* of insurance. The *Hampton* case[44] can therefore be read as turning on a point of statutory construction.[45] The present definition in Schedules 1 and 2 of the Insurance Companies Act 1982 refers merely to *contracts* of insurance, and it is suggested therefore, that these older cases are of no relevance to the construction of the modern statute and to a modern definition of insurance at least for regulation purposes.[46] It would indeed be most strange if a business could escape from regulation as insurance merely by introducing less formality, even if in all respects the contracts it entered into fell within a definition of the sort that has been given here. The legislature has deemed that insurers should be more closely scrutinised as regards their financial situation than most other businesses, because of the importance of insurance, the risks involved, and the need to ensure that insureds do not suffer at the hands of reckless or fraudulent insurers.

---

[42] (1932) 48 L.T.R. 240.
[43] Phillimore L.J. dissented strongly.
[44] The same must be true of the *Hall D'Ath* case.
[45] This also distinguishes the earlier case of *Nelson* v. *Board of Trade* (1901) 84 L.T. 565, where tea merchants who offered married women who bought their tea over a certain period annuities on the deaths of their husbands were held to be subject to the Life Assurance Companies Act 1870. Although "policies" appeared in that Act, this was only part of the relevant definition; the other part referred simply to the granting of annuities upon human life, with no reference to the necessity for a policy.
[46] Whether or not the *Hampton* case might be used as the basis for a definition for other purposes is discussed briefly below.

A wider view

It may indeed be arguable that there should be no great concern to find a formal definition of insurance for regulation purposes. It could be enough to say that any transaction that looks like insurance by displaying the necessary characteristics of assumption and distribution of risk, and which is transacted on a reasonable scale, should be the subject of regulation.[47] On this view, technical questions as to the enforceability of the right by the insured, and whether or not the benefit he is promised is worth money, may be irrelevant. If, in fact, the "insurer" regularly dispenses real benefit, he should be regarded as an insurer. As has been pointed out with respect to the *Medical Defence Union* case,[48] it is, in fact, extremely rare for that company to refuse assistance to its members, and it is unlikely that any member faced with an allegation of negligence would deny that he was getting his money's worth from the company. There are strong arguments that such a body is in fact in the business of insuring to such an extent that the protection of its members requires that it be subject to the regulatory provisions of the Insurance Companies Act.

Definition for other purposes

If, in order to qualify as insurance for the purposes of regulation, it is sufficient that a transaction displays the necessary characteristics, the question arises whether a similar description will suffice for other purposes. Take, for example, the sort of deal that involves the assumption of risk outside the control of the party assuming the risk, but which is not referred to, nor perhaps would most people think of it, as insurance. As well as the examples given earlier, a case which has been known to exist involved a manufacturer of engine lubricants who, when he sold these, also guaranteed that the purchaser's car would not break down from any cause for a certain period. Clearly this went beyond risks which were within his control. Could such a manufacturer claim, for example, that his contracts are exempt from the statutory control of exclusion clauses in the Unfair Contract Terms Act 1977, because they are contracts of insurance? It is suggested that he should not be able to do so. For regulation purposes, for the reasons mentioned, a wide definition of insurance should be used which would indeed catch

---

[47] See especially, for a full and persuasive argument on these lines, to which the text does no justice at all, the article by Hellner cited in note 34.
[48] Roberts (1980) 43 M.L.R. 85; Merkin (1979) 1 *Liverpool Law Review* 125.

this sort of case. However, the Unfair Contract Terms Act exemption was clearly intended to apply to contracts of insurance as normally understood and described.[49] The policy of the Act dictates that anything which does not choose to identify itself as insurance cannot claim the advantage of the exemption. It is suggested therefore, that for this purpose, and perhaps for the purposes of applying the special rules of insurance law such as the doctrine of *uberrima fides*, there is merit in the views expressed in the *Hampton* case and others that the transactions are accompanied by the usual incidents of insurance, namely some sort of policy and an identifiable premium.

---

[49] Because the insurance industry promulgated *Statements of Practice* in return; see p. 4, above.

Chapter 2

THE PARTIES TO THE CONTRACT OF INSURANCE

This chapter is devoted to a brief consideration of the parties involved in the insurance transaction, namely the insurer and the insured. So far as the latter is concerned, little needs to be said. He must have an insurable interest in what he insures, something which is examined in detail in the next chapter, and he must have the usual capacity to contract.[1]

By far the more important matter is the position of the insurer, since the ability to act in such a capacity is closely controlled by the state. Before this matter is considered, it should be noted that many contracts of insurance and subsequent dealings thereon are conducted through the agency of an intermediary. Full consideration of this question is deferred to Chapter 10.

THE REGULATION OF INSURERS

It was seen in Chapter 1 that the most important, albeit not the only, reason for defining the contract of insurance is because the carrying on of insurance business is regulated by statute. It should be noted that entry into one isolated contract of insurance, as defined above, would probably not mean that the "insurer" had to be authorised since the Insurance Companies Act 1982, section 2, requires that persons *carry on* insurance business before they must be authorised.[2] The entry into one insurance contract can hardly be so regarded, unless perhaps

---

[1] The detailed law on capacity may be found in any standard text on the law of contract.

[2] As to the consequences of a lack of authorisation on the contracts entered into by an unauthorised insurer, see p. 73, below. Note that, in respect of the classes of insurance business listed in Scheds. 1 and 2 to the 1982 Act, the Act refers to both the effecting and the carrying out of insurance contracts. It has been held that these are to be read disjunctively so that "effecting" means entering into contracts and "carrying out" means, *inter alia*, paying of claims. If either activity is performed in the United Kingdom, authorisation is required: *The Bedford Insurance Co. Ltd.* v. *Instituto de Ressaguros do Brasil* [1984] 1 Lloyd's Rep. 210; *Stewart* v. *Oriental Fire and Marine Ins. Co.* [1984] 2 Lloyd's Rep. 109.

the transaction and the risk assumed thereunder are of such magnitude that the affair cannot in reality be written off as not involving the carrying on of insurance business.

Closely linked with the statutory control of insurers is the law which exists to protect insured persons when this control fails and this will be examined below.

It must be stressed that the following account gives only the barest outline of what is, in part, a very complex area of law.[3]

The source of state control

State control of insurers began in 1870.[4] It followed the failure some two years previously of two sizeable life insurance companies. The pattern has been repeated until recently in the sense that the subsequent revisions and extensions of control have generally followed some major insurance collapse which drew attention to the defects in the existing law or the way that it was applied. For example, the circumstances surrounding the liquidation of the Fire, Auto and Marine Insurance Company in the mid-1960s led to a substantial amendment (by Part II of the Companies Act 1967) of the system then established under the Insurance Companies Act 1958. Even more disastrous was the failure of the "cut-price" motor insurer, the Vehicle and General, in 1971, when overnight approximately one million motorists found themselves without cover.[5] As a result, the 1958 Act was further amended by the Insurance Companies Amendment Act 1973. The legislation was then consolidated in the Insurance Companies Act 1974. However, this Act was premature because it almost immediately had to be amended in order to take account of requirements emanating from an EEC Directive.[6] The regulations effecting these amendments were then consolidated in the Insurance Companies Act 1981 which further amended the 1974 Act because of additional EEC

---

[3] For a detailed description, see Ellis and Wiltshire, *The Regulation of Insurance Business*. An annotated version of the legislation may be found in the *Encyclopedia of Insurance Law*.

[4] Life Assurance Companies Act 1870. This and amending statutes until the 1930s required only that insurers deposit a sum of money with the court as security.

[5] The Department of Trade was severely criticised over this by a Tribunal of Inquiry: 1972 H.C. Papers 133. See Chapman, "The Vehicle & General Affair: Some Reflections for Public Administration in Britain" (1973) *Public Administration* 273.

[6] The Directive regarding Freedom of Establishment in Non-Life Insurance, No. 73/239 (July 23, 1973), concerning the right of insurers from one EEC Member State to establish branches or agencies in other EEC States.

requirements.[7] These Acts were then consolidated in the Insurance Companies Act 1982, which is now the primary source of the law, but it must be added that a good deal of detail is still contained in regulations.

Added to the fact that the Department of Trade and Industry, the Government department charged with insurance supervision, now has more expertise and manpower in the insurance field than it once possessed, the 1982 Act provides a fairly watertight system for the financial regulation of insurers. Should this perchance fail, the Policyholders Protection Act 1975, which will be described later, will operate in the last resort to ensure that insureds are very little, if at all, out of pocket as the result of an insurance insolvency.

Authorisation under the Insurance Companies Act 1982

Under section 2, only the following are permitted to carry on insurance business: (a) bodies authorised under section 3 or (under section 4) existing prior to the Act by virtue of having been authorised under the earlier Acts; (b) members of Lloyd's; (c) registered friendly societies; and (d) for limited purposes only,[8] trades unions and employers' associations. For present purposes, authorised companies and Lloyd's underwriters are the important categories. Friendly societies, which are of no mean importance in a limited field, namely that of industrial life assurance, are under the control of the Registrar of Friendly Societies and generally outside the scope of this book. It should be noted that the Secretary of State has power to exempt from the authorisation requirement insurers who provide exclusively or primarily benefits in kind such as vehicle recovery services.[9]

The development and organisation of Lloyd's was noted briefly earlier.[10] It is a measure of the strength of that organisation that self-regulation was regarded as generally sufficient[11] until pressure from Europe necessitated its inclusion within

---

[7] The Establishment Directive on Life Business, No. 79/267 (March 5, 1979). It should be noted that proposals for Directives to establish freedom of services, that is the right of an insurer in one member state to sell insurance directly in another member state, have existed for some time. See Charpette, "Freedom to provide insurance services in the European Community" (1984) 9 E.L.R. 3.

[8] The provision of provident or strike benefits.

[9] s.2(5): see p. 11 footnote 36, above; s.15(6) excludes such insurers from Part II (continuing duties and the Secretary of State's powers).

[10] Chapter 1 at p. 2.

[11] But note the comments on p. 2, note 4, above.

some of the statutory provisions.[12] It is still the case, however, that membership of Lloyd's entitles an underwriter to transact insurance business without seeking the authorisation of the Secretary of State.

The applicant must submit its business proposals under section 5. With limited exceptions, an applicant whose head office is in the United Kingdom must be a registered company.[13] An outside applicant must be a body corporate entitled under the law of its own country to carry on insurance business and must nominate a general representative in the United Kingdom.[14] An applicant with its head office outside the EEC must possess a minimum of assets within the United Kingdom and must lodge a prescribed deposit.[15] The Secretary of State must refuse an application if it appears to him that any of certain people in the applicant organisation are not fit and proper persons to hold their positions.[16]

Insurance business is divided into a number of classes by the Act.[17] Applicants must state which class or classes of business they intend to run and authorisations are restricted to the classes specified.[18] Broadly, these classes divide into long-term business, that is, life and related sorts of insurance, and general business. It is no longer possible for new insurers to combine long-term and general business.[19] This provision was dictated by an EEC Directive, but its purpose is not immediately obvious, provided that other controls in respect of such composites are adequate.

An authorisation can be revoked by the Secretary of State,[20] whether wholly or partly, at an insurer's request, or

(i) if it appears to have failed to satisfy its obligations,
(ii) if there are grounds on which it would be refused authorisation, if that were being sought, for example, on the "fit and proper" person basis,
(iii) if, in the case of an insurer from another EEC state, its state has withdrawn its authorisation, or

[12] Principally the solvency margin requirement (see below); s.84. Note also s.85 regarding transfers of business.
[13] s.7.
[14] ss.8 and 9.
[15] s.9.
[16] ss.7(3), 8(2) and 9(5). The fit and proper requirement is a continuing one; see p. 21, below.
[17] s.1 and Scheds. 1 and 2.
[18] s.3.
[19] s.6.
[20] s.11.

(iv) if it has ceased to carry on insurance business or failed to commence business within a year of authorisation.

In all but the last case, the Secretary of State must serve written notice on the insurer giving the ground for the proposed action and one month for representations to be made.[21]

Once an insurer has been authorised, it is by no means out of the purview of the Secretary of State. The bulk of the 1982 Act is concerned with duties cast upon authorised insurers and powers of intervention vested in the Secretary of State. These are outlined below.

Continuing duties of insurers

The most important of these are as follows:

(a) Maintaining solvency margins. The concept of the solvency margin has been central to insurance company supervision for many years. Simply, insurers are required to maintain a minimum amount whereby their assets exceed their liabilities.[22] By this means, it is hoped, insurers will never approach actual insolvency. The actual calculation of the margin required is a complex business, involving, in addition, the application of statutory requirements as to the valuation of assets and liabilities.[23] There are differing requirements as to insurers authorised in other EEC member states and non-EEC insurers. The solvency margin requirements apply to the members of Lloyd's taken together.[24]

(b) Non-insurance activities. Insurers cannot carry on activities other than in connection with or for the purposes of their insurance business.[25]

(c) Localisation and matching of assets. The Act[26] contains power for the Secretary of State to take regulations to introduce into the law the provision of the EEC Directive requiring that the reserves of an insurer required to meet known and estimated liabilities must be covered by assets situated in the country where the business is carried on.

(d) Accounts, actuarial investigations and statements. More detailed accounts are required[27] of insurance companies than of limited companies generally and, *inter alia*, these must be

[21] s.12.
[22] s.32.
[23] These are done by Regulations.
[24] s.84.
[25] s.16.
[26] s.35.
[27] ss.17–24.

deposited with the Secretary of State. Companies which carry on long-term business are subject to actuarial investigation every year, and must appoint their own qualified actuary. All companies are required to prepare periodical statements of business in respect of each class of insurance business they underwrite.

(e) Separation of assets. Companies which combine long-term and general insurance business must maintain separate funds in respect of the different kinds of business and the assets representing the long-term fund are available only for that business and, on a winding up, are available only to meet liabilities attributable to that business.[28] In addition, a company is prohibited from declaring a dividend when its long-term liabilities exceed its long-term assets. These are important provisions aimed obviously at protecting the policyholders with life insurance.

(f) Changes in management and control. In accordance with the fact that the Secretary of State exercises wide powers over who manages and who controls an authorised insurer, insurers are obliged to notify him whenever there is a proposed change in this respect.[29]

The powers of intervention vested in the Secretary of State

Sections 37 to 48 of the Act give extremely wide powers to the Secretary of State. He is empowered to intervene in the affairs of an insurer for a number of reasons or grounds, among the most important of which are

(i) that he considers it necessary in order to protect a company's policyholders against the risk that the company may be unable to meet its liabilities,

(ii) that a company has failed to fulfill an obligation under the Act, which refers especially to the maintenance of the solvency margin,

(iii) that a company has furnished misleading or inaccurate information, and

(iv) that it appears to him that a director, manager or controller of the company is not a fit and proper person.

Once a ground to intervene exists, the Secretary of State has power to require a company to do or not to do a number of things. These include the maintaining of assets in the United Kingdom, limiting premium income, producing information

---

[28] ss.27–29.
[29] s.62.

and the making or realising of specified investments. In the last resort, where the specific powers are not considered sufficient, he "may require a company to take such action as appears to him to be appropriate for the purpose of protecting policyholders or potential policyholders against the risk that the company may be unable to meet its liabilities or, in the case of long-term business, to fulfill the reasonable expectations of policyholders or potential policyholders."[30] The breadth of these powers is obvious.

In general, no formality surrounds the exercise of a power to intervene except that when exercising it, the Secretary of State is required to state the ground upon which he is exercising it. Only in one case does the legislation require that notice of possible action be given to the company, which then has a chance to make representations. This is when the Secretary of State intends to take action on the ground of unfitness.[31] However, the principles of administrative law and judicial review should ensure that the powers are exercised fairly and in one notable instance of an allegation of unfitness, the Department of Trade was severely criticised by the Ombudsman for not allowing the person concerned fully to present his view, and for not presenting to him all the evidence against him.[32]

Despite these wide ranging powers, it is clear that the Department of Trade and Industry much prefers to operate informally.[33] That, of course, is easy to do when there are strong legal powers behind informal suggestion.

Finally, in the context of the Secretary of State's powers, it should be noted that he has special powers to petition for the winding up of an insurance company.[34]

Remaining provisions of the Act

The Insurance Companies Act contains a number of other provisions. Some of them are also concerned with the financial regulation of insurers. Notable in this connection are the provisions applicable to linked long-term policies, that is life insur-

---

[30] s.45.
[31] s.46.
[32] See the *Second Report of the Parliamentary Commissioner for Administration, Session 1976–1977,* H.C. Papers 116.
[33] A most useful account of the way the Department views its powers is given in the *British Insurance Law Association Bulletin,* No. 37, March 1976, by M. S. Morris, then Under-Secretary in the Insurance Division of the Department of Trade.
[34] ss.53–59.

ance combined with a substantial investment in securities and/or property, and the provisions which apply specially to Lloyd's. The former regulate in particular the types of property which can be used for investment.[35] The latter require, *inter alia*, that premiums received be kept in trust funds, with separate ones in respect of life and general business, that each underwriter's accounts be audited, and that the Committee of Lloyd's deposit every year with the Secretary of State a statement summarising the extent and character of the insurance business done by the members of Lloyd's in the year.[36]

Remaining provisions cover such matters as limited control of intermediaries, insurance advertisements, and formalities in life policies. Where relevant, these are considered in subsequent chapters.

The protection of policyholders

The regulatory powers which have been briefly examined obviously exist for the benefit and protection of insureds or policyholders. More substantial protection in the financial sense, where necessary, is provided under the Policyholders Protection Act 1975.

This Act, in the aftermath of a particular collapse which gave rise to much public concern,[37] established the Policyholders Protection Board. The Board has two prime functions. First, it has a power to assist an insurer who is in financial difficulties.[38] This may be done, for example, by arranging for substitute policies to be offered to the insureds of the insurer concerned. Secondly, it is under a duty to ensure that certain measures are taken when an insurance company goes into liquidation.[39] In this respect, it must ensure that the liabilities of the liquidated company in respect of compulsory insurances[40] are fully met, and that in respect of non-compulsory insurances, the policyholders receive 90 per cent. of the benefits that are due to them. In the case of life policies which have not matured, this must be

---

[35] See s.78 and the Regulations made thereunder (S.I. 1981, No. 1654, reg. 72). These resulted from the recommendations of the Scott Committee on Linked Life Assurance, 1973, Cmnd. 5281.
[36] ss.83 and 86.
[37] That of the Nation Life Insurance Company which featured widely in the press and on television. Rather curiously, perhaps, the 1975 Act was not retrospective and did not protect the unfortunate policyholders of this company.
[38] Policyholders Protection Act 1975, ss.16 and 17.
[39] *Ibid.* ss.5–12.
[40] As to these, see Chapters 19 and 20.

The Regulation of Insurers

done by securing the continuity of such insurances,[41] for example, by transfer to another insurer. The Board is financed by a levy on all authorised insurers in so far as it is necessary in any particular year; this levy must not exceed 1 per cent. of the companies' net premium income in that year.[42] It is unlikely in practice that the Board will be called into operation very frequently.

[41] *Ibid.* s.11.
[42] *Ibid.* ss.18–22.

Chapter 3

INSURABLE INTEREST

Insurable interest is a basic requirement of any contract of insurance unless it can be, and is, lawfully waived. At a general level, this means that the party to the insurance contract who is the insured or policyholder must have a particular relationship with the subject-matter of the insurance, whether that be a life or property or a liability to which he might be exposed. The absence of the required relationship will render the contract illegal, void or simply unenforceable, depending on the type of insurance. We have already stressed the essential differences between life and other insurances in many respects,[1] and the law regarding insurable interest is one situation where the differences can be crucial. A brief examination of the history of the insurable interest requirement[2] reveals this.

History of the requirement

Simply, a contract of life insurance was enforceable at common law despite the absence of any relationship between the insured and the life insured, and even in the face of judicial reluctance. The reason for this was that wagers in general were legally enforceable[3] and thus the courts had no option but to enforce wagers in the form of life insurance contracts. An increase in these practices, which were clearly distasteful[4] and which indeed could serve as an inducement to murder, led to growing concern and, ultimately, legislative action in the form of the Life Assurance Act 1774. As far as other types of insurance were concerned, namely indemnity contracts, there was abundant authority recognising as valid marine policies without interest,[5] which, as has been seen earlier, were the other common form of insurance at the time. However, statute, in the

---

[1] See Chapter 1.
[2] For more detail, see *MacGillivray and Parkington*, paras. 14–37.
[3] See, *e.g. March* v. *Piggott* (1771) 2 Burr. 2862, a bet as to which father of the parties would live longer. In certain instances wagers were not enforceable, particularly where public policy intervened or where the matter was regarded as a waste of the court's time.
[4] See the preamble to the Life Assurance Act 1774.
[5] See *MacGillivray and Parkington*, para. 15.

form of the Marine Insurance Act 1745, put a stop to this practice. The exact position with regard to non-marine indemnity policies is not clear. By analogy with life and marine policies, the mere fact of there being no interest, at least at the date of the contract, should not have rendered such insurances void. However, as such contracts were and are, in most cases,[6] contracts only to indemnify the insured against a loss he actually suffers, the insured could only recover if he showed that he had suffered a loss, in other words that he had an interest at the time of loss.[7] Further, there is authority,[8] preceding any statutory requirement, in the case of a fire policy on buildings, that interest was required by the common law both at the date of the contract and at the date of the loss.

In any event, the legislature intervened with a series of statutes, finally rendering all contracts by way of gaming or wagering void under the Gaming Act 1845, s.18. The details of the relevant provisions will be examined shortly, but it is useful at this stage briefly to summarise how the various statutory provisions apply to the various types of insurance:

(i) Marine policies are now governed by the Marine Insurance Act 1906, by section 4 of which such policies without interest are void[9];

(ii) Life Policies are governed by the 1774 Act and a failure to show interest renders a policy illegal.[10]

(iii) All other policies except those on "goods and merchandises"[11] may also be covered by the Life Assurance Act, despite the misleading short title.[12]

(iv) In respect of policies on goods, there is no statutory requirement of insurable interest *per se*. However, the Gaming Act 1845 will strike down any goods policy which is really a wager, and, it seems, the Marine Insurance Act 1788 still technically requires that every goods' policy contain the name of a person interested therein.[13]

[6] See Chapter 13.
[7] *Lynch* v. *Dalzell* (1729) 4 Bro.P.C. 431.
[8] *Sadler's Co.* v. *Badcock* (1743) 2 Atk. 554.
[9] But not illegal: *Edwards (John) & Co.* v. *Motor Union Ins. Co.* [1922] 2 K.B. 249.
[10] *Harse* v. *Pearl Life Ass. Co.* [1904] 1 K.B. 558; see further below, p. 35.
[11] s.4 of the 1774 Act exempts these expressly.
[12] *Re King* [1963] Ch. 459, 485; see the full discussion below, pp. 36–39.
[13] This Act applied to land policies on goods as well as marine policies. It was repealed by the 1906 Act but only in so far as it related to marine risks (see Sched. 2). It is a matter for doubt how far the requirement is ever consciously heeded. Certainly purely oral insurance policies on goods are recognised as valid despite it (see Chap. 4).

We shall now examine quite separately the requirement of insurable interest in life insurance on the one hand and in property insurances on the other. One general point should, however, be stressed at this stage, which is that the strict legal requirements may in some instances be honoured more in the breach than the observance, particularly in the field of life insurance. Illustrations of this are certain policies insuring the lives of children and some group insurances of employees. There is no justification for this state of affairs and more detailed examples and suggestions for reform will be made at the appropriate stages.

INSURABLE INTEREST IN LIFE INSURANCE[14]

Section 1 of the Life Assurance Act 1774 requires the insured to have an insurable interest in the life insured. The other relevant provisions of the Act require the names of persons interested to be inserted in the policy (s.2) and declare that when the insured has an interest, he can recover no more than the amount of the value of his interest (s.3). These provisions raise four basic questions: the time at which interest is required; the very nature of insurable interest; attempted evasions and the meaning of section 2; and the effect of a policy without interest.

The time when interest is required

It is convenient to consider this first, simply because it is the most straightforward question. There can be little doubt that section 1 of the Act on its own can be read as requiring interest at the time a policy is effected, but no more. However, section 3 of the Act, talking as it does in terms of the insured recovering only the value of his interest, might be thought to require interest at the time of loss, *i.e.* at the date of the death of the life insured. This was the decision in the old case of *Godsall* v. *Boldero*,[15] which held, in effect, that a policy by a creditor on the life of his debtor was a policy of indemnity because section 3 permitted recovery in language appropriate to the concept of indemnity against a loss.

However, *Godsall* v. *Boldero* was overruled in the landmark

---

[14] Life insurance here includes, it seems, pure endowment insurance—*MaGillivray and Parkington*, paras. 64–65. For a general critique, see Merkin, (1980) 9 Anglo-American L.R. 331.

[15] (1807) 9 East 72, followed in *Henson* v. *Blackwell* (1845) 4 Hare. 434.

case of *Dalby* v. *India and London Life Assurance Co.*,[16] a decision which has stood unchallenged for well over a century and which established beyond doubt that it is necessary for the insured to have an interest only at the time the policy is effected. The *Dalby* case was not strictly a case of life insurance, but rather the reinsurance of a life policy.[17] The plaintiff was the director of a company which had insured the life of the Duke of Cambridge, and which reinsured the risk with the defendant. The original policies were cancelled, but the plaintiff kept paying the premiums on the reinsurance policy until the Duke died. The defendant then denied liability on the ground that the plaintiff had no interest in the Duke's life at the date of his death, having himself nothing to pay out on it. The Exchequer Chamber found for the plaintiff, holding that section 3 of the 1774 Act applied only to require the insured to value his interest at the date of effecting the policy. As section 1 was satisfied, because the plaintiff did have interest at the time he reinsured, and as there was no common law requirement that the plaintiff prove interest at the date of loss, he was entitled to recover.

While there are difficulties with regard to the construction of section 3, which looks as though it refers to the time of loss, and while the *Dalby* case could lead to certain mischiefs to which we shall refer, there is no doubt that the decision is totally justifiable. To hold the contrary would be against justice and fair dealing, as the premiums paid on a life policy are calculated on actuarial principles according to the probable duration of the life. They are fixed just as the sum payable on death is fixed. There is no comparison with the assessment of a risk under an indemnity policy, even though it can hardly be denied that certain life policies are intended to indemnify against a possible loss, a point we shall return to again. To allow an insurer who has assessed the risk under a life policy in the usual way to resile from his bargain for these reasons would be quite absurd.

Consequences of Dalby
However, the *Dalby* case has consequences which may be regarded as mischievous. These will arise only where the

---

[16] (1854) 15 C.B. 365. In fact the insurers in *Godsall* v. *Boldero* repented and paid out, following the outcry against them after the decision: see Lord Blackburn in *Burnand* v. *Rodocanachi* (1882) 1 App.Cas. 333, at 340–341.

[17] See also on this, following *Dalby*, *Southern Cross Ass. Co. Ltd.* v. *Australian Provincial Assurance Association Ltd.* (1935) 53 C.L.R. 618 (High Court of Australia).

insured is not also himself the life insured or where an insured assigns[18] a policy on his own life to a party with no interest. An example will illustrate the point. As will be seen, a creditor may insure his debtor's life for the amount of his debt. Indeed it is not uncommon for financiers to effect group policies on their debtors. The debt may be repaid shortly thereafter, yet the creditor may keep up the policy until the debtor dies, which may be many years later. Is there not an element of gaming here? One of the reasons for requiring insurable interest has been said[19] to be the removal of an inducement to murder the life insured, yet the creditor has a strong motive for murder.[20] In essence, this sort of policy is surely intended to indemnify the creditor against the loss he may suffer by the debtor not repaying his debt before he dies, and the same can be said of other common types of policy, for example, by employers on the lives of their employees. It could be suggested that once the insured ceases to have an interest in the life insured, the latter should have the option of taking over the policy for his own benefit, subject to some compensation to the insured in respect of the premiums he has paid.[21] Thus, in effect, the consent of the life insured would be necessary for the continuation of a policy where interest had ceased. This is an area which deserves careful consideration at least in the context of the general examination of the insurable interest requirement which, it will be argued, is desirable.

The nature of insurable interest

Despite stipulating that an interest is required, the 1774 Act does not say, in so many words, exactly what is an insurable interest in a life. However, the provisions of section 3, to which we have already adverted, indicate that it means a pecuniary or financial interest, because the section talks of "the amount of the value of the interest of the insured." In general this has been the approach adopted by the courts.

There are two cases, though, where insurable interest is pre-

---

[18] As to assignment of a life policy, see Chapter 17.
[19] See *Worthington v. Curtis* [1875] 1 Ch.D. 419; McGovern, "Homicide and Succession to Property," (1969) 68 Mich.L.Rev. 65 at 78.
[20] Of course one would hope that he would be deterred by the criminal consequences, but not all murders are solved. Should the civil law permit the survival of an inducement to murder?
[21] An alternative would be to confine recovery by the insured to the surrender value of the policy at the time interest ceases.

sumed and where section 3 is regarded as inapplicable, the reason being that they are outside the mischief of gaming which the 1774 Act was passed to prevent.[22] Insurances on one's own life[23] or on the life of a spouse[24] are automatically valid regardless of the amount insured. However, this presumption does not extend to other family relationships, outside the special context of industrial life assurance.[25]

Apart from these cases the requirement of pecuniary interest means that the law is very strict, and, indeed, is no doubt stricter than common practice would indicate. Essentially, the insured must show that he would suffer financially by the loss of a legal right on the death of the life insured and it is only the amount of likely loss that can be covered. The law is perhaps best illustrated by examining separately family relationships, other than that of husband and wife, from other relationships.

Family relationships

So far as family relationships are concerned, it is clear that a child who is a minor would have an insurable interest in the lives of his or her parents, if they are legally obliged to support the child, as the latter would clearly therefore suffer financially, by the loss of a legal right on their death. Whether or not there is such a legal obligation is unclear. There is no such at common law,[26] but there may be a statutory obligation[27] which would found insurable interest. Certainly, if a maintenance order has been made, compelling a parent to provide for a child, the child must have an insurable interest in the parent's life. In all cases, though, there is the problem of valuing the interest as required under section 3 of the 1774 Act. It may be that an unlimited interest could be presumed as in the case of spouses. Insurance by an infant child on the life of a parent is surely outside the

[22] *Griffiths* v. *Fleming* [1909] 1 K.B. 805, esp. at 821.
[23] *Wainewright* v. *Bland* (1835) 1 Moo. & R. 481.
[24] *Griffiths* v. *Fleming*, above. *Cf.* Married Women's Property Act 1882, s.11. (see Chapter 17) which allows a married woman to insure her own and her husband's life. The presumption might well extend to unmarried couples living together.
[25] On this, see section 2 of the Industrial Assurance and Friendly Societies Act 1948 which permits limited insurances on the lives of parents and grandparents.
[26] *Bazeley* v. *Forder* (1868) L.R. 3 Q.B. 559. In Scots Law, there is such an obligation which extends quite widely throughout the family; see *MacGillivray and Parkington*, paras. 101–105.
[27] Supplementary Benefits Act 1976, s.17 provides for such an obligation, but only to the extent that supplementary benefit is paid or claimed to meet the requirements of the child (s.18).

mischief of the Act. However, on principle and authority,[28] an adult child can have no such insurable interest unless he can prove some legal obligation arising on the death of his parent. In *Harse* v. *Pearl Life Assurance Co. Ltd.*,[29] a son insured the life of his mother who lived with him and kept house for him. The insurance was expressly declared to be "for funeral expenses." It was held by the Court of Appeal that the policy was illegal for lack of interest, there being no legal obligation on the son to bury his mother when she died, and she not being legally bound to keep house for him. The existence of a legal obligation of any sort must in practice be extremely unlikely. In all these cases, of course, there is no objection to a parent insuring his or her own life and even naming a child as beneficiary, provided that the insurance is genuinely own-life, a point to which we shall return.

The converse situation of a parent insuring the life of a child raises interesting problems, for there is no doubt that such insurances are effected in practice. *Halford* v. *Kymer*[30] is authority for the fact a parent would not usually have the necessary interest, except possibly to cover funeral expenses,[31] because there is no other financial loss arising. There can be no other legal obligation on a parent to incur expenditure on the death of a child. Even if a parent is being supported by his adult child, there is no obligation and hence no interest (*Halford* v. *Kymer*), and it goes without saying that the parent who is not being supported has no interest. It appears that in practice parents do insure the lives of their children. One example[32] is a personal accident policy taken out when the family is travelling. Clearly such insurance is justified on the ground that extra expense would be incurred if the child died away from home. But as there is no obligation to incur such expense, it is difficult to see how there is insurable interest in this sort of case, and even if there is, under section 3 of the 1774 Act, the amount recoverable is only the actual costs incurred which should be valued when

---

[28] *Shilling* v. *Accidental Death Ins. Co.* (1857) 2 H. & N. 42; *Harse* v. *Pearl Life Ass. Co. Ltd.* [1904] 1 K.B. 558.
[29] Note 28, above.
[30] (1830) 10 B. & C. 724.
[31] While there used to be an obligation to bury one's children, this may now in fact be obsolete, as local authorities are now obliged to bury any person who dies in their area; see *MacGillivray and Parkington*, para. 92. Insurance of funeral expenses used to be permissible in the area of industrial life assurance.
[32] Another might be school fees insurance, depending upon how it is effected. The problems here have their parallels in cases involving trusts or alleged trusts of life policies. These are considered in Chapter 17.

Insurable Interest in Life Insurance 31

the policy is effected. Some statutory authorisation of these insurances, to a carefully defined extent, seems essential.

Outside the context of parent and child, there is one curious case[33] holding that a *de facto* guardian had an insurable interest in the life of her infant step-sister, on the ground that she had promised the child's dying mother that she would take care of her and thus incurred expenditure. This decision simply cannot be supported in the absence of an obligation, surely most unlikely in practice, on the child to repay the guardian, so that the latter would suffer financial loss in the event of the child's prior demise. It has never been overruled but there is a Privy Council decision to the opposite effect on similar facts.[34]

Business relationships

In respect of relationships of a business character, insurance may be effected by, for example, a creditor on the life of his debtor, an employer on the life of his employee, or vice versa, and a partner on the life of his partner. In all these cases, however, the amount of interest is limited again to the pecuniary interest of the insured. The point is nicely illustrated by the old case of *Hebdon* v. *West*.[35] A bank clerk insured his employer's life with two insurers, one policy being for £5,000, the other for £2,500. The clerk had a contract of employment for seven years at a salary of £600 per annum, and he owed his employer £4,700, the latter having promised that he would not call in his debt during his lifetime. When his employer died, the clerk received the £5,000 from the first insurer. The refusal of the second insurer to honour its contract was upheld by the court. It was accepted that the insured had an insurable interest in his employer's life to the extent of what he was contractually entitled to under his contract of employment, *i.e.* a maximum of £4,200, because he stood to suffer this loss by the loss of a legal right. However, he had no interest by virtue of the promise not to call in the debt as he had provided no consideration and hence the promise was not legally enforceable.[36] As his interest

---

[33] *Barnes* v. *London, Edinburgh & Glasgow Life Ass. Co. Ltd.* [1892] 1 Q.B. 864.
[34] *Anctil* v. *Manufacturer's Life Ins. Co.* [1899] A.C. 604; see also the comments of the Court of Appeal in *Griffiths* v. *Fleming*, above, at 819 and of Lord Alvestone C.J. in *Harse* v. *Pearl Life Ass. Co.* [1903] 2 K.B. 92 at 96, doubting the decision in *Barnes*.
[35] (1863) 3 B. & S. 579.
[36] *Quaere* whether the promise might not now be binding under the doctrine of promissory estoppel.

was more than satisfied by the payment of the first insurer,[37] the second was not liable.

Perhaps more than the decisions involving family relationships, *Hebdon* v. *West* illustrates that, in substance and despite what has often been said, the effect of section 3 of the 1774 Act is to render this sort of life insurance in law a contract of indemnity, the difference from the normal indemnity principle being that the measure of the insured's loss is judged at the time the policy is effected rather than at the time of loss. The result is hardly just, particularly when compared with that in the *Dalby* case. *Hebdon* was not a case of gaming or wagering and the insurer had received premiums based, one assumes, on usual actuarial considerations.

It seems most unlikely that in practice the decision is applied. Provided that the insured has an interest in the life insured, a valuation of that interest within the strict confines of section 3 is unlikely. Take, for example, the case of an employer insuring the life of an employee, a common practice particularly under group insurance policies. As a matter of strict law, the employer's interest will be only the value of the services which he will lose if the employee dies.[38] While in the case of a most valuable employee with a lengthy service contract that may be a substantial sum, in the case of a less exalted employee, it can be at most the equivalent of the period of notice that the employee must lawfully give to determine his employment. In fact employees are insured for sums which may bear no relation to the strict legal value. Two recent cases illustrate this, although in neither was the point the subject of any dispute between the parties. In *Green* v. *Russell*,[39] an employee architect was one of a group insured by the employer. The sum insured was £1,000. In law the employer received the money when the employee was killed and the latter's representatives had no claim.[40] It is difficult to believe that that figure was strictly the pecuniary interest of the employer. Similarly, in *Marcel Beller Ltd.* v. *Hayden*,[41] the relevant facts involved a group policy. Here the insurable interest point was adverted to, and the learned judge commented[42]

---

[37] Presumably the first insurer could not recover back the "excess" he had paid, as it was money paid under a mistake of law, which is generally irrecoverable: see Chapter 12 at p. 212.
[38] *Simcock* v. *Scottish Imperial Ins. Co.*, (1902) 10 S.L.T. 286.
[39] [1959] 2 Q.B. 226.
[40] See Chapter 17, p. 279.
[41] [1978] Q.B. 694. See further, Chapter 11, p. 172.
[42] *Ibid.* at p. 697.

that it was not in question that the insured employers had an insurable interest in their deceased employee's life. While this is perfectly correct, the amount of that interest *may* not strictly have been the £15,000 the employee was insured for, but the point was simply not considered. It cannot be said that a section of a statute which is so obviously ignored serves any useful purpose.

Attempted evasions and section 2

Section 1 of the Life Assurance Act 1774 does not require simply that the insured has an interest in the life insured. It also stipulates that any person "for whose use, benefit, or on whose account" a policy is made must have an interest, and by section 2,[43] the names of the insured and any beneficiaries must be inserted in the policy, on pain of the policy being illegal. The purpose behind these provisions is clearly to prevent evasions of the basic requirement so that if, for example, A appears to insure his own life, but in fact B is insuring A's life, or the insurance is for B's benefit, B must have an interest and B's name must appear in the policy. Benefit must not be taken too widely. The fact that a man in insuring his own life intends ultimately to benefit his wife and children, as must be common, does not mean that the latter must have an interest under section 1 and be named under section 2. Only if the direct purpose of effecting the policy is to confer an immediate benefit on another[44] can the requirement be applicable.

A strict application of section 2 can lead to unjust results. In *Evans* v. *Bignold*,[45] a wife appeared to insure her own life. In fact the insurance was effected because her husband borrowed money from the trustees of a will under which the wife was entitled to money when she became 21. The trustees insisted on the husband providing security, and the surety insisted that he insure his wife's life. The husband was not named in the policy. It was held that he should have been, as a person interested, under section 2, and the failure meant that the policy was illegal. In fact, of course, he had an insurable interest in his wife's life, so section 1 was satisfied, and the result is unnecessary. It is suggested that section 2 is in fact superfluous. If A

---

[43] Subject to Insurance Companies Amendment Act 1973, s.50, discussed below.
[44] As in *Evans* v. *Bignold* (1869) L.R. 4 Q.B. 622, below.
[45] Note 44 above.

insures his own life for the benefit of B, but B has an insurable interest, whether or not B is named in the policy should not affect its validity, as there is no element of gaming or wagering. If B has no interest in A's life, the policy is illegal under section 1, even if B is expressly named in the policy. If B is not named, and on the face of it the policy appears to be effected by A on his own life, the court can nonetheless enquire into the realities of the situation and find such a policy illegal under section 1 if it was really intended for B who has no interest. In *Shilling* v. *Accidental Death Insurance Co.*,[46] a father effected a policy on his own life, but the evidence showed that it was his son who was entirely instrumental in the transaction and who paid the premiums, and that the policy was for the benefit of the son, as the father immediately afterwards executed a will in his favour. It was held that in reality the policy was made by the son on the life of his father in which he had no insurable interest. It was therefore, illegal under section 1.[47]

However, as will be seen in detail later,[48] there is no bar to an insured's assigning a policy of life insurance to someone without interest. This would appear to be the easiest legal solution to the problem of cases without interest. Provided that A who effects a policy on his own life does so genuinely, when he has done so, he can assign the policy to whomsoever he pleases (to B) and there is no need at all for B to have an interest in A's life nor to have his name inserted under section 2.[49] The line appears to be a very fine one between A taking out a policy in order to benefit B, and A bona fide effecting a policy with an intention of assigning the benefit but with no particular assignee in mind. The first case would fall foul of section 2 if B's name were not inserted and of section 1 if it was really a case of B insuring A's life in which he had no interest. The second is perfectly valid.[49]

It has already been pointed out that section 2 of the 1774 Act appears superfluous. In certain instances it was clearly also a most inconvenient nuisance, particularly in respect of group policies, for example, a policy taken out by an employer to cover the whole of or the whole of a class of his employees. If the policy was solely for the employer's benefit, then of course section 2 would not apply. But if the policy were effected for the

---

[46] (1857) 2 H. & N. 42.
[47] It would also have failed s.2.
[48] See Chapter 17.
[49] *M'Farlane* v. *Royal London Friendly Society* (1886) 2 T.L.R. 755.

benefit of the employees, they would all have had to be named in it. Because of the inconvenience, section 50 of the Insurance Companies Amendment Act 1973 now provides that, in such a case, section 2 of the 1774 Act does not invalidate a policy for the benefit of unnamed individuals within a class or description if the class or description is stated in the policy and every member is identifiable at any time.

The effect of a policy without interest

There is a difference in the wording of sections 1 and 2 of the 1774 Act. Failure to comply with section 2 expressly renders the policy unlawful, but section 1 says merely that policies without interest "shall be null and void to all intents and purposes whatsoever." Despite this, there is clear authority[50] that a breach of section 1 does render a policy illegal. The only real practical consequence of this concerns the recovery of premiums paid on an illegal policy if the insurer in fact takes the point, a matter dealt with in Chapter 8. Except in such cases, of which in any event there is no modern reported example, insurers do not raise the point for the obviously sensible reason that to do so in respect of a policy on which premiums had been duly paid could rightly attract unfavourable publicity. If insurers have paid out under an illegal policy and there is a dispute between rival claimants to the money, the illegality is ignored.[51] If an insurer did not pay, not because of illegality but relying upon some other defence, the Court should raise the illegality point and refuse to enforce the contract on this ground.[52]

Reform of the law

The law on insurable interest in life insurances is clearly out of touch with reality in many respects, as has been pointed out in the preceding account. It is suggested that a general reform is necessary which might well follow the useful precedent set by the Australian Insurance Contracts Act 1984.[53] This assumes that a requirement of interest is still desirable, but sets out a list

---

[50] *Harse* v. *Pearl Life Ass. Co. Ltd.* [1904] 1 K.B. 558.
[51] *Worthington* v. *Curtis* (1875) 1 Ch.D. 419, *Carter* v. *Renouf* (1962) 36 A.L.J.R. 67.
[52] *e.g. Gedge* v. *Royal Exchange Ass. Corp.* [1900] 2 Q.B. 214.
[53] ss.18 and 19. See also the article by Merkin referred to in footnote 14 above and Tarr (1986) 60 A.L.J. 613.

of relationships in respect of which it is permissible for one person to insure the life of another.[54]

INSURABLE INTEREST IN PROPERTY INSURANCE

Statutory or contractual requirement

Turning to the law regarding insurable interest in property insurances, the first consideration must be an attempt to clarify the extent to which the statutory requirements apply. There is no doubt that section 18 of the Gaming Act 1845 applies to all such insurances,[55] so that any insurance on property with which the insured has no connection at all nor any prospect of a connection is void. This requirement cannot, however, be too difficult to satisfy and is certainly much easier to satisfy than the strict requirement of insurable interest which will be discussed shortly.

Application of the 1774 Act

The Life Assurance Act 1774 clearly does not apply to insurances of goods, for these are expressly exempted by section 4. Whether or not it applies to insurances of real property is a question of some difficulty which has occasioned opposing views and to which the answer is not settled. In one Court of Appeal case, *Re King*,[56] it was stated, *obiter*, that the Act did apply, while a more recent dictum of the same court in *Mark Rowlands Ltd. v. Berni Inns Ltd.*[57] is to the contrary effect. In the latter case, where the insurer of a landlord was arguing that the landlord's unnamed tenant could not benefit from the insurance because the tenant was not named in the policy as required by section 2, Kerr L.J. stated that "this ancient statute was not intended to apply, and does not apply to indemnity insurances,

---

[54] For discussion of other possibilities, namely abandoning the requirement of interest altogether and relying on the general prohibition on wagering and on public policy or imposing a requirement of consent by the life insured, see the Australian Law Reform Commission's Discussion Paper No. 7, paras. 26 and 27 and their Report No. 20, paras. 134–138.

[55] *Macaura v. Northern Assurance Co. Ltd.* [1925] 2 A.C. 619.

[56] [1963] Ch. 459 at 485 (*per* Lord Denning M.R.). This *dictum* is relied upon by MacGillivray and Parkington, para. 153, in support of the application of the Act to real property insurance, but is ignored in Ivamy's *Fire and Motor Insurance*, pp. 175–181, putting the opposite view. See also the Australian High Court decision in *British Traders' Insurance Co. v. Monson* (1964) 111 C.L.R. 86.

[57] [1986] Q.B. 211. The *ratio* of this case concerns an insurer's subrogation rights and this aspect of it is discussed below at pp. 251–252.

but only to insurances which provide for the payment of a specified sum upon the happening of an insured event."[58]

It is respectfully submitted that Kerr L.J.'s reasoning and the authorities on which he relied are not wholly convincing; further, he made no reference to the earlier *dictum*. The strongest support for his view comes from the decision in *Mumford Hotels Ltd.* v. *Wheler*,[59] a case where a tenant unnamed in a landlord's insurance policy was held entitled to compel the landlord to use insurance monies for reinstatement, this right being implied from the terms of the lease.[60] On the other hand, a literal reading of sections 1 and 2 seems clearly to suggest that they comprehend real property insurance, since they expressly refer, as well as to lives, to "other event or events." Although his dictum is terse, Kerr L.J. seems to be saying that indemnity insurances of real property were not within the mischief the Act was designed to prevent. While it is quite true to say that the primary reason for the Act was to prohibit wagering on lives and that, well before the Act was passed, there was authority that the common law required an insurable interest in insurances on buildings at the time of the policy,[61] it seems unlikely that there were in existence in 1774 non-indemnity, *i.e.* valued, insurances on buildings which could be caught by the Act. Given that section 4 expressly exempted marine and goods policies and that it is unlikely that in 1774 forms of insurance other than life, marine, goods and buildings insurance existed, the words "other event or events" must surely incorporate ordinary insurances of real property. It is also notable that when passing later legislation, Parliament seems to have assumed that the 1774 Act had a wider application than Kerr L.J.'s *dictum* would allow.[62]

The application of section 1 to real property insurances would in fact cause no problems, and there is an attractive construction of section 2 which would remove the difficulties faced by Kerr L.J. over the decision in the *Mumford Hotels* case. This was

---

[58] [1986] Q.B. at 227.
[59] [1964] Ch. 117.
[60] This case is discussed further below at p. 235.
[61] *Sadler's Co.* v. *Badcock* (1743) 2 Atk. 554.
[62] See especially s.148(4) of the Road Traffic Act 1972, discussed further at p. 298, below, where the words "Notwithstanding anything in any enactment" seem apt to refer to the 1774 Act by allowing enforcement of a motor policy by anyone named in the policy, notwithstanding that the actual insured has no insurable interest in a named person's liability. The fact that case-law reached the same result (see p. 45, below) does not destroy the force of this point. In fact

propounded in the Australian case of *Davjoyda Estates Ltd.* v. *National Insurance Co. of New Zealand*[63] and is to the effect that section 2 applies only when the insured himself has no interest to satisfy section 1 but is insuring on behalf of another with an interest who must therefore be named. This construction is consistent with the mischief which the 1774 Act was designed to prevent and does remove the inconvenience of having to list all the persons interested in an insurance, but it does run counter to the dictum in *Re King* as well as to the views of Kerr L.J.

However, there is a problem in applying section 3 to real property insurances. This provides that where the insured has an interest, no greater sum can be recovered from the insurer than the amount of the value of *his* interest. It thus appears to imply that even where another person is named in the policy, in accordance with section 2, and that other person's interest is insured, only the value of the insured's interest can strictly be recovered. If, for example, a tenant insures the house and names his landlord as interested, recovery is limited to the value of the tenant's interest, which may be much less than the value of the property or the sum insured.[64] Furthermore, section 3 is unnecessary in the case of property insurances for these, as will be seen, are usually contracts of indemnity and the insured can recover only the value of his interest at the date of loss. This principle clearly existed before the 1774 Act was passed. The solution to this problem may be either to read section 3 as not applying to property insurances, as not being within the mischief intended to be prevented, whereas the other sections must apply because of their wording, or to read "the insured" in section 3 as comprehending the insured and any interested person whose name is inserted in the policy. However, this latter solution could be misleading, because there is one clear case where, by statutory authority,[65] a person interested in real property may compel the insurer to expend the insurance monies on

---

in many of the cases on "waiver" of insurable interest (see pp. 44–45, below), it seems to have been assumed that the 1774 Act applied to all insurances except those on goods, as the argument has often turned on the meaning of "on goods" rather than on any wider point such as that propounded by Kerr L.J.

[63] (1967) 65 S.R. (N.S.W.) 381 at 428, *per* Manning J. This construction was cited with approval by the Australian Law Reform Commission, Report No. 20, para. 112, although, as noted elsewhere (p. 40), Australia has solved any problems in this area by a wide-ranging reform.

[64] The point was not considered in *Re King*, above, but there the tenant insured had an interest to the full value of the property, because he had covenanted to repair.

[65] Fires Prevention (Metropolis) Act 1774 s.83, see Chapter 14, pp. 232–234.

reinstatement, regardless of whether or not he was named in the policy and regardless of the insured's strict entitlement. Perhaps section 3 should be read as no more than confirmation of the principle of indemnity in property insurance.

Whatever the solution to the problem of section 3, it is respectfully suggested that there are strong arguments, not countered by the *dictum* in the *Mark Rowlands* case, that sections 1 and 2 do apply to real property insurance. This does seem unnecessary. As with life insurance, any dangers that the Act was intended to cover are amply guarded against by the prohibition on wagering; in addition, the principle of indemnity will ensure that no one profits from a loss in respect of which they have no interest. To make the point absolutely clear, the 1774 Act needs to be repealed in this respect.

For the present, however, it seems right to assume that the Act at least may to apply to real property insurances. Even if it does not, there is, as mentioned above,[66] a common law requirement of interest at the date of contract and this seems to mean insurable interest in the strict sense which will be described below. In the case of goods, however, all that is required at the date of contract is sufficient not to fall foul of the Gaming Act and here a genuine expectation of acquiring an interest will suffice. But in all cases of insurances of property, insurable interest is prima facie required at the date of loss, simply because such insurances are only contracts to indemnify the insured against a loss actually suffered.[67] This is merely a necessary incident of the contract and as such can be, and sometimes is, dispensed with.[68]

The meaning of insurable interest

We can now turn to consider exactly what constitutes an insurable interest in property, regardless of whether or when it is statutorily or contractually required. As with life insurance, the law in this country is stricter than is probably necessary.[69] The starting-point must be the classic decision in the marine insurance case of *Lucena* v. *Craufurd*.[70] Here the Crown Com-

---

[66] p. 37 at footnote 61.
[67] *Macaura* v. *Northern Assurance Co. Ltd.* [1925] A.C. 619.
[68] See pp. 44–45, below.
[69] For a useful critique, see Harnett and Thornton, "Insurable Interest in Property; A Socio-economic Re-evaluation of a Legal Concept" (1948) 48 Col.L.R. 1162.
[70] (1806) 2 B. & P.N.R. 269.

missioners insured a number of enemy ships which had been captured by British vessels but were still on the high seas. The statute giving them authority empowered them to take charge of such ships only when they reached British ports. A number of the ships were lost at sea before reaching port. Whether or not the Commissioners had an insurable interest in them caused a great division of opinion, and the matter was debated by the judges before the House of Lords whose decision was that there was no interest, at the time of loss the Commissioners having no present proprietary right to the ships. In the classic words of Lord Eldon,[71] insurable interest is "a right in the property, or a right derivable out of some contract about the property, which in either case may be lost upon some contingency affecting the possession or enjoyment of the party."

Factual expectation of loss?

A wider "factual expectation" test had been propounded by some of the judges, although it was clearly not accepted by the House of Lords. This wider test was expressed by Lawrence J. as follows[72]: "A man is interested in a thing to whom advantage may arise or prejudice happen from the circumstances which may attend it and whom it importeth, that its condition as to safety or other quality should continue. . . . To be interested in the preservation of a thing is to be so circumstanced with respect to it as to have benefit from its existence, prejudice from its destruction." Curiously, this *dictum* was cited by Kerr L.J. in the *Mark Rowlands* case,[72a] even though that it does not represent prevailing English law is obvious from many decisions, particularly that of the House of Lords in *Macaura* v. *Northern Assurance Co. Ltd.* which is discussed below. That it should perhaps represent the law is another question.[72b]

Proprietary or contractual right

As the law stands, therefore, a mere expectation or even a moral certainty of loss should particular property be destroyed

---

[71] *Ibid.* at 321.
[72] *Ibid.* at 302.
[72a] [1986] Q.B. at 228.
[72b] The wider test has been adopted judicially by the Canadian Supreme Court in *Constitution Insurance Co. of Canada* v. *Kosmopoulos* (1987) 34 D.L.R. (4th) 208, which decided that the time had come to refuse to follow any more the *Macaura* case (see below). It has also been adopted legislatively in the Australian Insurance Contracts Act 1984, s.17.

is not enough. There must be a present right to a legal or equitable interest or a right under contract. A remainderman whose interest is vested has an insurable interest,[73] but the person with a contingent interest does not, nor even does the beneficiary of property under the will of a dying testator.[74] The contingency may not happen; the testator may, in theory, revoke his will. In a famous American case,[75] a turnpike company insured a bridge spanning a stream which connected two parts of the company's road, but the company had no legal or equitable interest in the bridge, and it was held that they had no insurable interest in it.

In *Macaura v. Northern Assurance Co. Ltd.*,[76] the sole shareholder of a limited company, who was also a substantial creditor of the company, insured in his own name timber owned by the company. The House of Lords held that he had no insurable interest in the timber which had been subsequently destroyed by fire. As a shareholder he had no right to the property owned by the company, the latter being a separate legal person, albeit his shares would fall in value in the event of the destruction of the company's property. This was merely a moral certainty of loss. Similarly, as creditor, as Macaura had no right to the company's property in the sense of a mortgage or charge over it, or some other proprietary security interest,[77] he had no interest in it. One may wonder whether this is not too narrow a view. In both the above capacities, the insured did have a real economic interest in the company's property, and of course he could so easily have put matters right by arranging for the company to insure the timber.[78] It should be noted, though, that a shareholder can insure his shares against loss of value due to the failure of an adventure that his company is embarked upon,[79] and a creditor may insure against his debtor's insolvency,[80] so that

---

[73] Per Lord Eldon in *Lucena v. Craufurd*, above, at 314.
[74] *Ibid.* at 325.
[75] *Farmers' Mutual Ins. Co. v. New Holland Turnpike Road Co.*, 122 Pa. 37 (1888).
[76] [1925] A.C. 619.
[77] *e.g.* the statutory right in *Moran, Galloway & Co. v. Uzielli* [1905] 2 K.B. 555.
[78] Note that the insurer initially resisted Macaura's claim on the ground of fraud which, although the allegation failed, may have influenced their resistance. In the U.S.A. a shareholder does have an insurable interest in his company's property—see Vance, *Handbook on the Law of Insurance*, p. 175. In Canada, the *Kosmopoulos* case (note 72b above) concerned a "one-man" company and as already noted the Supreme Court decided that the time had come to depart from the narrow English law exemplified by *Macaura*.
[79] *Wilson v. Jones* (1867) L.R. 2 Ex. 139.
[80] *Waterkeyn v. Eagle Star Ins. Co.* (1920) 5 Ll.L.R. 12.

the practical results of the *Macaura* case can be substantially mitigated.

Possession of property

One other point of general interest which arises out of the *Macaura* case is that possession of property by itself is not enough to found insurable interest. The timber in question was standing on Macaura's land. There must be some right of enjoyment of the property or some legal liability in respect of it. However, it would only be on facts as unusual as *Macaura*,[81] where the insured had no right to enjoy the timber, that possession would not give interest. There is authority that a finder can insure the property he has found,[82] on the ground that possession in English law is a good root of title generally defeasible only by the true owner. What is clear beyond doubt is that possession with legal liability, such as that of a bailee, gives the possessor an insurable interest.

Sales of goods

The party to a contract for the sale of goods who either has property in the goods or bears the risk of their loss has an insurable interest.[83] So far as hire purchase agreements are concerned, the owner of the goods will retain an insurable interest so long as the property or the right to repossess the goods remain vested in him.[84] The hirer will also have an interest as bailee, in addition to a likely obligation to insure the goods.

People living together

Whether or not spouses, or other people living together have an insurable interest in what is solely the property of the other has never been decided. On principle the answer should be in the negative unless the non-owner has possession sufficient to insure, in other words use of the property is shared.[85] But, for

---

[81] Compare *Boehm* v. *Bell* (1799) 8 T.R. 154: the captors of a ship had an interest because of the rights and duties attaching.

[82] *Stirling* v. *Vaughan* (1809) 11 East 619.

[83] *Inglis* v. *Stock* (1885) 10 App.Cas. 263. It seems unlikely that an innocent purchaser of stolen goods, without good title to them, has an insurable interest: *Chadwick* v. *Gibraltar General Insurance Co.* (1981) 34 O.R. (2d) 488; *Thompson* v. *Madill* (1986) 13 C.C.L.I. 242; see Hasson, (1983–84) 8 *Canadian Business Law Journal* 114.

[84] Even if his right is liable to be defeated because of failure to comply with the statutory requirements of the Consumer Credit Act 1974.

[85] *Goulstone* v. *Royal Ins. Co.* (1858) 1 F. & F. 276.

example, a husband can hardly have an insurable interest in his wife's jewellery, though there may be other ways in which the law permits him in effect to insure it, as we shall see later.

Limited interests in property

The categories of legal or equitable interest which will support insurable interest otherwise include the interests of mortgagor and mortgagee, vendor and purchaser, landlord and tenant and trustee and beneficiary. But once the insured is not the sole unencumbered owner of property, whether real or personal, the question of the extent of his interest becomes of importance. This does not turn upon any statutory requirement of insurable interest, but stems from the fact that such insurances are contracts of indemnity. Anyone who has a proprietary interest in property may insure it up to its full value; any statutory requirement is thereby satisfied. However, contractually the insured must have an interest at the time of loss and the value of his interest is crucial. He can prima facie recover only sufficient to indemnify him.[86]

For example, any tenant of property has an insurable interest in it and can therefore insure it for up to its full value. If he is merely a weekly tenant with no obligation to insure or repair, his recovery is limited to the value of his insurable interest, which can at most be the equivalent of four week's rent, assuming the premises to be a dwelling house.[87] If he has a fixed term lease under which he is liable to pay the full rent regardless of the destruction of the property, he will have an interest at the time of loss to that extent. If he is under an obligation to insure or to repair, his interest will be the full value of the property. Conversely in all cases, it seems that the landlord's interest as reversioner extends to the full value of the property, even where the tenant is liable to repair, because of the risk of the tenant failing to comply with his obligation.[88]

The same points can be made in respect of all the other categories of limited owners which have been mentioned. Each has sufficient legal or equitable interest to insure, but they will prima facie recover only what they have lost. A mortgagee will

---

[86] The modern case which, it is suggested, most clearly explains the distinction between the existence of an insurable interest and the value of it is *Davjoyda Estates* v. *National Ins. Co. of New Zealand* (1967) 65 S.R. (N.S.W.) 381.

[87] Because of the statutory requirement of four weeks' notice to terminate such a lease (Protection from Eviction Act 1977, s.5).

[88] Important subrogation issues may arise—see Chapter 15.

recover only the value of his outstanding debt,[89] the vendor of land may recover nothing if he can still enforce the contract of sale against his purchaser.[90] Insurance by someone with a limited interest in property raises the further question whether there are any circumstances when such a person can recover more than the value of his interest in the property, in order to account for the balance to another. This will be considered shortly.

The insured is not necessarily confined to recovering the value of his proprietary interest in the property. He has an insurable interest in an expectancy based upon his proprietary interest, for example, in the profits he would expect to make from his ownership or occupation of the property.[91] This, however, has to be insured quite separately; the usual indemnity policy on property will not indemnify against consequential losses.[92]

Waiver of insurable interest

Assuming that the Life Assurance Act 1774 applies to insurances of real property, it is clear that the statutory requirement imposed thereby cannot be dispensed with. In respect of goods insurance, however, the only statutory requirement is the prohibition on gaming or wagering. Otherwise the requirement of insurable interest is merely implied into the contract as a consequence of the principle of indemnity and applies only at the time of loss. *Macaura* v. *Northern Assurance Co.*[93] illustrates this quite neatly. The insurers had initially referred the dispute to arbitration pursuant to a term in the policy. The insured argued that having done so they were precluded from alleging that the contract was void for want of insurable interest. It was held that the insurers were not alleging that the contract was void for failure to comply with any statutory obligation. They recognised the contract as valid, but denied (successfully) that the insured had at the time of loss the interest necessarily required in such a contract of indemnity.

On principle, there is no reason why, in an appropriate case, this contractual requirement should not be waived or dis-

---

[89] *Westminster Fire Office* v. *Glasgow Provident Investment Society* (1888) 13 App.Cas. 699.
[90] See this question discussed later, pp. 130–132 and 239.
[91] *City Tailors Ltd.* v. *Evans* (1922) 91 L.J.K.B. 379.
[92] See p. 182, below.
[93] Note 76, above.

pensed with, and there are clear authorities to this effect. In *Prudential Staff Union* v. *Hall*,[94] the plaintiff association of employees insured with Lloyd's against any loss suffered by any of its members of money held by them as agents or collectors of their employer. Clearly the association had no insurable interest in its members' liabilities, yet this was held to be no bar to its enforcing the insurance contract, the 1774 Act being inapplicable[95] and the contractual undertaking of the insurer to pay the association waiving any requirement of insurable interest.[96] Similarly, in *Thomas* v. *National Farmers' Union Mutual Insurance Society*,[97] the tenant of a farm insured the hay and straw thereon which was destroyed by fire, but after his lease had ended. The policy provided that it ceased to cover all property insured which passed from the insured "otherwise than by operation of law." The hay and straw had become the landlord's property on the expiration of the lease but only by operation of law owing to a provision in the Agricultural Holdings Act 1948. Thus, although the tenant no longer had any property in the goods, and thus no insurable interest, this was "by operation of law" and the insurer was contractually liable to pay him. What exactly is the obligation of the insured in cases like these with respect to the insurance monies he receives will be considered shortly.

If the insurable interest requirement in respect of goods' insurance can be waived, the question arises as to what are "goods" for the purpose of the exemption in section 4 of the 1774 Act. Obviously covered are the straightforward insurances of personal property.[98] However, there is also authority that the exemption extends to any policy of liability with respect to goods. So in *Williams* v. *Baltic Insurance Association of London*,[99] it was held that a liability policy on a car, or the liability section of a general motor policy, was exempted from the 1774 Act. While this may have been a rather benevolent construction,[1] it is well established[2] and obviously sensible as will be seen.

---

[94] [1947] K.B. 685.
[95] Money is goods for these purposes, although it would not be for the purposes of the Sale of Goods Act.
[96] In fact the action failed as it was held that the plaintiff suffered no loss.
[97] [1961] 1 W.L.R. 386.
[98] *Cf.* definition of "goods" in Sale of Goods Act 1979, s.61(1).
[99] [1924] 2 K.B. 282.
[1] But s.4 does refer to insurance *on* goods, not *of* goods.
[2] Although in the context of motor insurance it is not generally necessary: see Road Traffic Act 1972, s.148(4)—Chapter 19, p. 298.

Insurance of Third Parties' Interests

We must now return to the question of when a limited owner, or indeed someone without insurable interest in particular property, can recover on an insurance policy for the benefit of a third party not named therein. Because, as has just been seen, the requirement of insurable interest can be waived in respect of goods insurance, this situation clearly admits of the possibility. In respect of real property, the law is less developed, and that question is left to be considered quite separately.

Insurance on goods

If the insured has a limited interest in the goods insured, but has insured them for their full value, which is perfectly permissible as has been seen, he may, in certain cases, be entitled to recover the full value upon a loss, holding the balance on trust for the third party or parties entitled to the other interest or interests in the goods. Indeed if he himself has suffered no loss, he may recover the full value for the third party. The essential requirements are that the insured does have an interest in the goods and that as a matter of construction of the insurance contract, the policy does cover more than that limited interest. It is a question primarily of what the parties intend as derived from the construction of the contract, rather than from extrinsic evidence of actual intention.[3]

The insured with an interest

In *Waters* v. *Monarch Fire and Life Assurance Co.*,[4] the plaintiffs were flour and corn factors who effected a floating policy over the goods in their warehouse, whether their own or those held "in trust or on commission." A fire destroyed all the goods in the warehouse at a particular time. It was held that the plaintiffs were entitled to recover the full value of the goods; they would retain sufficient to cover their own interest and were trustees for the owners of the goods as to the rest. It was clear from the words of the policy cited above that it covered the interests of the owners. The fact that they were unaware of the policy was irrelevant. By contrast in *North British & Mercantile Insurance Co.* v. *Moffat*,[5] tea merchants insured chests of tea in their ware-

---

[3] *Hepburn* v. *Tomlinson* [1966] A.C. 451; *contra, British Traders' Ins. Co. Ltd.* v. *Monson* (1964) 111 C.L.R. 86.
[4] (1856) 5 E. & B. 870. See also *London & N. W. Railway Co.* v. *Glyn* (1859) 1 E. & E. 652.
[5] (1871) L.R. 7 C.P. 25.

houses which were their own or "in trust or on commission for which they are responsible." Fire destroyed certain chests which had been resold by the insured. It was held that because property in those chests had passed to the purchasers the insured had no interest in them. They could not recover for the purchasers because the words "for which they are responsible" qualified both the phrases "in trust" and "on commission". They could thus recover only for those third parties to whom they were in some way liable, which was not the situation.

The leading case is *Hepburn v. A. Tomlinson (Hauliers) Ltd.*[6] Carriers effected insurance on a quantity of tobacco which was stolen in circumstances attaching no legal liability to them. The policy was clearly expressed as a goods in transit policy, that is, insurance of the goods as such while they were being transported from one place to another, and not one simply insuring the carriers' potential legal liability. The owners of the goods were expressly named and the conditions were those appropriate to a first party and not a liability policy. In these circumstances the House of Lords held that the carriers were entitled to recover the full value of the tobacco for the benefit of the owners.[7] There was no gaming involved, the carriers did have an interest in the goods, because of their potential legal liability in respect of them if they were negligent, and the only question for decision was whether they intended to insure as it appeared from the construction of the contract.

The principle of *Waters* and *Hepburn* is most easily applicable to the situation where a bailee or carrier, for reasons of commercial convenience, insures goods on behalf of their owner as well as on his own behalf. It has, though, been recently applied, expressly for "commercial convenience," to an insurance of contract works under a contractors' all risks policy. In *Petrofina Ltd. v. Magnaload Ltd.*[8] it was held that an insurance effected by the owners and main contractors covering the construction of an extension to an oil refinery, under which all the sub-contractors working on the site were included within the definition of "the insured," enured to the benefit of each and every sub-contractor in respect of all the property insured. Arguably this point was unnecessary for the decision as the real issue was not whether the principal insured could recover for the benefit of a third party, but whether or not the insurer could exercise subrogation rights in the name of the principal insured against the

---

[6] [1966] A.C. 451.
[7] What if the owners had also insured? See Chapter 16, esp. at pp. 261–262.
[8] [1984] 1 Q.B. 127.

negligent sub-contractors responsible for the loss[9]; it was surely not necessary to find that the sub-contractors had an interest in the whole works in order to disallow subrogation.[10]

Third party's rights

Clearly the effect of the cases discussed so far is, practically speaking, to sanction an exception to the doctrine of privity of contract.[11] What is not entirely clear from the decisions is what is the relationship between the insured and the third party. If he claims on the policy and recovers, it is clear that he must account to the owner, whether as trustee or in quasi-contract for money had and received.[12] If the insured does not in fact claim, the third party will be able to recover only by showing that the insured contracted as his agent or as trustee for him. In the *Waters* case, the court appeared to treat the question as one of agency[13]; on this basis the third party can ratify and adopt the insured's act, provided that the latter contracted as agent and the third party is not an undisclosed principal,[14] and thus, if necessary, sue the insurer directly.

The insured without an interest

Turning to the case of insurance of goods where the insured has no interest, as we have already seen, there is clear authority that the insured can recover if the contract admits of the construction that the requirement of insurable interest was waived.[15] In *Williams v. Baltic Insurance Association of London*,[16] the plaintiff effected a motor policy on his car including cover against liability to third persons injured by use of the car. The policy was also expressed to cover any friend or relative of the insured driving with his consent. The plaintiff's sister, driving

---

[9] As to this aspect of the case, see p. 253, below.

[10] Further it is arguable that on the construction of the policy, the sub-contractors did not in fact have an interest in the whole contract works because the words "for which they are responsible" were expressed to limit the property insured; *cf.* the *Moffat* case (note 5, above). See further, [1983] J.B.L. 497.

[11] Whereby a third party cannot benefit by or be sued upon a contract between two others.

[12] Precisely which basis is applicable was left open in *Hepburn v. Tomlinson*, above.

[13] (1856) 5 E. & B. 870 at 881 (Lord Campbell C.J.). But if the insured insures as trustee, as in the *Waters* case and the *Glyn* case, it may be that the third party, as beneficiary, could sue the insurer, joining the insured as defendant: *Vandepitte v. Preferred Accident Ins. Corp.* [1933] A.C. 70.

[14] See below, p. 49 where this is discussed more fully.

[15] *Prudential Staff Union v. Hall*, note 94 above; *Thomas v. National Farmers' Union Mutual*, footnote 97, above.

[16] [1924] 2 K.B. 282.

the car with consent, negligently injured some people who recovered damages from her. The question was whether or not the insured could recover an indemnity in respect of these damages on his sister's behalf. Plainly, he had no insurable interest in his sister's legal liability, but, equally, the wording of the policy was expressed to cover that liability, so that the principal question was whether or not it was necessary for the plaintiff to have an insurable interest. Roche J. held that the policy was one on goods[17] so that it was exempted from any statutory requirement other than the prohibition on gaming and wagering, of which it clearly did not fall foul. As the common law did not require insurable interest in such a case, except as a consequence of the principle of indemnity, the very application of which was in issue, he was able to construe the contract as waiving any requirement of interest (and hence the principle of indemnity) because the policy expressly extended to the sister's liability.

It is plain that if the insured succeeds in this sort of case, he will hold anything he recovers for the third party, by analogy with the case of the insured with a limited interest which has already been discussed. However, whether or not the third party himself can sue, if the insured declines to do so, is open to some doubt, outside the context of motor insurance where there is a statutory right.[18]

Third party's rights

In *Vandepitte* v. *Preferred Accident Insurance Corporation of New York*,[19] the third party sued on facts very similar to those of *Williams*. The Privy Council held that he was prevented by the doctrine of privity of contract. The third party will therefore have to establish an exception to this doctrine. The possibilities of establishing that he was the beneficiary of a trust appear remote[19a], even though once the insured actually recovers, the proceeds thus recovered may be impressed with a trust. On principle, there is no reason why the third party cannot claim that the insured contracted as his agent. If a person expressly

---

[17] See p. 45, above.
[18] Road Traffic Act 1972, s.148(4); see note 2, above.
[19] [1933] A.C. 70.
[19a] However, the New South Wales Court of Appeal has recently allowed a person not party to the contract but described as one of the insureds under a contractor's liability insurance to enforce the contract directly on the basis of a trust: *Trident General Insurance Co. Ltd.* v. *McNiece Bros. Pty. Ltd.*, March 31 1987, (unreported) (see Reynolds [1987] J.B.L. 378).

contracts on behalf of another, even though that other is not actually named, who was in existence and capable of being ascertained at the time of the contract, that other, the principal, can ratify the acts of the agent and sue on the contract.[20] It may be, however, in non-marine insurance, that this ratification must occur before the loss. While this is possible, it is more likely that the third party will not discover the fact that the policy may benefit him until after a loss has taken place.[21]

The authority which decided that ratification is only effective if it takes place before a loss is *Grover and Grover Ltd. v. Mathews*,[22] which was not actually a case directly on insurable interest. The plaintiffs insured their piano factory through an agent at Lloyd's. Without consulting them, the agent wrote seeking renewal of the policy when it expired. A fire happened after this expiry and after the agent wrote, but before the plaintiffs knew what the agent had done. When they did find out, they purported to ratify his acts. It was held that the insurers were not liable. While ratification after loss is permissible in marine insurance,[23] Hamilton J. regarded this rule as anomalous and not to be extended to non-marine insurance.[24] It is arguable that this case is wrong in principle and that it conflicts with other authority,[25] but until it is expressly overruled, it stands as an effective bar to the third party directly enforcing an insurance contract made for this benefit by an insured without an interest in the property of the third party.[25a]

Insurance on real property

In respect of insurances on real property, the first crucial question is whether the Life Assurance Act 1774 applies.[26] If it does, then the insured without an interest in the property insured cannot recover for the benefit of another simply

[20] See, generally, *Bowstead on Agency*, 15th ed. pp. 51–81. The sister in *Williams v. Baltic* did ratify before the loss—see the finding of the arbitrators at p. 284 of the report, but curiously did not herself sue the insurers.

[21] e.g., a householder's policy may cover the property of the insured and members of his family permanently living with him. It is by no means certain that a spouse or mother-in-law, e.g., would be aware of this until a loss was suffered.

[22] [1910] 2 K.B. 401.

[23] *Williams v. North China Ins. Co.* (1876) 1 C.P.D. 757.

[24] He regarded himself as bound by the *Williams* case in which, he said, the court had recognised the anomaly of the rule. With respect, this is a curious reading of the *Williams* case, see, further, *MacGillivray & Parkington*, paras. 184 and 370.

[25] e.g. the dictum in *Waters v. Monarch*, referred to in the text above at note 13.

[25a] Note that in the *Trident* case (note 19a, above), the *Grover* case was held to be wrong, although a claim based on ratification failed for other reasons.

[26] This question is discussed earlier at pp. 36–39.

because the policy will be illegal.[27] Even if the insured has an interest, it may be that section 2 requires any third party to be named,[28] but it will be recalled that it has been said that section 2 is inapplicable to ordinary indemnity insurance contracts.[29] Further, the construction of section 2 propounded in *Davjoyda Estates Ltd. v. National Insurance Co. of New Zealand*[30] provides an alternative and sensible solution to this problem.

However, whether or not the 1774 Act applies, it seems less likely in respect of real property insurances, as compared with insurances on goods, that a policy will be open to a construction that allows the insured to recover for the benefit of a third party or allows the third party himself to sue on the policy. It must be stressed that we are here concerned with this limited question, the answer to which is not necessarily the same as the answer as to whether or not the third party has an interest in any insurance moneys actually recovered or as to whether he can use the compulsory reinstatement provisions of the Fires Prevention (Metropolis) Act 1774.[31] Just because, for example, the terms of a lease can be construed to entitle the tenant to the benefit of money received by his insured landlord[32] does not necessarily mean that the landlord was entitled under the insurance contract to recover for the benefit of the tenant nor that the tenant could sue on the insurance contract if the landlord chose not to.

Bearing this in mind, the same basic principle of construction as applies to insurances of goods for the benefit of third parties will apply to insurances of real property. Thus the contract as properly construed must reveal an intention to cover the third party's interest,[33] and the insurance will have to be of the full

[27] s.1 of the 1774 Act; see p. 37, above. If the Act does not apply, it seems that the common law reaches the same result: *Sadler's Co. v. Badcock* (1743) 2 Atk. 554; see p. 37 above.

[28] There are considerable difficulties if s.3 applies; see the earlier discussion at pp. 38–39. In Canada, where the 1774 Act does not apply, there are a number of authorities applying the *Waters* principle to insurances of real property on appropriate facts; see *e.g. Commonwealth Construction Co. v. Imperial Oil* (1976) 69 D.L.R. (3d) 558.

[29] *Mark Rowlands Ltd. v. Berni Inns Ltd.* [1986] Q.B. 211 at 227; see p. 36, above; contra, *Re King* [1963] Ch. 459 at 485; see *ibid*.

[30] (1967) 65 S.R. (N.S.W.) 381; see p. 38, above.

[31] As to these, see Chapter 14 below.

[32] As in, for example, *Mumford Hotels Ltd. v. Wheler* [1964] Ch. 117 and, it seems, *Mark Rowlands Ltd. v. Berni Inns Ltd.*, above; see p. 37, above. See also *Beacon Carpets Ltd. v. Kirby* [1985] Q.B. 755, note 38 below. Compare *Re King*, above.

[33] *Hepburn v. Tomlinson* [1966] A.C. 451; see p. 46, above. Compare the decision of the High Court of Australia in *British Traders Insurance Co. v. Monson* (1964) 111 C.L.R. 86, where, wrongly, the matter was said to turn upon whether

value of the property rather than merely of the interest of the insured as limited owner.[34] This seems to be fairly likely where the relationship between the insured and the third party is that of trustee and beneficiary[35] or mortgagor and mortgagee[36]; in the first case, the interests of the parties are similar, whereas in the second there is most likely to be a noting of both interests on the insurance policy. It seems less likely to be the case where the interests of the parties are quite distinct, as where they are vendor and purchaser[37] or landlord and tenant.[38]

or not the insured could show that he intended to insure for the benefit of the third party. Clearly though the decision in that case was correct. A tenant proposing to purchase the freehold of the property insured it for its full value and as freehold owner, making no mention of the landlord's interest. However, the purchase fell through before the fire which damaged the property. It was held that the tenant could recover only sufficient to indemnify him for his loss and nothing for the benefit of his landlord.

[34] Note that there is no rule of law requiring an insured to specify his interest in the insured property, although normally this would be required by the terms of the proposal form or stated in the policy.

[35] See *Davjoyda Estates Ltd.* v. *National Insurance Co. of New Zealand*, above, where the plaintiff company entered into a contract to purchase land as agent for another company and insured the land; the insurers were aware of the true principal, but the latter was not named in the policy. Before completion, fire damaged the property. Applying the analogy of the "bailee cases" (pp. 46–47, above) and getting round the problem posed by s.2 of the 1774 Act in the way described at p. 38, above, it was held that the plaintiff insured as trustee for the other company and could recover the full value of the property. On the construction of the policy, what was insured was the property itself and not merely the limited interest of the insured; there was no presumption of law, merely of fact, that an insured insures only his own interest and in the case of insurance by a trustee, he must also be insuring the interest of the beneficiary since their interests are essentially the same and of necessity the proceeds are held on the same trusts as the property is held.

[36] See *e.g. Hepburn* v. *Tomlinson*, above, at 481–482, *per* Lord Pearce.

[37] *Rayner* v. *Preston* (1881) 18 Ch.D. 1; see Chapter 9 at p. 129.

[38] In *Re King*, above, the Court of Appeal refused to apply the analogy of the "bailee cases" to an insurance by a tenant under a covenant to repair and reinstate. The case involved a dispute between landlord and tenant, the insurer not being involved. The tenant had a full insurable interest and could not be said to be insuring for the benefit of the landlord; the latter in fact was also named in the policy, but this was held to be merely to ensure that the landlord was able to control the receipt of the moneys and insist on reinstatement. Compare *Beacon Carpets Ltd.* v. *Kirby* [1985] Q.B. 755, where the relevant provisions in both the lease and the insurance policy were quite different. Again the dispute was between landlord and tenant, the insurer being quite unconcerned having paid out the insurance moneys. See also an interesting unreported Irish case, *Church and General Insurance Co.* v. *Connolly*, noted (1983) 5 D.U.L.J.(N.S.) 291, where a tenant at will recovered under a fire policy for the benefit of its landlord. The arrangement was a very informal letting of premises used as a youth centre and quite unlike the usual formal lease. The 1774 Act was held not to apply to Ireland.

Chapter 4

FORMALITIES AND FORMATION OF THE INSURANCE CONTRACT

In this chapter a number of matters are examined, some of which at least involve merely the application of general requirements of the law of contract to the particular context of the insurance contract. While we are first concerned with questions as to formation and formalities required, it is convenient to consider also a number of related matters, namely temporary cover and cover notes, and the law concerning the duration, renewal, cancellation and surrender of insurance contracts.

FORMATION OF THE INSURANCE CONTRACT

The insurance contract is no exception to the general rule requiring offer, acceptance, consideration and an intention to create legal relations in order to find a binding legal contract.[1] The last two requirements, however, will invariably be satisfied automatically and need not be considered further.

Offer and acceptance

An offer to enter into an insurance contract may be made by a prospective insured or by an insurer. At the initial stage,[2] it will in practice be made by the proposed insured,[3] usually, but by no means necessarily, by means of completing a proposal form.[4] Proposal forms are of course standard mass-produced documents prepared by insurers.[5] The insurer may simply accept the

---

[1] See generally Treitel, *Law of Contract*, Chapters 2 to 5.
[2] Compare the position on renewal, discussed later pp. 67–71.
[3] For a recent illustration, see *Rust* v. *Abbey Life Ass. Co.* [1979] 2 Lloyd's Rep. 334.
[4] Proposal forms are not used in all classes of business nor often in respect of temporary cover (see later). In *Adie* v. *The Insurance Corp.* (1898) 14 T.L.R. 544, the offer by the insured took the form of a letter attaching his old policy from a different insurer.
[5] Under the *Statements of Insurance Practice* (see p. 4, above), proposal forms issued to individual proposers must contain a statement that a copy of the completed form is automatically provided for retention at the time of completion, will be supplied as part of the insurer's normal practice or will be supplied on

offer made or may "accept" it with qualifications, in which case the "acceptance" may in law amount to a counter-offer. Assuming for the present that there appears to have been an offer and an unqualified acceptance of that offer, the question arises as to what must be comprised in this agreement for there to be a binding insurance contract.

Agreement on material terms

It was once suggested in the House of Lords[6] that all the terms and conditions of the contract must be agreed by both parties. Clearly there are certain essential matters on which there must be accord, namely, the amount of the premium[7]; the nature of the risk, including the subject-matter of the insurance[8]; and the duration of the risk.[9] But otherwise it is suggested that the better view, despite the authoritative dictum already referred to, is that these matters are the only ones upon which agreement is required, for the reason that the proposer for insurance is deemed to have applied for the usual form of policy issued by the insurer in respect of the particular type of insurance in question. He is thus deemed to have agreed to the usual terms and conditions to be found in the insurer's policy.[10] In *General Accident Insurance Corporation* v. *Cronk*,[11] the proposal form which the applicant completed did not contain some terms which were in the policy he subsequently received. He declined to pay the premium, arguing that the sending of the policy with different terms was merely a counter-offer which he chose not to accept. It was held that he was liable for the premium for the reasons already outlined. In practice nowadays, apart from the situation when an application is made orally, for

---

request within three months after completion. *Quaere* whether automatic supply should not be the rule, given the importance of the proposal form; see Chapters 6 and 7, below. However, the insurer must not raise an issue under a proposal form without supplying a copy; this relates to issues of non-disclosure and misrepresentation, as do other aspects of the *Statements* which are considered in those later chapters.

[6] *Alliss-Chalmers Co.* v. *Fidelity & Deposit Co. of Maryland* (1916) 114 L.T. 433 at 434.

[7] *Ibid.* In the case of an ordinary risk, however, the amount may be deemed to be in accordance with the insurer's usual tariff. The premium need not actually be paid.

[8] *Beach* v. *Pearl Ass. Co. Ltd.* [1938] I.A.C.Rep. 3.

[9] See generally *Murfitt* v. *Royal Insurance Co.* (1922) 38 T.L.R. 334 at 336.

[10] *General Accident Ins. Corp.* v. *Cronk* (1901) 17 T.L.R. 233; *Rust* v. *Abbey Life* [1979] 2 Lloyd's Rep. 334.

[11] Above.

example for a cover-note,[12] no difficulty is likely to arise on this point, as invariably proposal forms stipulate that the proposer's offer is subject to the insurer's usual terms and conditions.

Counter-offer

It may very likely be that the insurer does not simply accept the proposer's offer, but states that acceptance is subject to payment of the first premium. It is clear that in law this generally amounts to a counter-offer,[13] so that there is no binding contract until the premium is in fact paid.[14] On general principle, until this act of acceptance, either party should be free to withdraw. However, the law appears to be that the insurer's act constitutes a counter-offer which the proposer may decline to accept but which the insurer cannot revoke, unless there is a change in the risk involved between the time of the original offer and the insured's acceptance by payment of the premium. In other words, the insurer is bound by its counter-offer so long as the risk remains the same. If the risk changes, the tender of the premium by the insured constitutes a new offer which the insurer is at liberty to reject. In *Canning* v. *Farquhar*,[15] a proposal for life insurance was "accepted" on December 14 on the terms that no insurance was to take effect until the first premium was paid. The premium was tendered on January 9 but four days previously the proposer had fallen and suffered serious injuries from which he subsequently died. The Court of Appeal ruled that the insurer was not bound, the majority[16] reasoning along the lines already discussed.[17] However, it may be that the insurer is estopped from denying that there is a binding contract. This will be the case if, for example, the policy contains a

---

[12] See pp. 64–67, below.

[13] It may even be merely an invitation to treat, whereupon the proposer must make a new offer on this basis: *Locker* v. *Law Union and Rock Ins. Co. Ltd.* [1928] 1 K.B. 554.

[14] *Canning* v. *Farquhar* (1886) 16 Q.B.D. 727, 733.

[15] (1886) 16 Q.B.D. 727. See also *Harrington* v. *Pearl Life Ass. Co.* (1914) 30 T.L.R. 613.

[16] Lindley and Lopes L.JJ.

[17] Lord Esher M.R. decided the case primarily upon the ground that tender of the premium could never be acceptance of an offer by the insurers, even if there had been no change in risk. The tender would be an offer by the proposer requiring to be accepted by the insurers. With respect, this must be incorrect. The insurer's letter of December 14 was more than a mere statement of intent or invitation to treat. This is not to deny, of course, that such a reply by insurers to a proposal could not in an appropriate case be construed as merely an invitation to treat if matters other than the mere payment of the premium were left open; see *e.g. Locker* v. *Law Union*, above.

statement that the premium has been paid, as in *Roberts* v. *Security Co. Ltd.*,[18] where this overrode a condition that the insurance was not effective until the premium was paid.

Changes in risk

If there are any material changes in the risk between the date of proposal and the date of the conclusion of the contract, then these must be disclosed to the insurer in accordance with the general duty of disclosure.[19] Failure to do so renders the contract voidable at the option of the insurer. If, in *Canning* v. *Farquhar*, the insurer had accepted the premium tendered, not knowing of the insured's fall, they would have been able to avoid liability for this reason. However, this principle applies only so long as there is no contract in existence. If, for example, the insurer accepts the insured's offer unconditionally, he is thereupon bound, even if the contract provides that the risk will not run until the premium is paid.[20] Non-disclosure of a change in the risk before the premium is paid will not entitle the insurer to avoid the contract, although it would not be liable for any loss occurring before the premium was paid.

Communication of acceptance

It is a general rule of the law of contract that acceptance of an offer is not effective until communicated to the offeror, which will obviously apply to the insurance contract. There are some well-established exceptions to this general rule, three of which appear of particular relevance in the context of insurance. First, where an offer is unilateral, acceptance is constituted simply by performance in accordance with the terms of the offer. There are one or two examples of this in the insurance field. It used not to be uncommon for newspapers and diaries to offer accident insurance to people who having bought the article, filled in the relevant coupon. A modern example of such coupon insurance is cover against death or injury during aeroplane flights which can be purchased at airport counters. There can be no doubt that in law the provision of such insurance is a unilateral offer

---

[18] [1897] 1 Q.B. 111; see p. 57 below.
[19] See Chapter 6.
[20] See *MacGillivray and Parkington*, paras. 319–323. This position is unlikely in practice. A provision that the risk does not run is perhaps most likely to be construed as meaning that no contract is in force. It has indeed been held that there is a strong presumption, in the case of life insurance, that no contract comes into existence until the premium is paid and the policy issued: *Southern Cross Ass. Co. Ltd.* v. *Australian Provincial Ass.* (1939) 39 S.R. (N.S.W.) 174.

by the insurer which the proposer accepts simply by filling in the relevant details requested on the form.

The second exception to the communication of acceptance rule, which can be of some importance, is where a policy is issued under seal. Assuming that the insurer's acceptance is unconditional, or that any condition as to prepayment of the premium is waived, if the acceptance takes the form of the signing and sealing of a policy,[21] there is no requirement of communication to the insured. In *Roberts* v. *Security Co. Ltd.*,[22] the plaintiff filled in a proposal form for burglary insurance on December 14. On December 27 the directors of the insurer fixed the company's seal to the policy accepting the proposal, which provided that it was effective from December 14. On the night of December 26, obviously before he knew of the insurer's acceptance, since it had not then taken place, the insured suffered a loss. It was held that the insurer was liable.

Third, the rule requiring communication of acceptance obviously implies that silence or delay does not constitute acceptance. While this is certainly prima facie the case, an insured who acts in reliance on an offer from an insurer will be regarded as having accepted it even in the absence of express communication.[23] In *Rust* v. *Abbey Life Assurance Co. Ltd.*,[24] the proposer for a form of linked life policy retained the policy for seven months before disputing that she was bound by it. She alleged that she had never intended to enter into that sort of contract and had been misled by the insurer's agent. It was found that the nature of the contract had been fully explained to her and that she was bound by it. Even if she had not made an offer to the insurer which the latter had accepted by issuing the policy, which the court considered was the case,[25] the insurer's issue of a policy was an offer which she had accepted by doing and saying nothing for seven months.

Statutory requirements

Finally, in connection with the formation of insurance contracts, there are two statutory provisions which should be

---

[21] See generally *MacGillivray and Parkington*, Chap. 5.
[22] [1897] 1 Q.B. 111; a condition that the policy was not effective until the premium was paid was waived by a recital that the premium had been paid. See above.
[23] See, *e.g. Taylor* v *Allon* [1966] 1 Q.B. 304, discussed below, p. 64.
[24] [1979] 2 Lloyd's Rep. 334.
[25] Following *Adie* v. *The Insurance Corp.*, note 4, above, and *General Accident* v. *Cronk*, note 10, above.

noted. Under section 72 of the Insurance Companies Act 1982, which merely attracts criminal sanctions for failure to comply and has no civil consequences, regulations can be made as to the form and contents of insurance advertisements, defined as advertisements[26] inviting persons to enter into or offer to enter into insurance contracts, or containing information calculated to lead to such entry or offers.[27] The regulations[28] apply primarily to advertisements for life insurance by overseas insurers not authorised to carry on business in the United Kingdom and require that these facts be disclosed. The only regulation of relevance to authorised domestic insurers specifies that if any advertisement by them refers to their authorised capital, it must also state the amount of subscribed and paid up capital.[29]

Section 133 of the Financial Services Act 1986[30] provides that it is an offence for any person to induce or attempt to induce another to enter into a contract of insurance with an insurer by making dishonest or reckless statements or promises or forecasts or by dishonestly concealing material facts.[31] This is obviously aimed at misleading statements, promotional material and the like issued by insurers or their agents. An individual who was so induced to enter into an insurance contract could have a civil remedy, in addition to the criminal sanction in the section, if the representation was one of fact.

FORMALITIES

Subject to one or two exceptions,[32] there is no general requirement of English law that an insurance contract be in any particular form. Indeed, an oral agreement, provided that it can be proved, is binding, provided that there is the necessary agree-

---

[26] "Advertisement" itself is widely defined in subsection 6 as every form of advertising. It may well include any document sent out by an insurer, even to private addresses; cf. R. v. *Delmayne* [1970] 2 Q.B. 170.

[27] Section 72(5).

[28] Insurance Companies Regulations 1981 S.I. No. 1654, regs. 65 and 66.

[29] Note also the restriction on promoting insurance contracts which are investment contracts (as to this, see p. 59, below) in s.130 of the Financial Services Act 1986.

[30] Replacing s.73 of the Insurance Companies Act 1982.

[31] This section only applies to non-investment insurance contracts, but investment contracts (most forms of life insurance) are covered by the substantially similar s.47.

[32] Especially marine policies (Marine Insurance Act 1906, s.22) and guarantee policies (Statute of Frauds 1677, s.4).

ment on the material terms.[33] In practice, of course, apart from cases of temporary cover, insurance contracts are invariably recorded in a policy, but there is no magic in this, unless it is a term of the insurer's acceptance that they are not liable until a policy has been issued.

Life insurance contracts

There are requirements, however, applying to most contracts of life insurance, either under the Insurance Companies Act 1982, sections 75 to 77[34] or under the Financial Services (Cancellation) Rules 1977.[35] Both these sets of requirements impose a "cooling-off" period during which a life policyholder can change his mind and cancel a contract he has entered into or withdraw from an offer he has made. They exist to deter and penalise undue high pressure salesmanship.[36] Failure to comply with the requirements does not affect the validity of any contract,[37] but a breach of the Cancellation Rules is actionable as a breach of statutory duty.[38]

The Cancellation Rules provide greater protection to the life insured than the 1982 Act in terms of both the information with which he must be provided and the period allowed for cancellation. The Rules apply to all life contracts which fall within the definition of "investment" in Schedule 1 to the 1986 Act.[39] This definition is likely to comprehend the vast majority of life insurance contracts in practice. The life contracts which are not investments are principally (i) those which are pure life insurance, that is where the benefits are payable only on death, (ii)

---

[33] *Murfitt* v. *Royal Insurance Co.* (1922) 38 T.L.R. 334.

[34] And the regulations made thereunder, namely regs. 70 and 71 and Scheds. 10 to 12 to the Insurance Companies Regulations 1981 S.I. No. 1654.

[35] Hereafter referred to as the Cancellation Rules. These are made, under s.51 of the Financial Services Act 1986, by the Securities and Investment Board as the designated agency under the Act. They are contained in Chapter V of *The Regulation of Investment Business*. By Sched. 10, para. 5(3) to the 1986 Act, the 1982 Act's provisions are superseded where relevant by the Cancellation Rules. It should also be noted that the latter also apply to many unit trust schemes.

[36] They were originally introduced on the recommendations of the Scott Committee on Property Bonds and Equity Linked Life Assurance, 1973 Cmnd. 5281, and have their equivalent in the hire purchase and consumer credit legislation.

[37] Insurance Companies Act 1982, s.75(4); Financial Services Act 1986, s.62(4).

[38] Financial Services Act 1986, s.62(1).

[39] With some qualifications in respect of single premium policies. The distinction between what can be described as "investment insurance" and "non-investment insurance" under the 1986 Act is relevant in other contexts; see especially p. 58, above and p. 152, below.

those where the benefits on death (other than by accident) are payable within 10 years or before the life insured attains a specified age not exceeding 70, that is certain short-term policies, and (iii) those where the policy has no surrender value or where a single premium is payable and the surrender value does not exceed that premium. The 1982 Act's provisions will apply to most of these non-investment contracts.[40]

Under both regimes, a notice of the right to cancel must be sent to the insured.[41] The notice must be in the prescribed form[42] and contain the specified information relating to the salient features of the contract.[43] Attached to the notice must be the prescribed form of notice of cancellation.[44] The right to cancel[45] can be exercised up to a number of days after the insured receives the notice of the right or when he knows that the agreement is concluded and makes his first or only payment of premium, whichever is the later.[46] Under the 1982 Act the number of days is 10; under the Cancellation Rules it is the longer period of 14 days.

Notice of cancellation operates to rescind any concluded contract or to withdraw any offer not yet accepted. Any money paid by the insured must be returned to him.[47]

Forming the Contract at Lloyd's

Where the insurer is a member of Lloyd's, there are sufficient peculiarities concerning the procedure adopted in the formation of a contract to justify brief[48] separate consideration. We adverted earlier[49] to the special position of Lloyd's underwriters, whose procedure for the consideration of an offer for

[40] Note, however, the exemptions from the 1982 Act's provisions in reg. 71 of the 1981 Regulations.
[41] The 1982 Act requires that this be sent at the latest by the time of contract; the Cancellation Rules allow up to seven days thereafter.
[42] Sched. 10 or 11 to the 1981 Regulations; Sched. 1 to the Cancellation Rules.
[43] As stated above, the Cancellation Rules require more information than the 1981 Regulations.
[44] Sched. 12 to the 1981 Regulations; Sched. 2 to the Cancellation Rules.
[45] Notice of which is deemed to be served when posted under both the 1982 Act and the Cancellation Rules.
[46] Thus, if no notice of the right to cancel is sent, the right to cancel always exists.
[47] Subject to an allowance under the Cancellation Rules in respect of single premium policies.
[48] For a fuller account, see *MacGillivray and Parkington*, Chap. 20.
[49] Chapters 1 and 2.

insurance involves the submission of a slip with details of the risk etc. to each relevant underwriter in turn. It should be noted that the proposer himself cannot do this; he must act through a Lloyd's broker.[50] The legal conundrum is simply when the contract is concluded. Is each underwriter bound when he has accepted the offer by initialling the slip, even though later underwriters might decline the offer or amend its terms, or is there a contract only once the whole of the offer, the full amount of insurance requested, has been accepted?

It has now been authoritatively decided by the Court of Appeal[51] that the underwriter is bound from the moment he initials the slip, despite the fact that in theory this could lead to odd legal results, for example if a later underwriter accepts on different terms. Strictly therefore the insured may have separate contracts with different underwriters rather than the one whole insurance contract. In reaching this conclusion, the Court of Appeal applied the well-established customs of the London insurance market.

It also seems from the Court of Appeal's judgment[52] that the insured has no right to cancel a contract with an underwriter who has accepted his offer if a later underwriter refuses to accept the offer, so that the insured is only partially covered, or "accepts" it on terms unacceptable to the insured. Again in theory this could lead to odd results, though no doubt in practice disputes would rarely arise.

Temporary Cover and Cover-Notes

It is, of course, common practice in many different types of insurance, but most commonly in motor insurance, for insurers to agree to temporary cover upon first receipt of a proposal, pending full consideration and possible acceptance of the offer, and issue of a policy. Such "cover-notes," as they are usually called, are undoubtedly fully effective contracts of insurance.[53] There is a comparative dearth of legal authority concerning

---

[50] See Chapter 10. Brokers may have authority to grant temporary cover—*Praet* v. *Poland* [1960] 1 Lloyd's Rep. 416; see further below.

[51] *General Reinsurance Corporation* v. *Forsakringsaktiebolaget Fennia Patria* [1983] Q.B. 856; contra *Jaglom* v. *Excess Insurance Co. Ltd.* [1972] Q.B. 250. See also *Eagle Star Insurance Co. Ltd.* v. *Spratt* [1971] 2 Lloyd's Rep. 116.

[52] Compare the views of Staughton J. at first instance in the *General Reinsurance* case: [1982] Q.B. 1022.

[53] *Mackie* v. *European Ass. Soc.* (1869) 21 L.T. 102.

them, but a number of important legal questions arise which are examined in the following paragraphs.

Authority to issue cover-notes

Whereas the acceptance of an offer for a full contract of insurance can invariably be made only by the insurer, authority to conclude a binding cover-note will often be vested in an agent. Some of the relevant agency principles are examined in detail in Chapter 10. In this context, it is necessary merely to say that, regardless of whether or not an insurer has expressly conferred authority on an agent to issue cover-notes, the fact that an agent is entrusted with blank cover-notes or their equivalent appears sufficient to confer upon him either implied actual authority or ostensible authority.

In *Mackie* v. *European Assurance Society*,[54] the plaintiff insured his mill and warehouse through W, at the time an agent for the Commercial Union. Subsequently W became an agent of the defendant. The plaintiff's policy with the Commercial Union expired and he asked W for a new one. W gave him a cover-note, in the form of a receipt, for a month in the name of the defendant. Despite the fact that at the time the plaintiff did not realise that the insurer was different,[55] and despite the fact that the defendant no longer transacted fire business, Mallins V.C., in a judgment notable for its criticism of the defendant's attitude, held that there was a binding temporary contract of insurance between the parties. Having provided W with cover-notes, the defendant had conferred authority on him to bind them. The principle must apply to any agents entrusted with cover-notes, even if they are brokers and normally agents of the insured.[56]

An agent not entrusted with blank cover-notes will not usually be regarded as having authority to bind the insurer.[57] The decision in *Murfitt* v. *Royal Insurance Co.*,[58] where an agent was held to have implied actual authority to enter into temporary oral contracts of fire insurance, must be regarded as exceptional. The judge stressed that the facts were special, because the agent in question had been giving such cover orally for two

---

[54] See note 53.
[55] Though this should be irrelevant; the plaintiff merely wanted to be insured.
[56] See *Stockton* v. *Mason* [1978] 2 Lloyd's Rep. 430, discussed below and in Chapter 10.
[57] *Dicks* v. *S.A. Mutual Fire & General Ins. Co.* [1963] (4) S.A. 501.
[58] (1922) 38 T.L.R. 334.

years with the knowledge and consent of his superiors. However, it would appear that the position of brokers may be different. There is a clear dictum[59] that they have implied authority to issue interim contracts of insurance in a case where the only acknowledgement by the broker was oral. This appears to be a clear recognition of a common practice whereby insurers do confer such authority on brokers. It must be stressed, however, that this can apply only where there is a pre-existing arrangement between insurer and broker.

Conclusion of the temporary contract

In the ordinary case, this should be a simple matter, the contract being concluded by the insurer or its agent's temporary acceptance of the proposer's offer, provided that the material terms are agreed, as discussed earlier. It will then last for the stated period or until earlier termination by the insurer if, as is usual, this is permitted, or upon being superseded by a formal policy. There can be no objection, sufficient terms being agreed, to the conclusion of a temporary contract by telephone. It should be noted, however, that as a cover-note is a proper contract of insurance, the proposer is under a duty to disclose all material facts to the insurer prior to its conclusion, on pain of the contract being voidable at the latter's option.[60]

There is one contrasting situation where, it seems, this analysis of offer by the proposer being accepted by the insurer will not apply. This is where temporary cover is offered by the insurer upon the termination of a formal contract. In practice this appears to be confined to motor insurance in order to enable the insured to satisfy the compulsory insurance requirements of the Road Traffic Act 1972.[61] What happens is that the insurer, sometimes by way of a slip attached to the motor insurance certificate, alternatively by the notice sent out inviting renewal of the policy, offers to cover the insured for a short period, usually 15 days, upon expiry of the old policy.[62] Any legal problem surrounding this is likely to arise only when the insured does not renew his old policy or effect a new one with a

---

[59] *Stockton* v. *Mason*, above at 431, *per* Lord Diplock.
[60] *Mayne Nickless* v. *Pegler* (1974) 1 N.S.W.L.R. 228, criticised in (1977) 40 M.L.R. 79 (Birds); *Marene Knitting Mills* v. *Greater Pacific General Ins. Ltd.* [1976] 2 Lloyd's Rep. 631.
[61] See Chapter 19.
[62] This temporary extension is often only in respect of the compulsory requirements.

different insurer in time. This was the case in *Taylor* v. *Allon*,[63] where the insured's policy with the A Company expired on April 5, but he possessed the sort of temporary slip described. He had decided to change his insurer to Company B, and from B he obtained new cover from April 16. However, he drove his car on April 15, and was charged with driving without insurance.[64] The Divisional Court held that he had been rightly convicted of that offence. Obviously he was not insured by B on April 15. A's cover-note was, it was held, merely an offer by A to insure him from the expiry of the policy, which was binding only if he accepted it.[65] On the facts there was no evidence that the insured accepted that offer. Clearly the insured had not expressly communicated his acceptance to A, though the Court was prepared to assume that this was the sort of situation where the usual rule as to communication of acceptance did not apply. However, even on this assumption, acceptance by conduct was necessary and there was no evidence of this, which would usually be by the insured's driving his car in reliance upon the offer.

Terms incorporated into the cover-note

The question next arises as to what are the terms of the contract constituted by a cover-note. Here the question of when the contract is concluded may be crucial. Obviously, the material terms[66] must be agreed, but it may be important to know whether conditions regarding the claims process, for example, contained in the insurer's standard policy are incorporated.

The careful insurer will ensure that its acceptance of the insured's offer is expressly made subject to its usual terms and conditions for the class of insurance in question.[67] Alternatively, the cover-note may be issued following completion of a proposal form which incorporates the relevant terms.[68] However, it might be thought that this is unnecessary, by virtue of the rule examined earlier that a proposer's offer for insurance is deemed to be for the usual form of policy issued by the insurer. It would appear, though, that this does not apply to cover notes.

---

[63] [1966] 1 Q.B. 304.
[64] Under what is now Road Traffic Act 1972, s.145.
[65] Even though A stated in evidence that they regarded themselves as bound to the insured.
[66] See p. 54, above.
[67] See, *e.g. Dawson* v. *Monarch Ins. Co. of New Zealand* [1977] 1 N.Z.L.R. 372.
[68] See, *e.g. Houghton* v. *Trafalgar Ins. Co. Ltd.* [1953] 2 Lloyd's Rep. 18.

No implied incorporation

In *Re Coleman's Depositories Ltd. and Life & Health Assurance Association*,[69] a company applied for a policy of employer's liability insurance. They completed a proposal form on December 28 and on that day received a cover-note with no reference to any conditions. The insurers accepted the offer by the sealing of a policy on January 3 which was expressed to run from January 1, and which was delivered to the company on January 9. On January 2, one of the insured's employees was injured. At the time his condition was not considered dangerous, but he subsequently developed dangerous symptoms and died on March 15. On March 14 the insured gave notice of a possible claim against them to the insurers. The latter denied liability on the ground that the insured had failed to give immediate notice of the claim as required by a condition in the policy. By a majority, the Court of Appeal held that the insured was not bound by this condition, reasoning that it could not apply until communicated to the insured, which was not until January 9 and after the injury to the employee.[70] Although there is an obvious element of justice in the decision, the reasoning is not easy to follow. If the insured was simply relying upon the cover-note, and indeed the policy was not executed until after the accident, although it was stated to apply retrospectively, there is a case for saying that as it did not contain any reference to conditions, and in particular the condition requiring notice, the insured was not bound by any. Even this, however, runs contrary to the decisions in cases like *General Accident* v. *Cronk*[71] and there are contrary authorities.[72] However, the insured had relied upon the terms of the policy in agreeing initially to go to arbitration and there was no suggestion that they were not suing on the policy. In these circumstances, it is difficult to see how they could deny that they were bound by other terms in the policy, the fact that they may not have had actual knowledge of them, at the relevant time, being irrelevant.

While *Re Coleman* must stand as clear authority for the proposition that conditions imposing obligations on the insured apply to cover-notes only when expressly incorporated, it is

---

[69] [1907] 2 K.B. 798. See also *Inn. Cor. International Ltd.* v. *American Home Ass. Co.* (1974) 42 D.L.R. (3d) 46.

[70] The Court was also of opinion that in any event the condition was not a condition precedent to liability. On this distinction, see Chapter 7.

[71] (1901) 17 T.L.R. 233; see p. 54, above.

[72] *e.g. Wyndham Rather Ltd.* v. *Eagle Star & British Dominions Ins. Co. Ltd.* (1925) 21 Ll.L.Rep. 214.

perhaps safe to assume that it has survived largely unchallenged only because since then insurers have always stipulated expressly that their cover-notes incorporate their policy terms. In any event, it must be the case that terms of the usual policy defining the scope of the cover are impliedly incorporated into the cover-note.[73]

An oral contract?

It may be that the insured is able to argue that a contract was concluded before the written cover-note or any incorporation by reference on a proposal form was made available to him. The facts of the Australian case of *Mayne Nickless Ltd.* v. *Pegler*[74] illustrate this quite neatly. The insured purchased a car and the vendor immediately arranged for insurance, seemingly by telephone. The insured later received a cover-note bearing the date of purchase of the car and incorporating the insurer's usual terms. The case was decided upon other grounds, but it must be at least arguable that a binding insurance contract was concluded orally by telephone before the insured was aware of any express terms. The point was not argued, but if this is the correct legal analysis, and the situation may arise commonly in motor insurance, it is difficult to see, consistently with the decision in *Re Coleman* how an insurer can rely upon express incorporation of policy conditions, unless of course there is mention of this when the oral contract is being concluded.

The cover-note in the *Pegler* case also stated that it was "subject to . . . a satisfactory proposal for your insurance." It was held that the effect of this was to enable the insurer to avoid liability under the cover-note because of a misstatement in the proposal form subsequently completed by the insured. The proposal was not "satisfactory." With respect, it might be argued that the phrase simply warned the insured as to the need to complete a proposal form before a formal policy could be issued, or simply that "satisfactory" means proper in the formal sense rather than in the sense of everything being absolutely correct. There is at least some ambiguity which is surely sufficient to invoke the *contra preferentem* rule.[75] Further, the effect of the decision is that if a proposal form is never in fact completed, which may be for quite innocent reasons, for example, a subsequent accident[76] or the insured's decision to approach

---

[73] See *MacGillivray and Parkington*, paras. 294–295.
[74] (1974) 1 N.S.W.L.R. 228.
[75] See Chapter 11 at pp. 166–168.
[76] See (1977) 40 M.L.R. 79 at 82.

another insurer, the cover-note is technically worthless. It is suggested that in a case where such a qualification is attached to a cover-note, the court should disregard it on the grounds that it may render the protection allegedly provided useless.[77]

Termination of the cover-note and its relationship with a subsequent policy

Finally, it is necessary to consider when the contract contained in a cover-note comes to an end, otherwise than by the expiry of its stated period. In practice it may well provide that it can be terminated by the insurer, and there can be no objection to an insurer's acting in reliance upon such an express right, although the insured must receive notice of cancellation. In the absence of such a right, a cover-note would clearly not be terminable until it duly expired.[78]

It must frequently be the case, however, that a formal policy is issued before the cover-note's expressed duration has run. Here it would appear that the policy takes over from the date it is issued but not before. Even if the policy is expressed to be retrospective, it must be arguable that a claim arising before its issue falls under the cover-note only.[79] This can only be of any real consequence, however, if there is a relevant difference between the terms of the cover-note and the policy, which, as has been seen, is not very likely nowadays.

DURATION AND RENEWAL OF INSURANCE POLICIES

The question of the length of an insurance contract is a matter for the policy itself to provide. There are no rules of law. However, it is safe to state as a general rule that the life contract is quite different from other insurance policies. There must be at least a presumption that a life contract is entire, is one contract, existing until the death of the life assured, or a specified fixed date in the case of an endowment or term policy.[80] So, provided that the premiums due are properly paid,[81] the insurer cannot refuse to renew a life policy, nor can he allege non-disclosure of

[77] *MacGillivray and Parkington*, para. 289.
[78] *Smith* v. *National Mutual Fire Ins. Co. Ltd.* [1974] 1 N.Z.L.R. 278.
[79] *Re Coleman*, above. Rather oddly in that case, as we have seen, the insured appeared to be suing on the policy rather than the cover-note.
[80] *Stuart* v. *Freeman* [1903] 1 K.B. 47 at 53–54 and 55; compare *Pritchard* v. *Merchants' and Tradesmen's Mutual Life Ass. Co.* (1858) 3 C.B.(N.S.) 622 at 643.
[81] *Pritchard* v. *Merchants' and Tradesmen's*, above.

material facts which happen after the contract is first concluded. We shall advert to this question later under "days of grace."

In contrast, most other policies are of limited duration, normally of one year, though, of course, there is no bar to the agreement of a policy for a shorter or longer term. But upon expiry of such a policy, if the parties choose to renew the contract, the renewal is clearly in law a fresh contract[82] and thus, for example, the duty of disclosure arises again.[83]

Cancellation

Many non-life policies contain a condition entitling either party to cancel them upon giving notice to the other party, usually of seven or 14 days, but a clause permitting immediate cancellation would no doubt be valid. Some such conditions may require the insurer who seeks to cancel to show cause, but this is not essential and an absolute right to cancel is enforceable.[84] That such a right is capable of being abused, though it is an open question how often it may be abused, is evident from the cases.

In *Sun Fire Office* v. *Hart*,[85] the Privy Council upheld the cancellation of a fire policy under a clause providing for termination by the insurers "from any . . . cause whatever" after the insured had suffered several fires and had received an anonymous letter threatening arson.[86] More extreme perhaps are the facts in the Indian case of *General Assurance Society* v. *Chandermull Jain*.[87] There the insured's property was covered against loss or damage by flood. The River Ganges, which ran near the insured's property, had already started to flood further up its course when the insurers served notice of cancellation. The Supreme Court of India held that the insurers were perfectly justified in taking this action, there being nothing unreasonable

---

[82] *Stokell* v. *Heywood* [1897] 1 Ch. 459.
[83] *Lambert* v. *Co-operative Ins. Soc.* [1975] 1 Lloyd's Rep. 465; see Chapter 6.
[84] *Sun Fire Office* v. *Hart* (1889) 14 App.Cas. 98.
[85] See footnote 84.
[86] The Court of Appeal of Grenada had refused to uphold the clause, saying that it would permit cancellation for any reason, which would be absurd. The Privy Council justified their decision partly on the ground that the insured could go elsewhere. This must be somewhat unrealistic. What insurer would insure at anything like the same premium an insured who has been threatened with arson, and the fact of cancellation must be a material fact which should be disclosed to any subsequent insurer, which again is hardly likely to dispose it to look kindly on the insured.
[87] A.I.R. (1966) S.C. 1644.

about unrestricted cancellation rights,[88] provided that cancellation is effected before the risk insured against has run. This is a question of fact; presumably there has to be some danger to the property insured before a cancellation would be illegitimate. It should be noted that usually, upon cancellation, the insured is entitled under the standard condition to a *pro rata* return of premium. In the absence of such an express right, he would not be entitled to anything, the risk having run.[89]

One would imagine that nowadays insurers only rarely exercise their cancellation power arbitrarily,[90] but, even if this is so, there would appear to be an unanswerable case for the restriction of such rights, particularly in the field of motor insurance, where insurance is compulsory.[91] What is needed is a guaranteed minimum period of notice before cancellation can take effect, in order to enable the insured to seek fresh cover, and, particularly, a requirement that the insurer have good reason to cancel.

Life policies

Life policies do not, of course, contain cancellation clauses of the same kind but commonly, at least apart from term assurance, they do permit the insured to surrender the policy after a certain number of years, so that the insured then receives a lump sum, the surrender value, or they provide for the policy to become paid-up, so that no more premiums are due, but the benefits accruable on death are reduced to the appropriate sum according to the amount of premium actually paid. At the early stages of a life policy, these values are inevitably low and may be much less than the value of the premiums paid, the insurer having to take account of his administrative costs. What these entitlements are may or may not be spelt out in the policy. The law certainly does not prescribe any minima.[92]

---

[88] The insured had a similar right of cancellation which, it was said, complimented the insurer's. This is ridiculous. The insured who cancels does not jeopardise the position of the insurer who can retain at least the premium appropriate for the risk he has borne. As the facts of the case show, the insured may very easily be substantially harmed by the insurer's cancellation.

[89] See Chapter 8.

[90] A modern reported example of what appears to have been a fairly arbitrary cancellation is *J. H. Moore v. Crowe* [1972] 2 Lloyd's Rep. 563. The dispute concerned the consequences of a cancellation.

[91] Compare the position in the U.S.A.: see (1969) Duke Law Journal 327.

[92] Compare the Australian Life Insurance Act 1945–1973, ss.95–99 and Sched. 6, prescribing such minima.

Renewal and days of grace

Apart from life policies, there can be no right to renew an insurance contract in the absence of a term of the contract to that effect.[93] Nor is an insurer under any general obligation to send out a renewal notice,[94] or any form of warning that a policy is about to expire, though this is, of course, common practice. Nor need an insurer have any reason for not renewing.[95] As we have seen, the renewal of a non-life policy constitutes the effecting of an entirely new contract.

In practice of course insurers do generally renew, and they may allow a period of "days of grace" after the expiry of the old contract for the renewal premium to be paid. The precise effect of such a period depends upon the wording of the policy in question, but as a general rule, as this is a concession, it is unlikely that the insured is protected while the premium remains unpaid, so that a loss before payment would not be covered. It must also be doubtful whether an insured could, after a loss, insist upon renewal by tendering the premium within the days of grace and thus purporting to accept the insurer's offer.[96] However, there does appear to be a clear exception in the case of life policies which permit days of grace. As these are continuing policies, subject to lapse only upon non-compliance with conditions as to payment of premium, payment within the days of grace, but not of course after-

---

[93] For an example, see the policy in *Kirby* v. *Cosindit Spa* [1969] 1 Lloyd's Rep. 75; compare *Jones Construction* v. *Alliance Ass. Co. Ltd.* [1961] 1 Lloyd's Rep. 121 and *Webb* v. *Bracey* [1964] 1 Lloyd's Rep. 465.

[94] *Simpson* v. *Accidental Death Ins. Co.* (1857) 2 C.B.(N.S.) 257.

[95] Query whether an insurer should have, for the reasons suggested in connection with cancellation. In theory problems could arise when, as is common in motor insurance, an insured has the right to a "no claims" or "loyalty" bonus entitling him to a discount on the normal premium. For example, an insurer may promise that the bonus will adhere if the insured makes no more than a limited number of claims over a period of some years, that is spanning several legally separate contracts. The question may arise as to how such a promise is legally enforceable. A possible solution is that the insurer makes a standing offer to continue to insure, subject no doubt to there being no unacceptable or undisclosed material changes in risk; this would of course be contrary to the usual legal position governing non-life contracts, as explained earlier (p. 68). Another possibility might be an enforceable collateral contract, so that the insured would be entitled to damages, namely the extra cost of other insurance, if the insurer unjustifiably failed to renew, but not actually to any rights to a new contract of insurance. It is conceivable perhaps that the insurer failing to renew in these circumstances would be in breach of a general duty to act with the utmost good faith; see p. 80, below.

[96] *Cf. Canning* v. *Farquhar* (1886) 16 Q.B.D. 727, discussed earlier.

wards,[97] is effective, even if the loss, *i.e.* the death of the life assured, has already occurred.[98] The only situation where this would not be the position is where the insurer has the right not to accept payment of the premium after the renewal date,[99] but in this case it is hardly correct in any event to speak of there being days of grace.

---

[97] *Pritchard* v. *Merchants' and Tradesmen's Mutual Life Ass. Soc.* (1858) 3 C.B. (N.S.) 622.
[98] *Stuart* v. *Freeman* [1903] 1 K.B. 47.
[99] *Simpson* v. *Accidental Death*, above.

Chapter 5

VOID, VOIDABLE AND ILLEGAL POLICIES

This chapter gives a brief general description of the circumstances which may render an insurance contract void or voidable or entitle the insurer to repudiate the whole contract or to avoid liability in respect of a particular claim. The next two chapters are then concerned with a detailed discussion of the principal circumstances.

VOID CONTRACTS OF INSURANCE

The most obvious example of a void contract of insurance is a contract void by reason of illegality. It is also conceivable, although perhaps unlikely in practice, that an insurance contract could be void for mistake.[1]

The general maxim of the law, *ex turpi causa non oritur actio*, applies to insurance contracts as much as to any other contract. A very important application in insurance is the rules of public policy which may render performance of a contract illegal, although the contract itself is not tainted with illegality. This question is considered in Chapter 12. A contract of insurance may itself be illegal and void for the following reasons:

(1) the insured may not possess the insurable interest which statute sometimes requires; this has already been examined in Chapter 3;
(2) the contract may have been entered into to achieve a purpose which is illegal or contrary to public policy;
(3) the contract may be vitiated by the unlawful use of insured property.

There are few examples of the last two categories. One

---

[1] As to mistake, see Treitel, *Law of Contract*, Chapter 8.

example of (2) would be a contract of insurance on the property of an enemy national. It is also the case at common law that a contract with an insurer lacking the authorisation required under section 2 of the Insurance Companies Act 1982[2] is void for illegality,[3] but this result, which would very often be unfair to insureds who would most probably be innocent of the illegality, has been reversed by section 132 of the Financial Services Act 1986.[4] In essence, that section gives the insured the right to elect whether or not to treat such a contract as enforceable. If he elects not to enforce it, he can reclaim his premium etc. and claim compensation for any loss. The insurer can never enforce such a contract unless it persuades the court to exercise its discretion to allow enforcement under section 132(3).[5]

The fact that insured property may be used unlawfully may render the insurance contract illegal. There is a principle in marine insurance law that an unlawful voyage has this effect.[6] While the same principle may well in theory apply to non-marine insurance, so that if the property insured is always used unlawfully, the insurance contract might be vitiated, it is clear that occasional or temporary illegal use does not render the insurance contract void. In *Leggate* v. *Brown*,[7] for example, the use of a tractor in circumstances prohibited by the Road Traffic Act, but covered by the insured's motor policy, was held not to render that policy illegal. An insurance policy will not cover property unlawfully obtained, but here it is performance of the insurance contract that is against public policy, not the policy itself, and this particular case is considered in Chapter 12.

---

[2] See p. 17, above.
[3] *Phoenix General Insurance Co. of Greece S.A.* v. *Administratia Asiguraliror de Stat* [1986] 2 Lloyd's Rep. 552. For discussion of this and the other cases on what became a most controversial issue before the introduction of the statutory provision discussed below, see [1984] J.B.L. 298; [1985] J.B.L. 486; [1987] J.B.L. 49.
[4] This section does not apply to most life insurance contracts because they fall within the definition of investments under this Act (see p. 59, above); however, they are covered by the substantially similar provision of s.5.
[5] Because s.132(6) provides that a contravention of s.2 of the 1982 Act does not make a contract of insurance illegal or invalid to any greater extent than is provided in s.132, it seems to follow that an insurer can rely on any defence to a claim by the insured, *e.g.* for non-disclosure or breach of warranty or condition, and can pursue subrogation rights against a third party, since these are not matters of "enforcement" of the contract which is what s.132(1) strikes down; *cf. McCall* v. *Brooks* [1984] R.T.R. 99.
[6] See *MacGillivray and Parkington*, paras. 439–443.
[7] (1950) 66(2) T.L.R. 281.

Voidable Contracts of Insurance

Of the utmost importance in insurance law are those areas of law whereby in certain circumstances an insurance contract may be voidable at the option of the insurer or the insurer may have the right to repudiate the contract. These are where the insured is guilty of fraud or a material non-disclosure or misrepresentation, or of a breach of a term of the contract which upon its true construction entitles the insurer to repudiate the whole contract. Fraud, non-disclosure and misrepresentation will be considered in the next chapter.

In general contract law, the term upon breach of which the innocent party has the right to repudiate the contract is usually known as a condition. A lesser term is described as a warranty, and a breach only entitles the innocent party to claim damages.[8] While there is a certain amount of conceptual confusion in some of the cases, it is suggested that the better usage in insurance law is to reserve "warranty" for the description of those terms breach of which does render the contract voidable or entitles the insurer to repudiate it.[9] This is historically accurate and is the view adopted in the Marine Insurance Act 1906; it is also supported by the Law Commission's Report on Insurance Law[9a] to which reference will be made later. Full consideration of warranties will be made in Chapter 7.

It may be the case that an insurance policy refers to its becoming void in certain circumstances. It is clear that, unless this relates to a matter, whereby, as a matter of general law, a policy may be void, for example, for lack of insurable interest, this usage is inaccurate. The term in question will in law be a warranty, in the sense described, and the policy will not be automa-

---

[8] It is, of course, true that modern cases are reconsidering the whole question of the relationship between and description of the terms of a contract. This development, however, has not touched insurance law and it seems unlikely to do so; see also note 10 below.

[9] It must be more accurate to say that a breach of warranty entitles the insurer to repudiate the contract rather than renders it voidable, for a warranty is a term and voidability should strictly be reserved for those situations where a contract can be avoided by reason of general principles not confined to what the particular contract says. Misrepresentation (and non-disclosure in insurance) are the only situations where the general law entitles the innocent party to avoid in the strict sense. However, the cases not infrequently talk of avoidance for breach of warranty, perhaps because, as will be seen in Chapter 7, warranties often arise from the contents of a completed proposal form and thus are very similar to representations. This confusion has led to some curious results, as will be seen in Chapter 7.

[9a] Report No. 104, *Non-Disclosure and Breach of Warranty* (1980), Cmnd. 8064.

tically void, because it is clear that in all such cases the insurer has the right, or may be compelled on appropriate facts, to waive a breach.

Avoiding Liability under a Valid Contract

The insurer may be entitled to avoid liability for a particular loss, but not to repudiate or avoid the contract entirely. This is obviously the case if the loss does not fall within the cover provided by the policy, but this is not a circumstance we are directly concerned with here. Otherwise the terms of an insurance contract which do have this effect can be described as conditions precedent to liability or suspensive conditions. The latter are sometimes known also as conditions or clauses describing the risk.

Conditions precedent here must be distinguished from warranties and also from mere conditions. What a policy describes as a condition precedent may, on its true construction, be a warranty, if it provides that on breach the insurer is entitled to repudiate the policy. Breach of a mere condition, on the other hand, only entitles the insurer to claim damages for such loss as it has suffered. Full discussion of the relevant distinctions will be made in Chapter 7. The usual matters covered by conditions precedent are duties to be performed by the insured, often upon the making of a claim. As already indicated, an insured's failure to comply with such obligations will entitle the insurer to avoid the particular liability, provided that the breach is connected with the loss. The legal distinctions between warranties, conditions precedent and mere conditions are sometimes confusing and the questions involved are perhaps the most difficult to determine in insurance law.

Suspensive conditions or clauses describing the risk are terms which sometimes arise from the contents of a completed proposal form. Again the full circumstances will be described later. If such a term exists, its effect is that the insurer is not at risk, and therefore not liable for a loss, while the term is not being complied with, but the risk attaches or reattaches, as the case may be, when the term is being complied with. Such a term therefore operates in the same way as an exception properly so-called in the body of a policy.

It can usefully be noted at this stage that insurers have complete freedom as to the terms that they use in their policies and that certain matters can, and may well be, covered alternatively

76 Void, Voidable and Illegal Policies

by warranties or by conditions of any sort. What any term is, in any particular policy, will depend basically upon how the particular insurer concerned has chosen to draft its policy. There are no overriding rules of law.[10]

Loss of the Right to Avoid the Contract or to Avoid Liability

Finally, there are a number of circumstances in which an insurer may lose the right to rely upon a non-disclosure or misrepresentation, or a breach of warranty or condition. This can arise first by application of the doctrines of waiver or estoppel. The essence of the matter is that the insurer, by what it says or does, leads the insured to believe that it will not insist upon its strict legal rights. The law then precludes the insurer from doing so. Waiver and estoppel may be conceptually different. This is a question more fully discussed later,[11] as indeed are the principles surrounding the application of these doctrines. Other illustrations of cases of waiver and estoppel will be found in the next two chapters.

Indisputable policies

Sometimes insurers provide that their policies are to become indisputable after they have been in force for a particular time. In practice this is only likely to apply to life policies. The effect of an indisputability clause is that the insurer cannot rely upon defences which would entitle it to avoid the policy from its inception.[12] Thus it will apply to non-disclosure, misrepresentation and certain breaches of warranty, but not, for example, to

---

[10] This presupposes that insurance contracts will not be touched by certain developments in contract law generally (see also Note 8). It is not inconceivable, on the basis of authorities like *Schuler* v. *Wickman* [1974] A.C. 235, that the courts could review the classification of terms in insurance contracts without regard to what they are actually described as. This must be most unlikely in the area of warranties, at least those created by basis of the contract clauses (see Chapter 7), because of their sanction over many years, including by a number of House of Lords cases, but is perhaps possible in the area of conditions and conditions precedent. Note, however, that there was no suggestion of this in *Cox* v. *Orion Insurance Co. Ltd.* [1982] R.T.R. 1; see p. 104, below.

[11] See Chapter 12 at pp. 206–209.

[12] *Anstey* v. *British Natural Premium Life Ass. Ltd.* (1909) 99 L.T. 765.

conditions or the coverage or definition of risk in the policy.[13] Furthermore, it cannot be relied upon to cure the lack of an insurable interest whose absence renders the policy illegal and void.[14] In addition, an indisputability clause never precludes the insurer from alleging that a policy was obtained by fraud.

---

[13] See, *e.g.* Cardozo J. in *Metropolitan Life Ins. Co.* v. *Conway* 252 N.Y. 449, 169 N.E. 642 (1930). In some American states, indisputability clauses are compulsory. Compare the Australian Life Insurance Act 1945, s.84 which is to the same effect.
[14] *Anctil* v. *Manufacturers' Life Ins. Co.* [1899] A.C. 604.

Chapter 6

FRAUD, NON-DISCLOSURE AND MISREPRESENTATION

As described in the last chapter, an insurer has the right to avoid the contract of insurance in its entirety if the insured was guilty of fraud, non-disclosure or misrepresentation before the contract was entered into. The questions of fraud and misrepresentation are common to all contracts. Non-disclosure is peculiar to a class of contracts of which the insurance contract is the prime example.

It should be noted that in practice in many instances where the insured is an individual consumer, the law as to non-disclosure and misrepresentation is not applied strictly, largely because of the *Statements of Insurance Practice* mentioned earlier.[1] While this point should always be borne in mind, it is first necessary to describe the strict legal position and leave the question of practice and indeed of reform of the law to the end of the chapter.

Fraud

This topic can be disposed of quickly; more detailed discussion can be found elsewhere.[2] A proposer is guilty of fraudulent misrepresentation if he makes a statement which is false knowingly without belief in its truth or recklessly as to whether it is true or false.[3] In addition to the right to avoid a contract entered into by an insured who has been fraudulent, the insurer may also have the right to claim damages in the tort of deceit, and can in addition retain any premium paid.

Misrepresentation

An insurer can avoid an insurance contract if it was induced to enter into it by a misrepresentation of fact made by the pro-

---

[1] See p. 4.
[2] See *e.g. MacGillivray and Parkington*, paras. 570–575.
[3] *Derry* v. *Peek* (1889) 14 App.Cas. 337.

poser which was false in a material particular, whether the proposer acted negligently or quite innocently. This right differs little from that attaching generally in the law of contract.[4] Historically, misrepresentation in the strict sense has not been of particular importance in the insurance context. This is partly because the extreme width of the duty to disclose material facts, as described below, has meant that often non-disclosure has subsumed questions of misrepresentation. Cases have frequently failed to distinguish between the two defences taken by an insurer and indeed it appears to be standard practice for an insurer, where possible, to plead both defences. While this may be conceptually unsatisfactory,[5] it is well established, the rationalisation being that it is said to be part of the insured's duty of good faith to answer correctly questions on a proposal form.[6]

Another reason for the relative unimportance, historically, of misrepresentation is that it applies only to those statements made before a contract is concluded which are properly mere representations and not terms of the contract. The usual, although not the only, source of such representations by the insured will be the statements he makes on the proposal form. Traditionally, by the device known as the "basis of the contract" clause, which is examined in the next chapter, such statements have been made terms of the contract and the law of misrepresentation is therefore irrelevant to them. However, basis clauses are less common in modern practice, and indeed should not be used at all for proposals by individual insureds.[7] Misrepresentation therefore may be more relevant now than formerly.[8]

In any event, most of the legal questions that arise in the context of misrepresentation, in particular the need for the misrepresented fact to be material and how materiality is judged, are

---

[4] See *e.g.* Treitel, *Law of Contract*, chapter 9. *Quaere* whether in fact "inducement" is a necessary requirement in respect of insurance contracts as opposed to other contracts. It does not appear to be required under the terms of s.20 of the Marine Insurance Act 1906 which is no doubt a reflection of the general common law of insurance: see note 34 and p. 88, below.
[5] See Hasson (1975) 38 M.L.R. 89.
[6] *Everett v. Desborough* (1829) 5 Bing. 503.
[7] The *Statement of General Insurance Practice*, para. 1(b). See p. 120, below.
[8] However, by para. 1(a) of the *Statement of Practice*, the declaration at the foot of a proposal form should make it clear that the form is complete only to the best of the proposer's knowledge and belief. Where this is complied with, any statements on the form will be statements of opinion and not of fact and thus outside the realm of misrepresentation.

the same as apply to non-disclosure and these will be fully discussed shortly.

Finally, it should be noted that in theory at least section 2(2) of the Misrepresentation Act 1967 could operate as a restriction on the insurer's right to avoid for misrepresentation. That subsection gives the court discretion to award damages in lieu of rescission or avoidance. It has been held, *obiter*, that the discretion would never be used in respect of commercial contracts of insurance,[9] a *dictum* which clearly leaves open the possibility of it being available to individual insureds. On the other hand, since the insurer would, as noted above, probably be able in the alternative to rely upon a non-disclosure, the point seems academic, since it seems clear that the wording of section 2(2) cannot be applied to non-disclosures.[10]

NON-DISCLOSURE

The contract of insurance is the primary illustration[11] of a class of contracts described as *uberrimae fidei*, that is, of the utmost good faith. As a result, the potential parties to it are bound to volunteer to each other before the contract is concluded information which is material. The requirement of utmost good faith has also been held to apply throughout the contract[12]; this point is considered later.[13]

Insurer's duty

It has long been said[14] that the requirement of *uberrima fides* applies to both parties to the contract, in other words that it imposes a duty of disclosure on the insurer as much as on the insured. Until recently, this did not seem to have any real significance in practice. However, in *Banque Keyser Ullman S.A.* v. *Skandia Insurance Co.*,[15] it was applied in a meaningful and

---

[9] *Highlands Insurance Co.* v. *Continental Insurance Co.* [1987] 1 Lloyd's Rep. 109.
[10] See Hudson (1969) 85 L.Q.R. 524.
[11] Others are family arrangements and contracts to take shares in public companies, the disclosure obligations in the latter case being imposed largely by statute.
[12] *Black King Shipping Corporation* v. *Massie (The Litsion Pride)* [1985] 1 Lloyd's Rep. 437.
[13] See p. 210.
[14] See the founding judgment of Lord Mansfield in *Carter* v. *Boehm* (1766) 3 Burr. 1905; see also the judgment of Farwell L.J. in *Re Bradley and Essex and Suffolk Accident Indemnity Society* [1912] 1 K.B. 415, 430.
[15] [1987] Lloyd's Rep. 69. See [1986] J.B.L. 439 and Matthews "Uberrime Fides in Modern Insurance Law", chapter 3 in *New Foundations for Insurance Law*.

quite dramatic way. The plaintiff banks had agreed to lend money to someone provided that appropriate credit insurance policies guaranteeing the loans were obtained. The broker involved wrongly told the banks that full insurance cover had been obtained when in fact at the time it had not been; this fact later came to the knowledge of the insurers, but they failed to tell the insured banks which made further loans. Steyn J. held that the insurers were in breach of a duty of disclosure imposed on them by reason of the principle of *uberrima fides*.[16] He further held that the insureds' remedy was not limited to avoidance of the insurance contract and recovery of their premium. Justice and policy combined to require that the broken duty be remedied in a meaningful way by an award of damages.[17] It is in respect of this award of damages that the case is particularly significant. The result seems clearly right, albeit novel.[18] It may be that the case can be interpreted as supporting a broad duty of good faith and fair dealing imposed on an insurer.[19]

Insured's duty

Further applications of a duty of disclosure on an insurer are likely to be rare, so that the remainder of this chapter can be confined to the duty imposed on the insured. The basic effect of the duty can be stated quite simply. An applicant for insurance is under a duty to disclose to the insurer, prior to the conclusion of the contract,[20] but only up to this date, all material facts within his knowledge which the latter does not or is not deemed to know. A failure to disclose, however innocent, entitles the insurer to avoid the contract *ab initio*, and upon

---

[16] He also held the insurers liable in tort, but this was clearly a separate, albeit significant, *ratio*. Note that the decision of Steyn J. is being appealed.

[17] The banks could not recover on the policies because they contained an exclusion for fraud and the losses were caused by the fraud of the borrower. Further, the damages were awarded only in respect of loans made after the non-disclosure, in other words after the insurers knew of the broker's actions, since it was held that the first loan would have been made anyway.

[18] The only other case where the question of the remedy for a non-disclosure has been expressly considered is *Glasgow Assurance Corp.* v. *Symondson* (1911) 16 Com.Cas. 109, 121, where Scrutton J. stated that the only remedy was avoidance. However, this *dictum* was clearly *obiter*. As Steyn J. recognised, avoidance would normally be a sufficient remedy for an *insurer* alleging non-disclosure by the insured.

[19] There are other isolated examples of such a duty; see *e.g.* pp. 284, 291 below.

[20] The exact date when this occurs (see Chapter 4) may therefore be of the greatest importance.

avoidance it is deemed never to have existed.[21] The insurer must avoid within a reasonable time of becoming aware of the non-disclosure. The duty arises whenever a fresh contract is concluded and, most importantly, this includes upon a renewal of any contract except that of life insurance; this point has already been considered in an earlier chapter.[22] A number of important questions arise from this description and these are examined under the next following headings.

The rationale for the rule

In the leading case which established the duty of disclosure in insurance contracts, *Carter* v. *Boehm*,[23] Lord Mansfield said[24]:

> "Insurance is a contract upon speculation. The special facts, upon which the contingent chance is to be computed, lie most commonly in the knowledge of the insured only: the under-writer trusts to his representation, and proceeds upon the confidence that he does not keep back any circumstance in his knowledge, to mislead the under-writer into a belief that the circumstance does not exist, and to induce him to estimate the risque as if it did not exist."

There can be no doubt that the contract of insurance is a special one in the terms that Lord Mansfield expressed, but two comments can at this stage be made about his formulation of the doctrine of non-disclosure. First, it is by no means certain that he was intending to lay down as broad a doctrine as subsequent cases have established,[25] although this is a purely academic question today. Certainly the American courts developed a much narrower duty of disclosure from the same source.[26] It is also noteworthy that Lord Mansfield regarded his principle of good faith as he called it as applying to all contracts.[27] He could hardly have been referring to the broad duty of disclosure as it is known today. Secondly it is important to remember that *Carter* v. *Boehm* involved a contract entered into at a time when communications were poor and insurers were not equipped

---

[21] *Mackender* v. *Feldia A.G.* [1967] 2 Q.B. 590 appears to have decided to the contrary, but is distinguishable: see *MacGillivray and Parkington*, para. 656.

[22] See Chapter 4, p. 68.

[23] (1766) 3 Burr. 1905.

[24] *Ibid.* at 1909.

[25] See Hasson, "The Doctrine of Uberrima fides in Insurance Law—a Critical Evaluation" (1969) 32 M.L.R. 615.

[26] *Vance on Insurance* (3rd ed.) pp. 370 *et seq*; *Sebring* v. *Fidelity Phoenix Ins. Co.* 255 N.Y. 382 (1931).

[27] See (1766) 3 Burr. at 1910.

with means easily to discover by the asking of questions of the proposer all the information they needed to know. It must be concluded that the justification for an all-ranging duty of disclosure is not so apparent today and indeed this has been accepted by insurers themselves in respect of insurances effected by individuals. This is a question which we shall return to later.

Statements of fact

The duty of disclosure and the duty not to misrepresent require that statements made by the proposer be of facts not opinion. A misstated opinion is actionable only if not given in good faith.[28] However, the distinction between questions of fact and questions of opinion is not always an easy one and may not matter greatly in practice. This point can be illustrated particularly by the example of proposals for life insurance, where a proposer may very well not know highly material facts regarding his health, because he is not an expert, or if he does know something, may very well fail to appreciate its significance. In *Joel* v. *Law Union & Crown Insurance Co.*,[29] a statement as to the health of the proposer made by her was regarded as a statement of opinion. This accords with common sense, as the proposer who is not a medical expert or told specifically by such an expert of facts as to his health cannot be expected to give more than an opinion. However, in a later case[30] concerning a similar issue, a proposer who failed to disclose a visit to a specialist was held to be guilty of non-disclosure of a material fact, even though he did not know that there was anything seriously wrong with him. Thus, although a mere statement as to health without more is a statement of opinion, at least where the proposer does not know any relevant facts, if in fact a proposer for life insurance has consulted a doctor in more than an ordinary way, the fact of consultation will almost certainly be a material fact requiring to be disclosed.

Knowledge and opinion of the proposer

The question of the knowledge or the opinion of the proposer for insurance raises three further questions; first, his knowledge of the duty to disclose, secondly, whether his opinion as to materialty is relevant, and thirdly, what knowledge of the

---

[28] *Anderson* v. *Pacific Fire & Marine Ins. Co.* (1872) L.R. 7 C.P. 65.
[29] [1908] 2 K.B. 863. See also *Life Association of Scotland* v. *Forster* 1873 11 Macph. 351.
[30] *Godfrey* v. *Britannic Ass. Co. Ltd.* [1963] 2 Lloyd's Rep. 515.

material facts on his part is required. As to the first point, it is clear that whether or not the proposer knows that he is under a duty to disclose is totally irrelevant. Innocent non-disclosure is as actionable as negligent non-disclosure or concealment, as all the cases assume. Similarly, the insured's opinion as to the materiality of non-disclosed facts is irrelevant even though he may well have acted in good faith. As has been pointed out, it is the law that a man may act in perfect good faith within the ordinary meaning of the phrase, yet still be held not to have acted in the utmost good faith in the legal sense.[31]

Constructive knowledge

More problematic is the question as to whether or not the insured is bound to disclose only those material facts which he actually knows or whether his "knowledge" includes facts which he ought to know. Clearly he is not bound to disclose what he does not know, and some cases, particularly in the life insurance field, have assumed that only actual knowledge imposes a duty. In *Joel* v. *Law Union*, one of the issues was whether the proposer was bound to disclose the fact that she had suffered from acute depression, it being accepted that she was unaware of the fact. It was held not and the judges were at pains to point out that there is no duty to disclose what the proposer does not know.[32] However, it has later been said that the question as to disclosure of constructive knowledge is an open one so far as non-marine insurance is concerned.[33] It is arguable that a proposer is under a duty to disclose what he constructively knows, because that is the law in respect of marine insurance, and section 18 of the 1906 Act, which so provides, is merely a codification of the duty of disclosure in respect of marine insurance which reflected the common law rules in respect of all classes of insurance.[34]

Knowledge of proposer's agent

What cannot be disputed is that the knowledge of his agent, acquired in the course of his duties, is the knowledge of the

---

[31] See, *e.g.* McNair J. in *Roselodge Ltd.* v. *Castle* [1966] 2 Lloyd's Rep. 113 at 129.
[32] See especially Fletcher Moulton L.J., [1908] 2 K.B. at 884.
[33] McNair J. in *Australia and New Zealand Bank* v. *Colonial and Eagle Wharves Ltd.* [1960] 2 Lloyd's Rep. 241 at 252.
[34] But even this was left open by McNair J., *ibid*. More recent cases, *e.g.* *Highlands Insurance Co.* v. *Continental Insurance Co.* (note 9, above), assume in respect of other aspects of the duty of disclosure that s.18 merely codified the common law applying to all insurances. It is in cases of life policies that actual knowledge

proposer. If therefore, for example, the managing director of a company knows a material fact, but it is not known to the officer of the company who actually makes the proposal for insurance on the company's behalf, the company is deemed to know and the non-disclosure of the fact to the insurer will entitle the latter to avoid the contract. The same principle will apply if the agent is a broker, although in this case the proposer would almost certainly have an action in negligence against the broker who failed to disclose the fact to the insurer.[35]

What need not be disclosed

Facts which are material need not nonetheless be disclosed to the insurer if (i) they diminish the risk; (ii) they are facts which the insurer knows or is presumed to know or are matters of common knowledge; or (iii) they are facts of which the insurer waives disclosure. Many of the points under heads (i) and (ii) are self-explanatory. *Carter* v. *Boehm* itself was a case where the insurers could not rely upon the non-disclosure because, it was held, the material facts were a matter of common knowledge. The insurance was of a Fort in Sumatra by the Governor of the then colony. The material fact was that the Fort was likely to be attacked by the French. It was held that the underwriters in London should have known that as well as the insured; indeed it was said that they were more likely to know.

Knowledge of insurer's agent

An insurer will be deemed to have the knowledge that his agent has if that knowledge was acquired by the agent acting in the scope of his authority, actual or ostensible.[36] It is essential that the agent is in law the agent of the insurer, a question discussed more fully in Chapter 10. The device of imputing an agent's knowledge to his principal may be of great importance in the context of the duty of disclosure. For example, in *Ayrey* v. *British Legal & United Provident Assurance Co.*,[37] the district manager of the insurer knew the fact that the insured who effected a life policy and was by occupation and on the proposal form described as a fisherman, was also a member of the Royal Navy Reserve. It was held that this knowledge was imputed to

---

only has been required. This is not altogether surprising given the difficulties faced by the average proposer with regard to knowledge of his state of health (see p. 83, above). Perhaps the simplest and most logical solution would be to treat life cases as *sui generis*.

[35] See further, Chapter 10, pp. 148–151.
[36] For more detail on some principles of agency, see Chapter 10.
[37] [1918] 1 K.B. 136.

the insurer who could not therefore rely upon its non-disclosure by the insured. In *Blackley* v. *National Mutual Life Association of Australasia*,[38] the agent knew before the contract was concluded that the life insured had a brain tumor which had just been operated upon. Again this knowledge was imputed to the insurer.[39] It should be noted, though, that the fact that the agent could have known of the material fact, for example, by a proper medical examination, is not enough. Similarly, the fact that the insurers have the means of knowledge, for example, the name of the doctor of a proposer for life insurance, does not relieve the insured of his duty of disclosure.

It should also be noted that the position regarding imputation of an agent's knowledge will probably be different where the proposer warrants the accuracy of an incorrect statement even when the agent knows the true position. This question is discussed in the next chapter.

Waiver

Waiver of disclosure raises a number of points. First are those that arise from the fact that in the majority of cases insurance is effected following the completion by the proposer of a proposal form on which a great deal of information is in practice solicited. It is clear that the fact that many questions are expressly asked does not relieve the proposer of his duty to disclose facts outside the scope of the questions,[40] but in some cases the form of questions asked may reduce the scope of the duty of disclosure. Similarly, the proposer's leaving a blank in relation to a question which is accepted without inquiry by the insurer will normally be taken as a waiver by the insurer of any duty of disclosure in respect of the matters covered by the question.[41] This would not be the case, however, if in the circumstances, the blank space implies a negative answer to the question. If this is so, and a negative answer is incorrect, the insurers will be entitled to avoid the contract.[42]

---

[38] [1972] N.Z.L.R. 1038. The judgments in the New Zealand Court of Appeal contain a very comprehensive review of the principles governing the imputation of an agent's knowledge to his principal.

[39] For a more recent example, see *Woolcott* v. *Excess Insurance Co.* [1978] 1 Lloyd's Rep. 533, discussed at p. 139, below.

[40] *Glicksman* v. *Lancashire & General Ass. Co.* [1927] A.C. 139; *Schoolman* v. *Hall* [1951] 1 Lloyd's Rep. 139.

[41] *Roberts* v. *Avon Ins. Co.* [1956] 2 Lloyd's Rep. 240.

[42] *Ibid.* Properly, though, the grounds for avoidance will be misrepresentation or breach of warranty.

Waiver as a result of the form of questions asked will usually arise where an express question asks for some details of certain facts or types of facts.[43] Disclosure of other details will be waived if it is felt that a reasonable man reading the proposal form would consider that the insurer did not seek the other details. For example, a question asking the proposer for details of previous losses he has suffered within a five-year period would waive disclosure of losses outside that period even though such losses might well be material facts according to the usual test. Similarly, a question asking in respect of the claims history of the proposer in relation to the type of insurance for which he is applying might well be regarded as waiving any duty of disclosure of losses or claims in respect of other types of insurance which in some circumstances might be regarded as material facts.[44]

Where a question asked on a proposal form is ambiguous, a fair and reasonable construction must be placed upon it and it will be construed *contra proferentem* when the proposal form is incorporated into the contract. If, for example, the answer of the proposer is true according to a construction which a reasonable man might have put on the question, the insurers cannot rely upon its inaccuracy.

The test of materiality

Much of the criticism of the wide-ranging nature of the duty of disclosure has been directed at the test for determining materiality. A fact is material for the purposes of both non-disclosure and misrepresentation if it is one which would influence the judgment of a reasonable or prudent insurer in deciding whether or not to accept the risk or what premium to charge.[45] This test was conclusively adopted for non-marine insurance purposes in *Lambert* v. *Co-operative Insurance*

---

[43] *McCormick* v. *National Motor Accident Ins. Union Ltd.* (1934) 49 Ll.L.R. 361, 363, *per* Scrutton L.J.; *Schoolman* v. *Hall*, above, at 143, *per* Asquith L.J.

[44] In *Hair* v. *Prudential Assurance Co. Ltd.* [1983] 2 Lloyd's Rep. 667, it was held that the effect of a general warning on a proposal form of the need for disclosure, of the sort required by the *Statements of Insurance Practice*, was to waive the proposer's need to do any more than answer the questions put to him. However, this seems to be going too far (see [1984] J.B.L. 163).

[45] Or, possibly, whether to impose particular terms in the contract such as an exclusion or an excess. This may well be within the ambit of the present test; the Law Commission (Report No. 104, para. 4.48) thought so and that, in any event, it should expressly be brought within it.

Society,[46] the Court of Appeal holding that its statutory formulation in these terms in section 18 of the Marine Insurance Act 1906[47] was a codification of the common law applicable to all insurance contracts.

In the subsequent Court of Appeal decision in *Container Transport International Inc.* v. *Oceanus Mutual Underwriting Association (Bermuda) Ltd.*,[48] it was held that for the purposes of section 18, the requirement that a fact must be one which would "influence the judgment" of a prudent insurer did not mean that an insurer must have acted differently if he had known the fact, but merely that he would have wanted to know of the fact when making his decision; "judgment" was construed as meaning "the formation of an opinion," not "the final decision." While there is no doubt that this represents the prevailing law in all insurances,[49] it is arguable that it is based on a misreading of earlier authorities.[50] It certainly increases the burden on the insured. It is to be hoped that the House of Lords soon gets the opportunity to resolve this important issue.[51]

---

[46] [1975] 2 Lloyd's Rep. 485. See Merkin (1976) 39 M.L.R. 478. Some earlier non-marine cases, *e.g. Joel* v. *Law Union* [1908] 2 K.B. 863, suggested a test depending on the opinion of the reasonable insured. The Court of Appeal in *Lambert* did not like having to reach their decision and thought that the law should be changed. See also *Kelsall* v. *Allstate Insurance Co. Ltd., The Times.* March 20, 1987, where the test was accepted, but was modified by an express provision in the contract, "no known adverse facts," which had the effect of requiring the insured to disclose only those facts known by him, as a reasonable man, to be adverse.

[47] See also s.149(5)(*b*) of the Road Traffic Act 1972 which lays down the same test for certain motor insurance purposes; see p. 310, below.

[48] [1984] 1 Lloyd's Rep. 476.

[49] See *Highlands Insurance Co.* v. *Continental Insurance Co.* [1987] 1 Lloyd's Rep. 109, where the judge felt bound to accept it in a non-marine misrepresentation case, though clearly with some misgivings; see [1986] J.B.L. 420.

[50] See the excellent article by Brooke, "Materiality in Insurance Contracts" [1985] L.M.C.L.Q. 437 analysing all the earlier cases, especially the Privy Council case of *Mutual Life Insurance Co. of New York* v. *Ontario Metal Products Co. Ltd.* [1925] A.C. 344. This case concerned the construction of a Canadian statute which required, in respect of life insurance, not just that a misrepresentation be material but also that it induced the actual insurer to enter into the contract (*cf.* s.149(5)(*b*) of the Road Traffic Act 1972, note 47 above, which contains the same requirement). As Brooke points out, the Privy Council was careful to distinguish these two points and was clearly of opinion as regards the first that a non-disclosed or misrepresented fact must actually have influenced a reasonable insurer to decline the risk or to have stipulated for a higher premium in order to be material; see Lord Salveson at 351. See also the judgment of Lloyd J. at first instance in the *C.T.I.* case [1982] 2 Lloyd's Rep. 178.

[51] Leave to appeal in the *C.T.I.* case was granted but unfortunately the appeal was abandoned and the dispute was settled; see Brooke, *op. cit.* at 438.

It must follow from this test of materiality that it is irrelevant that the particular insurer considers a fact not to be material, if a reasonable insurer would think otherwise and this can be proved.[52]

Evidence of materiality

Because the test of materiality depends on the opinion of a reasonable insurer, the courts have long been prepared to accept as evidence of whether or not particular facts are material the opinion of other insurers.[53] In some cases, such opinions appear to have been accepted very readily, but some of the modern decisions emphasise that they are in no way binding on the court which must decide the issue as a question of fact. For example, in *Roselodge Ltd.* v. *Castle*,[54] an insurer's evidence to the effect that it would be material to an application for insurance many years later that the proposer was caught stealing apples at the age of 12 was ridiculed by McNair J. Similarly, the judgment of Forbes J. in *Reynolds* v. *Phoenix Assurance Co.*[55] is instructive. He rejected the arguments that if an insurer is telling the truth and he is held to be a reasonable insurer, the court must accept his evidence as conclusive. The evidence is expert evidence which assists the court but never binds it. This is particularly so, of course, where there is conflicting evidence from different insurers.

Examples of material facts

While the test to be applied to determine whether or not a non-disclosed fact is material is a question of law, the actual determination of the issue in any particular case involves the resolution of a question of fact.[56] As such, it is generally a question solely for the trial judge or arbitrator and not subject to appeal, and, furthermore, strictly no decision is actually binding in a later case under the doctrine of precedent. However, there are some categories of facts which are obviously material and others which have arisen so often in decided cases that they

---

[52] *Berger* v. *Pollock* [1973] 2 Lloyd's Rep. 442 at 463. Of course this is not the case if statute (see note 50) imports a requirement of inducement, nor if the policy otherwise provides.
[53] See, *e.g. Babatsikos* v. *Car Owners' Mutual Ins. Co.* [1970] 2 Lloyd's Rep. 314, for a general survey, but compare the comment of Lord Mansfield in *Carter* v. *Boehm* (1766) 3 Burr. 1905 at 1918. For a general criticism, see Hasson (1969) 32 M.L.R. 615. See also Evans (1984) 12 Australian Bus.L.Rev. 4.
[54] [1966] 2 Lloyd's Rep. 113 at 132.
[55] [1978] 2 Lloyd's Rep. 440 at 457–459.
[56] *e.g. Glicksman* v. *Lancashire & General Ass. Co.* [1927] A.C. 139.

would normally be so regarded. It is appropriate, therefore, to describe and illustrate some of these categories.

Material facts relate in general either to the physical hazard, that is the property, life or liability insured, or to the moral hazard. Facts relating to the physical hazard are those which are generally obviously material, for example, the nature, construction or use of an insured building, or whether it is particularly exposed to risk, in property insurance; health or a high risk occupation or hobby in life insurance; a bad accident record in terms of liability insurance. The modern cases rarely concern such issues, not least because they are invariably the subject of questions on a proposal form when the answers may be warranted and materiality is irrelevant.

Moral hazard

Facts as to the moral hazard of the proposer are, it seems, less likely to be the subject of express questions, although they should be in non-commercial insurances according to the terms of the *Statements of Insurance Practice*.[57] Moral hazard cases can perhaps be regarded as falling into three categories: (i) those relating to the insurance history of the applicant; (ii) those relating to his nationality or origins; and (iii) those relating to criminal convictions.

The insurance history of the proposer includes both previous refusals to insure by other insurers as well as his claims history. In *Glicksman* v. *Lancashire & General Assurance Co.*,[58] G and his partner applied for burglary insurance. It was held that the fact that G had when trading on his own previously been refused insurance was material, regardless of the reasons for the previous refusal and of the fact that there was on the proposal form a question which elicited such information in a way which could have been interpreted as applying to a previous proposal made by the applicants together. The House of Lords, in deciding the case, was full of regrets, but really there was nothing their Lordships could do. The materiality of the fact was a question of fact which had been conclusively decided by the arbi-

---

[57] *Statement of General Insurance Practice*, para. 1(*d*); *Statement of Long-Term Insurance Practice*, para. 1(*c*). This requirement seems to conflict with the trend in the insurance industry towards shorter proposal forms. There certainly do seem to be proposal forms in existence which do not solicit all material facts other than by general question.

[58] [1927] A.C. 139. See also *London Assurance* v. *Mansel* (1879) 11 Ch.D. 363 for an example in life insurance.

trator. It should be noted that, in vivid contrast, in marine insurance a previous refusal to insure is not material.[59]

Whether or not a previous refusal to insure in respect of a type of insurance other than that for which the proposer is applying is material is not so clear. In *Ewer* v. *National Employers' Mutual & General Insurance Association*,[60] Mackinnon J. clearly rejected such a wide proposition, but in *Locker & Wolf Ltd.* v. *Western Australian Insurance Co.*,[61] a previous refusal of motor insurance was held material to a proposal for fire insurance, quite apart from the fact that there was a general question on the proposal form. It would appear that such a previous refusal may be material when it relates in a general way to the integrity of the proposer.[62] A mere refusal would therefore not be material, but a refusal based on the insurance history of the proposer, for example, as to his claims experience, might well be.[63]

Previous losses of the sort which the proposer is seeking insurance against are clearly material,[64] although in practice these will be solicited by express questions and the answers warranted, and, quite possibly, any duty to disclose outside the scope of the question waived.

Many of the other facts relating to the moral hazard of the proposer are affected by legislation. Although the nationality of the proposer was held to be material in *Horne* v. *Poland*,[65] the decision cannot stand now in the light of the Race Relations Act 1976 which prohibits discrimination by insurers, among others, on "racial grounds."[66] Similarly, discrimination against an applicant on the grounds of sex is prohibited by the Sex Discrimination Act 1975, section 29, except in relation to certain matters in life and related policies.[67]

Criminal history

Perhaps the most important fact affecting the moral hazard of the proposer, apart from insurance history, is his criminal history. Certainly most of the modern cases have been concerned

[59] *Glicksman* in the Court of Appeal, [1925] 2 K.B. 593 at 608.
[60] [1937] 2 All E.R. 193 at 202–203.
[61] [1936] 1 K.B. 408.
[62] *Ibid.* at 414, *per* Slesser L.J.
[63] But what if the insurers were told of the claims experience, but not of the refusal based on it?
[64] *e.g. Arterial Caravans Ltd.* v. *Yorkshire Ins. Co.* [1973] 1 Lloyd's Rep. 169.
[65] [1922] 2 K.B. 364. But see the comment of McNair J. in *Roselodge Ltd.* v. *Castle* [1966] 2 Lloyd's Rep. 113 at 130.
[66] s.20; see ss.1 and 3 for the definitions.
[67] s.45.

with this question. This too may be affected by legislation, in this instance the Rehabilitation of Offenders Act 1974. A number of cases involving mostly the insurance of valuables establish that criminal convictions for offences of dishonesty are material, including those which relate to "a dim and distant past," 12 years[68] and, possibly, 20 years,[69] prior to the insurance application. In *Roselodge Ltd.* v. *Castle*,[70] though, a conviction for bribery was held not material to the insurance of diamonds, though a smuggling conviction was material. It appears also, logically enough, that the mere commission of an offence may be material, even if the proposer is acquitted by a jury, provided, of course, that the insurer can prove to the satisfaction of the civil court that the proposer did, in fact, commit the offence.[71] A wrongful conviction should also be disclosed,[72] but judicial opinion has been divided as to whether a proposer must disclose the fact of arrest where, in fact, he was innocent.[73] In *Lambert* v. *C.I.S.*[74] it was the convictions of the proposer's husband that were material facts. Although the result of this case has been criticised,[75] the offences were of dishonesty, and the insurance was an all risks one on jewellery, including some which was owned by the proposer's husband.

Woolcott v. *Sun Alliance & London Insurance*[76] appears to be a more extreme example because here there was no obvious connection between the non-disclosed conviction and the sort of insurance applied for. The plaintiff proposed for fire insurance on his house through the building society to which at the same time he was making a mortgage application.[77] He failed to disclose the fact that he had been convicted of robbery some 12 years previously. It was held that the insurers could avoid the policy.[78] The learned judge appears to have accepted, without

---

[68] *Schoolman* v. *Hall* [1951] 1 Lloyd's Rep. 139.
[69] *Regina Fur* v. *Bossom* [1957] 2 Lloyd's Rep. 466.
[70] See note 65.
[71] *March Cabaret Club & Casino Ltd.* v. *London Assurance* [1975] 1 Lloyd's Rep. 169.
[72] *Ibid.*
[73] *Ibid.* at 177; contra, *Reynolds* v. *Phoenix Ass. Co. Ltd.* [1978] 2 Lloyd's Rep. 440 at 460.
[74] [1975] 2 Lloyd's Rep. 465. See above at note 46.
[75] Merkin (1976) 39 M.L.R. 478.
[76] [1978] 1 All E.R. 1253.
[77] There was no proposal form; the insurance application was simply the answer to one question on the mortgage application form.
[78] But the building society which was also insured was able to recover as the policy was not a joint one. As to joint policies, see pp. 211 and 252 below.

demur, the evidence called for the insurers that the fact related to Woolcott's moral hazard. With respect, it is not at all obvious why a convicted robber should be more risky in relation to the insurance of a building than anyone else, even though it must be accepted that Woolcott's conviction was serious. In contrast, in *Reynolds* v. *Phoenix Assurance Co.*,[79] after perhaps a more thorough review of the law, Forbes J. held that a conviction for receiving was not a material fact in relation to fire insurance. Admittedly the matter was comparatively trivial and the insured was merely fined. It was held that the matter depended basically on the extent of the dishonesty and the age of the conviction. As the learned judge admitted, hard and fast rules cannot be laid down about this sort of case. This must be correct, even though it makes the application of the law somewhat uncertain, and the insured in the unenviable position of having to find evidence to challenge that of the insurers. One interesting comment in the judgment in *Reynolds* relates to the lack of experience among the experts called of actual disclosures by proposers of their previous convictions. Forbes J.[80] understandably found this surprising in view of the large numbers of crimes dishonestly committed every year and the almost universal adoption of some form of insurance for buildings. Clearly he did not believe some of the more extreme evidence as to materiality put forward in that case.[81]

It seems, in summary, that any conviction relevant to the insurance sought will be regarded as material unless it is both trivial and old. An irrelevant conviction, that is one not directly germane to the risk, will affect the moral hazard of the proposer certainly when it is serious, presumably meaning punished by imprisonment or a substantial fine. An ancient trivial offence would not be material. Whether a recent unconnected trivial offence would be, is less certain. In the decided cases of relevance, the offences were all quite old.

Spent convictions

However, regardless of the above, an applicant for insurance is never bound to disclose a conviction which has become spent under the terms of the Rehabilitation of Offenders Act 1974.[82] There are different periods laid down for rehabilitation

---

[79] See note 73 above. As to the other important issues in this case, see p. 222, below.
[80] [1978] 2 Lloyd's Rep. at 460.
[81] See also p. 89, above.
[82] s.4(3)(*a*).

depending on the seriousness of the sentence imposed. Most importantly, a conviction resulting in a sentence of two and a half years' imprisonment or more can never become spent. Otherwise, convictions with custodial sentences of between six months and two and a half years become spent after 10 years and those of less than six months after seven years. In respect of other sentences, the period is five years, except in relation to absolute discharges (six months) and conditional discharges and probation (one year).

There is one provision, though, in the 1974 Act (section 7(3)) which gives the court a discretion to admit evidence as to spent convictions if the court is satisfied that "justice cannot be done in the case except by admitting it." The issue arose in earlier proceedings in *Reynolds* v. *Phoenix Assurance Co.*[83] because the offence already referred to came to light only after the case commenced and the insurers sought to amend their pleadings to allege its non-disclosure. The Act did not apply when the plaintiff applied for the insurance in 1972, but it did when the matter came to trial. The Court of Appeal held that the pleadings should be amended on the ground that no prejudice would be caused to the plaintiff. Whether or not the evidence of the conviction should be admitted was then a matter for the trial judge. Forbes J. subsequently held that the evidence should be admitted, although this did not matter in the result as he held that the conviction was not material, as we have already seen.

It is unfortunate that in the *Reynolds* litigation the courts did not really decide the effect of section 7(3) on the duty of disclosure. They may have been influenced by the fact that the alleged non-disclosure took place before the 1974 Act existed. It can hardly be said to be just to admit evidence of spent convictions in relation to insurance effected after 1974 when, since that time, the proposer has been under no duty to disclose them.

Disclosure During the Contract

The duty to disclose material facts is cast upon the proposer or insured only before the contract or a renewal is concluded. At common law, there is no general duty to disclose material facts which occur when they occur during the period of insurance. The authority for this is the old case of *Pim* v. *Reid*[84] where the

[83] [1978] 2 Lloyd's Rep. 22.
[84] (1843) 6 M. & G. 1.

insured changed his trade and caused a large amount of highly inflammable material to be brought on to the insured premises. It was held that his non-disclosure of this fact to the insurer was not actionable. Certain contracts of insurance, though, most notably those of fire insurance, do, in practice, impose a duty on the insured to disclose facts occurring during the insurance which materially increase the risk.[84a] The term which imposes such a duty is usually, though not necessarily, a promissory warranty, since it provides that upon a failure to disclose, the insurer can avoid the policy. Although we shall be examining promissory warranties in general in the next chapter, it is appropriate here to consider this common type, since it clearly imposes a duty of disclosure analogous to that imposed by virtue of the principle of *uberrima fides*. Futhermore, the possible EEC directive on insurance contract law refers to this sort of disclosure as well as the more general sort.

Increase of risk clauses

A simple increase of risk clause, as it may be called, only operates when the increase is permanent and habitual. In *Shaw v. Robberds*,[85] a fire policy was effected upon a granary which contained a kiln for drying corn. On one occasion, the insured allowed a third party to dry some bark in the kiln and this, in fact, occasioned the fire which brought about the dispute. It was held that the insurers were liable, despite the presence of an increase of risk clause. The change was merely temporary. It mattered not of itself that drying bark was a much more hazardous business than drying corn.

If, therefore, an insurer wishes to be notified of merely temporary increases in risk, it must insert express clauses to that effect.[86] It is also notable that the standard clause in fire policies on buildings only relates to alterations to the building itself and not to any alteration of its contents which may increase the risk.[87] An analogous specific disclosure requirement often imposed in fire policies relates to the property being unoccupied for a specified period and requiring that fact to be reported to the insurer. Unoccupancy relates, it has been held, to the

---

[84a] There is evidence that such a duty is being imposed more widely by insurers, *e.g.* in household policies.
[85] Compare *Farnham* v. *Royal Ins. Co.* [1976] 2 Lloyd's Rep. 437.
[86] See, *e.g. Glen* v. *Lewis* (1853) 8 Ex. 607.
[87] *Exchange Theatre Ltd.* v. *Iron Trades Mutual Ins. Co. Ltd.* [1984] 1 Lloyd's Rep. 149; see [1984] J.B.L. 363.

absence of a physical presence in the building insured.[88] If, in fact, no-one is regularly and daily present therein, the building is unoccupied, unless the absence is merely temporary, for example, by reason of the insured being on holiday.[89]

An alteration in the risk is notifiable under the standard clause only if it does, in fact, increase the risk, but if the alteration causes the property to differ from the description given in the proposal or policy, that description may well have been warranted, and the unnotified alteration may well amount to a breach of warranty.

PRACTICE IN AND REFORM OF NON-DISCLOSURE AND MISREPRESENTATION

The point that the law is capable of operating harshly regarding the disclosure of material facts in particular has already been made earlier in this chapter. Indeed it has often been said that a proposer for insurance may act with perfect good faith and yet not satisfy the duty of disclosure which the law requires because he did not realise that particular facts were in law material or did not realise that he had to do any more than truthfully complete the answers to questions on a proposal form. It could be argued that there is no real need for a duty of disclosure in modern conditions other than one requiring the insured to answer honestly questions expressly put to him.[90]

Until fairly recently it seemed as though the law would be reformed in this respect. This was because recommendations for reform have been made by both the Law Reform Committee in 1957[91] and by the Law Commission in 1980.[92] The important and carefully considered recommendations of the Law Com-

---

[88] *Marzouca* v. *Atlantic and British Commercial Ins. Co. Ltd.* [1971] 1 Lloyd's Rep. 449.

[89] *Winicofsky* v. *Army and Navy General Ins. Co.* (1919) 88 L.J.K.B. 111.

[90] It must be doubtful whether the lack of a pure duty of disclosure would have any real effect on premiums, at least in typical "consumer" insurances. Certainly insurers in many countries, including the United States of America, manage without the law imposing any such duty.

[91] Fifth Report, Cmnd. 62.

[92] Report No. 104, *Insurance Law—Non-Disclosure and Breach of Warranty*, Cmnd. 8064. Note that the impetus for this report was the existence of a proposed E.E.C. Directive on certain aspects of insurance contract law, linked to a proposed Directive on Freedom of Services. The likelihood of these Directives being implemented seems to have virtually disappeared for the foreseeable future and no detail is given here. The relevant aspects of the Contract Law Directive are fully examined in the Law Commission's Report.

mission, which in practice would probably have meant the withering away of a pure duty of disclosure,[93] were accepted by the government, but were strongly opposed by the insurance industry particularly in respect of their application to business insurance.[94] The unfortunate result of this[95] has been that actual legal reform seems unlikely at present. Instead the government has accepted "reform" by way of self-regulation by the insurers themselves. For this reason, it is felt that detailed description of the Law Commission's proposals would be inappropriate in a book of this size.[96]

Statements of insurance practice

As has been noted earlier,[97] this self-regulation takes the form of declaratory Statements of Insurance Practice. In so far as they do, in practice, provide a measure of protection for the individual insured,[98] they are obviously to be welcomed.[99] Unfortunately one cannot be certain that they are universally complied with because those insurers who are not members of the Association of British Insurers or of Lloyd's are not party to them, although they are "expected" to comply. A brief review of their terms is necessary.[1]

---

[93] Because the duty to disclose would have been limited to what a reasonable man would think should be disclosed and this would surely have meant that, except in rare cases, a reasonable man would not have expected to do more than answer express questions. It may be that the Commission did not go far enough in terms of limiting the insurer's right of avoidance for non-disclosures or misrepresentations. Although they were no doubt right to reject the overly mathematical and unworkable proportionality approach of the proposed Directive, based on French law, it still does not seem right in non-fraud cases that the insured should forfeit all rights.

[94] One of the strongest arguments raised by insurers against legal reform is that they always apply the law fairly and use a technical defence like non-disclosure only when they suspect fraud. While this may be true of many reputable insurers, it is certainly not universally true and it is hardly acceptable that insurers should be such judges in their own cause.

[95] See North, "Law Reform; processes and problems" (1985) 101 L.Q.R. 338 at 349–350.

[96] For more detail, see the first edition of this book at pp. 99–104 and Birds, "The reform of insurance law" [1982] J.B.L. 449.

[97] See pp. 3–5.

[98] Though not for the business insured however "small" he may be. The lack of protection for such as the one-man business seems an unnecessary omission.

[99] Note that the terms of the *Statements* are binding on the Insurance Ombudsman, as to whom see p. 4, above.

[1] For a more detailed examination, see Forte, "The revised *Statements of Insurance Practice*," (1986) 49 M.L.R. 754 and Birds, "Self-regulation and insurance contracts," *New Foundations for Insurance Law*, Chapter 1.

The revised *Statements* issued in 1986 reflect the Law Commission's recommendations. As far as non-disclosure and misrepresentation are concerned, their effect is that insurers undertake not to rely on an innocent breach by the insured. By paragraph 2(b) of the *Statement of General Insurance Practice*,

"An insurer will not repudiate liability to indemnify a policyholder:
  (i) on grounds of non-disclosure of a material fact which a policyholder could not reasonably be expected to have disclosed;
  (ii) on grounds of misrepresentation unless it is a deliberate or negligent misrepresentation of a material fact."

Paragraph 3(a) of the *Long-Term Statement* provides rather more clumsily and ambiguously,

"An insurer will not unreasonably reject a claim. In particular, an insurer will not reject a claim or invalidate a policy on grounds of non-disclosure or misrepresentation of a fact unless:
  (i) it is a material fact; and
  (ii) it is a fact within the knowledge of the proposer; *and*
  (iii) it is a fact which the proposer could reasonably be expected to disclose.

(It should be noted that fraud or deception will, and reckless or negligent non-disclosure or misrepresentation of a material fact may, constitute grounds for rejection of a claim.)"

These paragraphs must be read in conjunction with the requirements that proposers must be warned on proposal forms and on renewal notices of the need for disclosure.[2] What is not certain is what effect warnings would be regarded as having on the reasonableness of a proposer's actions; could a plea of ignorance of the need for disclosure possibly be regarded as reasonable? How does a conscientious proposer read the warning in the light of the other requirement that insurers are expected to ask clear questions about facts which have generally been found to be material?[3]

---

[2] Warnings on proposal forms must be "prominent" (para. 1(c) and 1(a) of the *General* and *Long-Term Statements*, respectively). However, those on renewal notices need not be; *quaere* whether they ought not to be, as many people probably do not realise the importance of disclosure at the time of renewal. As to the possible legal consequences of a warning, see note 44 on page 87.

[3] See also the comment at note 57 on page 90.

Chapter 7

WARRANTIES AND CONDITIONS

In this chapter there fall to be described the terms of the contract of insurance other than those which are concerned with describing the risk covered and exceptions to it. The nature of these terms was described in a general way in Chapter 5. The contract of insurance will invariably in practice consist of not just the policy document itself, but also the completed proposal form where relevant, and often in addition other documents including in some cases renewal notices. This contract may contain three sorts of relevant terms, namely warranties, conditions and clauses descriptive of the risk. There is, however, no necessity for this, and it may be, for example, that a particular contract contains only conditions in the sense that they have been described earlier.

Clearly the most fundamental term, if it exists, is the warranty, since on a breach of warranty, the insurer can repudiate the whole contract. Warranties will therefore be considered first before we distinguish and describe clauses descriptive of the risk and conditions. Because, moreover, warranties are often created by means of declarations on a proposal form, and in practice it seems that proposal forms may be completed by agents rather than the proposer himself, the body of law relating to this particular situation will also be considered in this chapter. In addition, we must note that in practice the strict law is not always applied, by virtue of the *Statements of Insurance Practice*. This point is considered at the end of this chapter.

Warranties

It has already been pointed out[1] that a warranty is a term of the insurance contract upon breach of which the insurer can repudiate the contract. Warranties must be strictly complied with. It is quite irrelevant that the breach is unconnected with a loss that occurs. One of the oldest cases illustrates this point, which

---
[1] See Chapter 5, p. 74.

is thus of some antiquity, very neatly. *De Hahn* v. *Hartley*[2] involved a marine policy covering a ship and its cargo from Africa to its port of discharge in the West Indies. The insured warranted that the ship sailed from Liverpool with 50 hands on board. In fact it sailed with only 46 hands but it took on an extra six hands in Anglesey, very shortly out of Liverpool, and it thus had and continued to have 52 hands. It was held that the insurer could avoid all liability for breach of warranty, even though it was obvious that the breach could have had no connection with the loss which subsequently occurred.

The right to repudiate

The right to repudiate is from the date of breach which will differ, as will be seen, depending upon the type of warranty concerned. Upon a breach of warranty, the insurer's only option is to repudiate the contract or not. It cannot simply repudiate liability for a particular loss. If it purports to do so, it will be deemed to have waived its right to repudiate the contract. In *West* v. *National Motor and Accident Insurance Union*[3] the insured was alleged to be guilty of a breach of warranty by mis-stating the value of property he insured. When he subsequently suffered a loss, the insurers purported to reject the claim and to rely upon a term in the policy to refer the dispute to arbitration. It was held that by relying on the policy in this respect, they had waived any right to avoid the policy for breach of warranty which was the only right they might have had.[4] They had no right simply to reject the particular claim. The Law Commission has commented unfavourably on this decision, and recommended its statutory reversal.[5]

---

[2] (1786) 1 T.R. 343. See also the earlier case of *Pawson* v. *Watson* (1778) 2 Cowp. 785. Both cases were decided by Lord Mansfield, clarifying and establishing the distinction between warranties and representations.

[3] [1955] 1 All E.R. 800.

[4] This must be doubtful unless the warranty of value was incorrect when it was made, that is when the proposal form was completed. It was not a continuing warranty (see below), and warranties on a proposal form are not implied indefinitely into renewals of the contract: Winn L.J. in *Magee* v. *Pennine Insurance Co.* [1969] 2 Q.B. 507 at 517.

[5] Law Com. No. 104, 6.6 and 6.23. Since the Law Commission's Report appears unlikely to be enacted (see p. 97, above), this aspect of it will remain unimplemented. Compare the decisions on the validity of clauses relating to the forfeiture of premiums (see p. 124, below,) and the enforceability of arbitration clauses (see p. 205, below) despite a breach of warranty. Perhaps these cases are correct and *West* is wrong. After all a warranty is a term of the contract and in general contract law, a breach which justifies repudiation does not destroy the entire contract: *Heyman* v. *Darwins* [1942] A.C. 356. Or perhaps insurance con-

Warranties as promises

Warranties are essentially promises made by the insured relating to facts or to things which he undertakes to do or not to do, as the case may be. There are three sorts of warranties: warranties as to facts existing or past facts at the date they are made; warranties as to the future; and warranties of opinion.

Warranties of past or present fact

Warranties as to past or existing facts will usually, but not necessarily, arise as a result of a completed proposal form. The exact legal mechanism for this will be examined shortly. It is probably correct to say that the statements and questions and answers thereon, if they are warranted, will be presumed to be as to existing or past facts.

Promissory warranties

Warranties as to the future are known as promissory or continuing. They are continuing promises by the insured that facts will or will not exist in the future or will or will not continue to exist for the future. Common examples are warranties to maintain alarms or sprinkler systems in commercial fire policies and a warranty to maintain property in a reasonable condition which may be found in all sorts of policies. Whereas a breach of warranty as to past or present fact will entitle the insurer to repudiate the contract *ab initio*, since inevitably the breach occurred at the commencement of the contract, breach of a promissory warranty entitles the insurer to repudiate the contract from the date of breach, but it is valid up to that date. The insurer would thus, for example, be liable for a loss which occurred before the breach.

Promissory warranties may arise from completed proposal forms or from the body of the policy. Whether a warranty is promissory or simply present depends on the language used.

tracts are *sui generis* in this respect. Certainly many of the cases refer to avoidance *ab initio* in connection with breaches of warranty, which is not altogether surprising in view of the fact that insurers have often drafted their policies in this sort of way and in the light of the fact that proposal form warranties are akin to representations, and would be these in the absence of a basis clause (see below), as to which it is, of course, proper to speak of avoidance *ab initio* rather than repudiation. In this chapter, despite any logical difficulties, we shall adhere to the traditional usage and refer to breaches of warranties as to present and past facts as leading to avoidance of the whole contract. It is clear that if a term is described simply as a condition precedent to recovery, *i.e.* for a particular loss, the insurers can repudiate the claim and affirm the contract: see *e.g. Mint Security* v. *Blair* [1982] 1 Lloyd's Rep. 188, distinguishing *West* on this basis.

There appears to be no bar to its being both,[6] but in order to be promissory, it must, in general, contain in its wording a clear reference to the future. In *Woolfall & Rimmer* v. *Moyle*,[7] the insured warranted when it completed a proposal form for employers' liability insurance that its machinery, plant and ways "are . . . properly fenced and guarded, and otherwise in good order and condition." The Court of Appeal had no difficulty in rejecting the argument of the insurers that the warranty was promissory. The use of the present tense rather than the future tense was decisive. Similarly, in *Kennedy* v. *Smith*[8] a warranty in a proposal form for motor insurance which read: "I am a total abstainer from alcoholic drinks . . . " was held to relate simply to the past and the time it was made.

However, there appear to be two exceptions to the requirement of futurity in the language used. First, it has been held that if a provision can only be read as to the future, it will be promissory. In *Beauchamp* v. *National Mutual Indemnity Insurance Co.*,[9] the plaintiff, a builder, effected a policy to cover the demolition of a mill. He had never previously done demolition work. He warranted that he did not use explosives in his business in words which were clearly in the present tense. This was true at the time it was made, but the insured did later use explosives and this was held to be a breach of warranty. In the circumstances, because he had not used explosives before, the question addressed to him and his answer could only be read as referring to the future.

Secondly, there appears to be a principle that in fire and other policies on property, warranties as to the nature of the premises and precautions taken against loss will prima facie be read as to the future, on the ground that otherwise they would be of little or no value to the insurer. In *Hales* v. *Reliance Fire and Accident Insurance Co.*,[10] the warranty was as follows on a proposal form for fire insurance taken out by a shopkeeper: "Are any inflammable oils or goods used or kept on the premises? Lighter Fuel." Subsequently, the insured took delivery of a small quantity of fireworks. It was held that this amounted to a breach of a promissory warranty constituted by the question and answer

---

[6] This is implied in *Dawsons Ltd.* v. *Bonnin* [1922] 2 A.C. 413, as to which see below.

[7] [1942] 1 K.B. 66.

[8] 1976 S.L.T. 110. See also *Sweeney* v. *Kennedy* [1950] Ir.R. 85; *Kirkbride* v. *Donner* [1974] 1 Lloyd's Rep. 549.

[9] [1937] 3 All E.R. 19.

[10] [1960] 2 Lloyd's Rep. 391.

cited. The reasoning was as above. With respect, a similar argument put forward by insurers, admittedly not in the context of property insurance, was convincingly rejected in *Woolfall & Rimmer* v. *Moyle*, where Lord Greene M.R. said:[11] "If the underwriters intended to refer to the future, it is most unfortunate that a printed document of this kind . . . should not be so expressed. Had they intended that . . . , nothing would have been easier than to say so. If they did not mean it, I am at a loss to understand how the point comes to be taken." Furthermore, in *Hales*, there were other reasons why the same result could have been more logically achieved, in particular, a specific term declaring all warranties to be continuing and an increase of risk clause. It is suggested that the decision as it stands is open to serious objection.[12] In contrast, in *Hair* v. *Prudential Assurance Co. Ltd.*,[13] a warranty in a fire policy that the property was occupied, worded clearly in the present tense, was held not to have continuing effect.[14]

Warranties of opinion

Warranties of opinion are less severe than warranties of facts because if the insured merely warrants that facts are or will be true to the best of his knowledge and belief, there will be a breach of warranty only if he dishonestly or recklessly supplies an incorrect answer. The insured must exercise due care when making his warranty, but that is sufficient.[15] This is of particular importance in the context of "consumer-type" insurance because proposal forms, following the *Statement of Insurance Practice*,[16] should now be worded so as to require only warranties of opinion rather than warranties of fact.

Creation of warranties

There are a number of ways in which warranties may be created. Some of these may be found in the body of the policy whereas one in particular is found in proposal forms, namely

---

[11] [1942] 1 K.B. at 71.

[12] See further, Birds, "Warranties in Insurance Proposal Forms" [1977] J.B.L. 231 at 237.

[13] [1983] 2 Lloyd's Rep. 667.

[14] According to Woolf J. (*ibid.* at 672–673), any other construction would have been unreasonable. The decision in *Hales* does not appear to have been cited.

[15] *Huddleston* v. *R.A.C.V. Ins. Pty. Ltd.* [1975] V.R. 683; cf. *Mammone* v. *R.A.C.V. Ins. Pty. Ltd.* [1976] V.R. 617. See also *Macphee* v. *Royal Insurance Co.* 1979 S.L.T. 54.

[16] See p. 120, below, for other relevant parts of the Statement.

the "basis of the contract clause." We shall consider this device separately.

The policy may create warranties by the use of the word "warranty" itself, such as in the phrase "the insured warrants . . . ," but even this may not be conclusive if the court concludes that as a matter of construction the parties could not have intended a warranty.[17] A provision whereby the insurer has the right to repudiate the contract on breach or whereby the contract is declared to be void or voidable in certain circumstances has the same effect. A classic illustration here is the standard increase of risk clause in fire policies which was discussed in the previous chapter.[18] In addition, it must be open to the court to conclude that on the construction of the policy, the wording of a particular term gives rise to a warranty.[19]

Warranty or condition?

The use of the words "condition precedent" can give rise to difficulties. As has been seen,[20] there is a legal distinction between warranties and conditions precedent to a particular liability, but in fact, a warranty may equally be referred to as a condition precedent, provided it is clear that performance of the condition is precedent to the validity of the *policy*. Modern policies do not appear always to make the distinction clear. It seems clear that a general declaration making the terms of the policy conditions precedent to the validity of the policy is not sufficient to create warranties or fundamental terms of all of these terms, because by their nature some of them will be of the sort that cannot conceivably be regarded as precedent to the liability of the insurer, for example terms which after indemnity confer rights on the insurer such as subrogation rights. It does seem, however, that even matters which cannot objectively be regarded as fundamental to the validity of the contract, such as conditions relating to the claims process, can be made so fundamental by appropriate wording and equivalent to warranties in the sense we have described them.[21]

---

[17] See *e.g. De Maurier (Jewels) Ltd.* v. *Bastion Ins. Co.* [1967] 2 Lloyd's Rep. 550, discussed below.
[18] See p. 95.
[19] Law Com. No. 104, 6.3.
[20] Chapter 5, pp. 74–75.
[21] See *e.g. Cox* v. *Orion Insurance Co.* [1982] R.T.R. 1, where the Court of Appeal held that a breach of a condition relating to the furnishing of particulars of loss entitled the insurer to treat the whole contract as repudiated because the policy contained a provision making its conditions "conditions precedent to

Insurers, though, cannot be blamed entirely for this confusion by reason of the wordings they adopt. Some of the decided cases are equally unclear. For example, judges have sometimes used the description "condition" in referring to what here are meant by warranties. Even a similar term has attracted different appellations and different legal consequences in decided cases. Two contrasting examples will suffice. In *Conn* v. *Westminster Motor Insurance Association*,[22] a term in a motor policy requiring the insured to maintain his vehicle in an efficient condition appears to have been regarded as a warranty in the proper sense. While the Court of Appeal did talk in terms of its being a condition precedent, they appear to have regarded the term as precedent to the validity of the policy because they held that upon any breach the insurers could repudiate liability. In *W. J. Lane* v. *Spratt*,[23] on the other hand, a term in a goods in transit policy requiring the insured to take all reasonable precautions for the protection and safeguarding of the goods was regarded as a term, breach of which could be relied upon only if there was a causal connection between the breach and a particular loss.[24] The ground for the distinction between what on the face of them appear to be the same sort of term is not obvious. It is suggested that this sort of conceptual confusion is not satisfactory. Even though it may not matter in all cases to an insured or an insurer whether the latter can repudiate the policy or merely a particular claim, there are some situations where the distinction is vital[25] and it would become of the utmost importance if ever the recommendations of the Law Commission were implemented,[26] for the latter are concerned solely with warranties in the sense that they have here been defined.

---

any liability of the company to make any payment under this policy." The general trends in modern contract law on terms, mentioned in Chapter 5, especially at note 10, do not, unfortunately, seem to be taken account of in the insurance context.

[22] [1966] 1 Lloyd's Rep. 407. See p. 305, below, for more detail on this decision.

[23] [1970] 2 Q.B. 480.

[24] In fact Roskill J. referred to the term as a warranty, but it is clear that he was using the terms condition and warranty in the opposite sense to what is the usual practice and the practice adopted here (and by the Law Commission). See also the unreported case of *Port-Rose* v. *Phoenix Assurance p.l.c.*, see p. 162, below, where a "condition" requiring the taking of reasonable care was held not to be actionable unless the breach caused the loss.

[25] See, *e.g.* p. 116, below.

[26] As to these, see p. 119, below.

The basis of the contract clause

Historically, perhaps the most common and easiest way of creating warranties was the basis of the contract clause contained at the foot of the proposal form. While this device may not be so wide-ranging in its effects as it has been, because of the provisions of the *Statement of Insurance Practice* mentioned earlier, it is still of importance in areas where the *Statement* does not apply and still appears to be used in "consumer-type" insurances to create warranties of opinion.[27]

By making the questions and answers and declarations on a proposal form the basis of the contract, and providing that in the event of any untruth the contract could be voidable, insurers succeeded in equipping themselves with a potential defence to an action on the policy much wider than that arising by virtue of the duty of disclosure.[28] The device was first adopted in proposal forms for life insurance in the last century. In *Thomson* v. *Weems*[29] a question on a proposal form asked: (a) "Are you temperate in your habits and (b) have you always been strictly so?" The proposer answered "(a) temperate; (b) yes." The form contained a basis clause which expressly said that in the event of untruth, the policy would be void. As the proposer was in fact a heavy drinker, the House of Lords had no difficulty in upholding the insurers' repudiation of the policy. Materiality, they said, was irrelevant, even though, in fact, the matter must have been material on the facts of the case.[30]

In contrast, in *Dawsons Ltd.* v. *Bonnin*,[31] it was accepted that

---

[27] Further, it still appears to be acceptable to use a basis clause to create promissory warranties: see the rather ambiguous para. 1(b) of the *Statement of General Insurance Practice*, discussed at p. 120, note 87, below.

[28] For a persuasive attack on the device, see Hasson, "The Basis of the Contract Clause in Insurance Law" (1971) 34 M.L.R. 29. Hasson points out that the warranties held to be created by basis clauses in the early cases were material to the risk and these cases could therefore have been distinguished in later cases where the warranties were not material, of which *Dawsons Ltd.* v. *Bonnin*, below, is a classic example. This, however, would have been most unlikely at a time when the prevailing doctrine was freedom of contract.

[29] (1884) 9 App.Cas. 671. Earlier cases are *Duckett* v. *Williams* (1834) 2 C. & M. 348; *Anderson* v. *Fitzgerald* (1853) 4 H.L.C. 483.

[30] But was not the question really asking for the proposer's opinion rather than a statement of fact? See Hasson, *op. cit.* at pp. 34–35. It is difficult to justify the view taken in most of the cases that questions asked of the health of a proposer for life insurance can be answered factually by a non-expert: see the trenchant comment of Fletcher Moulton L.J. in *Joel* v. *Law Union and Crown Ins. Co.* [1903] 2 K.B. 863 at 885, cited in Hasson, *loc. cit.* See also the related problem in the area of non-disclosure, discussed in Chapter 6 at p. 83.

[31] [1922] 2 A.C. 413. The other leading case is *Yorkshire Ins. Co.* v. *Campbell* [1917] A.C. 218.

Warranties

the incorrect answer was immaterial.[32] A motor proposal concerning a lorry asked where it was garaged. The proposer wrongly answered that it was garaged at an address in central Glasgow, whereas, in fact, it was garaged at an address on the outskirts of the city. The proposal form merely declared that it was to constitute the basis of the contract; there was no reference to the policy being void or voidable in the event of an untrue answer, something which in the dissenting judgments was regarded as of great significance.[33] Despite this, by a bare majority, at least one of whose members[34] was not happy with the result, the House of Lords held that the insurer could repudiate the policy. "Basis" was sufficient to render the contents of the proposal form into fundamental terms of the contract. With respect, "basis of the contract" by itself could simply have been interpreted as the starting point on which negotiations were to be based, rendering wrong answers on the proposal form justifying repudiation only if they amounted to material misstatements.[35] However, whatever criticisms may be made, the decision has long stood as authority for the simple proposition that a basis of the contract clause converts all statements on a proposal form into warranties.[36] It follows that in addition to materiality being irrelevant, unless there is a term in the contract which requires this, it is also irrelevant that the proposer has answered the questions in good faith and to the best of his knowledge and belief if, in fact, answers are inaccurate. An even more harsh example of this is the decision in *McKay* v. *London General Insurance Co.*[37] The proposer for motor insurance stated that he had never been convicted on the proposal form which contained a basis clause. In fact he had been fined ten shillings many months previously for driving without efficient brakes because a nut had become loose on his motor cycle. Even though this was held not to be a material fact for the purposes of the duty of disclosure, the insurers were entitled to repudiate the policy for breach of warranty.[38]

---

[32] But see *MacGillivray and Parkington*, paras. 607–608.
[33] See Viscount Finlay at 430–431, and Lord Wrenbury at 436–437.
[34] Lord Dunedin at 434–435.
[35] This point is strengthened by the fact that the policy contained a condition expressly providing that *material* misrepresentation or non-disclosure would render it void; see Hasson, *op. cit.*, at p. 36.
[36] See, *e.g.* the later decision of the House of Lords in *Provincial Ins. Co.* v. *Morgan* [1933] A.C. 240, discussed below.
[37] (1935) 51 Ll.L.R. 201.
[38] Swift J. did not like the result, though; see his comments at 202.

Needless to say, this strict legal position has attracted considerable criticism, and it is noteworthy that judges have been as critical as other commentators.[39] Proposals for reform will be considered later.

Interpretation of warranties

Some mitigation of the strictness of the law of warranties, and in particular of the effects of a basis clause, has been effected by the courts adopting strict rules of interpretation. In particular, as it is usually the insurer who formulates the wording, in the event of any ambiguity, the warranty will be construed *contra proferentem*. The leading example is the decision of the House of Lords in *Provincial Insurance Co.* v. *Morgan*.[40] A firm of coal merchants insured a lorry under a standard motor policy. Part of the completed proposal form, which was the basis of the contract, read as follows: "State (*a*) the purposes in full for which the vehicle will be used; and (*b*) the nature of the goods to be carried. (*a*) Delivery of coal; (*b*) coal." One day the lorry was carrying some timber, as it did occasionally, as well as five hundredweight of coal. After the timber and three fifths of the coal had been delivered, and while the lorry was being driven to deliver the remaining coal, it was damaged in an accident. It was held that the insurers could not repudiate the policy for breach of promissory warranty. The insured warranted only that the lorry would in general be used for carrying coal, which was complied with; he did not, on the wording of the question and answer, warrant that the vehicle would be used to carry only coal. "In insurance a warranty . . . , though it must be strictly complied with, must be strictly though reasonably construed."[41]

Another example of the reasonable interpretation of warranties is afforded by the cases concerning obligations imposed on a liability insured to take reasonable precautions. These are considered in Chapter 18.[42]

---

[39] The leading criticisms are referred to by the Law Commission, Report No. 104, at 7.2 and 7.3. Even if it is the case that insurers have not generally relied on their strict legal rights, it is suggested that this fact is no answer to the necessity for reform of the law.
[40] [1933] A.C. 240.
[41] Lord Wright at 253–254; and see his comments at 254–256. The other point which arises from the case is considered below.
[42] p. 289.

CLAUSES DESCRIPTIVE OF THE RISK

In a number of cases, courts have construed statements on proposal forms with a basis clause not, or not just, as warranties, whether present or promissory, but as statements or clauses descriptive of the risk. Sometimes these terms have been described as warranties describing the risk,[43] which is a rather confusing appellation. This sort of term relates to the use of property insured. Its effect is rather like the effect of an exception to the risk properly so called, namely the risk is suspended while the term is not being complied with, but non-compliance does not entitle the insurer to repudiate and the risk re-attaches when the term is being complied with. It is therefore a less harsh device than a warranty in the strict sense, which may be why certain terms have been categorised in this way by the courts.[44]

For example, in *Farr* v. *Motor Traders' Mutual Insurance Society*[45] the plaintiff insured his two taxi-cabs. In answer to the question on the proposal form—"State whether the vehicles are driven in one or more shifts per 24 hours," he answered—"Just one." For a short period, because one of the taxis was being repaired, the other was driven in two shifts in the course of one day. The relevant accident occurred much later when both cabs were on the road and neither was being used in more than one shift per day. It was held that the insurers were liable in respect of this accident. The statement was not a promissory warranty, for breach of which they could repudiate the policy, that each cab would only ever be driven in one shift per day. It was merely descriptive of the risk. Had the accident occurred at the time when only one cab was in use, the insurers would not have been liable. Presumably also, if the statement had been untrue at the time it was made, it could have been relied upon as a warranty of present facts.

In *De Maurier (Jewels) Ltd.* v. *Bastion Insurance Co.*,[46] an all risks insurance effected by jewellers contained the following term: "Warranted road vehicles fitted with locks and alarm systems approved by underwriters and in operation." The insured suffered two losses. At the time of the first, the locks on

---

[43] *e.g.* in *De Maurier (Jewels) Ltd.* v. *Bastion Ins. Co.* [1967] 2 Lloyd's Rep. 550 (see below).
[44] See Baer (1978) 2 Can.Bus.L.J. 485.
[45] [1920] 3 K.B. 669.
[46] [1967] 2 Lloyd's Rep. 550.

the car in question were not of the required sort; at the time of the second, there were no faults. At first the insurers repudiated the policy, and hence liability for both losses, seemingly on the ground that a promissory warranty had been broken before the first loss. Subsequently, however, they admitted liability for the second loss.[47] It was held that the insurers were not liable for the first loss, as the risk was suspended because the locks were not approved. The term cited, despite the presence of "warranted," was not a warranty in the full sense, but merely a warranty descriptive of the risk.

The basis for the reasoning in these cases seems to be that in neither could the terms in question be clearly construed as promissory warranties, presumably because the language did not sufficiently refer to the future, and they thus attracted the lesser categorisation of statements descriptive of the risk, because they related to the use of property insured. There has been no suggestion that this categorisation would attach to statements on a proposal form not of this sort. The holding in the *De Maurier* case is a little curious because the term was drafted not by the insurers but by brokers acting for the insured. It seems that the insurers could have repudiated the policy on the ground of breach of warranty of present facts because the car which was involved in the first loss did not have the required locks at the time the warranty was made, but on the facts it was held that the insurers had waived this right.

If a statement on a proposal form can be both a warranty as to past or present facts, and descriptive of use for the future, as these decisions suggest, the question remains whether it can be both a promissory warranty and a statement descriptive of the risk. The point arose in *Provincial Insurance Co. v. Morgan*,[48] the facts of which have already been given, where the decision of the Court of Appeal[49] was firmly based on the ground that the relevant question and answer were descriptive of the risk. On this analysis, the insurers were liable because the lorry was carrying only coal at the time of the accident. In the House of Lords, this view was taken by Lord Russell, for whom it was the only reason for the decision, and by Lord Wright as subsidiary to his main reason which rested, as we have seen, on the interpretation of the question and answer as a promissory warranty. The question arises as to what would have been the result of the

---

[47] They were criticised by Donaldson J. for not having done so earlier.
[48] See note 40 above.
[49] [1932] 2 K.B. 70.

case if the lorry had been carrying timber as well as coal at the time of the accident. On a strict view of Lord Buckmaster's reasoning, with which Lord Blanesburgh agreed,[50] the insurers would still have been liable because there was no breach of promissory warranty as he interpreted it. Against that are the views of Lords Russell and Wright and those of the members of the Court of Appeal which point to the opposite result. The latter is presumably the correct view, although it can be criticised as not designed to let the insured clearly know where he stands.

Agents and the Proposal Form

As we have seen, a common source of warranties is the proposal form which contains a basis clause. It is not uncommon for an insurance transaction to be negotiated through an agent of one sort or another and frequently it would seem, in this case, the agent actually fills in the proposal form. Normally this would of course be done in consultation with the proposer, but there are reported cases which show that occasionally this is not the case. If an answer is incorrect due to the fault or with the knowledge of the proposer, then obviously the policy can be repudiated according to the law that has been considered. If, however, the proposer tells the agent the truth, but the latter chooses to falsify an answer, and the proposer does not become aware of what has happened, because he does not check what the agent has done, the question arises whether the proposer is bound by what the agent has done. Certainly he is if the agent is in law his agent at all times, and it has even been held that in this case he has no right to sue the agent in damages.[51] If, however, the agent is a full-time agent of the insurer, for example, a canvassing agent or another full-time employee, it might be argued that his knowledge of the truth should be imputed to the insurer.

It has already been seen[52] that in the context of the disclosure of material facts, this is the legal position. In the context of the answering of questions on a proposal form, however, the law has in general taken the opposite view. This is an area which has given rise to a comparatively large number of reported cases

[50] Lord Warrington agreed with both Lords Wright and Buckmaster.
[51] *O'Connor* v. *Kirby* [1972] 1 Q.B. 90, discussed in Chapter 10 at p. 150. Compare, however, *Dunbar* v. *A. & B. Painters Ltd.* [1986] 2 Lloyd's Rep. 38, which is also discussed later. See that Chapter also for a fuller discussion of whose agent in law a particular agent is, and the question as to imputation of knowledge.
[52] Chapter 6, p. 85.

Warranties and Conditions

in all common law jurisdictions. We shall here concentrate on the English decisions, but make reference to some particularly apposite Commonwealth cases.

Knowledge imputed

The first authority which must be examined is perhaps the earliest in time, a Court of Appeal decision which appears at first sight to be out of line with subsequent cases. *Bawden* v. *London, Edinburgh & Glasgow Assurance Co.*[53] concerned a proposal for accident insurance by a proposer who was illiterate and had only one eye. This fact was known to the agent of the insurers who completed the form for him. That form, however, warranted that the proposer had no physical deformity, which was obviously incorrect. Subsequently the insured suffered an accident in which he lost the sight of the other eye. It was held that he could recover under the policy for total loss of sight. The agent's knowledge of the truth at the time of the proposal was imputed to the insurer.

Knowledge not imputed

Bawden was, however, distinguished in a number of subsequent cases[54] and in particular in the leading case of *Newsholme Bros.* v. *Road Transport & General Insurance Co.*[55] Here the proposal was for motor insurance and the incorrect answers, which related to previous losses, were warranted to be true. It was found as a fact that the agent who filled in the form knew of the true facts. He was an agent employed by the insurers to canvass for proposals, but he was not authorised to effect insurance whether temporary or permanent. The arbitrator held that the agent's knowledge of the truth was imputed to the insurers who could not therefore repudiate the policy, but his decision was overruled by the trial judge and the Court of Appeal. The leading judgment was delivered by Scrutton L.J. who gave two principal reasons for the decision. First, he said,[56] if the agent filled in the form at the request of the proposer, for that purpose he must have been acting as the agent of the proposer and not of the insurers. Secondly,[57] "I have great difficulty in understanding how a man who has signed, without reading it, a

---

[53] [1892] 2 Q.B. 534.
[54] See, e.g. *Biggar* v. *Rock Life Ass. Co.* [1902] 1 K.B. 516; *Keeling* v. *Pearl Ass. Co.* (1923) 129 L.T. 573.
[55] [1929] 2 K.B. 356.
[56] *Ibid.* at 369 and 375.
[57] *Ibid.* at 376.

document which he knows to be a proposal for insurance, and which contains statements in fact untrue, and a promise that they are true and the basis of the contract, can escape from the consequences of his negligence by saying that the person he asked to fill it up for him is the agent of the person to whom the proposal is addressed." Greer L.J. also relied upon the agency point,[58] but he laid greater stress upon another reason, namely, that to allow evidence of what the agent actually knew to be introduced would be a violation of the parol evidence rule whereby oral evidence is generally inadmissible to vary the terms of a written contract.[59] Here the proposal form was part of the contract because, as usual, it formed the basis of it and its terms were warranties.

Greer L.J. was thus able to distinguish the *Bawden* case on the grounds that in the latter, because of the special circumstances of the proposer's illiteracy, the court could rightly ignore the parol evidence rule or put a special meaning on the words used in the contract.[60] In contrast, Scrutton L.J. came very close to saying that the *Bawden* case was wrong.[61]

Agency

As to the agency point, the judges seemed particularly impressed by the fact that the agent did not have actual authority to fill in proposal forms. With respect, this should not be conclusive. The fact that agents are armed with such forms and frequently complete them, probably to the knowledge of insurers, must arguably give them ostensible authority to do so, unless any such authority is negatived, for example, by a notice on the proposal form,[62] yet the principles of ostensible authority were ignored in the *Newsholme* case. Further, even if an agent does become the agent of the proposer, or at least his amenuensis, for the purpose of filling in the form, at that stage the form is merely an offer to enter into an insurance contract and it is not easy to see why the correct knowledge of the agent should not be imputed to the insurer if the facts warrant it.[63] On

---

[58] *Ibid.* at 382.
[59] *Ibid.* at 379–380.
[60] See *ibid.* at 381.
[61] The *Bawden* case had previously also been subjected to considerable criticism in a number of cases in different jurisdictions. These are cited in the judgment of Scrutton L.J.
[62] See *Facer* v. *Vehicle & General Ins. Co.* [1965] 1 Lloyd's Rep. 113.
[63] See Tedeschi, "Assured's Misrepresentation and the Insurance Agent's Knowledge of the Truth" (1972) 7 Israel L.R. 475.

this basis the strict parol evidence rule could be ignored, as the court has already admitted extrinsic evidence for the insurer that the answer on the form was incorrect.

Signing of form

However, the second reason of Scrutton L.J. as described above must still be valid and strictly in accordance with the law governing the signature of documents, which holds a person bound by what he has signed, except in the limited circumstances when he can plead *non est factum*.[64] Therefore, it is suggested that *Newsholme* is correct, and cases to the contrary must either be wrong or regarded as exceptions, a point to which we shall return. Whether the result is a fair one is an entirely separate question. The Law Reform Committee[65] certainly thought not and recommended statutory reversal of the rule. However, their recommendation, framed in terms that the agent should be regarded as at all times the agent of the insurer may not go far enough. If the analysis of the true ratio for the rule given here is the correct one, the parol evidence rule and the rule relating to the signature of documents would still present problems if the contents of the proposal form are part of the written contract. The need for some reform was also pointed out in a Government White Paper in 1977,[66] but hitherto, there have been no more concrete proposals.

Newsholme overruled?

It has, however, been decided in Canada[67] that the decision in *Newsholme* has been effectively overruled by the most recent English case, namely the Court of Appeal decision in *Stone* v. *Reliance Mutual Insurance Society*.[68] Here the plaintiff's fire

---

[64] See Treitel, *Law of Contract*, Chapter 8. The *Bawden* case might thus be regarded as a case where the insured could plead *non est factum* because of his illiteracy and consequent inability to check the form.

[65] Fifth Report, 1957 Cmnd. 62.

[66] *Insurance Intermediaries*, Cmnd. 6715, para. 16. The comment here was rather ambivalent. Having supported the Law Reform Committee's recommendation, the White Paper then says; "But it is not the Government's intention that the proposer should be relieved of responsibility for the accuracy of statements made by him in response to questions expressly put to him in the proposal form."

[67] *Blanchette* v. *C.I.S. Ltd.* (1973) 36 D.L.R. (3d) 561. This Supreme Court case, in fact, involved the slightly different situation referred to below, namely the agent filling in a blank form *after* signature by the proposer.

[68] [1972] 1 Lloyd's Rep. 469. See also Timmins, "Misrepresentation in Insurance Proposal Forms Completed by Agents" (1974) Vict.Univ. of Wellington L.R. 217, who is also, it is suggested, over-optimistic.

policy with the defendants had lapsed. An inspector employed by the defendants called on the plaintiff's wife and persuaded her to effect a new policy. On the proposal form, the answer "none" was put to a question asking for details of lapsed policies and previous claims. This was incorrect. The plaintiff had made a claim on the defendants and had previously, obviously therefore, insured with them. The inspector had filled in the proposal form as indeed he was instructed to do by the insurers. It was held that the policy subsequently issued was not voidable. Megaw and Stamp L.JJ regarded the case as turning on its special facts, namely that the inspector was actually authorised to fill in proposal forms. Lord Denning's judgment could be more widely interpreted, but equally it is suggested that his decision really turned on the authority of the agent, not simply as regards the imputation of knowledge of the agent, but also because he had authority to represent that the form had been correctly filled in, particularly because it was accepted that the plaintiff's wife with whom he dealt was a person of little education. This is sensible. If an agent is fairly senior within an insurer's hierarchy, the circumstances should be such as to allow the admittance of what he did and said and to regard him as having authority to vary the terms of a written contract.

Another reason for regarding *Stone* as merely an exception to the general rule is that the insurers themselves must have known that the answers were false and what the truth was, because they were the insurers with whom the previous lapsed policy had been held and against whom the previous claim had been made.[69] To have allowed them to repudiate the policy in such circumstances would have been ridiculous. This point was not actually taken in the case itself, but it must be correct.

It is suggested therefore, that there is no mandate for regarding *Stone* as overruling *Newsholme Bros*. The latter remains the governing decision, but there are exceptions in the case of illiterate and possibly poorly educated proposers and, possibly, where the agent in question is more than a mere canvassing agent but can be regarded as having some authority to vary the terms of the contract.

Form signed in blank

There is some Commonwealth authority which supports a further exception, namely where the agent fills in the proposal form after it has been signed in blank by the proposer, the latter

---

[69] See Ritchie J., dissenting, in *Blanchette* v. *C.I.S. Ltd.*, note 67 above, at 572.

relying upon the agent's representation that he has the necessary information.[70] This is perhaps tenable, assuming that the proposer acts quite innocently and in the circumstances the agent can be regarded as having the authority to represent that the insurer would be estopped from relying upon a breach of warranty. On the other hand, it is clear that if the proposer signs the form after the agent has filled it in himself without asking any information of the proposer, the latter is bound by what he signs.[71]

CONDITIONS

It has already been pointed out that insurance policies almost universally list a number of terms of the contract under the heading "Conditions." While it is difficult to generalise, it is probably accurate to say that at least some of these terms do not relate directly to the risk covered or to statements of fact, but are in the nature of collateral promises or stipulations. Some "conditions" may, of course, be warranties in the sense described earlier in this chapter, as has been seen. One further important reason for distinguishing warranties from conditions other than those already considered, even when both terms might appear in the same part of a policy, is that it has been held that compliance by an insured with a condition may be dispensed with if it is unnecessary, for example, by reason of information which the insurer possesses from another source. The actual decision which may establish this[72] will be considered in a later chapter. It can hardly apply to warranties properly so called which, as we have seen, must always be strictly complied with.[72a]

Nature of conditions

Conditions which are in the nature of collateral terms seem to be of two kinds. First, there are promises or obligations imposed on the insured, primarily with regard to the claims

---

[70] *Blanchette* v. *C.I.S. Ltd.*, above. See also *Western Australian Ins. Co.* v. *Dayton* (1924) 35 C.L.R. 355.

[71] *Biggar* v. *Rock Life Ass. Co.*, note 54, above.

[72] *Lickiss* v. *Milestone Motor Policies at Lloyd's* [1966] 2 All E.R. 972; see Chapter 12 at p. 202.

[72a] In addition, a breach of condition is said to be actionable only if it causes the loss (see p. 105, above), whereas, as we have seen, there is no such requirement as regards warranties.

procedure, which are not made fundamental to the validity of the contract.[73] Second, are conditions conferring rights on the insurer, often repeating or enlarging rights given by the general law. Examples here include conditions governing subrogation rights and the rights of insurers to control proceedings by or against their insureds, and conditions concerning double insurance. Detailed consideration of the usual obligations and rights conferred by this sort of condition will be given in subsequent chapters. The questions to be considered here are the effect of conditions imposing obligations on the insured, namely whether they are precedent to the insurer's liability for a particular loss or whether upon breach the insurer has merely the right to claim damages for such loss as it has suffered, and the onus of proof in respect of such conditions.

Conditions precedent or mere conditions

If there is no reference to the sorts of condition in question being precedent to the insurer's liability, then it is clear that a breach does not entitle the insurer to repudiate liability.[74] This, however, seems unlikely to be the case nowadays. Policies will usually contain some general reference to their conditions being conditions precedent, if not a specific reference in a particular condition. The only legal problem which then appears likely to arise is where there is a general declaration, but within a particular condition there are parts which cannot conceivably be precedent to the insurer's liability, perhaps because the obligation thereunder can only be performed after the insurer has paid or because a relevant part does not actually impose an obligation on the insured.

In *London Guarantee Co.* v. *Fearnley*,[75] for example, a fidelity policy effected by an employer to protect himself against the risk of embezzlement by an employee had a condition which required the insured to prosecute the employee suspected when a claim had been made and which provided that he should give all information and assistance to the insurer to enable the latter to obtain reimbursement from the employee of any sums which the insurer was liable to pay. Clearly the second part of this condition could not be precedent to the insurer's liability since it could only operate when that liability

---

[73] As seen earlier (p. 104 at note 21), even these sorts of obligations can be made the subject of fundamental terms.
[74] *e.g., Stoneham* v. *Ocean, Railway and General Accident Ins. Co.* (1887) 19 Q.B.D. 237.
[75] (1880) 5 App.Cas. 911.

was established. Despite that, the majority of the House of Lords, with some hesitation, held that the first part was a condition precedent since the policy contained a general declaration to that effect and the two parts were separate and independent.

In contrast is the decision in *Re Bradley and Essex and Suffolk Accident Indemnity Society*.[76] This concerned a condition in a workmen's compensation policy taken out by a farmer, condition 5. There was a similar general declaration to the effect that the conditions were precedent to the liability of the insurer. Condition 5 contained three sentences. The first provided that the premium was to be regulated by the amount of wages and salaries paid by the insured, the second required the keeping of a proper wages book and the third required the insured to supply information to the insurers regarding wages and salaries paid. The insured, who only had one employee, his son, failed to maintain a wages book and the insurer relied upon this to deny liability for a particular claim. By a majority, the Court of Appeal held that the insured was not guilty of a breach of a condition precedent. According to Cozens Hardy M.R., the first and third parts of condition 5 were incapable of being conditions precedent. While the second, the one in issue, could be, "I think the fifth condition is one and entire, and it is to my mind unreasonable to hold that one sentence in its middle is a condition precedent while the rest of the condition cannot be so considered. A policy of this nature, in case of ambiguity or doubt, ought to be construed against the office."[77] The judgment of Farwell L.J. is to the same effect, though his reasoning is much broader; he would have required that the insured be informed of and consent to conditions precedent to liability before the policy was effected before they could be binding. With respect, this is too wide, however laudable, to constitute the law, and it conflicts with other authority.[78] Fletcher Moulton L.J., dissenting, followed the decision in *Fearnley* which he clearly regarded as conclusive.

Although one can applaud the Court of Appeal's determination to ensure that insurers frame their conditions precedent clearly and separately, it is difficult to distinguish the decision in the *Bradley* case from that in the earlier one. Perhaps all that

---

[76] [1912] 1 K.B. 415.

[77] *Ibid.* at 422.

[78] See the cases concerning offer and acceptance in the insurance context, discussed in Chapter 4 at p. 54.

can be said is that each decision turns on questions of construction and that other decisions are of small assistance unless the wording is identical.[79] It is probably fairly safe to suggest that a general declaration as to conditions precedent would normally be effective in so far as particular conditions or parts of them are clearly capable of being separated.

The onus of proof

In relation to an alleged breach of condition, "it is axiomatic in insurance law that, as it is always for an insurer to prove an exception, so it is for him to prove the breach of a condition which would relieve him from liability for a particular loss."[80] It is, however, possible for the wording of a policy to affect this, but it is clear that very clear words would be required to place the onus of proving that he complied with a condition on the insured.[81]

PRACTICE IN AND REFORM OF THE LAW OF WARRANTIES AND CONDITIONS

As we have seen at various points in this chapter, many aspects of the law of warranties, in particular the basis of the contract clause, have attracted criticism from judges and others. The whole matter was examined by the Law Commission[82] along with their examination of the duty of disclosure. As explained earlier,[83] implementation of their report seems regrettably unlikely for the foreseeable future and detailed consideration of it will not be attempted here.[84] Briefly, the Commission wanted all warranties to have to be material and they wanted the abolition of the basis clause. They would have allowed an insurer to

---

[79] See MacKinnon L.J. in *Welch* v. *Royal Exchange Assurance* [1939] 1 K.B. 294 at 311.
[80] *Per* Lord Goddard C.J. in *Bond Air Services Ltd.* v. *Hill* [1955] 2 Q.B. 417 at 427.
[81] *Ibid.* at 428.
[82] Report No. 104, 1980 Cmnd. 8064. Warranties were considered because of their obvious links, when arising from the contents of a proposal form, with disclosure and because the proposed E.E.C. Directive on insurance contract law contained provisions modelled on the French law of *aggravation du risque* corresponding in some ways to the English law of warranties.
[83] See pp. 96–97.
[84] For a little more detail, apart from the Report itself, see the first edition of this book, pp. 118–120 and Birds, "The Reform of Insurance Law" [1982] J.B.L. 449. The recommendations on warranties were more widely accepted as fair than were those on the duty of disclosure.

repudiate a claim on discovering a breach of warranty only if the breach was causally connected with the loss.[85]

Statements of insurance practice

This is in fact the position in practice when the *Statements of Practice* are relevant and are followed.[86] Paragraph 1(*a*) of the *Statement of General Insurance Practice* provides "The declaration at the foot of the proposal form should be restricted to completion according to the proposer's knowledge and belief," thus abolishing the full effect of any basis clause, and paragraph 1(b) provides, "Neither the proposal form nor the policy shall contain any provision converting the statements as to past or present fact in the proposal form into warranties. But insurers may require specific warranties about matters which are material to the risk."[87] Paragraph 2(*b*)(iii) states that an insurer will not repudiate on grounds of a breach of warranty or condition where the circumstances of the loss are unconnected with the breach "unless fraud is involved," thus mitigating one of the harshest potential consequences of a breach of warranty.[88]

---

[85] Difficulties might have arisen in connection with the Commission's recommendations because they were limited to warranties in the strict sense and might have been easily evaded by insurers resorting to the use of conditions precedent to loss to cover obligations traditionally the subject-matter of warranties.

[86] For more detail on these, see the sources cited at p. 97, note 1, above. Remember that the *Statements* apply only to individual non-business insureds and that there is no guarantee that they will be followed by insurers who are not members of the Association of British Insurers or Lloyd's.

[87] See also para. 1(*b*) of the *Statement of Long-Term Insurance Practice* which is to generally similar effect. The second sentence is a little odd as no-one has ever denied insurers' rights to impose continuing obligations of a material nature. Insurers may still feel that they can make the contents of a proposal form into continuing warranties. *Quaere* whether this should in fact be allowed; there seems no reason why such terms should not be required to be contained in the body of the policy.

[88] As mentioned earlier (pp. 105 and 106), the law imposes a causal connection requirement for breaches of condition. *Cf.* para. 3(*b*) of the *Long-Term Statement* which is similar but further qualified. Para. 2(*b*) does not apply to marine or aviation policies, an exclusion which could work hardship on private aeroplane and boat owners. The exception for fraud is perhaps unfortunate; an insurer can always reject a fraudulent claim (see pp. 209–211, below); why should it not have to prove fraud instead of retaining the right to rely on an unconnected breach of warranty?

Chapter 8

PREMIUMS

"Premium" can be described as the consideration given by the insured in return for the insurer's undertaking to cover the risks insured against in the policy of insurance.[1] It need not, although, of course, it usually will, take the form of a money payment; for example, it could be the liability to contribute to the funds of a mutual society insuring its members, imposed by membership of that society. Furthermore, if a policy is under seal, and hence does not require consideration to support it, strictly no premium is necessary, but needless to say, this is hardly likely to arise. The amount of premium is entirely a matter for the insurer, though in certain classes of business there are broadly agreed tariffs.[2] This can be contrasted with the position in some civil law countries where tariffs are standard, and with the position in some countries, including some states in the United States of America, where state approval of premium rates is required.[3]

Payment of premium

We have seen[4] that there is no general rule requiring the actual payment of the premium before the insurer is at risk, although this will frequently, particularly in life insurance, be required by a term of the policy. Prima facie, the proper mode of payment of premium is in cash, but of course it is just as common nowadays to find payment by cheque. The latter is only conditional on the cheque being honoured. Indeed, other modern forms of paying money are also, with the insurer's consent, frequently used. Predominant here are the systems of bank giro, standing order and direct debit, their use depending upon the type of insurance concerned. For example, a renewal notice for motor or property insurance will commonly contain a

---

[1] *Lewis* v. *Norwich Union Fire Ins. Co.* [1916] A.C. 509 at 519.

[2] *e.g.* in life and motor business. For a comprehensive criticism of the tariff system that used to exist in respect of fire insurance, see the Monopolies Commission Report on the Supply of Fire Insurance (H.M.S.O. 1972).

[3] See, *e.g.* Franson, *The Prior-Approval System of Property and Liability Insurance Rate Regulations: A Case Study*, (1969) 4 Wisconsin L.R. 1104.

[4] pp. 55–56, above.

bank giro form for the insured's use if he chooses, while premiums on certain endowment policies, particularly those used in conjunction with a mortgage for house purchase, may well be paid by standing order or direct debit. There has been no case law on the use of such methods generally for payment for any goods or services, and no problems can arise unless the bank responsible is for some reason late in making payment. It seems likely that, if the insured has sufficient funds in his account, the insurer who permits the use of one of these methods of payment would be held to be bearing the risk of any default by the bank, despite the fact that the bank is acting as agent of the insured rather than of the insurer. If not, the bank would in any event be liable to the insured for any loss suffered.

Payment on credit

The effect of inflation on premiums, so that the renewal premium on, for example, a motor policy can amount to hundreds of pounds, has prompted insurers in this and some other classes of business to offer their insureds the chance to pay premiums by instalments. Provided that the insured is an individual or a partnership, rather than a company or some other corporate body,[5] it is clear that such an arrangement falls prima facie within the Consumer Credit Act 1974 where the amount of credit, that is, of the deferred payment of premium, does not exceed £15,000.[6] It would be a restricted use credit agreement within section 11(1)(*a*) of that Act and a debtor-creditor-supplier agreement within section 12(*a*). Therefore, *inter alia*, the licensing machinery of the Act and the provisions as to rate disclosure and advertising[7] would apply. However, one effect of section 16(5) of the Act and paragraph 3 of the Consumer Credit (Exempt Agreements) Order 1977[8] is to exempt from the operation of the Act agreements for the payment of premiums on credit where the number of payments to be made to the insured does not exceed four. It appears that, in practice, insurers take advantage of this exception by limiting the number of payments on credit to a maximum of four, so that more detailed consideration of the Act here is unnecessary.

Apart from these issues as to payment, the other major legal

---

[5] Consumer Credit Act 1974, s.189.

[6] *Ibid.* ss.8 and 9, as amended.

[7] See generally, Goode, *The Consumer Credit Act, A Student's Guide*, Chapters 11 and 13.

[8] S.I. 1977 No. 326.

point concerning premiums is the situations when in law the insured is entitled to a return of premiums he has paid. It is to this that we shall devote the remainder of this chapter.

Return of Premium

An insured is basically entitled to a return of premium where there has been a total failure of consideration[9] and his action is in quasi-contract for money had and received. If the insurer has been at risk in any way or for any period, there is no entitlement at common law to a recovery of any part of the premium paid. In *Wolenberg* v. *Royal Co-operative Collecting Society*,[10] the insured had effected several policies of industrial assurance with different insurers to cover the cost of funeral expenses to be incurred on her mother's death. Having recovered that cost from one insurer, she sought to recover back the premiums paid on the policy effected with the defendant. It was held that as the insurer had been at risk there could be no return of premiums, even though, by reason of the principle of indemnity, the plaintiff had no claim on the policy. *Wolenberg* was thus a case of over-insurance. The same principle will apply to any situation where the insurer has been at risk at all, for example, where liability under the policy, though not the policy itself,[11] is avoided for breach of condition, where the policy is cancelled by either party after it has been in operation, and where the policy is avoided for breach of a continuing warranty,[12] the breach not being such as to avoid the policy *ab initio*. In practice, the principle is expressly reversed in some of these cases, and usually, for example, the cancellation clause in a policy[13] will provide for a rateable return of premium following cancellation.

There are two broad heads of case where there will or may be a total failure of consideration entitling the insured to recover his premiums. The first is where the policy is never concluded, is cancelled *ab initio*, or is void or voidable *ab initio*. The second, which is the less certain category, is where the policy is illegal.

---

[9] *Tyrie* v. *Fletcher* (1777) 2 Cowp. 666.
[10] (1915) 83 L.J.K.B. 1316.
[11] As to this distinction, see Chapter 5.
[12] See Chapter 7.
[13] See Chapter 4.

Non-existent, cancelled and void or voidable policies

If an insured pays a premium in respect of a contract of insurance which, in fact, is never concluded, he is obviously entitled to its return. The result is the same if a life policy is cancelled, or a proposal withdrawn, under the statutory procedures.[14] A policy may be void for mistake[15] or because it is *ultra vires* the insurer, or it may be voidable at the insurer's option for non-disclosure, misrepresentation or in certain circumstances, breach of warranty by the insured,[16] or at the insured's option for misrepresentation or non-disclosure on the part of the insurer.

Where a policy is avoided *ab initio* by the insurer, it seems, although there is no clear non-marine insurance authority, that the insured is entitled to recover premiums paid in all cases except where his non-disclosure or misrepresentation was fraudulent.[17] This would certainly be in accordance with principle. The same might be thought to apply prima facie to avoidance *ab initio* for breach of warranty. However, it is not uncommon for an insurer to provide for forfeiture of premiums where a policy is avoided for breach of warranty. Such a provision has been upheld,[18] even in a case where it appears quite clear that the insured did not act fraudulently.[19] It might be thought that avoidance of a policy entirely by the insurer would disentitle it to rely upon any of the terms. While this must be the result in cases of non-disclosure *stricto sensu*, avoidance for breach of warranty may not have the same result. Here, in effect, the insurer is repudiating the contract by relying on its terms, rather than rescinding it in the strict sense.[20] Hence, any term as to the forfeiture of premiums can equally be relied upon.[21]

---

[14] See pp. 59–60, above.

[15] See *MacGillivray & Parkington*, paras. 555–569.

[16] See Chapters 5, 6 and 7. Not all breaches of warranty entitle the insurer to repudiate the contract *ab initio*; see pp. 101–103, above.

[17] *Anderson* v. *Fitzgerald* (1853) 4 H.L.Cas. 484.

[18] *Duckett* v. *Williams* (1834) 2 Cromp. & M. 348; *Thomson* v. *Weems* (1884) 9 App.Cas. 671; *Sparenborg* v. *Edinburgh Life Ass. Co.* [1912] 1 K.B. 195.

[19] *Kumar* v. *Life Ins. Corp. of India* [1974] 1 Lloyd's Rep. 147 at 154; here the insurers undertook to return the premium *ex gratia*.

[20] See the discussion in Chapters 5 and 7, especially p. 100.

[21] *Quaere*, though, whether it might not be unenforceable as a penalty clause, as not being a genuine pre-estimate of the insurer's loss. Kerr J. in the *Kumar* case (above, at 154) clearly inclined to this view, but felt that he was constrained to uphold the clause by the weight of authority, particularly the cases cited in note 18.

It must be a fairly rare occurrence where an insured is entitled, and wants, to avoid a policy for misrepresentation of fact by the insurer, but a notable instance is the case of *Kettlewell* v. *Refuge Assurance Co.*[22] Here the insured was minded to let lapse the life policy she had with the defendant insurers, but she was persuaded to continue with it by the false representation of an agent of the defendant that after four more years, she would obtain a free policy, that is, that the policy would remain in force but she would have no more premiums to pay. The Court of Appeal held that the insured had the right to avoid the policy and recover the premiums paid since the date of the misrepresentation as money had and received,[23] it being irrelevant that the defendant had been at risk during the period that the premiums were paid and the policy in effect, albeit voidable. Avoidance by the insured operated *ab initio*.

Illegal policies

Where a policy is void because of illegality, somewhat different considerations apply. It should be noted that here we are concerned with contracts that are themselves illegal, not those situations where recovery under a valid policy is illegal for reasons of public policy.[24] In the latter case, the premium is never recoverable.

While there are a number of circumstances which could, in theory, render an insurance contract illegal,[25] easily the most common, and that which has given rise to the problems in this area, is illegality due to lack of insurable interest required by statute.[26] The general rule with regard to illegal contracts, whether of insurance or otherwise, is that the court will not entertain any action in respect of them, except in three exceptional cases.[27] Thus, premiums paid under an illegal insurance

---

[22] [1908] 1 K.B. 545; affirmed [1909] A.C. 243.

[23] Lord Alverstone C.J. considered that the money was also recoverable as damages in an action in deceit (p. 550). Buckley L.J. rested his decision on another ground entirely, considering that there had not been a total failure of consideration since the insured had had the right to enforce the contract until she avoided it. According to him, the money was recoverable as obtained by the insurers only by the fraud of their agent.

[24] For the distinction, see Chapter 5, and for avoidance on public policy grounds, see Chapter 12.

[25] See Chapter 5. Note the insured's statutory right, where the insurer is acting without authorisation, to recover the premiums: section 132(1) of the Financial Services Act 1986: see p. 73, above.

[26] *i.e.* the Life Assurance Act 1774; see Chapter 3.

[27] See further, Treitel, *Law of Contract*, Chap. 11.

contract are irrecoverable unless one of the exceptions applies. These exceptions are (i) where the party bringing the action was less blameworthy than the defendant, or, as it is more traditionally put, where the parties were not *in pari delicto*; (ii) where he is one of the class protected by the statute which makes the contract illegal; and (iii) where he has repented in time, that is before the contract was executed. The second exception is inapplicable to insurable interest cases[28] and the third is unlikely to apply except in the rare case where the insured relents before the risk begins to run. The first exception thus raises the only notable issues.

Parties not in pari delicto

It must be said that in their consideration of this, the cases are somewhat conflicting. Clearly, if there is no element of fraud or trickery on the part of the insurer or his agent, the parties will be *in pari delicto*, since it is a general principle that everyone is presumed to know the law, and there can be no recovery of premium. The problem concerns the degree of improper conduct on the part of the insurer or his agent which will suffice to negate this. In the badly reported case of *British Workmen's & General Assurance Co.* v. *Cunliffe*,[29] an agent of the insurers induced the insured to effect a policy on the life of his brother-in-law, in which he had no insurable interest. The Court of Appeal allowed the insured to recover the premiums he had paid. The headnote to the report states that the agent acted without any fraud but it does seem that the judges took the view that, even if he did not act fraudulently, his conduct was sufficiently improper as he knew what the law was and that the insured had no insurable interest, and despite this, assured the insured that the policy would be all right.[30]

This decision was distinguished in *Harse* v. *Pearl Life Assurance Co.*,[31] where the plaintiff insured the life of his mother in which he had no interest. Again, he had been persuaded to effect the insurance by an agent of the insurer, but the Court of Appeal held that the agent had acted quite innocently, the parties were *in pari delicto*, and there was no recovery of premiums. It was found that the agent had either forgotten or mistaken the law, and it does appear that policies of the sort in question were

---

[28] Though it would apply, at common law, to contracts with unauthorised insurers. Statute (see note 25) now makes express provision.
[29] (1902) 18 T.L.R. 502.
[30] *Ibid.* at 503, *per* Vaughan Williams and Romer L.JJ.
[31] [1904] 1 K.B. 558; as to this case, see p. 30, above.

being regularly sold at the time. The *Cunliffe* case was distinguished on the ground that it involved fraud. If these conclusions of fact were correct, then the decision in *Harse* is correct in principle, and distinguishable from *Cunliffe*, although it is somewhat difficult to accept without demur, the dictum of Romer L.J.[32] that agents of insurance companies must not be treated as under any greater obligation to know the law than ordinary persons whom they approach with a view to persuading them to effect insurance.

In the last important case on this question, *Hughes v. Liverpool Victoria Legal Friendly Society*,[33] a differently constituted Court of Appeal was somewhat troubled by the decision in *Harse*. *Hughes*, though, was a clear case of an agent fraudulently persuading the plaintiff to take over existing policies on the life of someone in which he could not conceivably have had an insurable interest, there being no relationship at all between them. The plaintiff was held entitled to recover his premiums. All three judges were prepared to assume that there was no fraud or impropriety on the part of the agent in the *Harse* case, because until that case was decided, it was a genuinely open question whether or not a son had an insurable interest in the life of his mother, but Swinfen Eady L.J. commented: "[That decision] must not be regarded as deciding that where a person is induced to insure a life in which he has no interest, by an agent making a misrepresentation of fact, or of mixed fact and law, the parties are necessarily *in pari delicto*." It would seem safe to assume that, at least where the insured has acted quite innocently, the decision in *Harse* would be of little practical importance nowadays.[34]

---

[32] *Ibid.* at 564.
[33] [1916] 2 K.B. 482.
[34] See, *e.g.* the decisions of the Industrial Assurance Commissioner referred to in *MacGillivray & Parkington*, paras. 1015–1019. It is only in the context of industrial life assurance that the point appears ever to have been litigated, perhaps because the usual purchasers of such insurance are more gullible than insureds generally. Certainly, from the dearth of modern reported cases, it would seem that the area is rather academic nowadays.

Chapter 9

ASSIGNMENT

A number of very important questions in insurance law and practice arise under the general heading of Assignment. Essentially, though, there are three distinct, but closely related topics involved. The first concerns the effect of an assignment by the insured of the subject matter of his insurance policy. The second is the assignment of the benefit of a contract of insurance and the third concerns the assignment of a contract of insurance itself. Various points within these topics overlap, but the basic distinctions are crucial. We shall consider each one in turn. On the whole in this chapter we shall not be concerned with assignment in the context of life insurance. This is a suitably self-contained topic more aptly considered in the later chapter (Chapter 17) on life insurance.

ASSIGNMENT OF THE SUBJECT-MATTER OF INSURANCE

The point that arises here concerns insurance of property when that property is sold or otherwise disposed of by the insured. It has been most often considered in connection with the sale and purchase of land, and for this reason we shall concentrate initially on this area, but the principles established in the cases are equally applicable to dealings with personal property. The assignment of the subject-matter of an insurance policy cannot operate to assign the insurance.

Once contracts for the sale of land are exchanged, the purchaser obtains an equitable interest in the property, although the vendor retains the legal estate. At this stage, both parties clearly have an insurable interest in the property and, in practice, both may well be insured as it is standard conveyancing practice, for reasons which will become obvious, for the purchaser to effect insurance on the exchange of contracts. On completion of the purchase, or, where the title to the land is registered, upon registration of the purchaser as proprietor, the legal estate vests in the purchaser and obviously the vendor

Assignment of the Subject-Matter of Insurance 129

ceases to have an insurable interest.[1] If the property is then lost or damaged, he can recover nothing for this reason.

Claim by the purchaser

If, between contract and completion, the purchaser does not insure, the question arises as to whether, in the absence of an assignment of the benefit of the vendor's policy, which we shall consider shortly, he can claim the benefit of the vendor's policy. It is clear that the vendor can recover,[2] as he still has an insurable interest to the extent of his unpaid interest in the property, but the suggestion in one of the cases that supports this[2] that he holds any money received for the benefit of the purchaser was soon dispelled by the decision in the leading case of *Rayner* v. *Preston*.[3]

Here fire destroyed the property which was the subject-matter of the insurance policy effected by P, after P had contracted to sell it to R. Despite this, the contract was completed in accordance with the general rule in conveyancing of real property that the property is at the purchaser's risk from the date of contract, and P received the full agreed purchase price from R. P also received money from his insurers and the action was brought by R claiming that the assignment of the property to him operated also to assign the benefit of the insurance. R argued that, following the contract of sale, P held the land and the insurance contract on trust for him. By a majority, the Court of Appeal denied R's claim, holding that the insurance contract was merely collateral to the main contract and that the relationship between vendor and purchaser of land was not generally that of trustee and beneficiary. In the absence of an express assignment of the insurance policy or monies, which was not in issue, there was no reason to say that P held the money for R.[4] As a result of this decision, P was of course in effect paid twice for the property, but his liability to repay the insurance monies was subsequently established in *Castellain* v. *Preston*,[5] a decision which is examined further in Chapter 15.

---

[1] *Ecclesiastical Commissioners* v. *Royal Exchange Ass. Corp.* (1895) 11 T.L.R. 476.
[2] *Collingridge* v. *Royal Exchange Ass. Corp.* (1877) 3 Q.B.D. 173.
[3] (1881) 18 Ch.D.1.
[4] Note though that R could have used the provisions of the Fires Prevention (Metropolis) Act 1774 to compel reinstatement; James L.J. (1881) 18 Ch.D. at 15. Although James L.J. was the dissenting judge, there has never been any suggestion that his opinion on this point was incorrect. See further, Chapter 14.
[5] (1883) 11 Q.B.D. 380.

Consequences of Rayner v. Preston

The effect of the decision in *Rayner* v. *Preston* may, as we shall see, be mitigated by an assignment of the benefit of the policy, but this may not be possible, for example, because the insurers refuse their required consent. If so, the decision hardly appears justifiable, because it requires that it is advisable that both vendor and purchaser insure, the former at least to the amount he is unpaid, and the latter at least to the amount of the full purchase price for which he will remain liable. This is surely wasteful, and it can hardly matter greatly from the insurer's point of view, if, in fact, the property insured is destroyed and the insured has an insurable interest, to whom the policy monies in fact go. This point is reinforced by the fact that fire policies do often contain a condition giving the purchaser the benefit of the insurance in this sort of case.[5a] Insurers have recognised the harshness of *Rayner* v. *Preston*, and would presumably rely on it only rarely. Despite this, it must not be forgotten that vendor and purchaser do have different interests, and the vendor will generally be concerned to recover in total only the market value of the property, whereas the purchaser will probably want sufficient to rebuild. We shall take up this point again.

Position of the vendor

We have already noted that after completion of the contract for the sale of land, or, indeed, upon receiving full payment,[6] the vendor can no longer recover because he no longer has any insurable interest, unless very exceptionally, he is allowed to and did insure for the purchaser.[7] Indeed his policy will lapse automatically once the subject-matter disappears.[8] This applies equally to the insurance of goods which are sold. In the case of a sale of specific goods, the contract itself may operate as a conveyance of the property,[9] in which case the seller will be able to insure only if he retains actual possession, section 39 of the Sale of Goods Act 1979 giving him a lien for the price despite the transfer of ownership. However, once the seller surrenders possession, the policy will lapse. Thus in *Rogerson* v. *Scottish Auto-*

[5a] It is thought that such a provision would also have the effect of disallowing the insurer from exercising subrogation rights in the vendor's name against the purchaser; see p. 252 below.

[6] *Ziel Nominees Pty. Ltd.* v. *V.A.C.C. Ins. Co. Ltd.* (1976) 50 A.L.J.R. 106.

[7] See the discussion in Chapter 3 at pp. 50–52.

[8] *Rogerson* v. *Scottish Automobile & General Ins. Co. Ltd.* (1931) 48 T.L.R. 17.

[9] Sale of Goods Act 1979, s.18, rule 1. It is open to the parties to agree to the contrary, which often happens in practice.

mobile & General Insurance Co. Ltd.,[10] the insured had a motor policy covering a particular car. He exchanged that car for a new one of a similar type without informing his insurers. The House of Lords held that thereupon his policy lapsed.

It should be noted, though, that this applies only where the insurance policy has a defined subject-matter. Most policies do and must have, simply in order to satisfy the requirement of insurable interest, but it is perfectly possible for a liability policy to exist covering the insured against defined heads of liability to third parties without tying it to particular property. For example, a third party motor policy need not be referable to any particular vehicle; it could cover the insured when driving any vehicle. In *Boss* v. *Kingston*,[11] the insured held a policy insuring third party liabilities in respect of his own described motor-cycle, and when he was driving a motor-cycle not belonging to him with the owner's consent. He sold his motor-cycle, but kept up his policy. One day he drove a friend's motor-cycle, and was charged with driving without insurance.[12] The magistrates convicted him on the ground that his policy had automatically lapsed when he sold his motor-cycle, following the *Rogerson* case, but the Divisional Court held that there was no such automatic lapse. The policy was merely a third party policy and it was not necessarily attached to any property. However, reluctantly they held that the insured had been rightly convicted. On the construction of the policy it had lapsed when the insured sold his motor-cycle, simply because it contained conditions precedent to the insurer's liability which could not be complied with if the motor-cycle was no longer owned by the insured. The distinction from the *Rogerson* case is no doubt a valid one theoretically, but in practice it is unlikely to matter very much. The point is perhaps likely to arise only in the context of motor insurances and such third party policies are likely to contain conditions as in *Boss* v. *Kingston*, compelling the conclusion that on the insured's selling the vehicle the policy lapses, even though strictly the vehicle might not be the subject-matter of the insurance.

In the case of the sale of goods insured where property does not pass at the time of the contract for sale, principally of unascertained goods, there should be no problems. Property[13] and

---

[10] Note 8. See also *Tattersall* v. *Drysdale* [1935] 2 K.B. 174.
[11] [1963] 1 W.L.R. 99.
[12] Road Traffic Act 1972, s.145; see Chapter 19.
[13] Sale of Goods Act 1979, s.18, rule 5.

risk[14] will usually remain with the vendor who can therefore recover if the goods are damaged or destroyed. The purchaser can have no interest in claiming the benefit of any insurance. Once property passes, and the price is paid, the insurance will lapse.

ASSIGNMENT OF THE BENEFIT OF AN INSURANCE POLICY

If the assignment of the subject-matter of an insurance policy does not of itself assign any benefit under the policy to the assignee, the question next arises as to whether or not that benefit might not itself be assigned. It must be stressed that we are not here considering the assignment of the policy or contract itself, but merely of the right to recover any benefits payable under it. There is no doubt that this benefit is a chose in action, one of those intangible pieces of property which can be assigned either at law, under section 136 of the Law of Property Act 1925, or in equity.[15] To bind the insurer, and make the latter directly liable to pay the assignee, notice will have to be given to it so that the assignment is legal. Otherwise the assignee can proceed only by suing the assignor to compel him to claim from the insurer. Such an assignment can take place before or after a loss[16] and the consent of the insurer is irrelevant.[17] What the insured is doing is simply saying that the proceeds from any claim he has or may have are to go to a third party.

However, the assignee will recover only what the assignor/insured is entitled to, that is the measure of the latter's insurable interest, and he will take subject to any rights the insurer may have, for example, to avoid the policy for non-disclosure or breach of warranty. For these reasons, express assignment of the benefit may not avail the purchaser to the extent he would wish in the sort of case of which *Rayner* v. *Preston* (above) is an example.

Statutory assignment

Section 47 of the Law of Property Act 1925 appears to remove the need for this sort of express assignment where the parties

---

[14] Sale of Goods Act 1979, s.20.
[15] For a fuller description of the assignment of choses in action, see Treitel, *Law of Contract*, Chapter 16.
[16] *Cf. Tailby* v. *Official Receiver* (1888) 13 App.Cas. 523; *Peters* v. *General Accident* [1937] 4 All E.R. 628 at 633, *per* Goddard J.
[17] *Re Turcan* (1888) 40 Ch.D. 5.

are the vendor and purchaser of property, whether land or goods. It was clearly intended to overrule the decision in *Rayner v. Preston* and provides, by subsection (1):

> "Where after the date of any contract for sale or exchange of property, money becomes payable under any policy of insurance maintained by the vendor in respect of any damage to or destruction of property included in the contract, the money shall, on completion of the contract, be held by or receivable by the vendor on behalf of the purchaser and paid by the vendor to the purchaser on completion of the sale or exchange, or as soon thereafter as the same shall be received by the vendor."

By subsection 2, the section has effect subject to (*a*) any stipulation to the contrary contained in the contract, which must refer to the contract of sale not the contract of insurance; (*b*) any requisite consents of the insurer; and (*c*) the payment by the purchaser of the proportionate part of the premium from the date of the contract.

The first point to note is that the section does not give the purchaser any direct rights against the insurer, as an express assignment under section 136 would. Secondly, and fundamentally, the question arises as to what section 47 purports to assign. Is it the contract of insurance itself or merely any benefits payable under it? In the absence of any judicial authority, it is suggested that there is no reason to regard the section as purporting to effect an assignment of the policy, as it refers merely to the money becoming payable under any contract of insurance. If this is so, the next question is as to the meaning of the second requirement ((*b*) above) in subsection 2. The ordinary understanding of "any requisite consents" would surely be "any consents as are actually required in the policy," but this is not the view that some of the leading works take.[18] It is often argued that the requirement specifies the need for express consent of the insurer. It is true that in practice this is usually impliedly given by the standard clause in fire policies on buildings to which we have already referred. But it is submitted that, in fact, the consent of the insurer is required only if it is expressly required. The section does not say that it operates "only with the consent of the insurer" and there is no reason to construe it other than with its literal meaning. As we have

---

[18] See, *e.g. MacGillivray and Parkington*, para. 1849; Emmet, *Title*, pp. 42–43.

already argued, section 47 does not purport to assign the contract of insurance itself, in which case, as will be seen shortly, the consent of the insurer would be necessary. It must not be forgotten though, that if the consent of the insurer is, in fact, required, it may well be very difficult for the purchaser to discover this.

It is argued, therefore, that section 47 overrules the decision in *Rayner* v. *Preston* in all but those cases where the insurers' consent is required and is not obtained. However, it may still not be safe for a purchaser to rely upon the section. In the case of contracts for the sale or exchange of land, the purchaser is entitled to only what the vendor is entitled to, in the words of section 47(1), only money that "becomes payable" to the vendor is impressed with the trust. Thus the insurer may have a defence to the vendor's claim and, in any event, the amount of the vendor's insurable interest, the amount which he is entitled to claim, may, following the contract of sale, be less than the full value of the property or the cost of its reinstatement. The vendor's loss can only be the amount for which he has contracted to sell the property less the deposit he has already received from the purchaser. As we noted earlier, it is therefore standard conveyancing practice, and clearly wise practice, for the purchaser to effect his own insurance upon exchange of contracts. As we have argued earlier, this, however, is wasteful and furthermore, it can lead to the problems associated with double insurance.[19] It is clearly time that something was done to alleviate these problems.[20]

Effect of section 47 on goods insurance

As far as contracts for the sale or exchange of goods are concerned, there is no doubt that section 47 applies. However, in the case of specific goods where property may well pass at the time of the contract, it is irrelevant simply because the vendor will have no claim and will have no insurable interest to recover anything to which the purchaser can claim entitlement, unless, exceptionally, the risk remains with him. But in this latter event, the purchaser will not suffer any loss anyway. Where, however, property does not pass at the date of the contract, and a loss occurs before it does, there is no reason why the purchaser should not claim the benefits of any insurance main-

---

[19] See Chapter 16.
[20] See, *e.g.* Aldridge (1974) 124 N.L.J. 966; Adams and Aldridge, *Law Society's Gazette* April 16, 1980.

tained by the vendor, if he in fact chooses to go ahead with the contract, subject to any consent expressly required by the insurer and to the other conditions in section 47(2).

Assignment of the Policy

Prima facie, any insurance policy is freely assignable, being itself a chose in action. This is statutorily confirmed in respect of life policies, which we shall consider separately,[21] and marine policies.[22] However, in respect of all other forms of insurance there are two conditions which must be satisfied before an assignment will be valid.

The first arises out of the personal nature of the insurance contract and requires the consent of the insurers. The result is that, in effect, non-life and non-marine policies are not really assignable, since insurers would consent to an "assignment" to a new insured only in circumstances which would amount to the creation of a new contract or a novation. In *Peters* v. *General Accident Fire and Life Assurance Corporation Ltd.*,[23] the vendor of a van handed over his insurance policy with the defendant insurers to the purchaser. The latter subsequently injured the plaintiff by the negligent driving of the van and the plaintiff sued the insurers under what is now section 149 of the Road Traffic Act 1972.[24] It was held that the insurers were not liable to satisfy the judgment awarded against the purchaser, as the insured vendor could not simply assign his motor policy to the purchaser without the insurers' consent.[25] The policy would in fact, have lapsed upon the sale of the van for the reasons and under the authorities mentioned earlier.

The second necessary condition for a valid assignment of a policy is that it must be contemporaneous with the assignment of the subject-matter of the insurance. Obviously a non-life policy cannot be assigned in the absence of the assignment of

---

[21] See Chapter 17 at pp. 270–273.
[22] Marine Insurance Act 1906, s.50.
[23] [1938] 2 All E.R. 267.
[24] See Chapter 19, at pp. 308–310.
[25] It was also held that the clause in the policy extending the cover to a third party driving with the insured's consent was not applicable as the van was the purchaser's property and he was driving it therefore not with the insured's consent, but by virtue of his ownership.

its subject-matter otherwise the assignee would have no insurable interest. The requirement of strict contemporaneity is well-established in marine insurance[26] and there is no reason to doubt that it applies equally to non-marine policies.

---

[26] *North England Oil Cake Co.* v. *Archangel Marine Ins. Co.* (1875) L.R. 10 Q.B. 249.

Chapter 10

INTERMEDIARIES

The law concerning insurance intermediaries is of special importance since in effect all insurance business is conducted through the medium of agents of one sort or another. Most insurers are and have to be companies or, in exceptional cases, other associations[1] and such bodies can of necessity act only through agents, ranging from directors and senior management down to junior employees. The only category of individual who can be an insurer is a Lloyd's underwriter and by custom he can act only through the agency of a Lloyd's broker. Quite apart from the sorts of intermediary already mentioned, much insurance business is transacted through insurance brokers and other "independent" agencies.

This wide variety of types of agent raises important questions concerning their suitability and qualifications and has led to a number of different mechanisms for their regulation. These are considered at the end of this chapter.[2] It may be helpful though for purposes of identification to attempt a rough classification of the different sorts of agent employed in insurance business. The following is suggested[3]:

(i) Lloyd's Brokers; those brokers recognised by Lloyd's as the people through whom only can a Lloyd's policy be effected. An insured may, of course, act through another intermediary in approaching a Lloyd's broker.

(ii) All other Insurance Brokers; those brokers other than Lloyd's brokers registered under the Insurance Brokers' Registration Act 1977,[4] and hence genuinely independent of any particular insurer or insurers.

(iii) Other "independent" agents, namely those agents not tied to particular insurers, but not registered under the 1977 Act, and hence not entitled to call themselves "insurance brokers."

---

[1] See Insurance Companies Act 1982, ss.2 and 7; see p. 17, above.
[2] See pp. 151–156, below.
[3] See also O'Neill, "Insurance Brokers and their Commission" [1978] J.B.L. 339.
[4] See below pp. 153–155.

(iv) Agents tied to particular insurers, such as their employees and full-time agents such as the canvassing agent. In law the latter may or may not be technically "employees."

(v) Occasional "brokers," meaning people such as motor dealers, solicitors, building societies and estate agents, whose main job is clearly not insurance, but who may sell insurance part-time or as an incidental part of their major work, often having pre-existing links with particular insurers.

Agent of Insurer or Insured

The first question to which we must turn is that of determining whose agent in law a particular intermediary is. This is not something about which it is easy to be dogmatic. As a general rule, only the agent under the direct employment or control of the insurer is the agent of the insurer, and even he may not at all times be such.[5] For most purposes, all other agents are in law the agents of the insured, and this is even so in respect of Lloyd's brokers.[6] However, recent cases have regarded particular brokers as agents of the insurer.[7]

Position of the broker

There is thus an element of uncertainty in an area which is of the greatest practical importance. This is particularly so in the case of brokers and their relationships with the parties to the insurance contract. There are clear decisions which will be examined in detail later that the broker is the agent of the insured. If, therefore, he has notice of certain matters pertaining to the insurance contract, or purports to act on behalf of the insurer, the latter should logically not be deemed to know or be bound by his actions. However, two recent decisions have assumed the contrary. In *Stockton* v. *Mason*[8] M's father, the insured, through his wife, instructed his brokers to transfer his

---

[5] See the line of authority of which *Newsholme Bros.* v. *Road Transport & General Ins. Co.* [1929] 2 K.B. 356 is the leading case, discussed fully in Chapter 7 at pp. 111–116.

[6] *Rozanes* v. *Bowen* (1928) 32 Ll.L.Rep. 98; *Anglo-African Merchants* v. *Bayley* [1970] 1 Q.B. 311; *North & South Trust* v. *Berkeley* [1971] 1 W.L.R. 470; *McNealy* v. *Pennine Ins. Co. Ltd.* [1978] 2 Lloyd's Rep. 18.

[7] *Stockton* v. *Mason* [1978] 2 Lloyd's Rep. 430; *Woolcott* v. *Excess Ins. Co.* [1978] 1 Lloyd's Rep. 633 (original trial), [1979] 1 Lloyd's Rep. 231 (Court of Appeal), [1979] 2 Lloyd's Rep. 210 (retrial).

[8] See note 7 above.

existing motor policy from a Ford Anglia to an M.G. Midget. An employee of the brokers said that this would be all right for a temporary period, which the father naturally assumed meant that the previous policy, which covered the driving of the car by any authorised driver, was thereby transferred to the new car. Subsequently, the brokers wrote saying that cover on the M.G. was restricted to the insured only. M was driving the M.G. when he negligently injured the plaintiff. The issue was whether under the Road Traffic Act 1972,[9] the plaintiff was entitled to sue M's father's insurers[10] and thus it depended on whether the latter were bound by the oral statement of the broker's employee purporting to authorise the M.G. to be substituted entirely for the Anglia. The Court of Appeal, consisting of three Lords of Appeal, held that the insurers were bound. "A broker in non-marine insurance has implied authority to issue on behalf of the insurer, or enter into as agent for the insurer, contracts of interim insurance . . . it seems to me to be quite unarguable that in saying 'Yes, that will be all right. We will see to that, Mrs. Mason,' the brokers were acting as agents for the insurance company and not merely acknowledging an order or request by Mrs. Mason to negotiate a contract with the insurance company on his behalf."[11]

In *Woolcott* v. *Excess Insurance Co. Ltd.*,[12] a case which involved much dispute as to the facts, being referred back by the Court of Appeal to the trial judge on this issue, it was clearly assumed beyond argument by the Court of Appeal that the knowledge of a material fact by the broker in question was imputed to the insurers, and that the latter's defence of non-disclosure of that fact failed, even if the insured did not know that the insurer had the knowledge or was deemed to know.[13]

These two decisions are clearly welcome as according with the reality of the situation, particularly as that is how it is no doubt perceived by insureds. Obviously the extent of the broker's authority to bind the insurer will depend upon considerations which we shall discuss further, later. What is not clear is the extent to which the principles of these cases are generally applicable. In both of them there was a close relation-

---

[9] s.149; see Chapter 19, at pp. 308–310.
[10] The brokers were also sued in the alternative.
[11] [1978] 2 Lloyd's Rep. 430 at 431–432, *per* Lord Diplock.
[12] See note 7 above.
[13] [1979] 1 Lloyd's Rep. 231 at 241–241 (*per* Megaw L.J.); see also [1979] 2 Lloyd's Rep. 210 at 211 (*per* Cantley J.).

ship between the brokers and the insurers, the former being actually authorised to conclude at least interim contracts of insurance. Suppose, however, that an insured negotiates through a broker with an insurer with whom the broker does not have such a relationship, or negotiates through one of the other sorts of agent other than a linked agent of the insurer. If we assume that such a broker or agent may not have actual authority from the insurer, is the insured entitled to rely on principles of apparent authority[14] if, for example, the broker or agent is in possession of proposal forms given to him by an insurer or if the latter has previously regarded itself as bound by representations of the broker or agent as to the cover provided by the insurer?

Broker's duties to the insured

Furthermore, does the broker remain the agent of the insured in any circumstances, so that, for example, he owes fiduciary duties and duties of care and skill to the insured? The answer must be in the affirmative in respect of the latter,[15] but there appears to be a potential conflict otherwise. The decisions in *Anglo-African Merchants* v. *Bayley*[16] and *North and South Trust* v. *Berkeley*[17] established, at least so far as Lloyd's brokers are concerned, that they cannot act for the insurer in investigating a claim without being potentially in breach of duty to their principal, the insured. The issue arose in both cases in relation to documents which, following a claim on the policies, the brokers had prepared for the insurers, which they refused to hand over to the insureds. This was regarded as a clear breach of duty on the ground that their true principals were the insureds and that they could not therefore act in accordance with the insurers' instructions without the consent of the insureds. This must continue to be the law, so that it appears that a broker may indeed be the agent of both insured and insurer. He may on appropriate facts be authorised to act for the latter in terms of granting cover or receiving knowledge of material facts, but otherwise he cannot act for the insurer in the context of investigating a claim without full disclosure of his position to the insured and the latter's consent.

---

[14] For a brief description of apparent or ostensible authority, see below at pp. 142–143.
[15] See the recent cases which are discussed at pp. 146–151.
[16] [1970] 1 Q.B. 311.
[17] [1971] 1 W.L.R. 470.

RELEVANT AGENCY PRINCIPLES

We cannot, in the space available, deal by any means comprehensively with all the principles of agency law which may be applicable to the insurance transaction.[18] We must therefore concentrate on those which appear to be of particular relevance, namely, the question of when a principal is bound by his agent's acts in favour of a third party; the question of when an agent's knowledge is imputed to his principal; and the relationship between principal and agent, especially when the principal is the insured.

Principal and third party

A principal is bound by any of the acts of his agent within the latter's actual, apparent (or ostensible) or usual authority and by an unauthorised act which he ratifies. The problems surrounding the concept of usual authority[19] do not appear to have been considered or indeed to be likely to arise in the insurance context, and need not detain us here.

Actual authority

Actual authority may be expressed or implied. What an agent is expressly authorised to do raises no problems. Implied actual authority arises where in the circumstances it must be the position that the agent had actual authority, but it was never conferred on him in so many words. If an insurer gives his agent blank cover-notes, he impliedly authorises him to effect binding temporary insurance contracts.[20] Similarly, the continuing adoption by the insurer of temporary oral contracts entered into by its agent will confer implied authority on that agent.[21] An example of the principle where the insured was principal is *Zurich General Accident and Liability Insurance Co. Ltd.* v. *Rowberry*,[22] where the brokers were instructed to effect a policy in respect of the insured's forthcoming journey to France. The brokers mistakenly inserted in the proposal form that the

---

[18] See, generally, *Bowstead on Agency* (15th ed.) and Markesinis and Munday, *An Outline of the Law of Agency* (2nd ed.).

[19] See, *e.g.* Markesinis and Munday, *op. cit.*, pp. 24–29.

[20] *Mackie* v. *European Ass. Soc.* (1869) 21 L.T. 102; *Stockton* v. *Mason*, note 7, above.

[21] *Murfitt* v. *Royal Ins. Co.* (1922) 38 T.L.R. 334.

[22] [1954] 2 Lloyd's Rep. 55.

insured's destination was Paris, whereas, in fact, he was going to Nice. The insured attempted to get out of the policy issued on the grounds of this mistake, but it was held that he was bound by the broker's actions, having given them authority to negotiate the proposal with no specific instructions as to his destination.

Ostensible authority

Ostensible or apparent authority arises where the principal, by words or by conduct, holds out his agent as having a particular authority.[23] It is really relevant only when the agent is exceeding his actual authority. The essence of ostensible authority is the representation made by the principal to the third party; it matters not what the agent says, nor whether he is acting fraudulently.[24] Thus, ostensible authority depends upon an estoppel, usually the representation being the conduct of the principal rather than anything expressly said.[25] Appointing an agent to a particular position confers on him ostensible authority to bind his principal in respect of the usual acts which someone in that position would have authority to do, and it is irrelevant, unless the third party is aware of this, in which case there can be no reliance on the representation,[26] that the agent is actually not authorised to do some of the usual acts.

Someone who holds the position of inspector in an insurance company will probably be regarded as having ostensible authority to vary the terms of a proposal form.[27] The payment of premiums to an agent will bind the insurer even if he is not authorised to accept them, if, nonetheless, he is held out as having authority to receive them.[28] The receiving of notice of loss by an agent, if he is the person with whom the insured has always dealt, should bind the insurer, unless there is an express indication to the contrary; the latter would negate any representation allegedly made by the insurer.[29] An agent held out as

---

[23] See generally, *e.g. Freeman & Lockyer* v. *Buckhurst Park Properties* [1964] 2 Q.B. 480.

[24] *Lloyd* v. *Grace, Smith & Co.* [1912] A.C. 716.

[25] An insurance example is *Eagle Star Ins. Co.* v. *Spratt* [1971] 2 Lloyd's Rep. 116.

[26] *Wilkinson* v. *General Accident Fire & Life Ass. Corp. Ltd.* [1967] 2 Lloyd's Rep. 182.

[27] *Stone* v. *Reliance Mutual Ins. Soc. Ltd.* [1972] 1 Lloyd's Rep. 469; see pp. 114–115, above.

[28] *Kelly* v. *London and Staffs. Fire Ins. Co.* (1883) Cab. & E. 47.

[29] *Brook* v. *Trafalgar Ins. Co.* (1946) 79 Ll.L.Rep. 365.

having authority to make alterations in a policy or to waive a breach of condition will bind the insurer.[30] Similarly, the furnishing of an agent with cover-notes gives that agent ostensible authority to conclude such temporary contracts, even if the insurer has expressly forbidden this so that implied actual authority is not available. On the other hand, an agent will never, it seems, unless of course authorised, as the directors would be or a branch manager might be, have authority to bind the insurer by the issue of a formal policy,[31] nor will he have authority to fill in a proposal form on behalf of the insured at least if he is a mere canvassing agent,[32] although this rather curious rule has been commented on earlier.[33] An agent of the insurer has no authority to bind his principal as to the meaning or construction of a policy, though this is not so much as a result of a lack of authority as of the rule that such a representation would be a representation of law, and in general these are not binding.[34]

Ratification

Even an unauthorised act not binding a principal by virtue of the principles of ostensible authority may, however, be ratified by the principal, provided that the agent was purporting to act as an agent[35] and that the principal was in existence and identifiable at the time of the agent's act. Ratification dates back to the time of the original act of the agent,[36] but it appears that in non-marine insurance it is not possible to ratify after a loss has taken place. Thus, in *Grover & Grover* v. *Mathews*,[37] where a broker effected without authority a renewal of the insured's policy, and the insured suffered a loss before he knew about the broker's actions, it was held that the insurer was not liable even though the insured ratified what the broker had done. It is, however, strongly arguable that this case was wrongly decided.[38]

---

[30] *Wing* v. *Harvey* (1854) 5 De G.M. & G. 265, see p. 144, below.
[31] *Stockton* v. *Mason*. Note 7, above; *British Bank of the Middle East* v. *Sun Life Assurance Co. of Canada (U.K.) Ltd.* [1983] 2 Lloyd's Rep. 9.
[32] *Newsholme* v. *Road Transport & General Ins. Co.*, [1929] 2 K.B. 356.
[33] See Chapter 7 at pp. 113–114.
[34] *Re Hooley Rubber & Chemical Man. Co.* [1920] 1 K.B. 257; cf. *Harr* v. *Allstate Ins. Co.* 54 N.J. 287 (1969).
[35] An undisclosed principal can sue and be bound only if the agent had actual authority: see generally, Bowstead, pp. 51–84..
[36] *Bolton Partners* v. *Lambert* (1888) 41 Ch.D. 295.
[37] [1910] 2 K.B. 401.
[38] See p. 50, above.

Imputing the agent's knowledge

Of particular importance in the context of insurance are the rules whereby, in certain cases, the knowledge of an agent is imputed to his principal so that the latter is deemed to know what the agent knows. These will be examined here only in the context of the agent being the agent of the insurer, that is where an insured is seeking to rely upon them.

Most commonly, the issue will relate to material facts of which the insurer alleges non-disclosure by the insured, but which the latter claims are deemed to be known by the insurer by virtue of its agent's knowledge. *Woolcott* v. *Excess Insurance Co.*,[39] which was described earlier,[40] is an example, and the matter was considered fully in the context of non-disclosure.[41] In general the agent's knowledge will be imputed to the insurer, because he will have been held out as having authority to receive it, but the position may well be different if an incorrect answer is given on a proposal form, even though the agent knows the truth.[42]

Another illustration would be where the agent knows of something which constitutes a breach of warranty or condition by the insured. His knowledge of the breach may be imputed to the insurer who may therefore, by subsequently accepting premiums, be deemed to have waived the breach. In *Wing* v. *Harvey*,[43] a life policy provided that it would become void if the assured travelled beyond the limits of Europe without the insurer's consent. An assignee of the policy subsequently informed an agent of the insurer that the life assured had taken up residence in Canada. For some time after this, before the life assured died, premiums were received by the insurer. It was held that the insurer had waived the breach of warranty; they were deemed to know what their agent knew and having accepted premiums subsequently, could not rely upon the breach.

What knowledge will be imputed depends upon the status of the agent receiving it, in other words, upon his actual or ostensible authority. In *Wing* v. *Harvey*, the agent was the local representative of the insurer at a branch office. A mere canvassing or soliciting agent would probably not be regarded as having

---

[39] [1979] 1 Lloyd's Rep. 231.
[40] p. 139.
[41] See pp. 85–86, above.
[42] *Newsholme Bros.* v. *Road Transport & General Ins. Co.*, above; Chapter 7 at pp. 112–114.
[43] (1854) 5 De G.M. & G. 265.

such a wide authority, which is after all tantamount to varying the terms of the policy, but such an agent probably has authority to receive disclosures of material facts.[44]

Relationship between principal and agent

If, for some reason, a principal cannot enforce a contract against a third party or he is liable to a third party because of the unauthorised acts of his agent, he may well have a remedy against the agent. Equally the relationship of principal and agent is a fiduciary one and duties arise as a result.

For example, the insurer bound by a contract which he could have avoided for non-disclosure had his agent not known the non-disclosed facts and his knowledge been imputed to the insurer, can sue the agent for damages, being the amount of money which he has had to pay the insured.[45] Similarly, if an agent acts beyond his actual authority, but the insurer is liable by virtue of the principles of ostensible authority, the insurer will have a damages remedy against the agent.

It is more likely in practice, however, that it is the insured seeking a remedy against his agent, commonly, but not necessarily, his broker. Indeed brokers must now themselves be insured against this potential liability.[46] In this context, it is usual and convenient to split up the heads of liability into two; that arising by virtue of the fiduciary relationship between the insured and his agent, and the duties of care and skill required of an agent.

Fiduciary duties

A fiduciary relationship carries with it strict duties, in particular the overriding one that the fiduciary, the agent, must not put himself into a position where his own interests do or may conflict with his duties to his principal.[47] This means, *inter alia*, that he must not act for another in a matter relating to his principal without full disclosure to and the consent of his principal. It used to be standard practice for Lloyd's brokers to act for the underwriter in certain matters, despite the fact that, as was mentioned earlier, they are in law agents of the insured. This

---

[44] *Ayrey* v. *British Legal & United Provident Ass.* [1918] 1 K.B. 136; *Blackley* v. *National Mutual Life Ass. of Australasia* [1972] N.Z.L.R. 1038; see Chapter 6 at pp. 85–86.
[45] *Woolcott* v. *Excess Ins. Co.*, above.
[46] See p. 155, below.
[47] *Boardman* v. *Phipps* [1967] 2 A.C. 46.

practice was condemned in *Anglo-African Merchants* v. *Bayley*[48] as clearly constituting a breach of fiduciary duty, unless the insured consented. Shortly afterwards the point arose again in *North and South Trust* v. *Berkeley*,[49] where a claim by the insured was investigated by assessors instructed by the brokers. Their report was handed to the brokers who showed it to the underwriters, but refused to let the insured have sight of it or know what it contained. They were thereupon sued by the insured who relied upon the earlier decision as establishing that the brokers had acted in breach of duty. Donaldson J. again condemned the practice of brokers acting for both parties and held that what had been done was a breach of duty, but, apart from admitting the possibility of a claim for damages by the insured, which was not, in fact, sought,[50] he refused to give the insured the remedy they did seek, namely, an order for delivery of the documents. This is rather curious,[51] but as it was expressly stated by the learned judge that a remedy would be available in future cases, the unsatisfactory nature of this decision need not detain us further.

Duties of care and skill

In respect of the duties of care and skill, there is no doubt that an agent such as a broker owes a duty to his client, the insured, to take reasonable care and skill. A comparatively high number of recently reported cases reveals what an important head of liability this potentially is. It should be noted that the insured's cause of action is in damages for breach of duty in contract or tort.[52] If what the insured is claiming is in effect the damages he has to pay to an injured third party, for example, this relates only to the measure of the broker's liability. The claim is not in respect of damages for personal injury, so that the relevant limitation period is six years, not three years.[53]

In advising his client with whom to insure, the broker must take due care. In *Osman* v. *J. Ralph Moss*,[54] the defendant brokers recommended to the plaintiff that he effect a motor

[48] [1970] 1 Q.B. 311.
[49] [1971] 1 W.L.R. 470.
[50] *Quaere*, how valuable such a remedy might in practice be.
[51] See the trenchant criticism by Kay and Yates (1972) 35 M.L.R. 78.
[52] *Osman* v. *J. Ralph Moss Ltd.* [1970] 1 Lloyd's Rep. 313. It would require significant fault on the part of the insured before a negligent broker could successfully plead the defence of contributory negligence: *Mint Security Ltd.* v. *Blair* [1982] 1 Lloyd's Rep. 188.
[53] *Ackbar* v. *Green* [1975] Q.B. 582.
[54] Note 52, above.

policy with an insurer already well-known in insurance circles to be in a serious financial situation and which in fact was subsequently wound up, leaving the plaintiff uninsured. As a result, the plaintiff was convicted of driving without insurance and involved in an accident for which he was liable, with no insurer to foot the bill. The plaintiff was of Turkish origin and had difficulty in reading and understanding English. The only warning the defendants gave him was a letter asking him simply to insure elsewhere. It was held that the defendants were liable in damages for the amount he was fined and the damages he had to pay the third party. What is not completely clear is how much turned on the fact that the plaintiff was not really literate in English, so that the letter which the defendants sent could not possibly have been enough to satisfy the duty they owed him. The decision does not actually hold that a broker must always expressly warn his client of the impending insolvency of his insurer, if he is aware or ought to be aware of this, and there are passages in the judgments[55] referring to the particular position of the plaintiff. It is suggested that brokers ought to be under a duty at all times to all classes of insured to advise and warn about particular insurers, not just as to their financial stability but also as to the suitability of particular policies and their general record in treating their insureds, for example, as to their generosity in paying claims.[55a] It seems clear that a broker who fails to warn the insured of any special terms incorporated on renewal is negligent.[56]

Another instance of negligent advice arose in *Cherry Ltd.* v. *Allied Insurances Brokers Ltd.*[57] Here the defendants had been the plaintiff's brokers for some 50 years, but the plaintiffs became dissatisfied and proposed to put their business elsewhere. As a result, they wished to cancel all their policies held through the defendants well before their renewal date, and they instructed the defendants to seek to do so. The defendants cancelled most of the policies but advised the plaintiffs that the particular insurer concerned would not accept cancellation of the plaintiff's consequential loss policy. The plaintiffs having effected a new policy of this sort thereupon cancelled it to avoid

---

[55] Sachs L.J. at 315; Phillimore L.J. at 319.
[55a] There were many successful unreported claims on this basis in 1984 and 1985 against brokers who sold largely worthless life insurance policies issued by Signal Life, a Gibraltar-based concern not authorised to act in the United Kingdom.
[56] *Mint Security Ltd.* v. *Blair* [1982] 1 Lloyd's Rep. 188.
[57] [1978] 1 Lloyd's Rep. 274.

being doubly insured. Subsequently, however, that first insurer did agree to a cancellation of the original policy, but the defendants failed to advise the plaintiffs of this. The latter then suffered a loss for which, because both policies had been cancelled, they were uninsured. It was held that the defendants were negligent in failing to advise the plaintiffs of the first insurer's cancellation, and were liable in damages for the amount which the plaintiffs would have recovered from their insurer had they been insured.

Duty regarding disclosure of material facts

Several cases have been concerned with the broker's position in respect of the duty of the insured to disclose material facts and not to make misrepresentations. This is obviously a crucial area as the insured who is dealing with a broker will not, in practice, have any direct communication with his insurer, and thus the exact nature of the broker's duty with regard to advising his client about such matters is vital. If the broker fails to ask the insured questions about facts which he, the broker, knows are material, he will be liable in damages to the insured if the insurer subsequently avoids liability. In *McNealy* v. *Pennine Insurance Co.*,[58] the plaintiff effected motor insurance through brokers. He was a part-time musician, a fact which, it was held, was material to the risk. The insurance company with which the brokers effected the insurance in fact refused to cover musicians, among other groups, and was not told that the plaintiff was one. It was held that the brokers were liable in damages in respect of the plaintiff's liability to a third party, the insurer having avoided their policy. The brokers with their knowledge that the insurer refused to cover certain risks were under a duty to the insured to ask him whether or not he was affected by this.

It would seem to follow that the same result would apply if the broker actually knows of material facts which he fails to disclose to the insurer.[59] In this regard, though, there is a conflict between *dicta* in *McNealy* and the decision in *Woolcott* v. *Excess Insurance Co.*[60] which was considered earlier.[61] In the latter case it was held that the broker's knowledge was imputed to the insurer who could not therefore avoid the policy for non-

---

[58] [1978] 2 Lloyd's Rep. 18.
[59] *Woolcott* v. *Excess Ins. Co.*, [1979] 1 Lloyd's Rep. 231; *Ogden* v. *Reliance Fire Sprinkler Co.* [1975] 1 Lloyd's Rep. 52.
[60] See note 59.
[61] See p. 139, above.

disclosure. In *McNealy* the view was clearly expressed[62] that the broker was solely the agent of the insured. On this basis there is no ground for imputation of knowledge.[63] While such disparity is unsatisfactory, it may not matter greatly to the insured. On the *Woolcott* basis, he will recover from his insurer who, in turn, will recover from the broker as happened in that case. On the *McNealy* basis, he will recover from his broker directly. However, one situation where the conflict could be crucial is if the broker is insolvent and, following *McNealy*, the court held that his knowledge of a material fact was not imputed to the insurer. In practice the insured would be remediless.

If the broker is unaware of material facts, and there are no special circumstances as in *McNealy* requiring him to quiz the insured, it appears unlikely that the court would hold that the broker was under a duty to warn the insured of his duty of disclosure. In *Warren v. Sutton*,[64] the plaintiff had a motor policy with the Legal and General. He was going on holiday to France with a friend whom he wished to share the driving with him. So he arranged for the friend to be covered under his policy. However, the latter had an appalling driving record with several convictions, none of which was disclosed to the insurer, so that the latter was able to avoid the policy and not pay in respect of an accident that occurred in France.[65] The plaintiff had arranged the policy and the extension through the defendant brokers whom he sued for damages. The facts of the case were somewhat complex and there was a crucial conflict of evidence, but it was found that the broker actually said to the insurer that there were "no accidents, convictions or disabilities" when the extension was being arranged. On this basis, the majority of the Court of Appeal held the broker liable. He had made a false representation to the insurance company in breach of his duty to the plaintiff. Lord Denning M.R. dissented strongly on the ground that the fault all lay with the plaintiff who never told the broker or insurer about his friend's record. However, the majority were clearly influenced by the trial judge's much more favourable assessment of the plaintiff as

---

[62] Lord Denning M.R. [1978] 2 Lloyd's Rep. 18 at 20.
[63] See the discussion at p. 139, above.
[64] [1976] 2 Lloyd's Rep. 276.
[65] The friend was in fact driving at the time, though this was legally irrelevant. The insurer was liable in respect of the damages he had to pay for personal injuries, because of restrictions similar to those in the Road Traffic Act 1972 (see Chapter 19), but escaped liability in respect of third party property damage.

witness than the defendant broker. The broker's representation to the insurer was clearly false. He was under a duty to obtain cover for the friend and to make such enquiries as were necessary. Thus, not having made such enquiries, he was solely responsible for the representation he made, and it was this representation which was the cause of the insurer's repudiation. If, however, the broker had not made the representation, and the reason for the insurer's repudiation had simply been non-disclosure by the insured of which the broker was unaware, it appears that the result would have been the other way.[66] This supports the view that the court would not hold a broker under a duty to warn the insured of his duty of disclosure in the abstract.

Further support can perhaps be found in another Court of Appeal decision on a related point.[67] In *O'Connor* v. *Kirby*,[68] the plaintiff insured his car through the defendant broker. For some reason[69] the latter incorrectly answered a question on the proposal form relating to the garaging of the car and the insurer subsequently avoided the policy for breach of warranty. The plaintiff sued the broker for failing to complete the form properly. It was held that he was not liable, as the plaintiff had signed the form containing the mistake and was solely responsible because it was his duty to see that the information therein was correct.[70] It is suggested that this reasoning is suspect in the light of the consideration that the insured dealing with a broker does place great reliance, and naturally so, on the latter. Far more satisfactory, it is submitted, is the reasoning of Megaw L.J. to the effect that a broker who completes a proposal form does owe a duty to the insured to take reasonable care that its contents are correct, but that in the circumstances the broker had fulfilled that duty since the mistake was at most due only to a slip or misunderstanding and the broker had given the form to the insured to check.[71] That this is the better ratio seems to be supported by the recent decision in *Dunbar* v. *A. & B. Painters*

---

[66] See Browne L.J. at 281.

[67] This was relied upon by Lord Denning M.R. in his dissenting judgment in *Warren* v. *Sutton*; it was not cited by the other members of the Court of Appeal in that case.

[68] [1972] 1 Q.B. 90.

[69] There was some evidence of collusion between the parties in order to get cheaper cover; this can hardly have disposed the court to look favourably on the plaintiff's claim.

[70] Following the *Newsholme* line of cases; see Chapter 7 at pp. 111–116.

[71] Compare *Reid* v. *Traders' General Insurance Co.* (1963) 41 D.L.R. (2d) 148.

*Ltd.*⁷² Here brokers who inserted incorrect answers on a proposal form were held liable in damages since it was shown that the answers required fell especially within the broker's knowledge. However, it seems likely that this last factor is crucial. If the broker is not in possession of the relevant information, primary responsibility in respect of both non-disclosure of material facts and the answering of questions seems to fall on the insured rather than the broker.

Measure of damages

If a broker is liable in damages to the insured, the measure of damages will, as has been seen, usually be that sum which the insured would have recovered from the insurer had the latter been liable. If the breach of duty by the broker is a failure to effect insurance at all, the question has arisen whether it is open to him to say that even if he had obtained the cover, the insurer would still not have been liable, and hence he should not be liable, because of some breach by the insured. The point arose neatly in *Fraser* v. *Furman*,⁷³ where the broker had failed in his duty to effect employer's liability cover for the plaintiff. The broker argued, however, that the insurer would not have been liable for the loss that subsequently occurred, because the plaintiff would have been in breach of a condition in the policy to take reasonable precautions to avoid loss. The Court of Appeal held that the broker was liable for the full amount of loss suffered by the plaintiff. Even if the defence would have been available to the insurer, which was doubted,⁷⁴ the fact was that in the circumstances the insurer in question would not have repudiated liability. Therefore, the question depends on the likely attitude of the insurer rather than the strict point as to whether, in fact, the insurer would have been legally liable.⁷⁵

THE REGULATION OF INTERMEDIARIES

In an important study in 1970, the Consumer Council drew attention to the plethora of advice-giving intermediaries in the

---

⁷² [1986] 2 Lloyd's Rep. 38, affirming [1985] 2 Lloyd's Rep. 616. The decision in *O'Connor* v. *Kirby* was not cited in this case.

⁷³ [1967] 1 W.L.R. 898. See also *Everett* v. *Hogg Robinson* [1973] 2 Lloyd's Rep. 217 and *Dunbar* v. *A. B. Painters Ltd.*, note 72, above.

⁷⁴ See further on this point, Chapter 18 at p. 289.

⁷⁵ But the position may be different if the insurance which the broker should have effected would have been void: *Thomas Cheshire & Co.* v. *Vaughan Bros. & Co.* [1920] 3 K.B. 240.

insurance industry and the consequently confusing picture facing the consumer. Anyone was entitled to set up in the business of selling insurance and call himself an insurance broker or give himself a similar fancy title, but this did not by any means necessarily imply competence or completely independent and impartial guidance. Also well documented is the potential conflict between the intermediary's duty to get the best deal for his client and his own interests in getting the best deal for himself. For example, where insurance is sold on a commission basis, the intermediary may well try to persuade the client to accept the policy that pays him the best rate of commission, rather than that which is best suited to the client's needs. There was an overwhelming case for the regulation of insurance intermediaries[76] and now the position has been remedied to some extent at least. Whether enough has yet been done we shall consider later. The regulatory provisions in existence at present can be examined under two heads; first those applying generally to all intermediaries, and secondly the requirements surrounding the registration and regulation of insurance brokers. What are described here are the relevant statutory provisions concerning general insurance. Space precludes detailed examination of the provisions applying to the selling of most forms of life insurance[77] or of the self-regulatory control on non-broker intermediaries selling general insurance.[78]

General regulation

The provisions applying generally seek to ensure that intermediaries who are not genuinely independent of a particular insurer reveal that fact. Regulations 67 to 69 of the Insurance Companies Regulations,[79] made under section 74 of the Insurance Companies Act 1982, require any intermediary who is connected with the insurance company with which he is suggesting that a proposer for insurance, ordinarily resident in

---

[76] See the British Insurance Brokers' Association Consultative Document (1976); *Insurance Intermediaries* 1977, Cmnd. 6715; see generally, Morgan (1978) L.M.C.L.Q. 39.

[77] These are governed by the Conduct of Business Rules made by the Securities and Investment Board under the Financial Services Act 1986. As to the forms of life insurance covered by this Act, see p. 59, above.

[78] See the *General Insurance Business—Code of Practice for all Intermediaries (Including Employees of Insurance Companies) other than Registered Insurance Brokers*, promulgated by the Association of British Insurers in 1987, revising the earlier code issued in 1981. For a brief description see Birds, "Self-regulation and insurance contracts," *New Foundations for Insurance Law*, 1987, pp. 8–11.

[79] S.I. 1981 No. 1654, replacing regulations first made in 1976.

the United Kingdom, contracts,[80] to disclose in writing details of his connection, and require information of a similar sort where the insurer is not authorised under the 1982 Act, *i.e.* where it is an overseas insurer.[81] Failure to comply with either of these requirements is a criminal offence. "Connection" for these purposes is defined quite widely in regulation 67, and comprises the cases where the intermediary or any partner, director, controller or manager of the intermediary is a partner, director, controller or manager of the insurer or of any controller thereof; the converse case where the insurer etc. is a partner etc. of the intermediary; the case where the intermediary or controller thereof has a significant interest[82] in the shares of the insurer or any controller thereof and vice versa; and the case where the intermediary, under any contract or arrangement whether legally enforceable or not, other than a contract of employment, with an insurer or associated company, undertakes not to perform any services relating to any sort of insurance business for any other insurance company. Under the last case, the employee of an insurer is excluded but not, for example, an agent under a contract for services who is tied to a particular insurer.

Where the suggestion from the intermediary to insure is written, the information must be sent or delivered at the same time. Where the suggestion is oral, the information must be disclosed orally there and then, and confirmed in writing, either immediately where the person is present, or as soon as reasonably practicable by post where the person is not present, in other words, where the matter was discussed by telephone. An easy way of satisfying these requirements, sanctioned in regulation 68(4), where the suggestion to insure is on notepaper, is to include the relevant details on the notepaper. In the case of a Lloyd's Broker, a simple statement of that fact suffices.

Regulation of brokers

The Consumer Council study mentioned above recommended the licensing of brokers as a safeguard against the

---

[80] The wide wording of reg. 68(1) of the Regulations is [invite] "to make an offer or proposal or to take any other steps with a view to entering into a contract of insurance with an insurance company."

[81] The Regulations do not apply to reinsurance contracts nor to industrial assurance or marine, aviation or transport insurance. Furthermore, there are a number of exceptions in reg. 69, particularly relating to certain renewals.

[82] Basically 5 per cent., or more; the Regulations apply certain provisions of the Companies Act 1985 for this purpose.

dangers already outlined. At the suggestion of the Department of Trade, this was taken up in 1976 by the then main association representing brokers, the British Insurance Brokers' Association. Their Consultative Document was approved by the Government,[83] and formed the basis of a Private Member's Bill which had Government backing and became the Insurance Brokers (Registration) Act 1977. Widely hailed as an important advance in protecting the interests of consumers of insurance, which it undoubtedly is, albeit by itself it may be incomplete, the Act effects with statutory backing a self-regulatory machinery not dissimilar to that which exists with respect to solicitors. In other words, the profession has statutory power to regulate itself, but Government approval is required of the Code of Conduct issued under the Act, and there are Government nominees on the Insurance Brokers Registration Council, the body charged with supervising the regulating machinery.[84]

Briefly, the Act requires that all brokers be registered with the Council. Acting as an insurance broker without registration is by section 22 a criminal offence, punishable on conviction on indictment by an unlimited fine. Rather curiously, however, the use of any other title, for example "insurance consultant" or "insurance advisor,"' and acting under such a title by an unregistered "broker," is not prohibited. This is arguably an unnecessary loophole. Mr. Average is unlikely to be aware of the provisions and effect of the 1977 Act, and may be equally as impressed by someone describing himself as "insurance consultant" as by the title "insurance broker."

The Council is under a duty to etablish and maintain a register of insurance brokers (s.2). To be registered, an applicant basically has to possess a recognised qualification and have three years' experience in the profession, and the Council must be satisfied as to his character and suitability and compliance with solvency and independence from insurers. An unqualified applicant may apply for registration if he has five years' experi-

---

[83] *Insurance Intermediaries* (1977) Cmnd. 6715; note also the EEC developments in this area, described by Morgan in the article referred to in note 76.

[84] See the Schedule to the 1977 Act. Note that the 1977 Act is amended in certain respects by the Financial Services Act 1986, s.138, primarily to ensure compatibility between the 1977 Act and the system of self-regulation in the financial services sector, including most forms of life insurance, established by the 1986 Act. The rules under the latter Act will regulate the selling of most forms of life insurance by other than registered brokers or full-time employees of insurers.

ence.[85] There is provision for appeal against a refusal to register (s.4).[86]

Under section 10, the Council has drawn up a Code of Conduct[87] and under sections 11 and 12, has made rules as to the conduct of insurance brokers' businesses.[88] Essentially, these rules require brokers[89] to have a minimum working capital of at least £1,000 and a margin of solvency of at least the same figure, to maintain independence from particular insurers, regarding which a questionnaire has to be completed every year, to keep insurance money in a separate bank account, to submit annual accounts to the Council, and to take out specified professional indemnity insurance. In addition, there is a scheme under section 12(2) of the Act whereby people who suffer loss from the bankruptcy, negligence or fraud of a registered broker are entitled to compensation.

Sections 13 to 20 of the Act provide for disciplinary proceedings,[90] the Council being empowered, *inter alia*, to investigate complaints from the public and, if necessary, to remove the name of a broker from the register.[91]

Future regulation

We have already noted the gap in the 1977 Act, and it is clear in general that that Act provides for only a partial regulation of insurance intermediaries. Bearing in mind the rough categorisation which we gave at the beginning of this chapter, it is clear that there are categories of intermediary who are still in a position to mislead the public, although of course this is not to suggest that all, or even most, of them would do so. A Government White Paper, *Insurance Intermediaries*,[92] promised to take the matter further. Among its tentative proposals[93] was the crucial one that insurance ought to be allowed to be sold only by regis-

---

[85] That the Council can insist on full-time experience during the five years was confirmed in *Pickles v. Insurance Brokers Registration Council* [1984] 1 All E.R. 1073.

[86] See further as to the qualifications, etc., S.I. 1978 No. 1395, S.I. 1979 No. 490 and S.I. 1985 No. 1804.

[87] S.I. 1978 No. 1394.

[88] S.I. 1979 No. 489, as amended by S.I. 1981 No. 1680, and S.I. 1987 No. 1496.

[89] Lloyd's brokers are exempted from some of the requirements.

[90] See also, S.I. 1978 Nos. 1456, 1457 and 1458.

[91] The court is slow to interfere with the exercise of these powers: *James v. Insurance Brokers Registration Council, The Times*, February 16, 1984.

[92] 1977, Cmnd. 6715.

[93] It also envisaged the reversal of the *Newsholme* rule; see Chapter 7 at p. 114.

156 *Intermediaries*

tered brokers, insurers or their employees and agents of either of these, for whom their principals would be fully responsible. The clear intention was that part-time agents and unregistered "brokers" would disappear except in circumstances where insurers were prepared to take full responsibility for them. Since the White Paper, insurers have undertaken a measure of self-regulation in this respect.[94] It remains to be seen whether this will prove sufficient.[95]

---

[94] See note 78, above.
[95] For a valuable paper on the sales techniques adopted by insurance intermediaries, see the report of the Office of Fair Trading, *The Selling of Insurance Policies* (December 1986).

Chapter 11

CONSTRUCTION AND CAUSATION: RISKS COVERED AND RISKS EXCEPTED

Introduction

It may fairly be surmised that the average consumer, and quite possibly a fair number of businessmen, do not read and fully understand their insurance policies at the time they receive them.[1] When the possibility of a claim arises, no doubt many people do make an attempt to discover whether or not they are covered for a particular loss, but even then, it may be doubted whether they actually sit down and read through and fully comprehend their policy from cover to cover. The same must be true of many other contracts, but at least in so far as the other classic consumer-type or standard-form contracts are concerned, whether relating to sales of goods, for cash or on credit, or to the provision of services, for example, there is a broad range of statutory control of one form or another.[2] In the insurance field, freedom of contract survives untramelled, and thus the only way to know whether or not a particular loss is within the ambit of a particular policy is to apply to the insurance contract the general principles of construction applicable to all written contracts. It is to the description and illustration of such principles that this chapter is partly devoted. Even then, however, to refer to the rules of construction as affecting only risks covered and risks excepted is misleading, because these principles may well apply to the other contents of the insurance contract, for example, the meaning of questions and answers on a proposal form, or the warranties and conditions in a policy.

It must also be pointed out that in certain respects, it is not

---

[1] In a survey of motor insureds conducted on behalf of Sentry Insurance in 1977, 64 per cent. claimed to have read their policies and 47 per cent. to have had them explained to them, but high percentages were still mistaken in respect of important aspects of the cover provided.

[2] From, *e.g.* the Sale of Goods Act 1979, the Consumer Credit Act 1974 and the Unfair Contract Terms Act 1977 controlling contract terms, to the Fair Trading Act 1973 vesting wide administrative powers in the Director General of Fair Trading. Recently the Office of Fair Trading has shown more interest in insurance: see especially its report on *Household Insurance* (September 1985) and its report on *The Selling of Insurance Policies* (December 1986).

strictly accurate to refer to the construction of words, rather the problem is one of describing their scope. For example, what "loss" means in the context of an insurance policy, a question which is considered later in this chapter, is not so much a question of construction, but of description or definition. The same can be said of the word "accident," another word commonly found in insurance policies, which we shall also consider later. The rules of construction do not help in finding out what these words mean, but some principles must be found to assist in explaining or defining them. This, it is suggested, justifies the consideration of those standard words in this chapter.

It is self-evident, given the great range of actual and potential sorts of insurance and the variety of insurers, that the actual number of words or phrases whose meanings may not be immediately apparent in all the insurance contracts which exist may be very large. Here, it is impossible to cover the whole ground, and the general points only can be illustrated. Some slight further guidance may be found in the later chapters dealing with specific types of insurance. In any event, it is felt that the approach adopted is justified on the ground that this is an attempt to elucidate the principles, not to give a totally comprehensive A-Z guide. Full citation of the authorities actually available on particular wordings can be found in the standard larger works on insurance law.

Although as a matter of construction, a loss may fall within the risks covered by a particular policy, it may still be necessary for the insured to show that the loss was caused by such a risk and not predominantly by an uninsured risk. This problem of causation it is convenient to consider also in this chapter. In addition, there are some general considerations regarding the nature of risks under an insurance contract which will be examined.

General

It is suggested that there are two points that can usefully be made at this stage before we examine the rules of construction in detail. To an extent these follow from comments already made in the introductory remarks. These are that there is no requirement that an insurance policy be reasonably intelligible in terms of content, and there is no requirement that it be especially legible. Insurance policies are still on the whole notoriously complex documents riddled with jargon, their layout is often muddled to the untrained eye, and the print, or some of it, may be very small. In one marine insurance case, *Koskas* v. *Standard Marine Insurance Co. Ltd.*,[3] the judge at first instance refused to allow the insurer to rely upon a particular condition on the grounds that the print was so small that it was barely legible. The Court of Appeal,[4] however, overruled this bold attempt to interfere because the print was legible, albeit with difficulty.

Judges have on occasion railed against insurers for not producing their policies in a form intelligible to the ordinary consumer,[5] and consumer representatives and bodies, including the Director General of Fair Trading[6] and the Insurance Ombudsman have frequently made the same point. The Law Commission clearly intended that conditions and exceptions in insurance contracts should be brought within the ambit of what became the Unfair Contract Terms Act 1977,[7] but pressure from the insurance industry secured their exclusion from that Act[8] in return for their agreeing to promulgate the Statements of Insurance Practice.[9] We have already commented on the terms of these Statements,[10] and it must be quite clear that they are no substitute for statutory control. Such detailed control in this country must be regarded as extremely unlikely ever to occur, so it is pleasant to record that the sort of pressure on insurers mentioned can pay off. A number of insurers have introduced policies for individual insureds which are clearly worded in modern English and which the average man ought to be able to read and understand. This, of course, does not ensure that he will read and understand, nor does it necessarily mean that construction problems will not arise, but it does illustrate what can be done by a concerned insurer.

American approaches

While certain judges may have complained occasionally about the form of insurance policies, there are very few signs of any attempt to give weight to criticism by the adoption of rules

---

[3] (1926) 25 Ll.L.R. 363.
[4] (1927) 27 Ll.L.R. 61.
[5] See, *e.g.* Lord Wright in *Provincial Ins. Co.* v. *Morgan* [1932] A.C. 240 at 252.
[6] See the reports referred to in note 2 above.
[7] Second Report on Exemption Clauses (No. 69).
[8] Sched. 1, para. 1(a).
[9] See pp. 4–5, above.
[10] See Chapters 6 and 7 in particular, at pp. 96–98 and 119–120.

of construction more favourable to the insured.[11] This contrasts quite vividly with the position in many of the States in the United States of America. Here doctrines described as "fulfilling the reasonable expectations of the insured" and "disallowing the insurer any unconscionable advantage" are well established,[12] following early recognition of the contract of insurance as a "contract of adhesion" par excellence,[13] in other words, as one of the classic cases in which there is absolutely no chance of the party which does not produce the standard form bargaining over the terms of the contract. One most interesting example of this approach, of particular relevance because it has been reported in this country, is the decision of the Supreme Court of New Jersey in *Gerhardt* v. *Continental Insurance Companies*.[14] Here the plaintiff held a householder's comprehensive insurance policy issued by the defendant. A section of the policy provided for indemnity against any sums which the insured would become legally liable to pay to a third party for personal injury or property damage arising out of his occupation of his house, but set out on a separate page were certain exclusions to this section, one of which provided that the cover did not apply with respect to bodily injury to a resident employee arising out of and in the course of his employment by the insured. Such an employee was injured in the insured's house and sued the insured who called upon the insurers to conduct her defence. The latter relied on the exclusion mentioned, but it was held that they were not entitled to do so. Read by itself, the exclusion appears to have been clear and, on ordinary principles of construction, applicable. However, the court said that, on a simple reading of this policy, which was prepared unilaterally by the company and sold on a mass basis as affording broad coverage to homeowners, the average insured, noting the section covering third party liability, would assume that an injury to a domestic employee was covered. The exclusion was not conspicuous, and as in earlier cases[15] the cover was described as comprehensive, and, while the insurer

---

[11] A notable exception is the judgment of Farwell L.J. in *Re Bradley and Essex and Suffolk Accident Indemnity Soc.* [1912] 1 K.B. 415.

[12] See especially, Keeton, "Insurance Law Rights at Variance with Policy Provisions," (1970) 83 Harv.L.R. 961 and 1281.

[13] See generally, Kessler, "Contracts of Adhesion—Some Thoughts About Freedom of Contract" (1943) 43 Col.L.R. 629.

[14] [1967] 1 Lloyd's Rep. 380.

[15] *e.g. Bauman* v. *Royal Indemnity Co.* 36 N.J. 12 (1961).

had the right to exclude particular types of liability, the doctrine of honouring the reasonable expectations of the insured required that it did so unequivocally.

It must be regarded as most unlikely that an English court would adopt such an approach. While it has attractions, such as that it might cause insurers more often to clarify their policies, there are also other factors to be borne in mind. Decisions of this nature depend entirely upon cases coming before the courts for decision. A principle of this sort is so vague that it would be difficult, if not impossible, to predict the result on the facts of any particular case, and a system which depends on the courts' adjudicating every dispute may be undesirable. Far better, it is submitted, would be a regime of prior approval of policy forms within guidelines laid down by statute.

Risk

As has been pointed out before, the essence of insurance is that it provides protection against the risks of uncertain events befalling the insured, normally events which would be adverse to him.[16] The concept of risk is fundamental, and there are a number of general points of universal application that must be made, as they may well apply, regardless of whether a loss appears to be covered as a matter of construction.

Intentional and negligent losses

First, as a general rule, the fact that a loss is occasioned by the negligence of the insured is irrelevant, but insurance does not cover losses deliberately caused by him. There are innumerable authorities confirming, for example, that the deliberate arson by the insured of property covered by a fire policy,[17] or the sane suicide of a life insured under a life policy, is not covered.[18] This point ties in very much with principles of public policy applicable to insurance contracts, which we shall examine in a subsequent chapter, but leaving these aside for the moment, it

---

[16] See the discussion in Chapter 1 as to the definition of the contract of insurance.
[17] *Britton* v. *Royal Ins. Co.* (1866) 4 F. & F. 905.
[18] *Beresford* v. *Royal Ins. Co.* [1938] A.C. 586; see pp. 191–192, below.

is clear that express policy terms can, if appropriately worded, cover deliberate losses, so that the general rule is not an absolute one. In practice, however, this is likely to apply only in respect of suicide under a life policy. In addition, the general rule excludes only losses caused deliberately by the insured himself. The fact that his wife[19] or employee,[20] for example, intentionally destroys property he has insured does not prevent the insured who is not a party to the act from recovering.

The point that the insured who is negligent can recover is subject to the important qualification that a term of the policy may in effect exclude the insurer's liability in this situation. It seems that increasingly insurers insert and rely on terms requiring the insured to take reasonable care of insured property or to maintain it in a reasonable condition.[21] Such terms will be warranties or conditions and a breach will entitle the insurer to repudiate either the whole contract or the particular claim.[22] While the right of insurers to insert such terms is acknowledged, it could be argued that the insured should not be penalised to the extent of recovering nothing but that there ought to be a mechanism which would allow him to recover some proportion of his loss.[23]

Perils never insured

A number of perils are never covered by indemnity insurances. Primarily these are wear and tear and inherent vice, in

---

[19] *Midland Ins. Co.* v. *Smith* (1881) 6 Q.B.D. 561.

[20] *Shaw* v. *Robberds* (1837) 6 Ad. & El. 75 at 84.

[21] As to such terms in motor policies, see pp. 303–306, below. When such a term appears in a liability policy, *i.e.* a policy protecting the insured against, *inter alia*, his negligence, it is construed so as to cover only reckless conduct: see p. 289, below. In a New Zealand case (*Roberts* v. *State General Insurance Manager* [1974] 2 N.Z.L.R. 312) such a term appearing in a motor policy has been similarly construed, even though the claim was not in respect of third party liability.

[22] See Chapter 7 above. For an example of a recent case where the insurer's repudiation was disallowed, where the insured under an all risks policy took her eyes off her jewellery at an airport for a brief moment while she helped a fellow passenger, during which time it was stolen, see *Port-Rose* v. *Phoenix Assurance Co. Ltd.* (1986) 136 N.L.R. 333. The Insurance Ombudsman has often had to deal with cases of negligence by the insured, particularly regarding household and travel insurance, and has taken a fairly strict view of the insured's duty; see his Annual Reports for 1984, 1985 and 1986, pp. 5–6, 7–8 and 6–8, respectively.

[23] *i.e.* something akin to the way in which the defence of contributory negligence in tort operates.

other words, natural behaviour. Simply these are not fortuitous and are not therefore capable of being covered by an insurance contract, the essence of which is to cover uncertain risks. So, for example, decay in food or the rusting of a car or the natural wear of tiles on a roof cannot be insured against. The major exception here, of course, is in the field of contingency insurance, that is life and related contracts. A life contract obviously covers the natural process of dying; a health insurance contract obviously covers what may be inevitable illness.

Principles of Construction

Attention must now be turned to the detail of the rules of construction applicable to insurance policies. It should be noted that the question of construction is a question of law, and once a word or phrase has been judicially considered, that decision should be followed according to the usual rules of precedent.[24] It seems that up to 13 rules of construction can be found.[25] What may be regarded as the most important of these will be summarised in the following paragraph, before some examples are cited.

Primarily it is the intention of the parties, as discovered objectively from the whole of the policy, that prevails. Written parts, if present, prevail over printed parts as more likely to express the agreement of the parties, and parol evidence is not in general admissible to vary or contradict the written document. The policy is construed according to its literal meaning; only if that is unclear can extraneous circumstances be examined. Words are normally understood in their ordinary meaning, but this is not the case where they have a technical legal meaning; here the latter prevails. Similarly, the context of a word may dictate a departure from its ordinary meaning. Words appearing in the one phrase are prima facie to be construed *eiusdem generis*. Finally, in the event that there is any ambiguity, the policy is construed *contra proferentem*, that is, against the person who drafted it and in favour of the other. This will normally, of course, be against the insurer and in favour of the insured.

---

[24] See, *e.g.* W. J. Lane v. Spratt [1970] 2 Q.B. 480 at 491–492, *per* Roskill J.
[25] See for a comprehensive list, Ivamy, *General Principles of Insurance Law*, 5th ed., Chapter 35.

It may be that different of these canons conflict in the sense that the application of different ones to the same facts may produce a different result. We shall see a good example of this later. In addition, it must be pointed out again that the primary rule, that the intention of the parties must prevail, is, in the majority of cases, founded on the incorrect premise that the insurance contract is the result of bargaining between parties of equal strength, who having bargained, reduced their agreement to writing. Bearing such considerations in mind, we shall now examine just a small selection of the cases on some of the more important canons of construction.

Ordinary meaning

The words in a policy are prima facie to be understood in their ordinary meaning. For example, in *Thompson* v. *Equity Fire Insurance Co.*,[26] a fire policy taken out by a shopkeeper exempted the insurers from liability for loss or damage occurring "while gasoline is stored or kept in the building insured." The insured, in fact, had a small quantity of gasoline for cooking purposes, but no other. It was held that the insurer was liable for a fire that occurred, as the words "stored or kept" in their ordinary meaning implied fairly considerable quantities, and imported the notion of warehousing or keeping in stock for trading. This was not the case and so the exception was inapplicable. In *Leo Rapp Ltd.* v. *McClure*,[27] metal was insured against theft "whilst in warehouse." Some of the relevant metal was stolen from a lorry parked in a locked compound surrounded by a wall topped by barbed wire. It was held that the insurer was not liable, as the ordinary meaning of warehouse implied some sort of covered building, and not a yard, however secure.[28]

Technical meaning

In two respects, however, the ordinary meaning of words will not prevail. The first is where a word has a technical legal or other meaning. This will generally be the case in respect of words describing cover or exceptions to it which are also the names of criminal offences, such as theft, or have acquired a

---

[26] [1910] A.C. 592.
[27] [1955] 1 Lloyd's Rep. 292.
[28] See also *Langford* v. *Legal and General Assurance Soc. Ltd.* [1986] 2 Lloyd's Rep. 103, where it was held that a car was "attended" within the "sensible and practical meaning" of the word where it was left by the insured in her driveway for only a few seconds and was visible from her kitchen window.

Principles of Construction

particular meaning.[28a] The meaning in the latter respect applies to the word in an insurance policy. The classic example is the decision of the House of Lords in *London & Lancashire Fire Insurance Co.* v. *Bolands*.[29] Here a policy on a baker's shop against loss by burglary, housebreaking and theft exempted the insurers from loss caused by, or happening through, or in consequence of, *inter alia*, riot. Four armed men entered the shop one day, held up the employees with guns, and stole all the money they could find. There was no actual violence used, and no other disturbance nearby, yet it was held that the event constituted a riot, and thus the insured could not recover. The stated, and not unattractive,[30] reason for the decision was that riot is a technical term which in a criminal context requires only three people executing a disturbance such as might cause alarm to a reasonable person.[31] Applying this meaning to the insurance policy, there was clearly a riot on the facts of the case. However, it may not be entirely insignificant that the shop was in Dublin and the robbery took place at a time of great disturbances involving the I.R.A. and others. It is not impossible that such a body was behind the robbery, and to talk in terms of riot becomes a little more understandable. It is instructive to compare the views of an American court[32] in holding that riot in an insurance policy meant what ordinary people would normally regard as a riot, distinguishing the decision in *Bolands* for these reasons. In the light of the well-established rules applying to technical words, the decision in *Bolands* is clearly correct. What may be questioned is whether it is a necessary or fair rule to apply to an insurance policy the meaning from another context when such a meaning may be totally different from the ordinary meaning. Fortunately, riot no longer commonly appears as an exception on the British side of the Irish sea, though it does so on the other.[33]

Context

The second way in which the ordinary meaning of a word may not be adopted is where the context requires otherwise. Frequently, the list of perils covered by, for example, a fire policy does not list each peril individually but groups a few

---

[28a] As to words which are the names of crimes, see Wasik [1986] J.B.L. 45.
[29] [1924] A.C. 836.
[30] But see Kemble (1976) 126 N.L.J. 1133.
[31] See, *e.g. Field* v. *Receiver of Metropolitan Police* [1907] 2 K.B. 853.
[32] *Pan Am* v. *Aetna Casualty* [1974] 1 Lloyd's Rep. 232; [1975] 1 Lloyd's Rep. 77.
[33] Where, however, state compensation is available.

together. This is what happened in a fairly recent case, *Young* v. *Sun Alliance & London Insurance*,[34] the plaintiff's household policy insuring him against loss arising from a number of causes, one group of which was "storm,[35] tempest or flood." His house was built on a meadow. Several times water seeped in and caused damage to the ground floor lavatory. On one occasion, the water was three inches deep on the lavatory floor. The plaintiff claimed that this constituted a "flood" and that the insurers were therefore liable to indemnify him in respect of the damage. The Court of Appeal rejected his claim. At least two of their Lordships[36] appeared to accept that in the ordinary sense of the word there was a flood in the case, but they concluded in favour of a contextual approach. As "storm" and "tempest" both import notions of the abnormal, by analogy "flood," appearing in the same phrase, meant a much larger movement of water than natural seepage to a level of three inches. They were almost persuaded, in view of the two possible meanings of "flood," to apply the *contra proferentem* maxim and have been criticised for not doing so.[37] *Young* is an illustration of the point made earlier that the application of different canons of construction to the same words can easily produce different results. It has therefore been suggested that the traditional rules be replaced by an enquiry as to what cover the parties really thought was being provided by the policy and as to the purposes behind the insurance in question.[37] This is perhaps an approach rather similar to the American rules of construction that were referred to earlier, and is, it is suggested, open to the same difficulties. As a minimum measure of clarification and reform, insurers could surely be urged to provide a glossary of terms in their policies explaining their understanding of standard words of coverage like "flood."

Contra proferentem

The maxim that provides for ambiguities to be construed against the party responsible for drafting them may be brought to the aid of the insured as two leading Court of Appeal decisions show.

In *English* v. *Western*,[38] a motor policy effected by a 17 year-

[34] [1977] 1 W.L.R. 104.
[35] As to storm, see *Anderson* v. *Norwich Union* [1977] 1 Lloyd's Rep. 253.
[36] Shaw and Cairns L.JJ. Lawton L.J. regarding the problem as more straightforward, holding that flood ordinarily meant something violent and abnormal.
[37] Merkin (1977) 40 M.L.R. 486.
[38] [1940] 2 K.B. 156.

old youth covered his liability for injury to all persons except, *inter alia*, in respect of "death or injury to any member of the assured's household" travelling in the car with the insured. He negligently injured his sister when she was his passenger. The insurers argued that they were not liable to indemnify the insured against his liability to her by virtue of the above exception. It was held that the expression "any member of the assured's household" was equally capable of meaning "any member of a household of which the assured was the head" as "any member of the same household of which the assured was a member." It was therefore ambiguous and the meaning more favourable to the insured, the former meaning, was adopted, so that the insurers were liable.

Houghton v. *Trafalgar Insurance Co. Ltd.*[39] also involved an exception in a motor policy which excluded liability when the car was conveying "any load in excess of that for which it was constructed." Here the insurer argued that the carriage of six persons in a car designed for five was within the exception. It was held that this was not a "load." While the carriage of persons could be so considered, it equally, indeed more naturally, referred to the carriage of goods.

The application of the *contra proferentem* maxim can hardly be said to be free from doubt. It is clear that there must be a genuine ambiguity; ambiguity must not be created simply to apply the maxim. However, whether or not a word or phrase is in fact ambiguous is not always apparent. It could be said that there was ambiguity over the meaning of the word "flood" in the *Young* case, and two of the judges admitted that counsel for the insured had very nearly so persuaded them. A classic illustration of the difficulties which gave rise to a difference of judicial opinion is *Alder* v. *Moore*.[40] Here the dispute arose not from the wording of a policy itself, but of an undertaking extracted from an insured following a payment under a policy. The defendant had been a professional footballer and a member of the relevant footballers' union when he suffered an injury to an eye which it was thought would prevent him from playing professionally again. The union had an accident policy under which its members who sustained permanent total disablement would receive £500 from the plaintiff insurer. The defendant received such a payment, in return for which he agreed that he would not take part "as a playing member" in any form of pro-

---
[39] [1954] 1 Q.B. 247.
[40] [1961] 2 Q.B. 57.

fessional football. Subsequently he recovered sufficiently to take up occasional professional football, though at a much lower level than before. The plaintiff sued for return of the £500. It was argued for the defendant, *inter alia*,[41] that the undertaking was ambiguous, because "playing member" could mean either simply "player" or "player who is a member of the union." Moore was not, when he returned to football, a member of the union. The latter interpretation was reinforced by the argument that if the former were correct, the word "member" in the undertaking was superfluous and that in the original policy, "member" was expressly defined as a registered member of the union. Despite this, a majority of the Court of Appeal[42] held that the plaintiff should succeed and regarded the undertaking as perfectly clear. With respect, the dissenting judgment of Devlin L.J. is much more persuasive.[43] For the reasons outlined he held that the phrase was ambiguous, and, although he adopted what he termed a wider rule than *contra proferentem*, he was clearly of opinion that the phrase should be construed against the insurer. Whichever view is the better on the facts of the case, it does illustrate how even the judges cannot always agree as to whether or not sufficient ambiguity exists.[44]

Specific Descriptions and Specific Words

It is appropriate to turn now to consider how some of the specific descriptions sometimes applied to insurance policies and some of the standard wordings have been defined in the context of the cover afforded by an insurance policy. Looking first at descriptions, it is well known that insurers, no doubt at least partly for marketing reasons, sometimes attach descriptions like "Comprehensive," "Invincible," "Homeguard" or "Maxplan" to their appropriate policies. While judges have occasionally commented adversely on such descriptions because they give a somewhat misleading picture and may lead an insured to consider that his cover is complete and not subject to exceptions, which it usually will be, it is clear that descriptions of the sort mentioned above are not terms of art and do not carry any legal

---

[41] It was also argued that the forfeiture was a penalty clause and void for this reason, but the court held against this argument by a majority.
[42] On this point, Slade J. simply agreed with Sellers L.J.
[43] See Goff (1961) 24 M.L.R. 637.
[44] Even in *English* v. *Western*, above, which seems a pretty clear case of ambiguity, Goddard L.J. dissented on the grounds that it was not.

meanings.[45] The one exception to this is the description "All Risks." Frequently, for example, policies on valuables and contractors' policies are "all risks." The nature of an "all risks" policy was explained in the marine insurance case of *British and Foreign Marine Insurance Co. v. Gaunt*.[46] Basically, it covers all loss to the property insured as occurs through some accidental cause, but not "such damage as is inevitable from ordinary wear and tear and inevitable depreciation"[47] or from inherent vice. The other significant feature of "all risks" cover is that the insured has to show only that a loss is accidental; he need not show the exact nature of the accident or casualty which occasioned the loss.

However, even an "all risks" policy can be subject to exceptions which will be upheld on usual principles of construction if they are clearly stated. In the Australian case of *Queensland Government Railways and Electric Power Transmission Pty. Ltd. v. Manufacturers' Mutual Life Insurance Ltd.*,[48] the plaintiffs held a contractors' all risks policy covering the construction of a bridge, but the policy excluded loss or damage arising from "faulty design." The bridge was being constructed to a design which, at the time, was the best available, but nevertheless, its piers were swept away by flood water after exceptionally heavy rains. It was held that the insurers could rely upon the exception. Even though the design was not negligent, because it was the best available, it was still "faulty" since otherwise the piers would never have collapsed.[49]

Fire

Insurance against loss or damage by fire is, of course, one of the standard and one of the oldest forms of cover, and the major part of any policy on real property. As fire does not have a technical meaning like, for example, theft or burglary, and because of its prominence, its meaning is worth exploring. Apart from obvious losses by fire, the actual burning of property insured, the problems that have arisen have been whether it is necessary

[45] Compare the attitude of some American cases; see, *e.g. Gerhardt v. Continental*, above, where the fact that the policy was described as a comprehensive one was one of the factors in the decision. Note also the strictures of the Insurance Ombudsman on the use of such titles; see his Annual Report for 1986, pp. 25–26.
[46] [1921] 2 A.C. 41.
[47] *Ibid.* at 46, *per* Lord Birkenhead.
[48] (1968) 118 C.L.R. 314; [1969] 1 Lloyd's Rep. 214.
[49] This definition of faulty has been trenchantly criticised by Merkin (1977) 40 M.L.R. 486 at 489.

that there be actual ignition of the property insured and whether loss or damage occurring in or as a result of a "proper" fire is covered. Actual ignition is necessary and damage from excessive heat is not enough. In the old case of *Austin* v. *Drewe*,[50] the stock in a sugar refinery was insured against damage by fire. A flue passed up through all the floors of the refinery from a stove on the ground floor. At the top of the flue was a register which was closed at night to retain heat, but opened when a fresh fire was lit in the morning. One morning an employee of the insured forgot to open the register. The intense heat in the flue damaged sugar being refined on the top floor, but, although there was smoke and sparks, the fire itself was confined to the flue and the sugar did not ignite. It was held that there was no loss by fire.

On the other hand, if there has been actual ignition of some property, the fact that the insured property itself does not catch fire is irrelevant if it is damaged in such a way that the proximate cause of the loss was the fire.[51] This point we shall return to later.

There is no distinction in English law between a "friendly" fire and a "hostile" fire. In other words, the fact that the damage is caused by a fire in its proper place does not matter so long as the loss is accidental. In *Harris* v. *Poland*,[52] the plaintiff's personal property was insured against loss or damage caused by fire. One day, as a security measure, she concealed her jewellery in the grate under coal which was ready for lighting. Later she inadvertently lit the fire without removing the jewellery and the latter was damaged. It was held that there had been a loss by fire. "[The] risks against which the plaintiff is insured include the risk of insured property coming unintentionally in contact with fire and being thereby destroyed or damaged, and it matters not whether that fire comes to the insured property or the insured property comes to the fire."[53]

Damage caused merely by explosion or lightning is not damage by fire,[54] but explosion caused by fire, or fire following an explosion or lightning will be covered, subject to the rules about causation which will be examined later, because here

---

[50] (1816) 6 Taunt. 436.
[51] *Symington* v. *Union Ins. Soc. of Canton* (1928) 97 L.J.K.B. 646.
[52] [1941] 1 K.B. 462.
[53] *Ibid.* at 468, *per* Atkinson J.
[54] *Everett* v. *London Ass. Co.* (1865) 19 C.B.(N.S.) 126. As to "explosion," see *Commonwealth Smelting* v. *Guardian Royal Exchange* [1984] 2 Lloyd's Rep. 608.

Accident

Loss caused by or arising out of an accident or by accidental means or some similar phrase is a fairly common form of wording in insurance policies, and an essential one in particular types. The considerable problems involved in defining "accident" have occasioned the courts difficulties many times,[56] and it is considered worthwhile, therefore, to devote space to this question. Particular policies where these problems arise are policies of personal accident insurance or policies such as motor policies which may well contain a personal accident component, and some policies of liability insurance.

As we have seen, insurance prima facie covers only unintentional acts anyway, so one problem is how the presence of the word "accident" qualifies this. Another is that even a deliberate act by someone may well be accidental from the point of view of the victim. Similarly, an insured may be engaged in a deliberate course of conduct when something happens which he did not intend. Is this an accident? It is suggested that the answers to these and other problems are best considered by a separate examination of first, those first party insurances where the description "accident" is to be found, and secondly, cases of third party or liability insurance where the liability of the insurer to indemnify exists only if the insured acted accidentally. It must be pointed out, however, that the cases do not necessarily adopt this distinction.

First party insurances

In the first sort of case we find predominantly policies of personal accident insurance.[57] Leaving aside for the present the issue of causation which can be of importance in this field, it would appear that injury arising from accident can be defined as injury which arises from some unexpected or unintended

---

[55] *Stanley* v. *Western Ins. Co.* (1868)) L.R. 3 Ex. 71.

[56] The classic illustration is perhaps the decision in *Trim Joint District School Board of Management* v. *Kelly* [1914] A.C. 667, a workmen's compensation case where the House of Lords split 4–3.

[57] Common also at one time were policies issued under the Workmen's Compensation Acts which gave birth to a considerable amount of litigation; see below.

event, which is not natural. So, for example, in *Hamlyn* v. *Crown Accidental Insurance Co. Ltd.*,[58] the insured bent down to pick up a marble dropped by a child. In doing so, he wrenched his knee. As he had no history of knee trouble it was held that his injury was accidental. Although obviously he intended to bend down, he did not intend or expect to hurt his knee. The fact that the insured is negligent is by itself irrelevant, so that being knocked down by a train when crossing a railway line without due care will be covered by a personal accident policy.[59] Death or injury from sunstroke or exposure would not normally be regarded as accidental, being the result of natural events.[60]

In *Marcel Beller Ltd.* v. *Hayden*,[61] the plaintiff company insured their employees against death consequent upon "accidental bodily injury" being the sole cause. An employee having consumed alcoholic drink to the extent that he had much more than the permitted level of alcohol in his blood, was driving his car too fast when approaching a corner; he lost control, crashed and was killed. One of the points for decision was whether this was an accident. It was argued for the insurers that it was not, because the death was a reasonably foreseeable consequence of a deliberate act by the employee, that is, the consumption of a considerable quantity of alcohol. The judge rejected this argument and distinguished the difficult case of *Gray* v. *Barr*,[62] a decision on liability insurance which will be examined shortly. In his view, accident should be interpreted in its ordinary sense as an ordinary person would understand it. As, on the facts, an ordinary person would have said that the employee's death was an accident, because he did not intend to kill himself nor expose himself to deliberate risk, the death was prima facie covered by the policy.

If the insured does take a deliberate risk, an injury resulting may fairly be said not to be accidental. In one Canadian case,[63] cited in *Marcel Beller Ltd.* v. *Hayden*, the insured balanced himself on the coping of a hotel patio 13 floors above the street in order to demonstrate to a friend that he had not lost his nerve. Unfortunately he lost his balance and fell to his death. This was held not to be an accident. In the words of the learned judge in

---

[58] [1893] 1 Q.B. 750.
[59] *Cornish* v. *Accident Ins. Co.* (1889) 23 Q.B.D. 453.
[60] *Sinclair* v. *Maritime Passengers' Ass.* (1861) 3 E. & E. 478.
[61] [1978] Q.B. 694.
[62] [1971] 2 Q.B. 554.
[63] *Candler* v. *London & Lancashire Guarantee & Accident Co. of Canada* (1963) 40 D.L.R. (2d.) 408.

Marcel Beller Ltd. v. *Hayden,* "It seems to me that a clear distinction can be drawn between cases where the predisposing cause is the deliberate taking of an appreciated risk and the cases such as the present where the predisposing cause, although it leads to the taking of risks, involves risk which was neither deliberately run nor actually appreciated."[64]

Sometimes, though probably rarely, to be found are cases where property damage is covered under a first party policy only if caused by or arising out of accident. In the Australian decision of *Lombard Australia Ltd.* v. *N.R.M.A. Insurance Ltd.,*[65] an approach similar to that of the personal injury cases was taken. There a car, the subject of a hire purchase agreement, was jointly insured against loss by accident by the hirer and the owner. The hirer deliberately committed suicide by driving it into a tree. It was held that the loss of the car was accidental so far as the owner was concerned and thus covered, as the latter certainly did not intend the loss.

Accidental means

One final point to consider in this context is whether subtle changes in wording can affect the interpretation of words. For example, a personal accident policy may not simply cover death or injury "caused by accident," but one "caused by accidental means" or, in the fuller phrase often employed, "by violent, accidental, external and visible means." Here it could be argued not just that the final event or injury must be accidental, but also the "means," in other words, the prior act of the insured, so that if a deliberate act led to the final "accident," the insured is not covered. An argument along these lines was in fact rejected in the *Hamlyn* case, which we have already examined, where the wording was of this sort and the bending over of the insured was clearly deliberate, but it has prevailed in decisions in other jurisdictions, including a leading American case.[66] It is suggested that the former approach is to be preferred. As that great judge, Cardozo J., dissenting, said in the latter case: "The

---

[64] [1978] 2 Q.B. at 705.
[65] [1969] 1 Lloyd's Rep. 575.
[66] *Landress* v. *Phoenix Ins. Co.* 291 U.S. 491 (1933); see also, the Scottish case of *Clidero* v. *Scottish Accident Ins. Co.* (1892) 19 R. 355 supporting the distinction between means and results, and the Victorian case of *Robinson* v. *Evans Bros.* [1969] V.R. 885 (p. 175, below), following the view of Cardozo J. See also *Glenlight Shipping Ltd.* v. *Excess Insurance Ltd.,* 1983 S.L.T. 241, where the Court of Session ignored the distinction, contrary to the *Clidero* case; see Davidson [1984] J.B.L. 391.

attempted distinction between accidental results and accidental means will plunge this branch of the law into a Serbian bog."

Liability insurances

Turning to consider the cases on the meaning of accident in a liability policy, it is convenient to examine separately cases on property damage and those on personal injury or death. Here a particular problem is that even an intended act by an insured may be accidental from the point of view of the third party victim, but it is clear that this is irrelevant and indemnity will not be provided if what the insured did was not from his point of view an accident. However, in considering what is the degree of foresight necessary to prevent the insured from recovering, it appears that the courts have taken a stricter view in the case of injury to third parties than in the case of property damage.

Personal injury

The classic decision concerning personal injury is *Gray v. Barr*.[67] The insured's wife had been having an affair with the plaintiff's husband which the insured was led to believe had ended, which indeed may have been the case. However, on discovering one day that his wife was not at home, he suspected her to be with Gray and he set off for the latter's house with a loaded shotgun in order to frighten him. When he arrived there, he and Gray were involved in a struggle on the stairs as the result of which two shots were fired from the gun, the second one killing Gray. The insured was acquitted of murder and manslaughter, but was sued in court by Mrs. Gray. He brought in his insurers as third parties, claiming that they were liable to pay. The relevant liability aspect of his policy provided such an indemnity if the loss was "caused by accident." Tied up very much with the question of defining accident in the context were questions of causation and public policy which will be considered later, but it does appear that the majority of the Court of Appeal held that what happened was not an accident within the policy, on the ground that the death of Gray was a foreseeable consequence of Barr's intentional act of taking a loaded shotgun into the deceased's house.[68] With great respect, it is submitted

---

[67] [1971] 2 Q.B. 554.
[68] This was clearly the view of Phillimore L.J. Lord Denning M.R. seemed to base his decision more on the ground of causation, as to which see below, p. 189.

that the opinion of the trial judge[69] and Salmon L.J. to the contrary is to be preferred. On the facts as found there was no intention to fire a shot nor to kill. Most people would surely regard what happened as an "accident" therefore, and to introduce questions as to prior acts is to bring in that confusing distinction between means and results upon which we have already commented. It may still be the case that the result in *Gray* v. *Barr* was correct, but here we are only concerned with the meaning of the word "accident," not with the inevitable issues of causation and public policy which arose also in that case.

Property damage

So far as property damage is concerned, the Australian decision of *Robinson* v. *Evans*[70] is a good example of the use of what it is suggested is a sensible test, that the event must be unintended and unexpected from the point of view of the insured. Here the plaintiff sued the defendant company in tort for damages for the destruction of his crop of brussel sprouts. The plaintiff was a market gardener, the defendant owned a neighbouring brick works. The plaintiff's claim, which involved two separate incidents, was settled and the dispute concerned the defendant's claim to be indemnified by its public liability insurers, the terms of the policy providing such indemnity in respect of accidental damage only.[71] The court found that the damage to the plaintiff's crop was caused by the emission of fluoride. In respect of the first incident, the defendant's managing director knew about the danger. It was held that this claim was not for accidental damage. While it may have been unintended by the defendant, it could not be said to be wholly unexpected because of the managing director's knowledge. The test to be applied was whether an ordinary reasonable sensible man, in the position of the insured (or, in this case, its responsible officers), would or would not have expected the occurrence. The second incident in respect of which the plaintiff claimed arose after the defendant had built a much higher stack on its chimney which it was genuinely believed would cure the problem, but which did not. It was held that the defendant's

---

[69] [1970] 2 Q.B. 626; see also the comments in *Marcel Beller Ltd.* v. *Hayden*, note 61, above.

[70] [1969] V.R. 885.

[71] In fact the policy's actual wording was "damage caused by accidental means," but the court sensibly rejected the distinction between means and results.

insurers were liable to indemnify it in this respect. This damage was unintended and unexpected and hence accidental.

In contrast, the decision of the Canadian Supreme Court in *Canadian Indemnity Co. v. Walkem Machinery & Equipment Ltd.*[72] is rather surprising.[73] W. Ltd. was the agent and distributor for a company which manufactured a special type of crane. It negligently sold to a customer a crane which had been inadequately repaired and which was in a dangerous condition. This crane collapsed and W. Ltd. was held liable to pay damages to a third party. Its comprehensive business liability policy, issued by the appellant insurer, indemnified it against liability to third parties arising from accident. It seems clear that W. Ltd. took a calculated risk in selling the crane, so that the subsequent collapse could hardly be said to be quite unexpected, even if unintended, but the court held that the liability of W. Ltd. arose from accident. It followed in particular some of the English Workmen's Compensation cases[74] in holding that accident means "any unlooked for mishap or occurrence," thus deciding that an unintended occurrence, however risky, was within the cover. The court laid great stress upon the fact that the policy was a comprehensive business liability policy and upon the fact that a narrower construction of accident would deny the insured recovery if an occurrence is the result of a calculated risk or of a dangerous operation. With great respect, this misses the point. Of course an insured can be covered against a calculated risk; a third party policy which indemnifies simply against legal liability to third parties without any limitation by reference to accident will cover all except deliberate risks. However, the inclusion of "caused by accident" must make a difference, especially it might be thought where the insured is a well advised businessman. It is suggested that this case would not and should not be followed here. It contrasts most strongly with the decision in *Gray v. Barr* which, it has already been suggested, goes to the other extreme.

Natural causes

An important point in this context concerns the relevance of natural causes to a third party policy insuring against liability caused by accident. As has been seen, in the context of personal accident policies, if the real cause of the loss is natural, it will

[72] (1975) 52 D.L.R. (3d.) 1.
[73] See Hasson (1976) 14 Osgoode Hall L.J. 669.
[74] *Fenton v. Thorley & Co. Ltd.* [1903] A.C. 443 and *Clover, Clayton & Co. Ltd. v. Hughes* [1910] A.C. 242.

not be covered, indeed it will usually be expressly excepted, and of course it is a general principle that insurance does not cover natural wear and tear. In *Mills v. Smith*,[75] a householder's liability policy indemnified the insured against liability for "damage to property caused by accident." The insured was held liable in damages to a neighbour for settlement damage to the neighbour's house caused by the root action of a tree in the insured's garden taking water from the soil on the neighbour's land. It was held that this was caused by accident. The learned judge was clearly disposed to give a wide meaning to these words in a householder's policy and the insured obviously did nothing which was intended or expected in any way. On the other hand, it could be argued that the real cause of the insured's liability was entirely natural, namely the action of the tree roots, albeit there was an "accident" when the neighbour's foundations dropped. Paull J. regarded it as significant that the insurers had chosen to use the same words as used to appear in the Workmen's Compensation Acts and felt able to rely on leading decisions under those Acts with appropriate adjustments. That led him to the conclusion that there were two questions to be answered on the facts. The first was whether there had at any moment in time been some unexpected event leading to damage. Here the settlement was this event, being more than the natural movement of foundations. The second was what was the cause of this. His answer was that it was the action of the roots of the tree and that this meant that the insurers were liable. With respect, this reasoning is difficult to follow. If the real cause of the loss was the action of the tree, that was surely natural and not "caused by accident." If the *causa proxima* rule means anything in this sort of case, a question to be discussed later in this chapter, the decision can hardly be supported on this ground. If it can be supported, it must be on the ground that the event must be looked at solely from the point of view of the insured, ignoring underlying "natural" factors. If, so far as he was concerned, the event was unexpected and unintended, then the loss was caused by accident. Perhaps underlying this is a rationale of providing broad support to the individual insured without too much regard to narrow principles of definition and causation.

Two further points can be made. The first is that changes in wording might make a difference to the result in a case like *Mills v. Smith*. If, for example, the policy had provided an

---

[75] [1964] 1 Q.B. 30.

indemnity in respect of damage "caused by *an* accident" or "caused by accidental means," it would have been more difficult to reach the same result.[76] Accident by itself is much more capable of a wide meaning than "an accident," and "accidental means" implies that the entire causal history must be accidental. In the latter respect, however, it might be hoped that the courts would follow the line we have seen and steer clear of the distinction between results and means. This was certainly the line adopted in *Robinson* v. *Evans*.[77]

The second point concerns the relevance of Workmen's Compensation cases, which, as we have seen, have been relied on in some of the third party policy cases.[78] Clearly these cases must be relevant when the wording of a policy is the same as that used in the Workmen's Compensation Acts, in other words "injury or damage caused by accident." But it is also true that workmen's compensation policies were construed more liberally than other insurance contracts because they were the system of first party insurance established for the benefit of employees before the days of state insurance under the social security system. For example, death or injury from natural phenomena has been held covered under a workmen's compensation policy, whereas it would not be so regarded under a personal accident policy. While workmen's compensation cases may be useful, therefore, they are not absolutely binding authorities.[79]

Conclusions

The cases that have been reviewed here illustrate, if nothing else, that "accident" is a difficult concept accurately to define. The following tentative conclusions can perhaps be drawn. First, that the meaning of accident is wider in the context of personal accident cover than in third party cover. In the former, the event need be only either unexpected or unintended, provided that the insured does not expose himself to a deliberate risk. In the latter it should be both unexpected and unintended. However, the degree of foresight which is relevant to determining whether or not an event is unintended is not clearly established. *Gray* v. *Barr* suggests that not a great deal of foresight of an event is needed before it is so regarded as intended for these

---

[76] See the judgment of Paull J. [1964] 1 Q.B. 30, 36.
[77] See p. 175, above.
[78] Particularly *Mills* v. *Smith* (note 75) and *Canadian Indemnity* v. *Walkem* (note 72).
[79] See the fuller discussion in *MacGillivray and Parkington*, paras. 1881–1908.

purposes, whereas *Robinson* v. *Evans* held that the insured as a reasonable man must have foreseen the event before he is denied indemnity. It may be that *Gray* v. *Barr* should be regarded as incorrect on this point[80] and treated solely as an authority on causation and public policy. What is clear is that disputes over the meaning of accident will continue to be the subject of litigation.

Loss

The word "loss" appears frequently throughout this book and in policies of insurance, for obvious reasons. It is the risk of loss that is central to the concept of insurance. In some contexts, "loss" appears merely as a part of a wider phrase, such as, for example, "loss by fire" or "loss by theft." In these cases, the meaning of loss itself is not important. Whether or not the insured can recover depends upon the meaning of fire or theft, and on whether his loss was caused by that insured peril. However, in other contexts, particularly perhaps in insurances of goods, "loss" is itself one of the forms of cover provided. A standard description is insurance against "loss, damage or destruction." The latter two words raise no problems of construction or definition, but the meaning of "loss" does, and it has exercised the courts on a number of occasions.

Constructive total loss

In marine insurance law, there is a doctrine of "constructive total loss" whereby, even if a ship or other property insured is not actually lost or cannot be proved to be so lost, the insured can by giving notice claim as for a total loss, the insurer thereafter becoming entitled to the ship or property if it should turn up.[81] This is because traditionally marine insurance has been regarded as insurance of the adventure as much as of the ship or other property insured. The same result can be achieved in non-marine insurance by agreement between insurer and insured, for example, an insurer might agree to pay in respect of a stolen car even if it cannot be shown to have been actually lost on the tests to be examined shortly, but it is well-established that there is no automatic doctrine of constructive total loss in non-marine insurance[82]; if necessary, the insured must prove an actual loss.

---

[80] See the comments in *Marcel Beller Ltd.* v. *Hayden*, note 61, above.
[81] See the Marine Insurance Act 1906, ss.60–63.
[82] *Moore* v. *Evans* [1918] A.C. 185.

Missing goods

Obviously, if goods are actually destroyed, they are lost, but cover in this respect falls more naturally under the "destruction" part of the standard phrase quoted above. If goods are mislaid or are missing or have disappeared, then they become lost if after a reasonable time and a fruitless diligent search, recovery of them is uncertain or unlikely. In Holmes v. Payne,[83] an insured necklace was mislaid and could not be found despite all the insured's efforts. The insurers agreed to replace it. Some months later the necklace was found in the insured's cloak, having probably fallen into the lining. It was held that it had been truly lost. The insurers were therefore bound by the replacement agreement, although, of course, the insured was not entitled to keep the necklace as well as the replacement jewellery. Indeed, she had, before the action brought by the insurers, offered it to them as salvage.

Irrecoverable goods

A rather different situation is where the insured knows where his property is, but he is unable to recover it. If it remains his property and is safely in the hands of parties who are bailees of it for him, then it is not lost even if physically he is temporarily deprived of possession. In Moore v. Evans,[84] just before the first World War, the insured jewellers sent a quantity of pearls to trade customers in Frankfurt and Brussels on sale or return. When war broke out, the Germans occupied Brussels. Thus for some four years, both sets of pearls were irrecoverable. However, the available evidence showed that they were being safely kept for the insured and had not been seized or interfered with by the German authorities. The House of Lords held that the goods were therefore not lost. If, however, the insured property has been interfered with or taken by someone without authority, then it may well be lost even if in theory the insured might have a legal remedy which would entitle him to reclaim the property. The test would seem to be whether, after all reasonable steps have been taken, recovery is uncertain. In London & Provincial Leather Processes Ltd. v. Hudson,[85] skins bought by the plaintiff company were as usual shipped from the seller directly to a German firm which was accustomed to process them for the plaintiff before sending them to the United King-

---

[83] (1930) 37 Ll.L.R. 41.
[84] Note 82.
[85] [1939] 2 K.B. 724.

dom. The German firm entrusted some of the skins to a subagent who retained them in purported exercise of a lien for money owed to them by the firm. The firm then went bankrupt, whereupon the equivalent of its trustee in bankruptcy sold more of the skins for the benefit of the estate. It was held that the insurers of the skins were liable for both losses, even though in theory, the plaintiffs might have had remedies in respect of them in the German courts. The policy here was an all risks policy, but that would appear to make no difference in principle. In *Webster v. General Accident Fire and Life Assurance Corporation Ltd.*,[86] the plaintiff's car was stolen and passed through the hands of a number of people before it reached a purchaser who probably, but not necessarily, received good title to it under the provisions of the Factors Acts.[87] On discovering his loss, the plaintiff had taken all reasonable steps to recover the car by contacting the police and the motoring organisations. It was held that the car was lost within the meaning of the plaintiff's insurance policy.

Loss of proceeds

Finally, it must be the insured property itself that is lost and not, for example, a sum of money received for it. If, then, the insured voluntarily hands over his property to another, intending to part with ownership, he cannot claim to have suffered a loss of it if the cheque which he receives in return for it subsequently bounces. What has been lost is the proceeds of sale, not the property.[88] This contrasts neatly with the facts of the *Webster* case to which we have already briefly referred. There, the circumstances were that the plaintiff entrusted his car to an auctioneer, when bidding for it had not reached the reserve price, upon the latter's saying that he had a private buyer. This statement was a lie, and the auctioneer intended at the time to deprive the plaintiff of the car. He subsequently sent several cheques which were dishonoured. Here there was a loss of the car because, apart from the point already mentioned, the plaintiff did not voluntarily part with property in the car. The auctioneer's dealings amounted to conversion and theft of the car.

---

[86] [1953] 1 Q.B. 520.

[87] The point was not decided. It was held that the plaintiff did not have to sue to find out, having taken legal advice to the effect that he would probably not succeed, and thus having acted reasonably.

[88] *Eisinger v. General Accident Fire and Life Assurance Corp. Ltd.* [1953] 2 All E.R. 897.

Cover Provided—Consequential Points

Having considered the principal rules of construction applicable to determining the cover provided by an insurance policy, and examined some of the common wordings used, it is convenient to look now at two points which are nothing directly to do with these questions, but which follow neatly from them. The first concerns the question of consequential losses, and the second the question of whether an insured peril must actually operate upon property insured and costs incurred in preventing an insured peril running.

Consequential losses

Insurance of property prima facie covers that property only in respect of the loss attributable to its own value. How that value is measured will be considered in Chapter 13. In other words, consequential losses are not recoverable unless they are separately insured. So, for example, in *Maurice* v. *Goldsborough Mort*,[89] where consignees of wool insured it as trustees for the owners, so that they were liable to account to them for the insurance money received following a loss, they could not recover in respect of their loss of commission. Similarly, in the old case of *Re Wright and Pole*,[90] an insured inn was destroyed by fire, but the insured was unable to recover in respect of the loss of custom and the hire of other premises, and in *Theobald* v. *Railway Passengers Assurance Co.*,[91] loss of business profits were not recoverable under an accident policy.

It is, of course, possible to effect insurance against loss of profits arising as the result of loss of property, and such cover, now known commonly as Interruption Insurance, is popular with businesses.

Must the risk run? Prevention costs

The question that arises here is perhaps partly a matter of cover provided and partly a matter of causation. Traditionally, it is considered under the latter heading, but it is suggested that it is better examined on its own.

The problem simply stated can be put in the following way. If

---

[89] [1939] A.C. 452.
[90] (1834) 1 A. & E. 621.
[91] (1854) 10 Exch. 45.

property is insured against a specific loss, can the insured recover if that loss does not actually operate upon the insured property, but it is lost or damaged in circumstances when the insured peril was imminent? Furthermore, if there is no loss, but only because the insured incurs expenditure in preventing what would have been a certain loss, can the insured recover this expenditure? We shall deal with these questions separately.

Insured peril imminent

As regards the first, there is clear authority in marine insurance cases that if the peril insured against has happened, and is so imminent that it is about to operate upon the insured property, loss to the property caused by measures necessarily taken to avert the risk happening to the insured property is covered. It can be said that the proximate or real cause of the loss is a peril insured against. In *Symington* v. *Union Insurance of Canton*[92] cork insured against loss by fire and stored on a jetty was jettisoned by being thrown into the sea to prevent an existing fire from spreading. It was held that the loss was covered, the real cause of it being the fire, an insured peril. It was stated clearly that the peril must have happened and be so imminent that the action was immediately necessary to avert the danger. Although there appear to have been very few non-marine cases on the point,[93] there is no reason to doubt that the same principle would apply, so that if, for example, house contents are insured against fire and are damaged by water to prevent an existing fire spreading, such damage would be covered even if water damage was not covered or was an expected peril.

Costs of prevention

The answer to the second question is more problematical, there being a clear distinction in that property insured is not actually damaged in any way. Suppose, for example, the case of a house by a river insured against damage by flood. Following heavy storms, the level of the river is rising and it is as certain as it can be that unless measures are taken, the house will be flooded. The insured incurs expenditure in buying equipment which successfully prevents such a flood. Can he recover such costs from his insurer? It might be regarded as a little strange if he could not, if he could prove that had he done nothing, the

---

[92] (1928) 97 L.J.K.B. 646.
[93] One such is *Glen Falls Ins.* v. *Spencer* (1956) 3 D.L.R. (2d.) 745.

house would have been damaged by an insured peril and the insurer would have been liable. In marine insurance, a "sue and labour" clause would permit recovery,[94] and by analogy the same principle was applied to the case of a charterparty involving marine risks: "sums paid to avert a peril may be recovered as upon a loss by that peril."[95] But in the absence of an express clause, it is not clear whether prevention costs are recoverable in marine insurance. In *The Knight of St. Michael*,[96] a cargo of coal from Newcastle, Australia, to Valparaiso was insured against loss by fire under a marine policy. Because of the overheating of part of the coal, some was discharged in Sydney. This was clearly necessary to prevent its spontaneous combustion. It was held that the consequent loss of freight was within the policy, and it was suggested that it was a "loss by fire," as there was an "actual existing state of peril of fire and not merely a fear of fire," although there was no actual fire. The problem with regarding this decision as clear authority is that there were also general words of cover in the policy covering "other losses" and the learned judge was clearly of the opinion and stated that if the loss was not by fire, it was within the other cover provided. In the United States of America there is clear authority that prevention costs can be recovered under a non-marine policy,[97] in the absence of express coverage. It is suggested that this principle could usefully be followed here,[98] and that such costs should be recoverable provided that there is an actual existing state of the peril insured, in other words that loss by a peril insured against is certain. Mere danger of such loss would clearly not be sufficient.[99]

---

[94] See, generally, Ivamy, *Marine Insurance*, Chapter 39; *Integrated Container Service Inc.* v. *British Traders Insurance Co. Ltd.* [1984] 1 Lloyd's Rep. 154.
[95] *Pyman Steamship Co.* v. *Admiralty Commissioners* [1919] 1 K.B. 49 at 53.
[96] [1898] P. 30.
[97] *Leebov* v. *United States Fidelity & Guaranty Co.* 401 Pa. 477 (1960) (Pennsylvania Supreme Court). A contractor caused a landslide, but, before it could do much damage, incurred expense in preventing it from causing certain further damage. It was held that his liability insurer was liable in respect of this expense. See further, Note (1971) 71 Col.L.R. 1309.
[98] However, in *Liverpool & London & Globe Insurance Ltd.* v. *Canadian General Electric Co. Ltd.* (1981) 123 D.L.R. (3d.) 513, the Supreme Court of Canada refused to permit the recovery of prevention costs where the insured risk had not actually begun to operate. Further, if prevention costs were claimed under a fire policy, and it was a loss by fire that had been prevented, there is the old authority of *Austin* v. *Drewe* (see p. 170, above), requiring that there be actual ignition, which would have to be distinguished.
[99] *Becker, Gray & Co.* v. *London Ass. Corp.* [1918] A.C. 101.

CAUSATION

As has been remarked several times in the course of this chapter, it is not sufficient in order that an insured should recover for a loss, that the loss falls within the cover provided as a matter of construction or definition. He must also show that the loss was proximately caused by an insured peril.[1] The proximate cause does not, however, mean the last cause, but the effective or dominant or real cause.[2] Working out what is the proximate cause in any situation is strictly a question of fact, so that decided cases cannot be binding but are merely illustrations. It should be noted that the doctrine can be excluded by appropriate wording.[3]

It has already been seen how the doctrine can operate to find an insurer liable where the insured peril is the real cause but not the actual instrument of the loss.[4] Otherwise it seems most relevant, and indeed it has been said to be relevant only really at all, in a case where, on the facts, there can genuinely be said to be competing causes of a loss, one of which is specifically covered by the policy and the other of which is expressly excepted.[5] Whether the doctrine can be at all relevant where there can be no question of an excepted peril is a matter to be considered later.

Determining the proximate cause

It has been said that determining the proximate cause of a loss is simply the application of common sense, and from many of the cases that would appear to be so. In *Marsden* v. *City & County Insurance*,[6] for example, a shopkeeper insured his plateglass against loss or damage arising from any cause except fire. Fire broke out in a neighbour's property, as the result of which

---

[1] For a useful review, see Clarke [1981] C.L.J. 284.
[2] The classical explanation of the doctrine of proximate cause is the judgment of Lord Sumner in *Becker, Gray & Co.* v. *London Assurance Corp.* [1918] A.C. 101.
[3] For an example in a household policy, see *Oei* v. *Foster* [1982] 2 Lloyd's Rep. 170; see [1982] J.B.L. 516.
[4] *Symington* v. *Union Ins. of Canton*, p. 183, above.
[5] Lord Dunedin in *Leyland Shipping Co.* v. *Norwich Union Fire Ins. Soc.* [1918] A.C. 350 at 363. This point is supported by the recent case of *J. J. Lloyd (Instruments) Ltd.* v. *Northern Star Insurance Co. Ltd.* [1987] 1 Lloyd's Rep. 32, where there were found to be two proximate causes of the damage suffered by a cruiser; adverse weather conditions and defective design. It was held that as defective design was not an excepted peril and adverse weather was not required to be the sole cause, the insurers were liable.
[6] (1865) L.R. 1 C.P. 232.

a mob gathered. The mob then rioted and broke the plate-glass. It was held that this riot, not the fire, was the cause of the loss and thus the insured recovered. In effect, the fire merely facilitated the subsequent loss rather than caused it. In *Winicofsky* v. *Army & Navy Insurance*,[7] goods were stolen from a building during an air raid. It was held that the theft not the air raid was the real cause of the loss; the latter merely facilitated it.

Two real causes

If there can really be said to be two real causes of a loss, discovering the cause which is the proximate cause is not always an easy matter. In a leading marine insurance case, *Leyland Shipping Co.* v. *Norwich Union Fire Insurance Society Ltd.*,[8] a ship was insured against loss from perils of the sea, with an exception in respect of loss due to hostilities. The ship was torpedoed by an enemy boat during the First World War. It was towed to Le Havre and moored in the harbour where it was quite safe. Subsequently, the authorities there required that it be moved to just outside the harbour. There, because of the action of the sea, it sank. It was held that the loss was not covered, the real cause being the torpedoing and not the perils of the sea. Yet had the ship not been moved outside the harbour, it would have been all right. The point is that the original cause predominates and is regarded as the cause of the loss unless it was merely facilitating a subsequent cause which totally changed matters. This analysis, however, does not appear to fit very well with some of what have been called the accident cases. There has been a great number of cases on questions of causation in accident policies, two of which will suffice here for detailed illustration.

In *Winspear* v. *Accident Insurance Association*,[9] the policy covered death or injury "caused by accidental, external and visible means" and excluded "any injury caused by or arising from natural disease. . . . " While crossing a stream, the insured suffered a fit, fell in and was drowned. It was held that the cause of death was accidental, namely the drowning, and not the fit, even though had it not been for the latter the insured would not have died as the stream was very shallow. *Lawrence* v. *Accidental Insurance Co.*[10] is even stranger in that the policy, while including the same wording, also required that accidental injury be the "direct and sole cause" of death. There the insured

[7] (1919) 88 L.J.K.B. 111.
[8] [1918] A.C. 350.
[9] (1880) 6 Q.B.D. 42.
[10] (1881) 7 Q.B.D. 216.

suffered a fit while standing on a railway platform. This caused him to fall on to the track, whereupon he was run over by a train. It was held that the accident of being run over was the proximate cause of death. Decisions like these can be interpreted in different ways. For example, it might be said that the natural cause, the fit, merely facilitated the real, accidental cause, but if that is so, surely it could be said of the *Leyland Shipping Case* that the torpedoing merely facilitated the sinking by the perils of the sea. Alternatively, the judges[11] may have been interpreting "proximate" as meaning latest, which subsequent cases[12] revealed clearly to be wrong. Or the cases can be justified on the ground that the accident superceded the prior, excluded, cause, to such an extent that it constituted a totally fresh cause,[13] but, with respect, this is difficult to understand on the facts. Perhaps the best explanation is the generosity of the English judges who decided these cases. Needless to say, insurers have been astute to draft changes in wordings so as to attempt to gain a more favourable result in this sort of case, and in what appears to be the latest reported accident case they succeeded.

In *Jason v. Batten*[14] the policy provided benefits to the insured if he sustained "in any accident bodily injury resulting in and being—independently of all other causes—the exclusive, direct and immediate cause of the injury or disablement." There was an exception in respect of "death, injury or disablement directly or indirectly caused by or arising or resulting from or traceable to . . . any physical defect or infirmity which existed prior to an accident." The insured suffered a coronary thrombosis after being involved in a motor accident, the clot blocking a coronary artery which had been narrowed by disease existing before the accident. It was held that the insurers were not liable. Stress associated with the accident had precipitated the thrombosis, but, assuming that the clot was an injury sustained in the accident, it was not "independently of all other causes" the exclusive cause of the insured's disablement. Equally efficient was the pre-existing disease. In addition, it was said, the loss fell clearly within the exception. It would appear therefore, that

---

[11] See, especially, Watkin Williams J. in *Lawrence v. Accidental Ins.*, above, at 221.
[12] Especially the leading House of Lords cases of *Becker, Gray*, above and *Leyland Shipping*, above. See also, *Wayne Tank Co. v. Employer's Liability Ass. Corp.* [1974] 1 Q.B. 57 at 66 (Lord Denning) and 72 (Roskill L.J.).
[13] See the explanation in *Jason v. Batten* [1969] 1 Lloyd's Rep. 281 at 291.
[14] [1969] 1 Lloyd's Rep. 281.

with the phrase "independently of all other causes" insurers have finally succeeded[15] in ensuring that they are liable under their personal accident policies only when there is an accident and nothing else. But it is important to remember, as was stressed earlier, that each case ultimately turns on its own facts.

Two proximate causes

It may be that in a case without such a clause qualifying the *causa proxima* rule, the court cannot genuinely say that one cause is more effective than another, so that an excepted cause and a covered cause are equally strong. This was a possible view of the facts in *Wayne Tank and Pump Co. Ltd.* v. *Employers' Liability Insurance Corporation Ltd.*[16] The plaintiff company was held liable to pay damages to Harbutt's "Plasticine" Ltd. for breach of a contract under which they installed new equipment in Harbutt's factory.[17] The equipment was defective and a resultant fire gutted the factory. Wayne Tank were insured by the defendants under a public liability policy which excluded indemnity for liability arising from damage caused by the nature or condition of any goods supplied by the insured. One cause of the plaintiff's liability was the defective nature of the equipment used, but another cause was the fact that one of its employees negligently and quite without authority turned on the equipment and left it on all night. Had this not happened, it was likely that the loss would not have occurred, as the equipment would have been tested under supervision and found to have been defective before any damage could be done. However, the Court of Appeal was unanimous in holding that the real cause of the loss was the defective nature of the equipment, a conclusion clearly in accordance with authority such as the *Leyland Shipping* case, whereby the original cause predominates unless it merely facilitates the subsequent cause and the latter totally alters the situation. The Court commented *obiter*, though, on the result if it could not genuinely be said that one of the two causes was predominant and held that the insurers would still

---

[15] For the other attempts, and for a fuller discussion of the accident cases, see MacGillivray and Parkington, paras. 1916–1925.

[16] [1974] 1 Q.B. 57.

[17] *Harbitt's "Plasticine" Ltd.* v. *Wayne Tank and Pump Co. Ltd.* [1970] 1 Q.B. 447. Had this case been decided correctly (see *Photo Production Ltd.* v. *Securicor Transport Ltd.* [1980] 2 W.L.R. 283), the subsequent insurance case would not have arisen. Harbutt's insurers rather than one of Wayne Tank's insurers would have borne the loss. It is clear that the insurance case was in substance a battle between two of the latter's insurers.

be protected, on the ground that they had provided for exemption from liability for one of the causes and the only way to ensure this was to exempt them totally. It is perhaps unfortunate that they did not consider the possibility in such a case of apportionment of the loss.[18]

Cause not expressly exempted

One final point remains to be discussed. As was seen earlier it was stated in one of the leading cases that the question of competition between causes becomes relevant only when there are two causes and one of them is expressly covered and the other is expressly exempted. In the case of *Gray* v. *Barr*, however, to which we have already referred in this chapter,[19] Lord Denning M.R. introduced the causation point where there was no express exclusion of a possible cause of the loss. In his view the proximate cause of the liability of the defendant Barr was not the shooting of the gun, whether that was an accident or not, but his deliberate conduct in approaching and grappling with the deceased while holding a loaded shotgun. Although neither of the other judges mentioned the causation point, and thus it cannot form part of the *ratio* of the case, consideration of it is logical. It seems unlikely though, that it will matter in practice if it is considered.[20] In a case like *Gray* v. *Barr*, the same result can be, and indeed was, reached simply on the construction of accident and/or the application of principles of public policy. This would seem likely to be the position in most cases, that is, that the same result can be achieved by considering whether the loss came within the cover provided as a matter of construction or definition. There is one type of case, though, where it is suggested that consideration of the causation rule, even though there is no question of an expressly excepted peril, might make a difference. This is where a possible cause of the loss is natural, whether from wear and tear or from the natural actions of living objects. An example, as pointed out earlier, is *Mills* v. *Smith*.[21] The learned judge in that case considered the matter as simply one of construction of "caused by accident," but if his attention had been directed towards the discovery of the proximate cause of the loss, might not the result have been different?

[18] See Ahmed (1974) 124 N.L.J. 592.

[19] See p. 174, above.

[20] Compare the case of *J. J. Lloyd (Instruments) Ltd.* v. *Northern Star Insurance Co. Ltd.*, described in note 5, above.

[21] See p. 177, above.

Chapter 12

CLAIMS UNDER THE POLICY

Claiming for a loss under an insurance policy may be considered to involve not simply the formal requirements usually imposed upon the insured, but also the question of the possible application of the rules of public policy and the law regarding the making of fraudulent claims. It is convenient also to examine some of the issues which may arise when claims are settled.

Public Policy

In a famous *dictum*,[1] a judge once referred to public policy as an "unruly horse," and it is clear that in the insurance field as much as in any other, care is needed in assessing the relevance of public policy considerations. There seem to be two relevant basic maxims which apply throughout the law: *ex turpi causa non oritur actio* (no action can arise from a wrongful cause) and a man may not profit from his own wrong or crime, the latter being probably merely a particular application of the former. The very application of these maxims to claims on insurance policies may be questioned in some instances, but, even assuming that it is sensible to apply them, how they actually apply is not always clear. It is convenient to subdivide the insurance cases into two basic groups, namely first and third party insurance.

First party insurances

If an insured is claiming in respect of a loss suffered solely by him, then it is clear, as we have already seen,[2] that he cannot recover if the loss was caused by his deliberate act. This may be simply the true construction of an insurance contract,[3] or it may alternatively be regarded as the application of a principle of

---

[1] Burrough J. in *Richardson* v. *Mellish* (1824) 2 Bing. 229 at 252.
[2] Chapter 11, p. 161.
[3] *Beresford* v. *Royal Ins. Co.* [1938] A.C. 586.

public policy.[4] In *W. H. Smith* v. *Clinton*,[5] an indemnity granted by a publisher against libel was held to be unenforceable, at least where the libel was intentional. But in addition, there is a general principle flowing from the maxims mentioned, that an insured cannot recover in respect of a loss caused by his own criminal or tortious act. This was neatly applied in the case of *Geismar* v. *Sun Alliance and London Insurance*.[6] Here the plaintiff smuggled into this country certain items of jewellery without declaring them and paying the legally required excise duty on them. As a result, they were liable to be forfeited. They were among items subsequently insured by him with the defendant and later stolen. It was held that the plaintiff could not recover in respect of this jewellery, as to allow such recovery would enable him to profit from his deliberate criminal act, even though the profit was sought indirectly under the insurance policy.[7]

It would seem that the commission of a crime or tort must be deliberate. It has often been recognised that insane suicide, when a crime, did not prevent recovery under a life policy.[8] So, for example, an insured might unintentionally commit a crime of strict liability in circumstances giving rise to a claim on his policy, but it is suggested that he would not be debarred from recovery.

A nice question arises concerning the inter-relationship of the two principles mentioned. The rule that deliberate acts *per se* are not covered can, because it is not an overriding requirement of public policy, be expressly excluded. The usual example is the inclusion of suicide, sane or insane, in the cover provided by a life policy, although normally only after the policy has run for a period of one or two years. If the commission of such an act, however, is also criminal or tortious, the question arises whether the maxims of public policy debar recovery. The answer would appear to be in the affirmative, following the leading case of *Beresford* v. *Royal Insurance Co.*[9] Here the life insured deliberately took his own life at a time when suicide

---

[4] Shand, "Unblinkering the Unruly Horse: Public Policy in the Law of Contract" (1972) 30 C.L.J. 144 at 161.

[5] (1908) 99 L.T. 840.

[6] See also Defamation Act 1952, s.11 confirming that indemnity or insurance against unintentional defamation is enforceable.

[6] [1977] 2 Lloyd's Rep. 62.

[7] Compare *Euro-Diam Ltd.* v. *Bathurst* [1987] 1 Lloyd's Rep. 178.

[8] *Beresford* v. *Royal Ins. Co.*, note 3, above.

[9] Note 3, above. For a more recent example, see *Husak* v. *Imperial Life Ass. Co. of Canada* (1970) 9 D.L.R. (3d.) 602.

was still a crime. It was arguable, and indeed was held, that on the construction of the policy death by suicide was covered, but the House of Lords nevertheless denied the insured's representative recovery. The principal ground for the decision was that recovery would permit a benefit to result to the insured from his criminal act,[10] although it was recognised that an assignee for value of the policy would have been entitled to recover, because then there could not be said to be such benefit. However, there must be a public policy in favour of enforcing contractual obligations which one party has freely undertaken. If the insurer had contracted to pay on the suicide of the life insured, why should they not have been held to that promise? This point was discussed by Lord MacMillan who concluded that the public policy considerations had to be weighed, finally concurring with the result in this way: "I feel the force of the view that to increase the estate which a criminal leaves behind him is to benefit him. . . . And no criminal can be allowed to benefit in any way by his crime."[11] It may be thought that this is slightly unreal, a point to which we shall return when assessing the public policy question in general. There can be little doubt now that the actual result of the *Beresford* case would be different, not least because suicide is no longer a crime.[12]

Further, in respect of life assurance, account must now be taken of the provisions of the Forfeiture Act 1982.[13] Section 2 of this Act gives the court a wide discretion to allow a claim by someone who has unlawfully killed another to the benefits of, *inter alia*, a life insurance policy. It cannot apply where the claimant is guilty of murder[14] nor does it apply to cases of suicide,[15] but it would be apt to cover a case of manslaughter where there was no intention or recklessness.

Third party insurances

Turning to consider the cases involving third party policies, the same general principles apply.[16] Thus, the intentional commission of a crime against the third party for which the insured

---

[10] As will be seen, Lord Atkin referred also to other public policy principles.
[11] [1938] A.C. 586 at 605.
[12] Suicide Act 1961; see the comment of Salmon L.J. in *Gray* v. *Barr* [1971] 2 Q.B. 554 at 582.
[13] See generally, Kenny, (1983) 46 M.L.R. 66.
[14] s.5.
[15] Because it only applies where the beneficiary has killed "another" (s.1).
[16] The Forfeiture Act is of no relevance here because of the requirement in s.2(4) that the claimant has an "interest in property."

is liable in damages in tort will not be covered by the insured's liability insurance. However, it is not clear what degree of deliberation is required, and it can be said again that there are competing public policy considerations involved.[17] In a sense, the idea of the insured benefiting from his own wrong in this sort of case is ridiculous, as any indemnity received goes to his third party victim. Furthermore, there is surely an important public policy consideration in attempting to ensure that the victims of tortfeasors receive any damages awarded to them, which in practice means in the majority of cases that the tortfeasor ought to be allowed to enforce his insurance policy. This has at least been recognised in the context of compulsory motor vehicle insurance, and there are four important cases which support this line of argument. These cases will be examined first, before it is sought to be discovered whether there are any differences in any other contexts.

Motor insurance

Both *Tinline* v. *White Cross Insurance Association*[18] and *James* v. *British General Insurance Co.*[19] concerned similar facts. The insured in both cases had third party cover in respect of injury or death arising out of the use of their cars, although this was not actually compulsory at the time. They were both involved in accidents resulting in the deaths of pedestrians in circumstances which led to their convictions for manslaughter. In *Tinline*, the insured was driving at an excessive speed; in *James*, he was drunk. Clearly both insureds were more than merely negligent, but on the other hand did not intend death or injury. In both cases it was held that their insurers were liable to indemnify them against the damages they were liable to pay in tort, despite the fact that, in the sense that the courts have used elsewhere, they would thereby profit from their own criminal actions. If the insured acts deliberately, however, it appears that public policy is still against his recovering. This was made clear in the judgments in *Hardy* v. *Motor Insurers' Bureau*.[20] This involved the deliberate injury of the plaintiff by an uninsured car thief. The plaintiff's claim against the defendant was resisted on public policy grounds. The Court of Appeal made it quite clear that had the tortfeasor himself been seeking to

---

[17] See generally the excellent analysis by Shand in the article referred to in note 4.
[18] [1921] 3 K.B. 327.
[19] [1927] 1 K.B. 311.
[20] [1964] 2 Q.B. 745.

enforce a motor policy, he would have been denied, but fortunately the Road Traffic Act 1972[21] permits a third party victim to sue the tortfeasor's insurer directly and, where the tortfeasor is uninsured, there is a right of action against the Motor Insurers' Bureau.[22] Thus, on the facts of the case, there was no question of the *ex turpi* maxim applying, and this will be the case in respect of all victims of car accidents. In the most lucid rationalisation by an English judge[23] of the place of public policy in the insurance context, Diplock L.J. referred to the importance of weighing up the different considerations:

> "I can see no reason in public policy for drawing a distinction between one kind of wrongful act, of which a third party is the innocent victim, and another kind of wrongful act; between wrongful acts which are crimes, on the part of the perpetrator and wrongful acts which are not crimes; or between wrongful acts which are crimes of carelessness and wrongful acts which are intentional crimes. It seems to me to be slightly unrealistic to suggest that a person who is not deterred by the risks of a possible sentence of life imprisonment from using a vehicle with intent to commit grievous bodily harm would be deterred by the fear that his civil liability to his victim would not be discharged by his insurers."[24]

The decision in *Hardy* has recently been approved and followed by the House of Lords in *Gardner* v. *Moore*,[25] where the facts were indistinguishable and it was held that the proper construction of the Road Traffic Act 1972 and the Motor Insurers' Bureau agreements, and the policy underlying them, required the M.I.B. to satisfy the motorist's liability to the innocent plaintiff.[26]

Other compulsory insurances
The immediate question that arises is how far this sort of reasoning can be applied outside the motor insurance field. It is

---

[21] s.149; see Chapter 19 at p. 308.
[22] See Chapter 19.
[23] Followed in Australia in *Fire & All Risks Co. Ltd.* v. *Powell* [1966] V.R. 513.
[24] [1964] 2 Q.B. at 769–770.
[25] [1984] A.C. 548.
[26] In the words of Lord Hailsham L.C., *ibid.* at 561–562, "To invoke, as [the M.I.B.] now do, the well-known doctrine of public policy that a man may not profit by the consequences of his own wrongdoing seems to me to stand the principle of public policy on its head."

suggested that it will be applied wherever else third party insurance is compulsory, and particularly therefore to employers' liability insurance.[27] The fact that an employee is injured in circumstances involving a criminal offence, for example under the Factories Act, should not entitle his employer's insurer to invoke the defence of public policy, if the employer is liable in tort to the employee, however great the degree of negligence or recklessness. Considerations as to the insured's profiting from his wrong or not being deterred if insurance monies are available, are outweighed by the consideration that Parliament deemed it of the utmost importance that injured employees should be compensated by making this insurance compulsory. If, however, the crime or tort was intentionally committed by the employer or someone for whom he is responsible, then it is possible that the claim for insurance indemnity could be denied, because there is no machinery equivalent to the Road Traffic Act provisions for the injured employee to sue the insurer directly, and thus any litigation would necessitate the insured employer directly enforcing the policy to recover in respect of a deliberate wrong, something which even under *Hardy* v. *Motor Insurers' Bureau* and *Gardner* v. *Moore*, the courts would not permit.

Other third party insurances

Outside these areas where the countervailing public policy considerations can be invoked, it seems that the courts will, despite the more liberal tenor of the judgments in *Hardy*, adhere to the traditional approach. In *Haseldine* v. *Hosken*,[28] for example, a solicitor sought to enforce his professional indemnity policy in respect of a loss he had suffered by entering into a champertous agreement. Despite his claim that he had not known that he was committing a criminal offence, a claim that in any event it might be difficult to believe, the Court of Appeal held that he was unable to recover.[29] Scrutton L.J. commented: "It is clearly contrary to public policy to insure against the commission of an act, knowing what act is being committed, which is a crime, although the person committing it may not at the time know it to be so." These are very wide words, appearing to make no distinction between negligent and intentional

---

[27] See Chapter 20.
[28] [1933] 1 K.B. 822.
[29] Another reason for the decision was that on its true construction the policy did not cover the loss in question.

crimes.[30] Whether such a distinction can be drawn must depend on the effect of the decision in *Gray* v. *Barr*,[31] although it is not easy to formulate precisely from the judgments here exactly what principles of public policy are to be applied. This case was considered in Chapter 11.[32] It will be recalled that it concerned the man who shot and killed his wife's lover. Although he was acquitted of both murder and manslaughter by a jury in a criminal trial, the Court of Appeal held in the civil action that he was in fact guilty of manslaughter, a conclusion that cannot itself be faulted. It was also held that, apart from any questions as to the construction of his insurance policy, public policy required that he could not recover from his insurers the damages he was liable to pay in tort to the deceased's widow. All three judges regarded as of the utmost significance the fact that Barr carried a loaded shotgun and threatened violence with it, thus engaging in a wilful and culpable act. The public conscience would be shocked, it was said, if he were allowed to enforce his insurance contract. Yet it may be noted that the public conscience of the 12 of the public who sat as the jury in the criminal trial can hardly have been shocked by Barr's actions as the wronged husband. Can it really be said that permitting him to recover would have encouraged the greater use of violence and guns, which is implicit in the court's reasoning? These more general questions will be returned to shortly. *Gray* v. *Barr* did at least recognise that the motor manslaughter cases were correctly decided, but the problem is whether these are *sui generis*, or whether there are other distinguishing features. The stress laid in the judgments on the intentional aspects of Barr's conduct, that is the use of a loaded gun quite deliberately, does support the view, perhaps, that genuinely negligent criminal acts by an insured will not invoke the defence of public policy if committed in the course of perfectly lawful behaviour. If, for example, a sportsman with an appropriate liability policy negligently shoots someone mistaking them for a deer, it is suggested that he should be able to enforce the policy in respect of any damages he has to pay.

The present public policy rules can therefore probably be

---

[30] In fact the court doubted the correctness of the decisions in *Tinline* and *James*, doubts that were not finally removed until the decision in *Gray* v. *Barr*, [1971] 2 Q.B. 554.
[31] [1971] 2 Q.B. 554. See also, *Co-operative Fire & Casualty Co.* v. *Saindon* (1975) 56 D.L.R. (3d) 556, justly criticised by Hasson in (1976) 14 Osgoode Hall L.J. 769 and *Meah* v. *McCreamer (No. 2)* [1986] 1 All E.R. 943 at 950–951.
[32] See p. 174, above.

summarised in this way. In motor insurance on the personal injury side, and probably in employers' liability insurance, only deliberate criminal conduct could possibly prevent an insured from enforcing a claim on public policy grounds. In all other cases, mere negligence in the commission of a crime or tort would not matter, but public policy will be a good defence where the act causing the loss was deliberate or reckless and where the insured deliberately, or possibly recklessly, engaged in a criminal course of conduct, even if the final act causing the loss was accidental.

It should be noted that there is also clear authority that insurance against the consequences of crime is strictly unenforceable for reasons of public policy.[33] Indeed, such insurance may itself be void, rather than merely a claim made under it. So, for example, insurance against parking fines would be against public policy. The same might be said of a very common form of insurance, namely that offered to motorists against the consequences of being "breathalysed." To drive with more than the permitted level of alcohol in the blood is a criminal offence. Policies offering chauffeur services, or an equivalent, for the period of the mandatory year's disqualification following such a conviction, might be said to fall within this prohibition. It is, of course, inconceivable that such an insurer would ever take the point.

Some general comments

Running through these cases appear to be a number of justifications for these principles of public policy. Some of these we have already briefly examined and they have all been the subject of detailed scrutiny elsewhere,[34] but it is appropriate here to make some general comments. The principles appear to rest particularly upon three points. First, there is the idea that refusing to allow indemnity will deter others. Secondly, there is the theme that it is right to punish an insured in this way. Thirdly, there is what has been called the absolute rule, that simply the courts should not allow someone to profit from their wrong. With great respect, it is suggested that deterrence and punishment should have no place in the civil law. While Mr. Barr was no doubt punished as a result of the Court of Appeal's ruling, which was tantamount to the imposition of a fine on him, is this

---

[33] *Hardy* v. *M.I.B.* [1964] 2 Q.B. 745 at 760.
[34] See, in particular, the article by Shand (note 4) and the note by Fleming (1971) 34 M.L.R. 176 on the first instance decision in *Gray* v. *Barr* which, on public policy, was to the same effect as that of the Court of Appeal.

proper when at a criminal trial he had been acquitted? Can it really be said that someone in his position would be deterred from using a gun when the prospect of life imprisonment did not do so? Furthermore, as has already been argued, the idea that insurance being available means that the insured will profit from his wrong is curious, at least in cases of suicide and third party insurance. "In most cases of insurance . . . the people most likely to be harmed by withholding indemnity are the innocent victims of the fault insured against, who more likely than not will be left with an empty judgment against a man of straw."[35] As has already been noted, there were signs of a more rational approach in *Hardy* v. *Motor Insurers' Bureau*, but the effect of this, other than in the motor insurance field, appears to have been quite overlooked in *Gray* v. *Barr*. It is submitted that in all these cases, all the factors should be weighed, in other words, the particular gravity of the conduct of the insured against the likely *real* consequences of refusing to enforce the insurance.[36] However, the prospect of the courts' doing this without legislative intervention appears remote.

The Claims Procedure

In the absence of any specific term in an insurance policy, it is unclear whether, upon suffering a loss, an insured is bound to claim for it within a reasonable time on pain of the claim being denied, or whether it is sufficient merely to claim before the statutory limitation period expires.[37] In practice, this is a purely academic question, as all policies contain conditions regarding such matters as when notice of a loss is required to be given and what claims procedure and what proofs etc. are required. Invariably, nowadays, such conditions will be conditions precedent to the liability of the insurer, a breach of which will entitle the insurer to avoid liability for the particular loss, or, possibly, conditions precedent to the validity of the policy.[38]

In general, as with any other part of the insurance contract, an insurer is free to insert whatever conditions it chooses in this

---

[35] Shand, *op. cit.* at 160.

[36] Applying these sorts of considerations to the facts of *Gray* v. *Barr*, Shand (*op. cit.* at 164) suggests that the result would and should have been different.

[37] Compare *MacGillivray and Parkington*, 7th edition para. 1584 with *ibid.*, 8th edition, para. 1704 and Ivamy, *General Principles*, p. 420.

[38] See pp. 116–119, above.

regard. However, the *Statements of Insurance Practice*[39] state that an insured will not be asked to report a claim and subsequent developments except "as soon as reasonably possible," and it is to be hoped that all relevant policies now have this wording rather than a strict time limit. In so far as they do, then obviously the relevant conditions will be legally binding, but it must be remembered that otherwise the *Statements* are not legally binding, so that there is no sanction if the wording of a particular policy has not been changed.

The matters which are usually contained in conditions governing the claims procedure can be examined under a number of heads.

Notice

The first basic obligation is to give notice of a loss. If the policy is a third party policy, the condition may well require that notice be given of any event that may give rise to a claim against the insured in addition to an actual claim. Oral notice is sufficient unless the policy provides otherwise.

Such conditions are strictly construed against the insurer. In *Verelst's Administratrix* v. *Motor Union Insurance Co.*,[40] a motor policy which covered the insured against death by accident required his representative to give notice in writing of a claim "as soon as possible" after it had come to his knowledge. This was construed subjectively so that the fact that notice was given nearly one year after the accident was irrelevant, as the existence of the policy was unknown until just before notice was given and all the circumstances of the representative had to be taken into account. It is suggested that a similar interpretation should be given to conditions inserted as a result of the *Statements of Insurance Practice*, so that "as soon as reasonably possible" means as soon as the insured (or his representative) could be expected to give notice taking all the circumstances into account.

Time-limits

It is unlikely that, in those situations where they are not constrained by the *Statements*, insurers retain conditions as generous to the insured as that in *Verelst*. Far more likely are those

---

[39] As to these, see pp. 3–5, above. They apply, of course, only to policies issued to individual insureds.
[40] [1925] 2 K.B. 137.

requiring notice within a specific time limit. If such a condition is clear, and is precedent to the insurer's liability, a failure to comply, however inadvertant or excusable, will entitle the insurer to avoid liability. An oldish example is *Cassel* v. *Lancashire & Yorkshire Accident Insurance Co.*,[41] where an accident policy required notice within 14 days. It was not until eight months after an accident that the insured became aware that he had been injured as a result of it, and he then gave notice, but it was held that the insurer was not liable. The term was clear and simply, was not complied with. Similarly, in *Adamson* v. *Liverpool London & Globe Insurance Co.*,[42] a cash in transit policy had the following condition: "The insured shall, immediately upon the discovery of any loss, give notice thereof to the company. . . . The company shall be under no liability hereunder in respect of any loss which has not been notified to the company within 15 days of its occurrence." Over a period of two years before the loss was discovered, an employee of the insured embezzled money entrusted to him for the purchase of National Insurance stamps. When the loss was discovered, the insured immediately notified his insurers. It was held that the latter were liable only in respect of the losses which occurred within the 14 days prior to notification, by reason of the latter part of the condition. It does seem though that there was an element of ambiguity in the condition, the first part of which referred to the giving of notice immediately upon discovery. The insured had done this and indeed had done all that he could do in the circumstances. The decision can only be regarded as a little harsh.

The result of conditions such as these, if strictly relied upon, and it is not suggested that they always are, may be that an insured is treated harshly without real justification. There appears to be an unanswerable case for giving a court power by statute to relieve a breach of such a condition in favour of an innocent insured, or to prescribe that a breach can be relied upon only when the insurer can show that it has been prejudiced thereby, or alternatively that a breach can never be used to defeat a claim *per se*, but entitles the insurer to counterclaim for such loss as it can show that it has suffered as the result of the breach.[43]

---

[41] (1885) 1 T.L.R. 495.
[42] [1953] 2 Lloyd's Rep. 355.
[43] Provisions such as these are common in the United States of America and Australia, for example.

Place of notice

In addition to stipulating time-limits, a condition as to notice may require that it is given to a particular place, for example, the insurer's head office. This will be upheld and a local agent will not have authority to waive the requirement,[44] but some power to relieve against technical reliance on a breach here seems desirable. In the absence of a specified destination, notice to any agent with usual authority to receive it will suffice. Notice need not be given by the insured himself, but by an agent of his authorised to do so. Whether or not a condition as to notice is satisfied if an unconnected third party informs the insurer of a loss depends on whether the decision in *Lickiss* v. *Milestone Motor Policies*[45] is followed. This will be discussed in the following section.

Particulars

The giving of notice of a loss is usually fairly informal, in the sense that it does not comprehend full details of a claim. These are normally separately required by a condition and frequently in practice consist of the filling in of a claim form sent by the insurer upon receipt of notice. In the absence of such a condition, the insured would simply have to prove his loss in the normal way if the matter were litigated.

The standard conditions imposing the legal obligation with respect to particulars appear to be of two types. One requires the insured to give full particulars of the loss, which has been defined as the best particulars he can reasonably give which must be sufficient to enable the insurer to ascertain the nature, extent and character of the loss.[46]

The other standard condition requires the insured to give such proofs and information as may reasonably be required by the insurer.[47] What an insurer reasonably requires must be a question of fact, but it will be virtually impossible for an insured to resist anything of relevance to his claim, and, if he is a businessman, he may well have to submit matters of general relevance to his business. In *Welch* v. *Royal Exchange Assurance*,[48] the plaintiff insured his stock in trade against fire. Following a claim, the insurers denied liability and the dispute

---

[44] *Brook* v. *Trafalgar Ins. Co.* (1946) 79 Ll.L.R. 365.
[45] [1966] 2 All E.R. 972.
[46] *Mason* v. *Harvey* (1853) 8 Ex. 819 at 820.
[47] "Proofs satisfactory to the insurer" will be interpreted in the same way; *Braunstein* v. *Accidental Death Ins. Co.* (1861) 1 B. & S. 782.
[48] [1939] 1 K.B. 294.

was referred to arbitration. The insurers, relying upon a condition of the sort mentioned, requested to see bank accounts which the insured used for the purpose of his business, but which were in his mother's name. The insured refused this until under cross examination in the arbitration proceedings. The arbitrator held that these details were reasonably required, and the Court of Appeal upheld that decision, the argument having centred on whether the condition was precedent to the insurers' liability. Having decided that it was,[49] the insured's claim was lost, as he had failed to comply before pursuing his claim to law, albeit, as it turned out, the bank accounts contained nothing of any relevance.

Personal compliance unnecessary?
One interesting point has arisen with regard to the insured's obligation to give full particulars, and a similar point could also arise with respect to the giving of notice. In *Lickiss* v. *Milestone Motor Policies*,[50] the insured motorcyclist was involved in an accident on May 17 in which he negligently damaged a taxi-cab. His policy covered him against such third party liability and required him to provide his insurers with full particulars of any accident as soon as possible and to forward immediately any summons, writ or similar matter relating to the accident. The insured never himself informed his insurers of the accident, but they learnt of it from the taxi driver. Neither did he forward a summons which he received, but the police on June 18 sent full details to the insurers. The main reason for the decision turned upon a point of waiver which will be examined later, but Lord Denning M.R., with whom Danckwerts L.J. agreed, held that the insured was not in breach of the condition mentioned on the ground that, although he himself did not comply, the insurers received all the necessary information, in particular from the police, within the necessary time. This aspect of the decision is difficult to justify as a matter of strict law, as the condition did expressly provide that *"the insured shall give* full particulars . . . ." (emphasis added),[51] though it is impossible to deny its justice, as the insurers were in no way prejudiced by the insured's failure. Assuming that the decision is followed, and there has as yet been no subsequent relevant case, its logic

---
[49] The condition provided for no liability "unless" it was complied with; compare the construction of "until" in a similar context in *Weir* v. *Northern Counties Ins.* (1879) 4 L.R.Ir. 689.
[50] See note 45.
[51] See, on this point, the dissenting judgment of Salmon L.J.

must apply to any condition concerning the claims procedure, including the giving of notice, even if such a condition expressly appears to require personal compliance by the insured (or his duly authorised agent).

Further co-operation

In addition to the requirement of particulars, conditions in appropriate policies sometimes require further co-operation by the insured. Examples of this will be seen in the context of liability policies in Chapter 18, but a particular example is worth citing at this stage. In *London Guarantee Co. v. Fearnley*,[52] a fidelity policy taken out by an employer covered him against the risk of embezzlement by an employee. A condition precedent provided that, if a claim was made, the insured should prosecute the employee concerned if the insurer so required. Following a particular claim, the insured refused to comply with such a request and it was held that the insurer was entitled to avoid liability.

Proof of loss

A condition may also require the insured to provide proof of his loss. This differs from particulars in that it means documentary proof of the loss, not merely a description of it. Sometimes the insured will be required to make a statutory declaration. Even though the proofs may show prima facie that the loss is covered by the policy, the burden of proving this should the matter be litigated still rests upon the insured.[53]

Contesting insurer's denial of liability

Finally, a condition may require the insured, if the insurer disputes liability for a loss, to contest this denial by legal proceedings within a stated period, on pain of liability being totally avoided. Such a condition has been upheld in a case which involved a claim against third party liability.[54] The insured failed to contest the insurer's denial of liability within the year stated and his claim was thus totally defeated even though his actual liability to the third party was not established until long after the year after the insurers repudiated. The only course of an insured in this position will be to seek a declar-

---

[52] (1880) 5 App.Cas. 911.
[53] *Watts v. Simmons* (1924) 18 Ll.L.R. 177.
[54] *Walker v. Pennine Ins. Co.* [1980] 2 Lloyd's Rep. 156.

ation that his insurers are liable to indemnify him, if he should be adjudged liable to the third party.

Arbitration

Despite the undertaking which will be referred to shortly, it is still usual to find in insurance policies of most sorts a condition precedent to the insurer's liability to the effect that any disputed claim must go to arbitration before a court of law. Such arbitration clauses can refer to disputes over liability, but more likely now they will cover only disputes over the *quantum* of a loss.

While arbitration may be cheaper than litigation, it naturally does not attract the attention that court action does, so that insurers might thereby be able to rely upon "technical defences" without public opprobium. Furthermore, legal aid is not available to a party to arbitration. Reporting in 1957, the Law Reform Committee[55] expressed concern and said that they had evidence that insurers had abused their position in certain cases against honest and careful insureds by insisting upon arbitration. However, they recommended no change in the law because at the time of their enquiry, the British Insurance Association and Lloyd's stated that their members had agreed not to enforce arbitration in cases of disputes over liability against the wishes of an insured. Excepted from this undertaking were reinsurance, marine insurance and certain aspects of aviation insurance where arbitration is specially negotiated and where the parties are perfectly capable of looking after themselves. In most cases, therefore, the law surrounding the use of arbitration clauses is of practical importance only at all in respect of disputes over the amount of a loss.[56]

The leading case of *Scott* v. *Avery*,[57] itself on an arbitration clause in an insurance policy, decided that such clauses in contracts generally are enforceable as conditions precedent provided that they do not purport ultimately to oust the jurisdiction of the court, and that they can cover disputes over liability as well as over quantum. If legal proceedings are brought by an insured in respect of a matter covered by an arbi-

---

[55] Fifth Report on Conditions and Exceptions in Insurance Policies, Cmnd. 62, para. 13.

[56] Note, though, that if an insured is able to, and does, take advantage of the services offered by Personal Insurances Arbitration Service (see p. 4, above, at note 15), he is bound by the result. This is not so in respect of the Insurance Ombudsman.

[57] (1856) 5 H.L.C. 810.

tration clause, the court has a discretion under section 4 of the Arbitration Act 1950 to stay the proceedings and thus enforce the clause. Obviously the onus is on the party seeking to keep the dispute out of arbitration. A number of insurance cases have considered the exercise of this discretion, and it seems that the legal proceedings will usually be stayed unless the dispute concerns difficult points of law or involves an allegation of fraud.[58]

Independent validity of arbitration clauses
The final question concerns what has been termed the independent validity of arbitration clauses.[59] It is clear that if the insurer is seeking to deny the validity or very existence of the policy in question, it cannot rely on any of its terms to enforce arbitration,[60] unless the arbitration clause itself is worded widely enough to cover the reference of a dispute as to the validity of the contract.[61] There are, it seems, three clear instances in the insurance context where, for this reason, an arbitration clause cannot be relied upon. These are (i) where the existence of the contract is disputed[62]; (ii) where the insurer alleges that the contract is void or illegal, for example, for lack of insurable interest required by statute[63]; and (iii) where it is alleged that the policy has been avoided *ab initio* for non-disclosure or misrepresentation.[64] Where, however, an insurer is simply relying on the terms of the contract to deny liability, then the contract and hence the arbitration clause still stand. Thus, an allegation of breach of condition, or breach of continuing warranty, or that a loss is not within the cover provided, does not affect the validity of an arbitration clause. It is not as clear whether breach of a warranty on the proposal form as to existing facts would have the same effect. Breach of such a warranty entitles the insurer to avoid the whole contract, and in substance, if not in form, the issue is the same as misrepresentation. However, it appears that the courts take the view that the insurer is simply relying

---

[58] See *Clough* v. *County Livestock Insurance Ass.* (1916) 85 L.J.K.B. 1185 and *Smith* v. *Pearl Assurance Co.* [1939] 1 All E.R. 95, holding that the cost of arbitration for the insured and the unavailability of legal aid are not valid grounds for disallowing it.
[59] Powell, [1954] C.L.P. 75.
[60] *Heyman* v. *Darwins* [1942] A.C. 356.
[61] *Ibid.* at 385 (Lord Wright) and 392, 398 (Lord Porter).
[62] *Toller* v. *Law Accident Ins. Soc.* [1936] 2 All E.R. 952.
[63] But not where the insured merely fails to have the interest required by the contract: *Macaura* v. *Northern Ass. Co.* [1925] A.C. 619 (see p. 44, above).
[64] *Stebbing* v. *Liverpool & London & Globe Ins. Co.* [1917] 2 K.B. 433.

upon the terms of the contract to deny its validity so that an arbitration clause is enforceable.[65]

One rather disputed situation is where the insurer avoids liability alleging a fraudulent claim. As will be seen, this has the effect of avoiding the policy rather than a particular claim, and it was suggested in *Jureidini* v. *National British & Irish Millers' Insurance Co.*[66] that the insurers could not therefore rely upon an arbitration clause. This dictum in a wider context has been subsequently disapproved of,[67] and it appears incorrect in principle. The avoidance of the policy is from the date of breach, and it still stands for the purpose of reliance upon its terms. In any event, under section 24 of the 1950 Act, it is likely that an allegation of fraud is a good reason for a court's refusing to enforce arbitration.

Waiver and estoppel

It is in connection with conditions regarding the claims procedure that most often are found allegations that an insurer is in some way precluded from relying upon a breach. Insurers may be so precluded by application of the doctrines of waiver and estoppel.[68] The use of the description "waiver" in this and similar contexts has been criticised, but it is well established and will be followed here.

While waiver and estoppel may have a common base, they are essentially different. Waiver is a form of election. The insurer who has the right to avoid liability may elect not to do so or may be deemed to have so elected, provided that it has knowledge of the breach and either expressly so elects or else acts in such a way as would induce a reasonable insured to believe that it is not going to insist upon its legal rights. Thus, waiver requires a conscious act by the insurer or its agent, but it does not require the insured to act in response in any way. Estoppel on the other hand requires a representation by words

---

[65] See, *e.g.* the *Stebbing* case, above, the discussion in Chapter 7 at p. 97, and the related problem as to whether a clause providing for the forfeiture of premiums paid upon avoidance for breach of warranty is enforceable (see Chap. 8, p. 124). As, in many cases, the same facts will involve breach of warranty and/or non-disclosure or misrepresentation, the insurer will have a choice and, by relying upon breach of warranty, can enforce the arbitration clause.

[66] [1915] A.C. 499 *per* Viscount Haldane; the other Lords decided the case on other grounds.

[67] *Heyman* v. *Darwins*, above; see Powell, *op. cit.* But see *The Litsion Pride* [1985] 1 Lloyd's Rep. 437, discussed at p. 210, below.

[68] As to the application of those doctrines in respect of non-disclosure or breach of warranty, see pp. 86–87, above.

or conduct to the insured that the insurer will not rely upon a breach of condition which the insured relies upon and acts upon to his detriment. It does not depend upon the knowledge of the person estopped and is a doctrine of much wider significance. Waiver and estoppel may very well arise upon the same facts, but in certain cases the distinction may be crucial, as will be seen.

Evidence of waiver

It is clear that for waiver to operate, the insurer must know of the breach, but that knowledge may be the knowledge of an agent which is imputed to the insurer under general principles.[69] Apart from express affirmation, the conduct of the insurer that can amount to waiver may be constituted by the acceptance of a renewal premium, but perhaps the most likely form in this context will arise simply from its handling of the claim. If, with knowledge of the breach, the insurer does anything such as writing for further particulars or continuing to process the claim without denial of liability or without reserving its position, that will amount to waiver. The facts of *Lickliss v. Milestone Motor Policies*, examined earlier,[70] provide a good illustration. The insured failed to forward any information to his insurers, but the police did so. Subsequently, the insurers wrote to the insured referring to the summons and indicating that they wished to arrange for his defence to it. It was held unanimously that this constituted waiver of their right to avoid liability. The insurers knew of the breach, yet had ignored it and written in terms indicating that they accepted liability.

On the other hand, a letter or an oral representation indicating that the insurers are still enquiring into the matter, without any indication that they regard themselves as bound, cannot amount to a waiver.[71]

The insurers may, knowing of a breach, continue to rely upon the policy to exercise a right given to them thereunder. If they do so without reserving their position, they will have lost their right to complain. In *Craine* v. *Colonial Mutual Fire Insurance Co.*,[72] a fire policy required the insured to deliver particulars of loss within 15 days of the loss as a condition precedent to recov-

---

[69] See Chapter 10 at pp. 144–145.
[70] See p. 202.
[71] See, *e.g. Farrell* v. *Federated Employers' Ins. Ass.* [1970] 1 W.L.R. 1400.
[72] (1920) 28 C.L.R. 305 (High Court of Australia). The decision was affirmed by the Privy Council, *sub nom. Yorkshire Ins. Co.* v. *Craine* [1922] 2 A.C. 541, but rather on the construction of the condition in question.

ery. This the insured failed to do. In the meantime, however, under another condition in the policy, the insurer took possession of the premises and remained there for four months. It was held that by reason of this action, the insurer was precluded from relying upon the breach. Normally, of course, this would have been a clear case of waiver, but a condition in the policy, apparently accepted as valid, precluded the application of this doctrine unless confirmed in writing by the insurer. Thus, the judgment proceeded upon the basis of estoppel and is a useful illustration of the point made earlier as to the importance of the distinction between the two doctrines. By its conduct in taking possession of the premises, the insurer represented that it would not rely upon the breach. The insured relied upon this to his detriment by being deprived of possession of his premises for the period stated.

Waiver of future performance

Just as an insurer may waive an existing breach, it may also waive future performance of a condition. In *Burridge* v. *Haines*,[73] a policy on horses contained a condition providing that in the event of death by accident, the insured should obtain the certification of a qualified vet to the effect that death was caused by a peril insured against. Following the death of one horse, the insurer's own vet examined the animal and the insurer told the insured that this was acceptable and that it would accept evidence of the horse's death other than that prescribed in the policy. It was held that the insurer had waived its right to rely upon a breach of the condition, because by its conduct it had implied that it would not enforce it, and it had rendered it impossible for the insured to comply by appointing its own vet who dissected and destroyed the horse before a vet chosen by the insured had the chance to examine it.

Agent's authority

Just as insurers may be deemed to have knowledge of a breach through an agent, so also in appropriate circumstances an agent may have authority actually to waive a breach. This will turn on the extent of the agent's actual or ostensible authority. An agent who has authority to accept premiums or settle claims will probably have at least ostensible authority to waive a breach of condition.[74] A mere canvassing agent will not. In

---

[73] (1918) 87 L.J.K.B. 641.
[74] See Chapter 10 at p. 143.

Brook v. Trafalgar Insurance Co.[75] the policy required notice of loss to be given to the company's head office, and it was held that a mere local agent had no authority by himself accepting notice to waive breach of that condition.

Delay as waiver

Mere delay by the insurers in dealing with, for example, a late claim does not amount to waiver. In *Allen v. Robles*,[76] a motor insured was obliged to notify his insurer of a claim against him within five days of the claim being made. Following an accident, he did not notify the insurers that a claim was made against him until two months later. However, the insurers did not deny liability to the insured for four months although they had informed the third party and had warned the insured one month after the claim that they reserved their position. It was held that the insurers had not lost their right to avoid liability merely by lapse of time. In the words of Fenton Atkinson L.J.: "The lapse of time would only operate against [the insurer] if thereby there was prejudice to the defendant or if in some way rights of third parties intervened or if the delay was so long that the court felt able to say that the delay in itself was of such a length as to be evidence that they had in truth decided to accept liability."[77]

Fraudulent Claims

The topic of fraudulent claims merits its own special treatment, as it appears that in this respect the duty of the insured to act with the utmost good faith survives beyond the effecting of the policy. Thus, if the insured makes a fraudulent claim, the whole policy, and not just the particular claim, is voidable.[78] It is not clear whether avoidance operates *ab initio* or from the date of the fraud; in the latter event, the insured would be able to keep or recover in respect of prior honest claims. It could be argued[79] that the latter is the legal position and this certainly seems to give the insurer sufficient protection. However, it has been held

---

[75] (1946) 79 Ll.L.R. 365.
[76] [1969] 1 W.L.R. 1193.
[77] *Ibid.* at 1196.
[78] *Britton v. Royal Ins. Co.* (1866) 4 F. & F. 905.
[79] Relying on the disapproval of the *dictum* in *Jureidini v. National British & Irish Millers' Insurance Co.* [1915] A.C. 999 in *Heyman v. Darwins* [1942] A.C. 356; see p. 206, above.

in a marine insurance case, *Black King Shipping Corp.* v. *Massie (The "Litsion Pride")*[80] that the insurer can avoid the whole contract *ab initio*. This was because the judge categorised a fraudulent claim as a breach of the general duty of utmost good faith imposed on an insured by section 17 of the Marine Insurance Act 1906 and construed the word "avoidance" in that section as meaning avoidance *ab initio*.[81] As the Marine Insurance Act is generally regarded as codifying the common law of insurance, presumably this decision should be followed in a non-marine case. In practice, a term giving the insurer the express right to repudiate for a fraudulent claim is invariably inserted in fire and similar policies. Clearly a breach of such a term only entitles repudiation from the date of breach, but this is an academic point if in fact the insurer can rely on a breach of the wider implied duty of utmost good faith.

Meaning of fraud

Clearly a claim is fraudulent if it can be shown that the insured intended to defraud the insurer, or put forward false evidence.[82] Otherwise, a fraudulent claim usually consists of an exaggeration by the insured of the amount of his loss. However, it is clear that mere exaggeration is not fraud. An insured may well claim higher than he knows he is entitled to as a bargaining device. Only, it seems, if he has a specific intent to recover more than he is entitled to is he fraudulent. In *Ewer* v. *National Employers' Mutual General Insurance Association*,[83] the insured under a fire policy claimed the current market price of goods destroyed, whereas he probably knew that all he was entitled to was their second-hand value. This was held not to be fraudulent. The figure claimed, which was "preposterously exaggerated," was merely a bargaining figure. On the other hand, in *Central Bank of India* v. *Guardian Assurance Co.*,[84] a claim figure

---

[80] [1985] 1 Lloyd's Rep. 437, at 514–516.

[81] However, as recognised *ibid.*, the insurers are not bound to avoid the whole contract; as s.17 merely provides that a policy *may* be avoided, they can choose simply to avoid the claim.

[82] The burden of proof in the insurers is a high one: *S. & M. Carpets (London) Ltd.* v. *Cornhill Insurance Ltd.* [1982] 1 Lloyd's Rep. 423, affirming [1981] 1 Lloyd's Rep. 677.

[83] [1937] 2 All E.R. 193; compare *Norton* v. *Royal Life Ass. Co.* (1885) *The Times*, August 12, where the finding at first instance ((1885) 1 T.L.R. 460) that a claim for £274 in respect of a loss of £87 was not fraudulent was reversed.

[84] (1936) 54 Ll.L.R. 247. See also the cases cited in Ivamy, *General Principles of Insurance Law*, 5th ed., pp. 410–411.

of nearly one hundred times the actual value of the goods destroyed was, naturally, held to be fraudulent.

Assignees and joint insureds

It appears that an assignee of the policy would not be defeated by the insured's fraudulent claim,[85] but that does not apply to the insured's trustee in bankruptcy,[86] nor to the case of a joint insurance where one insured's fraud will avoid the whole policy. However, joint insurance is only properly found where insurance is effected as regards property jointly owned by the insureds.[87] Insurance under one policy of composite interests, that is the different interests of the different insureds, for example, landlord and tenant or mortgagor and mortgagee, is not joint insurance, and fraud by one insured will not prevent the other who is innocent from recovering.[88]

Insurer's remedy

The insurer, who has paid out on what turns out to have been a fraudulent claim, may recover the money, but it is not entitled to recover as damages for breach of contract the costs incurred in investigating the claim.[89]

SETTLEMENT OF CLAIMS

Consideration of the precise legal rules governing the amount of compensation an insured is entitled to, following an insured loss, is deferred until the next chapter, but it is convenient to consider here some general points surrounding the settlement of claims other than the question of *quantum*. Frequently, of course, claims are settled following negotiations between insured and insurer, or parties acting on their behalf such as assessors and loss adjusters. The reported cases have been concerned with whether an insurer can reopen a settlement, but it is conceivable that an insured could do so on the ground of mis-

---

[85] *Central Bank of India* v. *Guardian Ass. Co.*, above, at 260.
[86] *Re Carr and Sun Ins.* (1897) 13 T.L.R. 186.
[87] *Central Bank of India* v. *Guardian Ass. Co.*, above.
[88] *General Accident Fire & Life Ass. Corp.* v. *Midland Bank* [1940] 2 K.B. 388.
[89] *London Ass.* v. *Clare* (1937) 57 Ll.L.R. 254. An action in the tort of deceit, though, might lie; Goddard J. at 270.

representation or undue influence by the insurer; this, though, would be difficult to show.[90]

A simple promise by the insurer to pay is not binding unless the insurer is actually legally liable, but once an insurer has actually made a payment, that is irrecoverable unless the claim was fraudulent or the payment was made under a mistake of fact. Payments made under a mistake of law are not recoverable as a matter of general principle, so if, for example, an insurer pays upon what is later realised was an incorrect construction of the policy, it is bound by that payment.

Mistake of fact

Payments made under a mistake of fact are recoverable by the action in quasi-contract for money had and received. This general principle was established in the insurance case of *Kelly* v. *Solari*.[91] Here a life policy provided for the quarterly payment of premiums, and in default the policy would lapse. The life insured died when one such payment had not been made, but the insurers paid the sum insured to his widow. It was held that, if the payment was made in ignorance or genuine forgetfulness of the facts, the insurers were entitled to recover it, and a new trial was order to ascertain this. "I think that the knowledge of the facts which disentitles the party from recovering must mean a knowledge existing in the mind at the time of payment."[92] The fact that the insurers may have been careless did not deprive them of their right to recovery.

Contracts of compromise

Somewhat different is the case where the insurer and insured enter into a contract of compromise. This might take the form of a replacement agreement, as in *Holmes* v. *Payne*,[93] where jewellery that was lost was replaced by the underwriters with jewellery of a similar value. Such a contract is binding unless one of the general grounds for rescission of a contract exists, such as misrepresentation or mistake. Fairly recently the question has arisen as to what sort of mistake will render such a contract void or voidable. The traditional view was that a contract was void only for a fundamental common mistake affecting the subject

---

[90] It is more likely when an insurer acting for its liability insured negotiates with the latter's victim as in *Horry* v. *Tate & Lyle Refineries Ltd.* [1982] 2 Lloyd's Rep. 416; see Merkin (1983) 46 M.L.R. 99 and p. 291, below.
[91] (1841) 9 M. & W. 54.
[92] *Ibid.* at 58, *per* Lord Abinger C.B.
[93] [1930] 2 K.B. 301; see p. 180, above.

matter of the contract.[94] A contract of compromise following an insurance claim could hardly ever be void on such grounds. The fact that an insurer entered into it under a mistaken impression that he was liable to the insured is a mistake as to the quality of the contract, the rights in respect of it. There is no mistake as to the nature of the contract. So, for example, the fact that an insurer need not have entered into it because he could avoid liability by reason of a right to avoid the policy for non-disclosure or misrepresentation or because the policy had lapsed would not render the contract of compromise void. Needless to say, the insurer could not possibly claim mistake if it compromised knowing of its right to avoid liability.

However, it now appears that whereas such a contract is not void for mistake, it is voidable in equity. In other words, the court has a discretion to set it aside. The leading case is *Magee* v. *Pennine Insurance Co.*,[95] where a motor policy was voidable for breach of warranty owing to mistatements by the insured on the proposal form. Following an accident, and unaware of this fact, the insurers agreed to a compromise. When the breach of warranty was subsequently discovered, they refused to pay the sum agreed. By a majority,[96] the Court of Appeal held that they were entitled to do so, Lord Denning M.R. following his earlier decision in *Solle* v. *Butcher*[97] to the effect that a contract can be set aside in equity if the parties were under a common misapprehension either as to the facts or as to their rights, provided that the misapprehension was fundamental and the party seeking to set the contract aside was not himself at fault. The other majority judge, Fenton Atkinson L.J., reasoned upon a different, and hardly supportable ground, but whatever the true *ratio* of the case, a question that has been fully discussed elsewhere, and whether or not it is strictly reconcilable with the House of Lords decision in *Bell* v. *Lever Bros.*,[98] the result is obviously sensible. It may be though that the insured should have been awarded at least some of the premiums paid. There does not appear to have been any fraud on his part. The proposal form that was incorrectly completed was filled in by the garage that sold him the car. The insurer was therefore never truly at risk

---

[94] *Bell* v. *Lever Bros.* [1932] A.C. 161. See generally, Treitel, *Law of Contract* Chapter 8.
[95] [1969] 2 Q.B. 507.
[96] Winn L.J. dissented strongly on the ground that the case was indistinguishable from *Bell* v. *Lever Bros.*, above.
[97] [1950] 1 K.B. 671.
[98] Note 94 above.

and under the equitable jurisdiction to rescind, the court could have allowed this.[99]

Ex gratia payments

If an insurer consciously pays out on a claim for which, in fact, it is not liable, then it is acting *ex gratia*. Such payments though are perfectly proper and not *ultra vires* an insurance company,[1] but it is established that they do not bind an insurer in the sense that the insurer who pays *ex gratia* is not bound to pay in subsequent similar or even identical circumstances.[2]

---

[99] In *Solle* v. *Butcher*, above, a lease was held voidable in equity for mistake at the landlord's suit, but only on terms that the tenant had the option to stay if he paid more rent.

[1] *Taunton* v. *Royal Ins. Co.* (1864) 2 H. & M. 135.

[2] *London & Manchester Plate Glass Co.* v. *Heath* [1913] 3 K.B. 411. For a powerfully argued case against the use in certain circumstances of *ex gratia* payments by life insurance companies, see Selmer (1966) 33 U. Chicago Law Rev. 502.

Chapter 13

THE MEASUREMENT OF LOSS

This chapter is concerned with the legal principles surrounding the actual assessment of an insured loss. It is possible first of all to exclude certain categories of insurance, wholly or partly, from consideration here, in particular all contingency policies, in other words, those of life and accident and their variations which are not generally speaking contracts of indemnity, or contracts to pay the insured strictly only what he loses.[1] In these cases, there are no difficulties as the policies themselves will provide the fixed sums that are payable in the event of a loss. Equally, although third party liability policies are contracts of indemnity, the amount recoverable raises no real problems, since that is simply the amount of the insured's liability, subject to any maximum sum insured and to any excess clauses, as to which more will be said below.

Essentially therefore, we are concerned with insurances on property of whatever sort, including both goods and land. The presumption is that such insurances are contracts of indemnity. This follows from the requirement of insurable interest at the time of the loss which is necessary in all such contracts unless it is waived.[2] Only in the case of valued policies is the principle of indemnity strictly irrelevant, and these will be examined separately. The modern "new for old" policies whereby insurers agree to pay the cost of replacing goods insured, are still indemnity policies, albeit of a different sort, and this despite the fact that there are not the same problems in calculating the measure of indemnity, as will be seen.

Sum insured

One overriding point is that the insured can never recover more than the maximum expressly stated in the policy. This is usually referred to as the "sum insured," and in property insurance, and to a lesser extent in liability insurance, the premium

---

[1] See Chapter 3. An accident or sickness policy may be a contract of indemnity (see Chapter 15 at p. 236), but even where this is the case, the measure of the insured's loss will not give rise to any legal problems.

[2] See Chapter 3.

payable is calculated very largely according to that figure. The problems that can arise from that figure being inaccurate, in the sense of being below or above the actual value of the property insured, will be considered later. For the present it is assumed that there are no such problems of under or over insurance.

Claim for damages

A further general point is that the following detailed consideration concerns only the measurement of the insured's basic loss. A claim under an insurance contract is a claim for damages for breach of contract,[3] and a wrongful refusal to pay by an insurer may render it liable in damages of more than this basic loss.[4] An example is the decision in *Grant* v. *Co-operative Insurance Society*,[5] where damages against an insurer who wrongfully repudiated liability were assessed on the normal contractual principles of remoteness and in addition to recovering the costs of repair to the insured house, the insureds (husband and wife) recovered the costs of protecting the house while it was unoccupied and the cost of alternative accommodation. They were not entitled, however, to damages for discomfort nor for the mental anguish suffered by the wife against whom a wholly unfounded allegation of arson had been made.

Total and partial loss

Property may be totally or partially lost. In more simple language, it may be totally destroyed or lost, or it may only be damaged. The measure of recovery may well differ according to this distinction. By total loss is not necessarily meant, in this context, complete destruction, although this is obviously included. A total loss includes the case where "the subject matter is destroyed or so damaged as to cease to be a thing of the kind insured."[6] For example, a house may after a fire be left with walls and foundations standing, but if none of it is usable, it must be regarded as totally lost. Similarly with the car that is a genuine "write off." It may be in practice that cars are written off because it is regarded as uneconomic to repair them, even

---

[3] *Jabbour* v. *Custodian of Israeli Absentee Property* [1954] 1 W.L.R. 139 at 143, *per* Pearson J.; *Edmunds* v. *Lloyds Italico & L'Ancora Compagnia di Assicurzioni & Riassicurazione SpA* [1986] 1 Lloyd's Rep. 326 at 327 *per* Donaldson M.R. In the *Jabbour* case, Pearson J. recognised that this was a somewhat odd classification, at least when the insurer admits liability to pay.

[4] In this respect, the limit of the sum insured on the basic measure must be inapplicable.

[5] (1984) 134 N.L.J. 81, available on LEXIS.

[6] *Halsbury's Laws of England* (4th ed.) Vol. 25, para. 298.

though they may not be so damaged as to cease to be cars, because they are capable of repair comparatively easily. Whether in law these would strictly be regarded as totally lost must be open to doubt, even though in practice they may be so treated. It is, of course, perfectly permissible for insurers to adopt this attitude, provided that the insured agrees. One or two problems that may flow from this sort of case will be discussed later.

TOTAL LOSS IN THE CASE OF GOODS

It is convenient to deal separately with the two classes of relevant property, namely goods and land, assuming for the present a genuine total loss. In respect of goods, the measure of what the insured has lost will prima facie be the market value of the property lost at the time[7] and place[8] of loss, in other words, its second-hand or resale value. This is because it is that sum that it will cost him to obtain equivalent goods. In *Richard Aubrey Film Productions Ltd. v. Graham*,[9] a policy was effected by a film producer against loss of negatives and films. A film that was almost completed was stolen. The evidence showed that on completion it would have had a market value of about £20,000 but that finally to complete it would have cost between £4,000 and £5,000. The insured therefore recovered the difference between those sums. This measure ignores feelings of lost effort and concentrates purely on loss in material terms. Similarly, in an appropriate case, nothing is recoverable to compensate for what can be called sentimental value or hurt feelings. A family "heirloom," for example, will only attract its market value even though its owners may have felt that it was worth much more than that to them.[10]

Value at time of loss

It is value at the date or time of loss that is recoverable, which, of course, may or may not correspond to the value at the date of

---

[7] *Re Wilson and Scottish Ins. Corp.* [1920] 2 Ch. 28; see below.
[8] *Rice v. Baxendale* (1861) 7 H. & N. 96.
[9] [1960] 2 Lloyd's Rep. 101.
[10] The strictness of the usual indemnity measure has no doubt astonished individual insureds from time to time; see the comments of MacKinnon J. in *Ewer v. National Employers' Mutual General Ins. Ass. Ltd.* (1937) 157 L.T. 16 at 21.

commencement or renewal of the policy. In *Re Wilson and Scottish Insurance Corporation Ltd.*[11] a car was insured in November 1915 for £250, which was its purchase price at the time and which was stated by the insured to represent his estimate of present value. The policy was renewed in subsequent Novembers until the car was destroyed by fire in June 1919. It was then worth £400. The policy covered the car "up to full value." The arbitrator reserved for the court the question whether the insured was entitled to £250 or £400, and Astbury J. held that it depended upon when the increase in value took place. If it was even partly before the last renewal, the insured was entitled to only £250, but if it occurred totally since the renewal, he was entitled to £400. There are a number of difficulties surrounding this decision. First, it is a little difficult to see how the insured could in any event be entitled to more than £250, as one would have thought that that figure, as it had never been changed, operated as the sum insured, the maximum recoverable. The answer to this must be that on the construction of the policy, there was no such sum insured, as none was expressly stated and the policy undertook to pay "full value." Assuming this to be the case, there is an inconsistency in the reasoning. At one point in his judgment, Astbury J. suggested that on each renewal, "the insured must be deemed to have continued or repeated his 'estimate of present value' at £250," and he implied that if this was incorrect on the renewal in November 1918, the policy was voidable.[12] Whether this was because of a non-disclosure of a material fact, that is, the increase in value, or a breach of warranty of value, is not made clear. It is suggested that it can only be the former, there being no authority and no reason for holding that statements in a proposal form not referable to the future are automatically rewarranted upon renewal; indeed there is a clear dictum to the contrary.[13] If, then, the increase in value occurred before renewal and non-disclosure of it amounted to non-disclosure of a material fact, the policy was voidable and there was no basis for holding that the insured was entitled to anything as a matter of strict law. However, the insurers had agreed to pay £250 in any event, and must therefore be deemed to have waived any right to avoid the policy. If, as has been seen, there was no sum insured in this case, so that the figure of £250 in the proposal

---

[11] See note 7.
[12] *Ibid.* at 31, citing Creswell J. in *Pim* v. *Reid* (1834) 6 Man. & G. 1 at 25.
[13] Winn L.J. in *Magee* v. *Pennine Ins. Co.* [1969] 2 Q.B. 507 at 517.

form was not to be taken as the maximum recoverable, the insured should have been entitled to the value of his car at the date of loss, namely £400, regardless of when the increase in value took place.

It is suggested therefore, that the decision itself in *Re Wilson* is open to question. However, the principle of value at the time of loss is clearly correct, and it would seem unlikely that the sort of facts there could recur, simply because estimates of value in a proposal form do usually correspond to the sum insured.

Replacement value

As the basic principle of indemnity is only contractual, it can be contractually varied. Policies on goods can and very often do, undertake to pay replacement value rather than market value, and indeed there may be cases where this is impliedly the measure, even if not actually spelt out.[14] Policies containing express undertakings to pay replacement value are increasingly common, and there can be no doubt that, subject to the sum insured, the insured is entitled to what it actually costs to replace the lost property by equivalent new property. These "new for old" policies are no doubt a major inroad into the traditional principle of indemnity, but it goes without saying that insurers demand higher premiums for such cover.

TOTAL LOSS IN THE CASE OF LAND

Until fairly recently, there was very little real authority determining what the insured whose house or office or factory is totally destroyed is entitled to claim, possibly because a total loss here is not that common. Logic might favour the market value approach as for goods, for the same reason that that should enable the insured to purchase an equivalent. In fact, an insured would not usually choose to do this; he would wish to be able to rebuild or reinstate. In some cases he may be compelled so to do.[15] For most of the time that insurance has been available, this probably did not matter, as the market value of property would cover the cost of rebuilding. Now it is notorious

---

[14] Particularly insurances of plant and equipment: *Roumeli Food Stores* v. *New India Ass. Co.* [1972] 1 N.S.W.L.R. 227 at 236–238.
[15] See Chapter 14.

that this is most unlikely. Hence, whether or not an insured is entitled to the cost of reinstatement is vital.

In most cases there will be such an entitlement as a result of the decision in *Leppard* v. *Excess Insurance Company*.[16] Here the Court of Appeal stressed that the insured is entitled to an indemnity against the amount of his loss and no more. There is no general principle dictating market value or cost of reinstatement. It is a question of fact and all the relevant facts of the particular case must be examined in order to ascertain the actual value of the loss at the relevant date. In the case itself, the insured had purchased a cottage which was worth some £4,500, including the site value, when it was burnt, but which would cost some £8,000 to rebuild. On the evidence the insured never intended to live in the cottage. He had purchased it from his in-laws solely for resale. It was held therefore that his loss was the market value of the cottage, that is what he lost by not being able to sell it. The judgments indicate, however, that in the normal case of the insured who lives in or otherwise occupies his house, office or factory, the measure of indemnity will be the cost of rebuilding, because otherwise his actual loss will not be made good.

In *Leppard*, the insured had argued in the alternative that his policy contractually provided that he was entitled to the cost of reinstatement. He placed particular reliance upon facts which are probably fairly standard. These were first, that in the proposal form he warranted that "the sums to be insured represent not less than the full value (the full value is the amount which it would cost to replace the property in its existing form should it be totally destroyed)," and second, that the policy contained a declaration by him that the sum insured represented and would at all times be maintained at not less than the full value of the buildings. The court held, no doubt correctly as a matter of law, that these could not affect the basic nature of the policy, which was otherwise in normal indemnity form. The effect of such declarations would be to constitute promissory warranties, on breach of which the insurer would have been entitled to repudiate the policy.[17] The insured had, in fact, complied with them and had insured the cottage for, eventually, £14,000. More about the effect of such warranties will be said later. All that remains to be said here is that the insured may have felt somewhat

---

[16] [1979] 1 W.L.R. 512. Noted in (1980) 43 M.L.R. 456 (Birds).
[17] See Chapter 7.

aggrieved, and understandably so, at being required to pay a premium calculated on £14,000 worth of insurance on pain of the insurer being able to avoid all liability, when he was entitled to substantially less.[18]

Partial Loss under an Indemnity Policy

In respect of a partial loss, there can be no case for treating goods and land any differently. A measure based on market value is generally inappropriate, since the insured cannot go into the market and restore himself to his pre-loss position, and payment based on the difference in market value before and after loss may well not compensate the insured. Therefore, the basis for an indemnity ought to be the cost of repair,[19] less perhaps any amount by which the insured is better off than before the loss, that is what is technically termed "betterment."[20]

Some potential difficulties

Before examining some of the cases, it must be pointed out that there may be difficulties arising from the adoption of the above measure. In the main, these stem from the problem in deciding whether or not a loss is to be regarded as partial or total. If a car is dented, however badly, or the roof of a house is damaged, these are clearly partial losses. But in practice a car may be so badly damaged that although it is capable of repair and can be still properly termed a car, it is regarded as uneconomic to repair it; it may then be written off. Similarly, the top floor of a house might be damaged to such an extent that although the bottom half is more or less intact and usable, in order to restore the house to its original condition, it is necessary to demolish the surviving part and start again. In the

---

[18] *Quaere* whether he might have had a remedy against the broker who advised him.

[19] This is implied in *Scottish Amicable Heritable Securities Assn.* v. *Northern Ass. Co.* (1883) 11 R. (Ct. of Sess.) 287 at 295 and *Westminster Fire Office* v. *Glasgow Provident Soc.* (1888) 13 App.Cas. 699, although the actual decisions turned on other points.

[20] In *Reynolds* v. *Phoenix Assurance Co.* [1978] 2 Lloyd's Rep. 440, (see below) Forbes J. held that the principle of betterment was well established. See the comments in *MacGillivray and Parkington*, para. 1688.

Leppard case, if Mr. Leppard's cottage had been so damaged, would he have been entitled to the costs of repairing it, which may well have been more than the market value of the cottage? It must be likely that the law would follow what is presumably insurance practice and look at what the insured actually loses, so that Leppard would have recovered no more than he did get, the fact of his non-occupation being crucial. However, in the case of a car or similar consumer durable, or any goods which tend to depreciate in value, the problem may be more complex simply because such depreciation is usual. A more complex problem, which is thought to be realistic, will further illustrate the point.

Imagine a modest family car some 10 years old but in very good condition for its age with low mileage and sound bodywork. Its market value will be reflected, however, primarily by its age, and, although it may attract the top price for a model of its kind of that age, this will hardly reflect its true worth to its owner. This top market price is £250. In an accident, the car is damaged on one side so that a wing and a door need replacement, there is some general tidying-up necessary, but the mechanics and the rest of the bodywork are sound. The work of restoring the car will cost £300 in total. Fairly clearly, the car is only partially lost, but is the insured entitled to £300, assuming this to be less than the sum insured, even though this is more than the market value of the car, which is all he would get if the car had been totally lost? It is suggested that he is and that the courts would in such a case follow the principles adopted in respect of insurance of buildings in recent cases, namely that a partial loss is assessed on the cost of repair or reinstatement save where the insured does not genuinely intend to reinstate.

Legal authorities

In *Reynolds* v. *Phoenix Assurance Co. Ltd.*,[21] the plaintiffs in 1969 bought an old maltings which they insured for £18,000, which was a little more than they had paid for it. Subsequently, on the advice of their brokers and valuers, the sum insured was increased to cover the likely cost of reinstatement in the event of a total loss, and at the material time that sum insured was £628,000. The plaintiffs had a sound business reason for purchasing the maltings. A fire occurred which destroyed about 70

---

[21] [1978] 2 Lloyd's Rep. 440. See also *Pleasurama Ltd.* v. *Sun Alliance & London Insurance Ltd.* [1979] 1 Lloyd's Rep. 389.

per cent. of the buildings. This was clearly a partial loss. There was some dispute in subsequent discussions involving assessors employed by the plaintiffs and loss adjusters acting for the insurers as to the cost of reinstatement and as to the plaintiffs' intention in this respect. The insurers elected not to reinstate as they were entitled to,[22] but it was accepted that the plaintiffs intended to do so, although the insurers were unwilling to pay over a provisionally agreed settlement figure except in stages as the rebuilding progressed. The plaintiffs were unwilling to proceed on this basis, the settlement fell through, and the matter came to trial. Forbes J. outlined three possible bases for indemnity. The first was market value, which would be difficult to assess, there being no ready market for buildings such as maltings, but which would probably be far less than the cost of reinstatement. The second was described as equivalent modern replacement value, namely the cost of building afresh a modern building for the purposes of the plaintiffs when commercially it would not be sensible to retain the original building. Again this would be considerably less than reinstatement cost. The third was the cost of reinstatement which worked out at something more than £200,000. The learned judge held that the policy was an ordinary indemnity policy and, as in *Leppard v. Excess Insurance*,[23] this meant that the plaintiffs were not automatically entitled under the contract to the costs of reinstatement. However, the plaintiffs were entitled to a genuine indemnity and the basis of that indemnity was the cost of reinstatement where, as on the facts, the plaintiffs did have the genuine intention to reinstate. The test to be adopted on this latter point was taken from an Irish case on compensation under statute[24]: "Would [the owner], for any reason that would appeal to an ordinary man in his position, rebuild [the property] if he got replacement costs, or is his claim for these a mere pretence?" Forbes J. held, therefore, that the plaintiffs were entitled to the largest sum, less an allowance for betterment which, he held, was a principle too well established in insurance cases of this kind to be upset.

Frequently insurers will have an option under the policy to reinstate or repair rather than pay money. The different considerations that may arise if this option is exercised are considered in the next chapter.

---

[22] See Chapter 14.
[23] See above p. 220.
[24] *Murphy* v. *Wexford C.C.* (1921) 2 Ir.R. 230.

The Insured with a Limited Interest

It has hitherto been assumed that the insured is the sole unencumbered owner of the property insured, but this may not be the case, and indeed the insured may not own the property at all but be, for example, tenant or mortgagee of real property or bailee, as under a hire-purchase contract, of goods. In certain exceptional cases, an insured may recover more than the value of his interest and hold the balance above his own loss for another. These circumstances were examined earlier in the chapter on Insurable Interest.[25] The measure of recovery here will be the value of the loss calculated in accordance with one or other of the ways already discussed.

Where someone with a limited interest insures or is entitled to recover in respect of only his own interest, problems may arise concerning the value of his interest and the amount of indemnity to which he is entitled. If a number of different interests in the same property are insured by the persons with those different interests, for example by different mortgagees, each insured is entitled to recover the value of his loss regardless of the position of the others and regardless of whether the total amount recovered by all the insureds exceeds the value of the property in question.[26]

In respect of certain insureds with limited interests, no problem will arise. For example, the indemnity claimable by a mortgagee will be the amount of his outstanding debt, and the same may be said of the hirer under a hire-purchase contract, unless the insured contracted for full value in order to cover his own and the owner's interests together. The case, though, of a tenant who insures the property which he has leased raises the problem quite neatly. If he has, in fact, covenanted to insure or to make good fire damage, he is only fully indemnified if he receives the full value of the property, which would normally, as has been seen, be the cost of reinstatement, regardless of the market value of his lease. Even if the tenant has not covenanted to insure or repair, it has been said that he is entitled to more than market value, since he will have been deprived of his home.[27] In *British Traders' Insurance Co.* v. *Monson*,[28] it was said

---

[25] See pp. 46–52.
[26] *Westminster Fire Office* v. *Glasgow Provident Soc.* (1888) 13 App.Cas. 699.
[27] *Castellain* v. *Preston* (1883) 11 Q.B.D. 380 at 400.
[28] (1964) 111 C.L.R. 86 at 92, 103–104 and 104–105. The case is considered further at p. 51, above.

The Insured with a Limited Interest

that the market value of a lease coupled with an option to purchase of which the tenant had the benefit would prima facie determine the amount of the tenant's loss, though that would not be all he was entitled to. The actual calculation, apart from that, would no doubt be somewhat speculative.

Loss Under a Valued Policy

Although, as a general rule, a contract of property insurance is a contract of indemnity, the parties are free to contract out of this by agreeing conclusively that a certain sum is payable in the event of loss. If this occurs, the policy is a valued policy and, unless the value is hopelessly excessive, it is enforceable.[29] Valued policies are more commonly found in marine than non-marine insurance, but no doubt there are some non-marine policies. If they are effected on buildings, it might be argued that section 3 of the Life Assurance Act 1774 prevents the insured from recovering more than the value of his interest strictly worked out,[30] but the point has never been taken. A policy is a valued policy only if the parties expressly agree that the property is assumed to have the value attached to it. The mere existence of a sum insured does not mean that a policy is valued.

In the case of a total loss, the amount recoverable is obviously the agreed value, whether that is more or less than the insured's actual loss.[31] In the case of a partial loss, the formula worked out in *Elcock* v. *Thomson*[32] is applied, the insurer being liable for that proportion of the agreed value as is represented by the depreciation in the actual value of the property, that is the difference between market value before and after loss. A property insured for £100,000 which is worth £50,000 before loss and £30,000 afterwards, will attract a recovery of £40,000, that is, two fifths of the agreed value. It matters not what it actually costs to repair the property, except that it was suggested in that case[33] that if, in fact, the insurers had exercised their option to repair,

---

[29] Excessive over-valuation might be non-disclosure of a material fact (see Chapter 6) or it might show that the policy was void as a gaming policy in contravention of the Gaming Act 1845 (see Chapter 3).
[30] See p. 38, above.
[31] This is also treated as the loss for subrogation purposes: *Burnand* v. *Rodocanachi* (1882) 7 App.Cas. 333.
[32] [1949] 2 K.B. 755.
[33] *Ibid.* at 764.

they would have been liable for those costs whether that sum was more or less than that produced by the formula.

Under-Insurance

Hitherto, it has been assumed that the sum insured is not less than the value of the property insured or possibly the cost of its reinstatement. There will frequently be an obligation on the insured to keep to the latter, as is evident from the facts of *Leppard* v. *Excess Insurance* as described earlier. Some nice questions arise if, in fact, the sum insured is less than either of these, that is, if there is under-insurance. Under-insurance is a problem that has concerned the insurance industry very much in recent times of high inflation.[34]

Insurer's right to avoid

The first point to note is that the insurers may well in such a case be entitled to avoid the policy or else to use a right to avoid to compel the insured to settle for a sum less than his actual loss. This may arise by virtue of the duty of disclosure or by virtue of a breach of warranty. Failure upon renewal to disclose a change in the value of the property insured could be regarded as the non-disclosure of a material fact,[35] as most renewals amount to the making of a new contract.[36] Alternatively, the initial estimate of value by an insured may well be warranted and if incorrect, entitle the insurer to repudiate upon this basis, although, if that is the only warranty, and it is not of a continuing nature, there is, it is suggested, no basis for repudiation simply because upon subsequent renewals the sum insured has not been increased.[37] Perhaps more likely nowadays is an express continuing warranty of the sort that existed in the policy in *Leppard* v. *Excess Insurance*.[38] In such a case, there is a clear basis for

---

[34] To such an extent that there has been a great deal of inertia selling of index-linked policies, and much publicity and exhortations to insureds to check their sums insured.

[35] This seems to be implied in *Re Wilson and Scottish Ins. Corp.* discussed above p. 218. In the case of buildings, where the problem of under-insurance has been especially acute, it might perhaps be possible to argue that the facts were common knowledge and hence, not required to be disclosed; see (1976) 126 N.L.J. 482.

[36] See Chapter 4, p. 68.

[37] See p. 218, above.

[38] See p. 220, above.

repudiation if the sum insured does not keep pace with the value or cost of replacement of the property.

Average

Quite apart from this, the insurer in a case of under-insurance may be able to rely upon the principle of average. This is irrelevant to a total loss, because the sum insured is the maximum recoverable. But an insured may suffer a partial loss below the sum insured where the property is under-insured. If so, and the policy is subject to average, he will recover only that part of the loss which the sum insured bears to the value of the property; the insured is deemed to be his own insurer with respect to the balance. For example, if a house worth £30,000 is insured subject to average for £20,000, the insured will be entitled to only two thirds of any loss. Commercial policies generally contain average clauses and it has been suggested that the principle of average would be implied, if not expressed, in commercial policies on goods.[39] However, average clauses are unusual, it seems, in household policies, except those issued by Lloyd's underwriters, and there is clear authority that the principle of average will not be implied in such a case.[40] Thus, in the absence of a breach of a relevant warranty, the insured in this case is entitled to recover fully up to the amount of the sum insured.

Excess and Franchise Clauses

It is convenient to mention here two devices often adopted which, if applicable, will limit the amount an insured recovers, although they raise few legal difficulties. Excess clauses or deductibles are common in motor, household and third party policies, among others. They provide that the insured is to bear the first amount of any loss, expressed either as an amount of money or as a stated percentage of any loss.[41] Franchise clauses are perhaps less common in non-marine insurance. These take the form of relieving the insurer from liability completely in respect of losses below a certain figure or percentage, and at this

---

[39] *Carreras Ltd.* v. *Cunard Steamship Co.* [1918] 1 K.B. 118.
[40] *Sillem* v. *Thornton* (1854) 3 E. & B. 868.
[41] As to possible consequences of motor policies having excess clauses, see *Hobbs* v. *Marlowe* [1978] A.C. 16, which is discussed in Chapter 15, especially at p. 254.

level operate in the same way as excess clauses, whereas losses above the specified figure or percentage are fully covered.[42]

Payment of Interest

A question of some importance in some contexts is whether or not an insured is entitled to claim interest on the policy monies payable to him. This can only arise of course, if there has been some delay in payment. There is no rule that interest is payable as a matter of course from the date when the money becomes payable, but the court has a discretion under section 3(1) of the Law Reform (Miscellaneous Provisions) Act 1934 to award interest if it thinks fit.

Interest will be so awarded when the insurer has wrongfully detained money which ought to have been paid. In an ordinary indemnity policy, it appears that it will normally be awarded from the date when the loss has been quantified, in other words when the insured called upon the insurer to pay, to the date of judgment.[43] A similar principle applies to life policies.[44] Interest is not due from the date of loss because, for a period after that, it is reasonable for the parties to negotiate to find out exactly how much money was due in respect of a claim.[45] If the insured is a commercial undertaking which has been deprived of money of which it could make good use, the rate of interest is likely to bear some relation to commercial rates. In the case of an individual insured, a lower rate may be appropriate.

Somewhat different considerations may apply in the case of an insurer claiming interest when suing by virtue of subrogation rights. These will be examined in Chapter 15 in the general context of subrogation.

---

[42] *Paterson* v. *Harris* (1861) 1 B. & S. 336; a number of truly separate losses on separate occasions, each falling below the figure or percentage, cannot be added together so as to bring the loss above the figure or percentage: *Stewart* v. *Merchants' Marine Ins. Co.* (1885) 16 Q.B.D. 619.

[43] *Burts & Harvey Ltd.* v. *Vulcan Boiler & General Ins. Co.* [1966] 1 Lloyd's Rep. 354.

[44] *Webster* v. *British Empire Mutual Life* (1880) 15 Ch.D. 169; *Re Waterhouse's Policy* [1937] Ch. 415.

[45] *Burts & Harvey Ltd.* v. *Vulcan Boiler & General Ins. Co.*, above.

Chapter 14

REINSTATEMENT

As was mentioned in the last chapter, it may in certain circumstances be the case that an insurer is entitled to or bound to reinstate insured property which has been damaged or destroyed. In so far as insurers may have a right to reinstate rather than pay money, this may arise under the terms of the policy or by statute. Reinstatement by contract will be permitted only if the policy expressly refers to it; if it does not, the insurers must pay money.[1] Insurers may become bound to reinstate by statutory provision. In this chapter, contractual and statutory reinstatement will be examined separately, together with one or two related matters. Of necessity, reinstatement is relevant only to property insurances.

CONTRACTUAL REINSTATEMENT

Clauses giving insurers the option to reinstate or repair have been common for a long time, particularly in insurances of real property,[2] but they are equally common nowadays in goods policies where they will often refer to replacement as well as to reinstatement or repair. Their purpose is obviously to protect insurers against excessive demands and fraudulent claims.

The option depends upon the insurer's election to reinstate, repair or replace rather than pay money, and it is a general principle that if a party with the benefit of such an option wishes so to elect, he must give unequivocal notice to the other party, that is the insured in this context, within a reasonable time or within the time, if any, fixed by the policy. Once the election is made, the insurer is bound by it, so that it is important to know when it occurs. There are two rather conflicting Scottish decisions on the point. In the first, *Sutherland* v. *Sun Fire Office*,[3] after investigation of a claim, the insurer offered a money pay-

---

[1] Brett L.J. in *Rayner* v. *Preston* (1881) 18 Ch.D. 1 at 9–10.
[2] An early example appears from the facts of *Sadler's Co.* v. *Badcock* (1743) 2 Atk. 554.
[3] (1852) 14 D. (Ct. of Sess.) 775.

ment, which the insured refused, and then offered to go to arbitration over the amount of the loss. This was also refused, whereupon the insurer elected to reinstate. It was held that this was a good election. By contrast, in *Scottish Amicable* v. *Northern Assurance*,[4] following the loss there were prolonged negotiations. The insureds claimed money or reinstatement; the insurers ignored the latter claim but disputed the amount of the loss and prepared for arbitration over it. Only when the insureds commenced proceedings 18 months after the fire did the insurers purport to elect to reinstate. It was held that this was too late. The distinction between the cases is, it seems, that in the latter the parties had agreed on a money payment, albeit the amount was disputed. Once this form of indemnity is agreed, it is too late for the insurer to elect to reinstate. In the former case, however, there had been agreement on nothing and therefore the election was still available.

Effect of election

At common law, once the insurer has made an effective election to reinstate, he is bound to restore the property to its original condition. In the old case of *Alchorne* v. *Favill*,[5] the premises when rebuilt were smaller than before the fire that caused the loss and, as a result, worth less. This was because of planning restrictions which prevented the insurer from rebuilding in the same manner. It was held, however, that having made their election, the insurers were bound by it and were liable to compensate the insured for the difference in value between the old and new buildings. It is likely nowadays that insurers protect themselves against the dangers of such planning restrictions by providing in the policy to the effect that reinstatement will be "as circumstances permit and in reasonably sufficient manner." Clearly they would still be liable in damages if the actual construction work were done badly, and the amount recoverable would be the cost of putting right the work and any foreseeable consequential losses, such as loss of rent or profit.

The effect of the election to reinstate is that the contract becomes a building or repair contract.[6] Presumably the correct legal analysis is that there is an offer in the insured's claim which is accepted by the insurer's election to reinstate. The

---

[4] (1883) 11 R. (Ct. of Sess.) 287.
[5] (1825) 4 L.J.(O.S.) 47.
[6] *Brown* v. *Royal Ins. Co.* (1859) 1 El. & El. 853 at 858–859.

insurer is bound to complete the work regardless of cost, unless this contract is discharged by frustration. However, there is authority that the insured's only remedy against a defaulting insurer is in damages; specific performance will not lie.[7] It matters not prima facie that reinstatement costs more than was originally estimated, that it costs more than the sum insured in the policy, nor that the insured receives a better building as a result, unless there is a clause in the policy whereby the insured is bound to pay towards the costs in this sort of situation. Because the insurers who have elected to reinstate are in the position of building contractors, they must bear any loss or damage occurring while they are in possession for that purpose. In *Smith* v. *Colonial Mutual Fire Insurance Co. Ltd.*,[8] the insurers elected to reinstate the insured house following a partial loss. While they were in possession, and when they had partly reinstated, a second fire occurred. The insurers claimed that they were entitled to deduct from the cost of reinstatement after the second fire the amount spent before that, but it was held that they could not do so. Having elected to reinstate, they had to complete the job properly, and were their own insurers while the work was in progress.

Impossibility

If it is impossible to reinstate before the insurers have made their election, for example, because planning permission will not be given, the insurers will be liable simply to pay the insured the amount of his loss.[9] If it becomes impossible after the election, there is authority that the insurer is nonetheless bound by his election and liable in damages for not reinstating despite the impossibility. Thus the insured might be entitled to compensation for the full value of the property, even if originally the loss was only a partial one. In *Brown* v. *Royal Insurance Co.*,[10] the only case directly in point, after the election to reinstate a partial loss, the Commissioners of Sewers under statutory authority ordered that the premises be totally demolished as being in a dangerous condition. It was held that the insured was entitled to the full value as damages for breach of the contract to reinstate. This case was decided, however, before the courts developed the doctrine of frustration[11]

---

[7] *Home District Mutual Ins. Co.* v. *Thompson* (1847) 1 E. & A. 247.
[8] (1880) 6 Vict.L.R. 200.
[9] *Anderson* v. *Commercial Union Ass. Co.* (1885) 55 L.J.Q.B. 146.
[10] See note 6.
[11] The founding case was *Taylor* v. *Caldwell* (1863) 3 B. & S. 826.

whereby a contract may be discharged where performance becomes impossible due to a supervening event which is not the fault of either party. In circumstances such as the *Brown* case, or where, for example, the property is compulsorily purchased by the local authority following the election, frustration could well be argued. It would not necessarily be applied, however, if, for example, the insurers could have discovered what was going to happen.

If the contract to reinstate is frustrated, the insurers would not be liable in damages, but they would not be relieved of their original liability under the insurance contract to pay for the loss.[12] Thus the insured should still recover monetary compensation in full, even though the insurers may have incurred expenditure before the frustrating event. It is possible to argue that the insurers might claim from the insured under section 1(1) of the Law Reform (Frustrated Contracts) Act 1943. Although that Act does not apply to contracts of insurance (s.2(5)(*b*)), the contract here, as has been seen, has become a contract to reinstate and in theory the Act might therefore apply.[13] Section 1(3) allows that the party who has received a "valuable benefit" before the frustrating event may be ordered to pay such sum as the court considers just to the other party. It may be thought, however, that it cannot really be said that the insured has received a valuable benefit if, in fact, he is deprived of his property by demolition or compulsory purchase.

STATUTORY REINSTATEMENT

Section 83 of the Fires Prevention (Metropolis) Act 1774 is a potentially important, but, it seems, little used provision. In essence it provides two things. Following a loss by fire, and only such a loss, it requires an insurance company, but not a Lloyd's underwriter,[14] to apply the policy monies, so far as they will go, towards rebuilding or reinstating an insured building at the request of any person or persons interested in the building; and it authorises an insurance company so to act if they have grounds for suspecting that the insured was guilty of fraud or arson. The second point is obviously a useful protection to insurers, though it seems to add little to the usual con-

---

[12] *Anderson* v. *Commercial Union*, above. See [1960] J.B.L. at 276–279.
[13] This is the view taken also in *MacGillivray and Parkington*, para. 1800.
[14] *Portavon Cinema Co.* v. *Price* [1939] 4 All E.R. 601.

tractual right they reserve which has just been examined. Of more interest is the obligation arising under section 83.

It should be noted first that the section applies only to fire policies on buildings,[15] but that it is not limited to London. There is clear authority that it applies throughout England and Wales,[16] but it does not apply to Scotland or Ireland.[17] Under section 83, reinstatement need only be to the extent of the policy monies available, which should be compared with the position under contractual reinstatement. However, this does mean the whole of the money potentially available under the policy, even if the "person interested" has, in fact, only a limited insurable interest in the building.[18]

Request to reinstate

The obligation on an insurer under section 83 arises only upon a clear and distinct request to reinstate by a "person interested" (see below) before the insurer settles with the insured. A mere request not to pay the insured, for example, is not enough. In *Simpson* v. *Scottish Union Insurance Co.*,[19] the tenant of premises insured them as he was obliged to do under his lease. Following a fire, the landlord wrote to the insurers asking them not to pay anything to the tenant and claiming that he was entitled to the benefit of the policy. Despite this, the insurers settled with the tenant. The landlord then proceeded to rebuild the premises and claimed that the insurers were liable to him. It was held that his claim was ill-founded. His request to the insurers was not sufficient to invoke the section; it was not a request to reinstate but rather a claim to the money, and he had no other right to the benefit of the policy. In any event, section 83 does not authorise a person to rebuild himself and then claim the cost.

Remedy against insurer

If an insurer fails to comply with a proper request under section 83, it is likely that the appropriate remedy is a mandatory injunction to compel them to do so. This was the opinion of Page-Wood V.C. in the *Simpson* case, and although, in the later

---

[15] See, *e.g. Ex Parte Gorely* (1864) 4 De G.J. & S., where s.83 was held inapplicable to a tenant's trade fixtures.
[16] *Ibid.* It also applies to much of the Commonwealth.
[17] *Westminster Fire* v. *Glasgow Provident* (1888) 13 App.Cas. 699; *Andrews* v. *Patriotic Ass. Co.* (1886) 18 L.R.Ir. 355.
[18] *Simpson* v. *Scottish Union Ins. Co.* (1863) 1 H. & M. 618 at 628.
[19] See note 18.

case of *Wimbledon Golf Club* v. *Imperial Insurance Co.*,[20] it was said that the only remedy is an injunction to restrain the insurers from paying the insured, it is submitted that the former opinion is the better one and certainly the one more in accord with the purpose of the section.

Person interested

Perhaps the most interesting question is who is a "person interested" for the purposes of compelling the insurer to reinstate. As has been seen, it is not necessary that such a person has a full insurable interest in the property, nor is it necessary that he has any contractual relationship with the insurer. On the other hand, the insured must be entitled to enforce the policy. The insured, however, is not such a person interested, so that he cannot compel reinstatement,[21] but otherwise it appears that anyone with a legal or equitable interest in the property can. Thus, in *Sinnot* v. *Bowden*[22] the mortgagee of the property whose debt was considerably less than the amount of the loss was held entitled to insist that the mortgagor's insurers reinstate, and there have been several cases where a landlord was held entitled to use section 83 against his tenant's insurer,[23] and conversely, where a tenant could compel his landlord's insurer to reinstate.[24] There is obviously here a possible practical solution to some problems raised by the requirement of insurable interest. If we take the facts of a case like *British Traders' Insurance Co.* v. *Monson*,[25] where a tenant who has insured for full value is entitled only to the value of his interest and cannot claim the full value for the benefit of his landlord, if the landlord invokes section 83 in time, the result contended for by the tenant on the facts of that case would, practically speaking, be achieved. It may also be the case that the purchaser of real property between contract and completion can invoke section 83 against his vendor's insurers. This was clearly stated, *obiter*, in *Rayner* v. *Preston*[26] and logically must be correct. If so, some of the difficulties surrounding the insurance position in this situation and the true meaning of section 47 of the Law of Property Act 1925[27] can be circumvented.

[20] (1902) 18 T.L.R. 815.
[21] *Reynolds* v. *Phoenix Ass. Co.* [1978] 2 Lloyd's Rep. 440, especially at 462.
[22] [1912] 2 Ch. 414.
[23] *e.g. Vernon* v. *Smith* (1821) 5 B. & Ald. 1.
[24] *e.g. Wimbledon Golf Club* v. *Imperial Ins. Co.*, above.
[25] (1964) 111 C.L.R. 86; see p. 51, above.
[26] (1881) 18 Ch.D. 1 at 15; see pp. 129–130, above.
[27] See pp. 132–135, above.

The insured's duty to reinstate?

Finally, there arise a number of questions not concerned with the position as between insured and insurer, but with those cases where the insured has recovered money from his insurer which a third party claims should be spent by the insured on reinstatement.

By section 108(2) of the Law of Property Act 1925, the mortgagee of property has the right to compel the mortgagor, who has insured and received money, to use it on reinstatement. Trustees who have received insurance money may reinstate trust property with it, but there is no obligation.[28]

Apart from these cases, it is likely that the insured and the third party are parties to a contract which, it is argued, expressly or impliedly, provides for reinstatement at the third party's option. A hire-purchase contract may, for example, contain such an express term for the benefit of the owner in respect of insurance he requires to be effected by the hirer. Another common example would be a covenant to reinstate in a lease. However, in the absence of an express covenant to reinstate, the court will not usually imply one even where the insured covenanted to insure.[29] It may be, however, that the circumstances including the imposition of a covenant to insure, show that the insurance was intended to be a joint one for the benefit of both parties, so that the third party may insist upon reinstatement. In *Mumford Hotels Ltd.* v. *Wheler*,[30] the tenant of property covenanted to pay what was called a "yearly insurance rent" equal to the premium necessary for a comprehensive policy on the premises. The landlord covenanted to effect such an insurance but did not covenant to reinstate. It was held that no such covenant could be implied, but the true inference from the circumstances was that the insurance was to be treated for the joint benefit of the landlord insured and the tenant, so that the latter had an interest in the policy monies and could oblige the former to use them for reinstatement.[31]

---

[28] Trustee Act 1925, s.20(4).
[29] *Lees* v. *Whitely* (1866) L.R. 2 Eq. 143.
[30] [1964] Ch. 117.
[31] As to the possible difficulties in this sort of case concerning the requirements of s. 2 of the Life Assurance Act 1774 and ways around these, see pp. 36–39 and 50–52, above.

Chapter 15

SUBROGATION

This chapter is concerned with the fundamental correlative of the principle of indemnity, namely, the insurer's right of subrogation.[1] Although often in the insurance context referred to as a right, it is really more in the nature of a restitutionary remedy.[2] The "fundamental rule of insurance law" is "that the contract of insurance contained in a marine or fire policy is a contract of indemnity, and of indemnity only, and this contract means that the assured, in the case of a loss against which the policy has been made, shall be fully indemnified, but shall never be more than fully indemnified."[3] A number of points arise simply from that oft-cited dictum and the doctrine of subrogation has many ramifications which must be examined. It is convenient first, though, to consider some general points.

Application of subrogation

Subrogation applies to all insurance contracts which are contracts of indemnity, that is, particularly to contracts of fire, motor, property and liability insurance. It does not apply to life insurance[4] nor prima facie to accident insurance.[5] However, although payments under an accident policy are usually of a fixed stated sum or according to a fixed scale, it is possible to have such policies whereby payments are made on an indemnity basis, in other words are related to specific heads of loss suffered by the insured. This might well also be the case in, for example, a health insurance policy or a medical expenses section of a larger policy. There can be no real doubt that these policies are indemnity policies and therefore should attract the

---

[1] An exhaustive and useful monograph is Derham, *Subrogation in Insurance Law*, Law Book Company, 1985.
[2] See Goff and Jones, *The Law of Restitution* (3rd ed.), p. 523.
[3] Brett L.J. in *Castellain v. Preston* (1883) 11 Q.B.D. 380.
[4] *Solicitors & General Life Ass. Soc. v. Lamb* (1864) 2 De G. J. & S. 251.
[5] *Theobald v. Railway Passengers' Ass. Co.* (1854) 10 Exch. 45.

right of subrogation.[6] It has indeed been argued[7] that many forms of life insurance have indemnity intentions, a point discussed earlier and reinforced by the requirement of section 3 of the Life Assurance Act 1774.[8] Notable examples are "keyman" policies effected by employers on the lives of their employees, and policies by creditors on the lives of their debtors. The only real purpose of such insurance is to indemnify against the risk of a loss. However, whatever the attractions of such an argument, it can be safely assumed that the law would not regard any form of life insurance as attracting the right of subrogation.

Origins of subrogation

There has been some dispute as to the true origins of the doctrine of subrogation. Some have claimed to find traces in Roman Law. It was probably first developed in this country in the Courts of Chancery and Admiralty,[9] but there are dicta in a number of the modern authorities, especially by Lord Diplock, to the effect that it is a common law doctrine.[10] Equally often expressed has been the view that it is a creature of equity.[11] Not much seems to turn on these different approaches.[12] Even if the better view is that subrogation is equitable,[13] it is clear that it can be modified, excluded or extended by contract; the extension of subrogation rights by express terms in insurance poli-

---

[6] See *Glyn* v. *Scottish Union & National Ins. Co.* (1963) 40 D.L.R. (2d) 929, where subrogation was held applicable to medical payments cover under a motor policy and *Gibson* v. *Sun Life Assurance Co. of Canada* (1985) 7 C.C.L.I. 65, where it was held applicable to a disability insurance policy; *Michigan Medical Services* v. *Sharpe* 339 Mich. 574, 54 N.W. (2d) 713 (1954), where there was an express term providing for subrogation; compare *Michigan Hospital Services* v. *Sharpe* 339 Mich. 375, 63 N.W. (2d) 638 (1954), a case which arose out of the same facts, where the absence of such a term was fatal. See generally, Kimball and Davis, "The Extension of Insurance Subrogation" (1962) 60 Mich.L.R. 841, especially at 860–861.

[7] Kimball and Davis, *op. cit.*

[8] See Chapter 3, especially at pp. 31–32.

[9] Goff and Jones, *op. cit.*, p. 523.

[10] *e.g. Yorkshire Ins. Co.* v. *Nisbet Shipping Co.* [1962] 2 Q.B. 330 at 339; *Morris* v. *Ford Motor Co.* [1973] 1 Q.B. 792 at 809–812; *Hobbs* v. *Marlowe* [1977] 2 All E.R. 241 at 254–255.

[11] *e.g. Burnand* v. *Rodocanachi* (1882) 7 App.Cas. 333 at 339; *Morris* v. *Ford Motor Co.*, above, at 800–801.

[12] Even where subrogation has been denied on "equitable" grounds (see pp. 255–257, below), the reasoning is suspect and the result supportable on other grounds.

[13] For the most thorough argument to this effect, see Derham, *op. cit.*, Chapter 1.

cies is commonplace.[14] If, on the other hand, the doctrine is legal in origin, there is no doubt that equity played an important part in its development, in particular, by compelling an insured to consent to the use of his name by the insurer in subrogation proceedings[15] and by imposing a constructive trust on the insured who has received money for which he is liable to account to the insurer.[16]

It should be noted that the doctrine of subrogation applies more widely than simply in the insurance context.[17] However, it is probably safe to proceed upon the understanding that, although the essential nature of subrogation applies in each context, each is self-contained, and in examining insurance subrogation, these other contexts may be ignored. Indeed it has been said in the House of Lords that it should not be assumed that principles which grew up in one area can be transplanted to another.[18]

THE TWO ASPECTS OF SUBROGATION

The passage cited earlier from the leading case of *Castellain* v. *Preston*[19] by itself gives a picture of only one aspect of the doctrine of subrogation, namely that the insured cannot make a profit from his loss and that for any profit he does make he is accountable to his insurer, either as constructive trustee or in an action in quasi-contract for money had and received.[20] Later passages, though, in the judgments in that case describe the second aspect of the doctrine. This is the right of the insurer who has indemnified his insured to step into the shoes of the insured—the literal meaning of "subrogation"—and in his name pursue any right of action available to the insured which may diminish the loss insured against. Typically, the insured's right will be to sue a third party liable to pay damages in tort or

---

[14] Examples of this appear throughout the chapter.
[15] *Morris* v. *Ford Motor Co.*, above, at 800.
[16] *Morely* v. *Moore* [1936] 2 K.B. 359.
[17] For a full description, see Goff and Jones, *op. cit.*, Chapter 27.
[18] *Orapko* v. *Manson Investments* [1977] 3 W.L.R. 229 at 234 (Lord Diplock).
[19] Note 3.
[20] The constructive trust basis has distinct advantages over the quasi-contractual basis which was relied upon in the leading cases of *Castellain* v. *Preston*, above and *Darrell* v. *Tibbits* (1880) 5 Q.B.D. 560. For example, when a corporate insured is put into liquidation, the insurers can recover monies which subrogation entitles them to in priority to other creditors: *Re Miller, Gibb & Co.* [1957] 1 W.L.R. 703.

for breach of contract, the third party's liability being in respect of the event for which the insured has recovered from his insurer. As already noted, the insurer can, if necessary, be compelled to lend his name for the purposes of the action.[21]

Although the purposes of these two aspects of subrogation are the same, namely, the prevention of the unjust enrichment of the insured, they are essentially different and it is suggested that to some extent different principles are relevant and different qualifications surround each aspect. They will therefore be examined separately.

THE INSURED CANNOT MAKE A PROFIT

The leading illustration here is still the case of *Castellain* v. *Preston*.[22] This was the sequel to the decision in *Rayner* v. *Preston*[23] which was examined in Chapter 9. It will be recalled that the insured vendor of a house which was burnt down between the contract and completion recovered money from his insurer for which he was held not accountable to his purchaser. The latter subsequently completed the purchase, as he was bound to do despite the fire, and paid the agreed price. It was held that the vendor was therefore bound to account to his insurer for the money the latter had paid. The Court of Appeal followed the slightly earlier decision in *Darrell* v. *Tibbits*[24] where the owner of a house which was let to a tenant insured it against fire. The local authority caused an explosion which damaged the house and paid compensation to the tenant. The insurers paid the insured, but then sought to recover this sum. It was held that they were entitled to succeed, as the insured had already been compensated by virtue of the tenant's receiving the compensation which had been used to repair the house. In respect of both cases, to have allowed the insured to keep the insurance money would have meant that he would have been doubly indemnified, and would have profited from his loss. In *Darrell* v. *Tibbits*, the tenant had covenanted to repair the house in the event of losses such as occurred. It was made clear that the same result would in effect have happened had the insurers, upon payment to the landlord, used his name to sue the tenant under this cov-

---

[21] *King* v. *Victoria Ins. Co. Ltd.* [1896] A.C. 250 at 255–256; *Edwards* v. *Motor Union Ins. Co.* [1922] 2 K.B. 249 at 254.
[22] See note 3.
[23] (1881) 18 Ch.D. 1.
[24] (1880) 5 Q.B.D. 560.

enant. This, of course, would have involved the other aspect of the doctrine of subrogation.

The rule that the insured cannot profit from his loss is subject to three limitations. First, he is accountable only when he has been fully indemnified. Second, if he receives a gift following the loss, this may not necessarily be taken into account. Third, if a surplus results after the insurer has recovered back its money, it seems that the insured is entitled to keep it. These three points must now be examined in detail.

Full indemnity

In *Scottish Union & National Insurance Co.* v. *Davis*,[25] the defendant insured's damaged car was handed to a garage for repair with the consent of the plaintiff insurers. After three attempts at repair by the garage, the insured was not satisfied with their work and took the car elsewhere. The garage nonetheless sent their bill to the insurers who paid it without getting a satisfaction note signed by the insured. The latter then recovered compensation from the party originally responsible for the damage and used this money to have his car properly repaired. The insurers claimed this latter sum, but the Court of Appeal had no difficulty in rejecting their claim. "You only have a right to subrogation in a case like this when you have indemnified the assured, and one thing that is quite plain is that the insurers have never done that."[26]

One point which is not clear from this case, nor from any other English authority, is whether the insured must be fully indemnified within the terms of the policy, or whether he must, in fact, be fully compensated, before the duty to account arises. That such a distinction might commonly arise can be illustrated quite simply. Imagine the case of property insured for £100 which is less than its value or replacement cost of £200. If the property is destroyed and the insured recovers £100 from his insurers, and then subsequently receives the other £100 from the party responsible for the loss, must he account for the latter to his insurers on the grounds that they have fully indemnified him under the terms of the insurance? Alternatively, suppose the case of a motor insured whose car is damaged in an accident. His insurers pay the costs of repair but have no interest in pursuing their right to sue the person responsible for the accident. The insured receives from that party what might be

---
[25] [1970] 1 Lloyd's Rep. 1.
[26] *Per* Russell L.J., *ibid.* at 5.

The Insured Cannot Make a Profit

termed consequential loss, for example, the cost of hiring a substitute car when his own is being repaired, a sum which was not recoverable under his insurance policy.[27] Can the insurers claim that he has profited because he was fully indemnified by them, even though he was not fully compensated? It is suggested that the insured's duty to account should arise only when he has been fully compensated. As mentioned earlier, the purpose of subrogation is to prevent unjust enrichment, and an insured can hardly be said to be unjustly enriched until he receives more than full compensation for a loss.

Support for this view can perhaps be found in the decision of the Supreme Court of Canada in *Ledingham* v. *Ontario Hospital Services Commission*.[28] L. and others were injured in a motor accident caused by a negligent uninsured driver. As a result they had a statutory claim on a Fund, but this was limited to 35,000 dollars, whereas their damages award against the driver amounted to 63,000 dollars. This latter sum included 15,000 dollars for the cost of medical benefits rendered by the respondent. The latter had a statutory right of subrogation to recover the cost of their services where possible, and the beneficiary such as L. in the present case was bound to claim that cost against a tortfeasor. This had been done. L., however, as mentioned, recovered only 35,000 dollars, whereas his loss was 48,000 dollars (63,000 dollars less the cost of the medical benefits). The question was whether the respondent was entitled to any of this 35,000 dollars. The court held that it was not entitled. Its statutory subrogation right, which was to be construed in accordance with the ordinary meaning of subrogation, arose only when L. and the others had been fully compensated. As they had recovered much less than their actual loss, the respondent had no possible claim.

Gifts

If the insured has been fully indemnified, but he also receives a gift from another to mitigate the effects of his loss, he will normally have to account to his insurers for the amount of the gift. In *Stearns* v. *Village Main Reef Gold Mining Co.*,[29] the defendant's insured gold was commandeered by the South African Government. The insurers paid the defendant for a total loss. The Government then returned a sum of money to the insured in

---

[27] See the facts of *Hobbs* v. *Marlowe* [1977] 2 All E.R. 241, discussed below at p. 254.
[28] (1974) 46 D.L.R. (3d) 699.
[29] (1905) 10 Com.Cas. 89.

return for the latter's agreeing to keep the mine open. It was held that the insurers were entitled to recover the equivalent of that money because it had been given in order to diminish the insured's loss. With this decision can be compared the earlier marine insurance case of *Burnand* v. *Rodocanachi*.[30] Here, during the American Civil War, the insured ship was destroyed by a Confederate cruiser. The insurers paid the agreed value. The insured subsequently received a gift from the United States Government. The House of Lords held that as, according to the construction of the relevant statute authorising the payment, this money was paid purely as a gift and intended to benefit the insured over and above any insurance money, the insurers were not entitled to claim it. It is clear that this case establishes the exception rather than the rule, and that the insured will be entitled to retain the gift only when it was intended as extra compensation for him.

A surplus

If, somewhat unusually perhaps, there happens to be a surplus after the insurers have recovered their money, the insured is entitled to keep it, in other words the insurers' subrogation rights extend only to the amount they actually paid to the insured. In *Yorkshire Insurance Co.* v. *Nisbet Shipping Co.*,[31] the point arose in a neat form. An insured ship was lost in 1945 as the result of a collision and the insurers paid its agreed value of £72,000. With the latter's consent, the insured started proceedings against the Canadian Government, owners of the other ship, and the Government was eventually in 1955 found liable. The damages awarded were some £75,000 which were properly converted into Canadian dollars at the rate of exchange prevalent at the time of the collision. That sum was paid to the insured in 1958, but when it was transmitted to this country and converted into sterling, it produced a sum of some £126,000, because the pound had been devalued in 1949. The insured could not of course deny the insurers' entitlement to £72,000, but disputed that they were entitled to the surplus of nearly £55,000. Diplock J. held that the subrogation rights of the insurers extended only to the sums they had paid out. Although he was construing the relevant section in the Marine Insurance Act 1906,[32] there can be no doubt that the decision is generally

---

[30] (1882) 7 App.Cas. 333.
[31] [1962] 2 Q.B. 330.
[32] s.79.

applicable. Although logically unimpeachable,[33] the result is somewhat unfair. After all, the insured had the benefit of prompt payment of the money in 1945. It was the insurers who were out of pocket for some 13 years or more. Had the insurer actually exercised their right to sue the Canadian Government in the insured's name, they would probably have been better off because they would have been entitled to claim interest on the money for their own benefit.[34]

THE INSURER'S RIGHT TO TAKE ACTION

The insurer's right to bring proceedings in the name of the insured is long established, being referred to as a commonplace occurrence as long ago as 1782 in *Mason* v. *Sainsbury*.[35] It is important to remember, however, that the action remains the insured's and that the defendant, if he is adjudged liable, gets a good discharge only if he pays the insured. If the insured should refuse to allow his name to be used, the insurer can, as an alternative to compelling it, bring proceedings against the wrongdoer and join the insured as second defendant.

A classic modern illustration of the insurer's right is the decision of the House of Lords in *Lister* v. *Romford Ice and Cold Storage Ltd.*.[36] There an employee of the respondent negligently injured another employee; in fact, they were son and father respectively. The respondent was therefore vicariously liable to pay damages to the father, an award satisfied by the respondent's liability insurers, who then used the respondent's name to sue the negligent employee to recoup the loss. The claim was that the employee had failed to exercise the reasonable care and skill impliedly expected as part of an employee's duty to his employer, and, by a majority, the House of Lords held that the claim succeeded. The majority regarded the fact that the action was in reality brought by the insurers as irrelevant. There was such an implied term in the employee's contract of employment

---

[33] But note the comments of Megaw L.J. in *Lucas* v. *E.C.G.D.* [1973] 1 W.L.R. 914 at 924, and the possible effects of express subrogation terms; see p. 250, below.

[34] *Cousins* v. *D. & C. Carriers* [1971] 2 Q.B. 230; see p. 248, below.

[35] (1782) 3 Doug.K.B. 61 at 64 (Lord Mansfield)—"Every day the insurer is put into the shoes of the assured." Note that if the insured is a company which has been wound up, the insurers have no rights since the insured's name no longer exists to be used: *M. H. Smith (Plant Hire) Ltd.* v. *D. L. Mainwaring* [1986] B.C.L.C. 342.

[36] [1957] A.C. 555.

and he had broken it. The main defence of the appellant was that, even if he should have acted with reasonable care and skill, if in fact his employer had insured against the consequences of a breach to a third party, there was equally to be implied in his contract of employment a term that he would be entitled to the benefit of that insurance. This persuasive reasoning was adopted by the dissenting judges, in particular by Lord Radcliffe, whose judgment is, it is suggested, much more realistic than those of the majority.[37] Although, as will be seen later, employers' liability insurers have, in fact, as a result of this decision, agreed to forgo their subrogation rights in this sort of case,[38] the decision does illustrate the wasteful consequences of this aspect of the doctrine of subrogation.[39]

There are a number of very important limitations surrounding, and consequences of, this aspect of the doctrine of subrogation. These will be examined under the following eleven heads.

1. The insured must be indemnified

As with the first aspect of subrogation, the insured must be indemnified by the insurer before the latter's right arises, and this is in respect of all claims made by the insured in respect of the particular event. In *Page v. Scottish Insurance Corporation*,[40] P, while driving F's car, negligently collided with and damaged T's car, as well as damaging F's car. F's insurers instructed P to have F's car repaired, but refused to pay these costs and, before indemnifying P against the claim of T, claimed to have the right to sue P in the name of F for damages for negligently driving F's car, and to be able to set off against the repair costs the damages payable to T. The Court of Appeal held that the insurers' exercise of their subrogation rights in F's name was premature: "The underwriter [has] no right to subrogation unless and until he [has] fully indemnified the insured under the policy."[41]

The question again arises whether it is enough for the insurer fully to have indemnified the insured under the policy, or whether the insured must be fully compensated. Similar

---

[37] See also Parsons, "Individual Responsibility Versus Enterprise Liability" (1956) 29 A.L.J. 714, a comment on the Court of Appeal decision which was decided the same way but again only by a majority.

[38] See Gardiner (1959) 22 M.L.R. 652.

[39] See also p. 257, below, and compare *Morris v. Ford Motor Co.*, [1973] Q.B. 792 discussed at pp. 255–257, below.

[40] (1929) 98 L.J.K.B. 308.

[41] *Ibid.* at 311, *per* Scrutton L.J.

examples to those given earlier[42] can be used to illustrate this point. Most apt, because of its likely occurrence, is the case of the insured car driver fully indemnified for car damage but with a claim for uninsured loss against the tortfeasor, which might be for consequential loss and/or the sum not recovered from his insurer because of an excess clause in his policy. In *Page*, Scrutton L.J. expressly reserved the question whether full compensation is necessary.[43] There is some authority that it is,[44] but it would seem likely that in this context the courts would hold that full indemnity only is necessary. If, as the result of a subrogation action, the insurer recovered more than it had paid the insured, the latter would be entitled to the excess. In any event, as will be seen, if the insurer declines to sue, the insured can himself bring proceedings. In practice, this question may be a rather academic one. This aspect of the doctrine of subrogation is frequently covered by an express clause in the policy vesting subrogation rights in the insurer upon indemnification under the policy or even, sometimes, before that.[45]

2. Who controls the proceedings?

It follows from the points just discussed that, until the insured is indemnified and in the absence of anything to the contrary in the policy, he has the right to sue the wrongdoer and control the proceedings. In *Commercial Union Assurance Co. v. Lister*,[46] the insured's mill was damaged by an explosion for which, it was alleged, the local authority was liable. He was insured for £33,000 but the damage was estimated at £55,000. The insured wished to sue the authority, but the insurers sought a declaration that they were entitled to the benefit of any such action. It was held that as he would not be fully indemnified by his insurers, the insured was entitled to bring and control the action, provided he acted bona fide and sued for the whole loss. In addition, before the insurers have the right to control, they must agree to indemnify the insured in respect of costs. It is also clear that even if the insured has been fully indemnified, he can if he wishes, sue the third party and control the proceedings if the insurer declines. The insurer has no right to stop the insured.[47]

[42] See p. 240.
[43] (1929) 98 L.J.K.B. 308 at 312.
[44] *e.g. Globe & Rutgers Fire Ins. Co. v. Truedell* [1927] 2 D.L.R. 659.
[45] See p. 250, below.
[46] (1874) L.R. 9 Ch. 483.
[47] *Morley v. Moore* [1936] 2 K.B. 359; *Hobbs v. Marlowe* [1977] 2 All E.R. 241.

In practice, though, many of these points may be redundant. Express subrogation clauses will often give the insurers the right to control the proceedings regardless of indemnification. One important question may then arise as to the position of the insurers who elect not to take control, in particular as to their liability for costs, as the standard term provides that if the insurers do take control, it is at their expense. Again the typical case may involve an under-insured insured who has been paid by his insurers and has a claim against a tortfeasor which he wishes to exercise to recover his uninsured loss. The insurers are not interested, save in the possibility of recovering anything if the insured is successful. The insured, as has been seen, must sue for his whole loss. Can he claim that the insurer must bear the costs of his action on the ground that, if he succeeds, it will be partly to the benefit of his insurers, and had they taken control, they would have been responsible for the costs? These facts arose in the New Zealand case of *Arthur Barnett Ltd.* v. *National Insurance Co. of New Zealand*,[48] where the Court of Appeal held that the insurers were not responsible. This result is also implied by the course of events in *Hobbs* v. *Marlowe*,[49] a case on similar facts which will be examined later, but where the point was not actually in issue.

3. The insured must not do anything to prejudice the insurer

It has just been seen that the insured who takes proceedings against a wrongdoer must sue for his whole loss, even if he has been partly indemnified by his insurers who decline to exercise their subrogation rights. This is perhaps one aspect of the general principle that once rights of subrogation exist or potentially exist for the benefit of the insurers, the insured must not do anything which might prejudice those rights on pain of his being liable to repay to the insurers as damages the amount which the insurers have paid or, where appropriate, of the insurers being able to avoid liability.

Therefore, while a compromise entered into between the insured and the wrongdoer will normally bind the insurers, such a compromise, whether agreed before or after indemnification by the insurers, will amount to a breach of this duty of the insured. However, the insured must actually prejudice the insurers' position, so that if his claim against the third party is a doubtful one and he acts bona fide in the interests of the

---

[48] [1965] N.Z.L.R. 874.
[49] [1977] 2 All E.R. 241. See p. 254, below.

insurers as well as himself, he will not suffer. In *West of England Fire Insurance Co.* v. *Isaacs*,[50] the defendant was the sub-tenant of property which he insured with the plaintiff. Following a fire, he recovered money from them which he paid to the tenant of the property who had covenanted with both him and the head landlord to insure. He undertook also not to sue the tenant for breach of this covenant, it appearing that the latter had not adequately insured. It was held that the insured was liable to return the equivalent money to the insurers, having prejudiced their potential right to use his name to sue the tenant for breach of the insuring covenant. There are a number of other illustrations in the cases of the same point, involving insureds who compromised a statutory claim or a claim in tort against a wrongdoer.[51]

It can perhaps be commented that this principle could unjustifiably penalise an innocent insured not aware of the intricacies of subrogation and tort actions. For example, following a car accident, an insured who was the innocent party might well, because his insurance is comprehensive, agree quite reasonably with the other driver that he will not pursue any claim against him. If that were a binding agreement, it would prejudice the insurers' subrogation rights and yet it seems a harsh application of the principle. This is not to suggest, of course, that an insurer would necessarily take the point, but the question remains as to whether it should be there to be taken.

4. The wrongdoer's position vis-à-vis the insurer

It is self-evident that a wrongdoing defendant cannot claim in defence that in reality the plaintiff is an insurer and that the nominal plaintiff has already been fully compensated for the defendant's wrong. Equally, it is no defence for him to claim that the insurer satisfied the plaintiff's claim when in law it was not bound to, for example, because the insurer had the right to avoid liability under the policy.[52] He can, however, rely on a prior agreement between himself and the insured that the latter would limit his rights. This would have been the result in *Lister* v. *Romford Ice*[53] if the reasoning of the minority had been accepted. There is County Court authority,[54] which appears

---

[50] [1897] 1 Q.B. 226.
[51] *e.g. Phoenix Ass. Co.* v. *Spooner* [1905] 2 K.B. 753; *Re Law Fire Ass. Co.* (1888) 4 T.L.R. 309; *Horse, Carriage & General Ins. Co.* v. *Petch* (1916) 33 T.L.R. 131.
[52] *King* v. *Victoria Ins. Co.* [1896] A.C. 250.
[53] See p. 243, above.
[54] *Haigh* v. *Lawford* (1964) 114 L.J. 208 (Salisbury County Court).

correct in principle, that the defendant cannot rely upon a purported waiver by the insured after he knows of the insurer's payment to the insured and thus, that the insurer's subrogation rights have crystallised.

It has also been held in a Canadian case[55] that a defendant can rely on an agreement between the plaintiff and his insurers that the latter would forgo their subrogation rights, but this must be doubtful as it amounts to an unrecognised exception to the doctrine of privity of contract.

5. Subrogation applies only when the insured has a right of action

If, quite apart from agreement or compromise, the insured has no right of action which he could pursue, the insurer can be in no better position. The leading illustration of this point is the decision in *Simpson* v. *Thomson*.[56] The insured owned two ships which collided due to the negligence of one of the masters. In respect of the ship which was negligently sailed, the insured paid money into Court, as he was statutorily bound to do, in order to compensate the various parties involved. The insurers paid for the other ship and then claimed the right to use the insured's name as owner of this ship to claim against the fund. It was held that the insurers had no such right, as it would be tantamount to the insured suing himself, which, of course, is impossible. It would have been different had the ships been owned by different companies, albeit they were both owned or controlled by the same person.[57]

6. The insurer's claim for interest

The question may often arise whether insurers suing in their insured's name are entitled to claim interest for their own benefit. Nominally, that award would go to the insured, the nominal plaintiff, but it is now clear that the insurers' subrogation rights include the right to appropriate interest under section 3(1) of the Law Reform (Miscellaneous Provisions) Act 1934.[58] In *H. Cousins & Co. Ltd.* v. *D. & C. Carriers Ltd.*,[59] it was argued in

---

[55] *Clark & Sons* v. *Finnamore* (1973) 32 D.L.R. (3d) 236.

[56] (1877) 3 App.Cas. 279. See also *Buckland* v. *Palmer* [1984] 1 W.L.R. 1109, where the principle was applied when the insured had lost her right of action because of rules of court. See [1985] J.B.L. 54.

[57] (1877) 3 App.Cas. at 294 (Lord Blackburn).

[58] See further on this, Chapter 13 at p. 228.

[59] [1971] 2 Q.B. 230.

an action for damages for breach of a contract of carriage that the plaintiff was entitled to interest only in respect of the period that he really suffered, namely until he was indemnified by his insurers. It was held that there was no reason why the plaintiff should not be awarded interest to the date of judgment on the usual basis, because the appropriate part of it would rightly enure to the benefit of the insurers.[60]

7. Assignment as an alternative to subrogation

The essence of subrogation is, of course, that the insurers sue in the name of the insured. It is, however, possible for the insurers to seek to adopt an alternative, namely, to persuade the insured to assign his cause of action to them. A bare cause of action, that is the right to sue another, is not assignable, but one enforced by an insurer is legitimate because it is supported by the insurer's interest in recouping himself in respect of the amount of the loss he has paid out as a result of the wrong of the defendant.[61] Provided that the assignment is complete, that is that notice is given to the defendant in accordance with section 136 of the Law of Property Act 1925, the insurer/assignee can sue in his own name.

Such assignments are probably rare. Insurers prefer to use the name of their insureds because of the consequent lack of publicity. However, assignment does have advantages over subrogation. In particular, there will be no requirement that the insured be fully indemnified before the insurer can sue, and it must be the position that the insurers can keep everything they recover from the action. The principle of *Yorkshire Insurance Co. v. Nisbet Shipping Co.*[62] will not apply simply because the cause of action is entirely the insurers' and the insured has forfeited all interest in it.

8. The effect of express terms[63]

It has already been seen in certain respects how express conditions in a policy may refer to subrogation rights. Such terms

---

[60] The contrary views expressed in *Harbutt's "Plasticine" Ltd.* v. *Wayne Tank & Pump Co.* [1971] 1 Q.B. 447 were clearly based on a misunderstanding. See (1970) 96 L.Q.R. 513.
[61] *Compania Columbiana de Seguros* v. *Pacific Steam Navigation Co.* [1965] 1 Q.B. 101.
[62] See p. 242, above.
[63] See further, Birds, *Contractual Subrogation in Insurance* [1979] J.B.L. 124.

appear common and there is no doubt that they can exclude or modify some of the conditions surrounding the exercise of subrogation rights at common law. If a policy does contain such a term, the correct approach is to consider it first for a determination of the parties' rights and to refer to general subrogation principles only if there is ambiguity in the term or if it is not all-embracing. In *Lucas* v. *Exports Credit Guarantee Department*,[64] the courts were faced with a subrogation term in a policy issued by the Department, which is a Government body. The issue concerned a question very similar to that in *Yorkshire Insurance Co.* v. *Nisbet*,[65] and it was held that whether or not the insurer was entitled to an excess resulting after the wrongdoer had paid, and arising because of a variation in the Exchange Rate, depended entirely on the construction of the relevant term. Indeed, in the House of Lords, general principles of subrogation were not considered at all.

Express terms will commonly entitle the insurers to take proceedings before or after indemnifying the insured, and may well entitle them to control or take over proceedings taken by the insured in which they have hitherto taken no interest. It has been seen how, under the general law, even if the insured has been fully indemnified, he is perfectly entitled to proceed against the wrongdoer if the insurers choose not to. In practice express terms may well permit the insurers to take control and thus abandon such an action. It is suggested that this should only be permissible if the insurers act in good faith and with due regard to the interests of the insured, which in practice means that it should not be if the insured has suffered uninsured loss for which he seeks compensation.[66]

An express term may also purport to give subrogation rights in the name of a party who is not the insured.[67] In certain circumstances,[68] the insured may recover on a policy for the benefit of a third party. If that third party has a claim in respect of the loss against a wrongdoer, the insurer will probably be unable to be subrogated to this right of action at common law simply because the third party has no direct right to sue the insurer.[68a] An express term of the sort mentioned is clearly an attempt to cure this problem, though it must be said that

---

[64] [1974] 1 W.L.R. 909.
[65] See p. 242, above.
[66] See further (1978) 41 M.L.R. 201 at 204 and [1979] J.B.L. 124 at 134–136.
[67] [1979] J.B.L. 124 at 129–130.
[68] See pp. 46–52, above.
[68a] But see the recent Australian Case mentioned in note 19a at p. 49, above.

The Insurer's Right to Take Action

enforcement of it would necessitate the sanctioning of an exception to the doctrine of privity of contract.

9. Two or more persons interested in the same property

Some nice subrogation questions may arise where two or more people have interests in the same property. This may happen, for example, in respect of landlord and tenant or mortgagor and mortgagee of real property, and it may well also involve questions of contribution to which we shall return in the next chapter. The parties may be separately insured, only one of them may be insured, or they may be jointly insured.

Where they are separately insured, the loss will fall on that party legally liable, and hence on that party's insurer. The other party's insurer alone can have subrogation rights if it indemnifies its insured first. If a bailor and bailee of goods are both insured and the goods are lost in circumstances whereby the bailee is responsible, his insurer bears the loss.[69] Similarly, if landlord and tenant are both insured, but the latter covenanted to insure or to repair in the event of a loss, the latter's insurer will bear the loss.[70] The converse will apply if the landlord covenanted appropriately.[71]

Even where only one of the parties is insured, it may be that the insurance enures to the benefit of the other so that the insurer can have no recourse against the latter. The point arose for the first time in this country in the important case of *Mark Rowlands Ltd. v. Berni Inns Ltd.*,[72] where property leased by the nominal plaintiffs to the defendants was damaged by the negligence of the defendants.[73] Under the terms of the lease the plaintiffs covenanted to insure and the defendants covenanted to pay a sum (an "insurance rent") of approximately one quarter of the premium. Further the defendants were relieved from their covenant to repair in respect of "damage by or in consequence of any of the insured risks." The Court of Appeal

---

[69] *North British & Mercantile Ins. Co. v. London, Liverpool & Globe Ins. Co.* (1877) 5 Ch.D. 569, discussed further at p. 260, below.

[70] *Darrell v. Tibbitts*, note 24 above.

[71] *e.g. United Motor Services v. Hutson* [1937] 1 D.L.R. 737.

[72] [1986] Q.B. 211; see p. 36, above for the insurable interest issues decided in this case and for a detailed note, Birds (1986) 6 Oxford J. Legal Stud. 304. Clearly the subrogation point was the primary issue.

[73] The defendants were in fact insured but against third party liability, not under an insurance of the property itself, so that this was not the sort of case discussed above.

held that the plaintiffs' insurers could not exercise subrogation rights against the defendants[74]:

> "An essential feature of insurance by fire is that it covers fires caused by accident as well as by negligence. This was what the plaintiffs agreed to provide in consideration of, *inter alia*, the insurance rent paid by the defendants. The intention of the parties, sensibly construed, must therefore have been that in the event of damage by fire, whether due to accident or negligence, the landlord's loss was to be recouped from the insurance monies and that in that event they were to have no further claim against the tenants for damages in negligence."[75]

It was clearly crucial to the result of the *Mark Rowlands* case that the terms of the lease made it clear that the insurance was for the benefit of both parties. Not all leases will be so worded. It may be that the reasoning can be extended to other relationships between persons interested in the same property, for example vendor and purchaser of land where the vendor's policy expressly enures to the purchaser's benefit between contract and completion,[76] and owner and hirer of goods where the owner has insured pursuant to a term of the contract of hire.[77]

A different situation is where both parties are insured under the same policy.[78] This point arose in *Petrofina Ltd. v. Magnaload*

---

[74] An odd feature of the case is the fact that it was openly admitted that the real plaintiff was the insurer. It could so easily have been fought as simply a landlord and tenant case, although it is not suggested that this would have made any difference to the result.

[75] Per Kerr L.J. at 232. The learned judge relied on a number of Commonwealth and American decisions on the same point, especially three cases in the Canadian Supreme Court: *Agnew Surpass Shoe Stores Ltd. v. Cummer-Yonge Investments Ltd.* (1973) 55 D.L.R. (3d) 248; *Ross Southwood Tire Ltd. v. Pyrotech Products Ltd.* (1975) 57 D.L.R. (3d) 248; *T. Eaton Co. Ltd. v. Smith* (1977) 92 D.L.R. (3d) 425. See Hasson (1976) 14 Osgoode Hall L.J. 769 at 779–782 and (1985) 5 Oxford J. Legal Stud. 416 at 430–433. See also *Marlborough Properties Ltd. v. Marlborough Fibreglass Ltd.* [1981] 1 N.Z.L.R. 464, commented on by Yates (1983) 3 Oxford J. Legal Stud. 431. Note that Canadian law does not excuse the actual negligent employee of the tenant; *Greenwood Shopping Plaza v. Beattie* (1980) 111 D.L.R. (3d) 257.

[76] *Cf. Rayner v. Preston* (1881) 18 Ch.D. 1 (p. 129, above) and *Castellain v. Preston* (1883) 11 Q.B.D. 380 (p. 239, above).

[77] See further Birds, *op. cit.*

[78] Note that this is not joint insurance in the strict sense since this arises only where the parties' interests in the property insured are the same: see *e.g. Re King* [1963] Ch. 459, where a policy in the joint names of landlord and tenant was not a joint insurance.

Ltd.,[79] where it was held that the insurers under a contractors' all risks insurance policy could not use the name of the principal insureds, the owners of the property and main contractors working thereon, to sue the negligent subcontractors responsible for the loss. The latter were held to fall within the definition of "the insured" in the policy, so that in effect it was a case of co-insurance and the principle applied was merely an extension of that which forbids the insurer from exercising subrogation rights to sue its insured.[80]

It is suggested that the same principle would apply to, for example, an insurance by both the hirer and owner of goods under a hire purchase contract, unless perhaps one of the insureds is guilty of a deliberate act causing the loss where subrogation would be permitted against him because he has forfeited his right to indemnity.[80a]

10. Waiver of subrogation rights

Insurers may voluntarily agree not to exercise rights of subrogation in certain circumstances. This may arise in the context of an agreement between insured and insurer, for example, it could be a term of the policy or of an agreement of settlement. Alternatively, insurers may simply undertake in general not to exercise their rights. The classic illustration of this is the undertaking by members of the British Insurance Association and Lloyd's that, as employer's liability insurers, they would not pursue claims in an employer's name against a negligent employee to recoup money paid out to indemnify the employer against a third party claim by a fellow employee based on the negligence of the employee.[81] This followed the decision in *Lister* v. *Romford Ice* which was discussed earlier.[82]

Insurers may also agree amongst themselves to waive their subrogation rights. The prime example is the "knock for knock" agreements between motor insurers, under which following an accident in which both damaged cars are insured against first party damage, that is, under the usual comprehensive motor

---

[79] [1983] 2 Lloyd's Rep. 91. See also p. 47, above and [1983] J.B.L. 497.
[80] See p. 248, above. In reaching his decision, Lloyd J. relied heavily on "commercial convenience" as did the Supreme Court of Canada on almost identical facts in *Commonwealth Construction Co. Ltd.* v. *Imperial Oil Ltd.* (1977) 69 D.L.R. (3d) 558, a case which Lloyd J. followed.
[80a] *Samuel* v. *Dumas* [1924] A.C. 431 at 445–446 (Viscount Cave). See further *MacGillivray and Parkington*, para. 1244.
[81] See note 38.
[82] See p. 243.

policy, each insurer indemnifies its own insured regardless of the strict legal position as to liability in tort. The existence of such an agreement does not prevent the innocent insured from pursuing his tort claim, at least unless and until his insurer takes it over and abandons it, a question which was discussed earlier. In *Hobbs* v. *Marlowe*,[83] the innocent car owner did indeed pursue this course because he wished to recover his uninsured loss, namely, his uninsured excess and damages for having to hire a substitute car while his was being repaired. In this, he was supported by the Automobile Association. The House of Lords had no difficulty in rejecting the argument for the negligent driver, in reality the latter's insurer, that the existence of the "knock for knock" agreement between the two insurers concerned removed the victim's right of action. In practice the damages recovered by the plaintiff would largely have to be repaid to his insurer, which was then under the agreement bound to pay them to the defendant's insurer. It was held, however, that the plaintiff (or really the A.A.) was entitled to only those costs appropriate to an action to recover his uninsured loss and as these were below the limits of the County Court Arbitration Scheme, he was not entitled to his own solicitor's costs.[84] The plaintiff had sued for his whole loss, and the result is somewhat harsh in the light of the fact that, had he not done so, he could have been penalised by his insurer.[85] On the actual facts of *Hobbs* v. *Marlowe*, it appears that this was no real danger because of the attitude of the plaintiff's insurer, but in a future case, an insurer might not be so unconcerned. If an insurer did indeed insist upon the insured's suing for full damages, it is to be hoped that the court would exercise the discretion permitted to award full costs.

The "knock for knock" agreements clearly have the substantial advantage of eliminating costly enquiries as to fault and wasteful subrogation actions. However, there appear to be some disadvantages so far as the innocent car driver is concerned. In particular, his no claims bonus may be affected as a result of something of which he was an innocent victim,[86] and he may be deterred from pursuing in law claims to which he is entitled such as the recovery of uninsured loss from the tort-

---

[83] [1977] 2 All E.R. 241.
[84] County Court Rules Ord. 47, r. 5(4).
[85] Upon the principles discussed earlier at pp. 246–247.
[86] Although this was not the case in *Hobbs* v. *Marlowe* and increasingly it seems that insurers will maintain no claims bonuses if there is no blame.

feasor. It is suggested that the system is in need of improvement in respect of such points.[87]

11. Denial of subrogation rights

It may be that the court has power to deny an insurer its subrogation rights in certain contexts. In *Morris* v. *Ford Motor Co.*,[88] Cameron Industrial Services Ltd. (Cameron) contracted to clean at Ford's works. A term of this contract provided that Cameron would indemnify Ford in respect of any liability attaching to Ford for the negligence of the employees of either of them. Morris was injured by an employee of Ford for whom Ford was vicariously liable. Ford claimed an indemnity from Cameron under the term described and Cameron in return claimed upon indemnifying Ford to be subrogated to Ford's right to sue its employee for failing to take reasonable care and skill. Although Cameron was not an insurer as such, though no doubt it was backed by one, its position was analogous to that of an insurer and in particular to the position of the insurer in *Lister* v. *Romford Ice and Cold Storage Ltd.*.[89] The undertaking given by insurers following the latter case, which has been referred to, was not relevant as that applies only when the injury in question is caused by one employee to another employee of the same employer. On the authority of the *Lister* case, Cameron should have succeeded in its claim. However, by a majority, the Court of Appeal held that subrogation would not be permitted. If the decision is correct, then its principles must apply to insurers directly and it cannot be written off simply as "not an insurance case."

One of the principal difficulties with *Morris* v. *Ford* is that the judges in the majority gave different reasons for their decisions, so that it is virtually impossible to say what the *ratio* is. Lord Denning M.R. claimed a broad jurisdiction to refuse to allow the enforcement of subrogation rights where it would not be "just and equitable." In his view, subrogation is an equitable remedy whose exercise is therefore subject to general equitable principles. To this there are the following objections, quite apart from the fact that the point was not relied upon in argu-

---

[87] See further (1978) 41 M.L.R. 201.
[88] [1973] Q.B. 793. See Powles (1974) 90 L.Q.R. 34. For another example, where the wrongdoer was the son of the insured and subrogation was denied at least partly on moral grounds, see *Morawietz* v. *Morawietz* (1984) 5 C.C.L.I. 11; see the useful comment thereon by Baer, *ibid*.
[89] p. 243, above.

ment. First, it is not certain that subrogation is an equitable remedy, and it is certainly wrong to imply that it is exclusively equitable.[90] Secondly, there is no precedent for such a broad ground for dispensation, and thirdly, even if there were, the "equity" ought strictly to refer to the position between insured and insurer, that is the merits of the insurer's claim as between them. The "equity" or rather "inequity" here was much more general, being the potentially harmful effects of permitting subrogation on industrial relations at Ford's. In the alternative, Lord Denning said that if subrogation depended on an implied term, the circumstances showed that such a term should not be implied.

The reasoning of James L.J. is somewhat more convincing. In his view, subrogation, which would normally attach to such a contract of indemnity, was excluded by an implied term in the contract between Cameron and Ford, because that contract was made against the background of the decision in *Lister* v. *Romford* and the possible implications of that decision. This is not really the same reasoning as Lord Denning's alternative. The latter held that subrogation should not be implied in the first place to a contract of this sort. James L.J. held that it would normally be so implied, but the circumstances negated that implication. While the reasoning of James L.J. that it is possible to exclude a normal incident of a contract by implication is no doubt legally sound, there is a difficulty in relating this to the facts of the case. As the dissenting judge, Stamp L.J., pointed out, to imply such a term in law the court must conclude that both parties would have said—"we did not bother to express it, it is too clear"—and there was no evidence to do so, the trial judge having found that Cameron did not know of the circumstances of the *Lister* case and the agreement resulting from it.

Despite this criticism, it is difficult not to sympathise with the result of the case. There are, it is suggested, sound reasons for not allowing risks of this sort to fall on individual employees when insurers have been paid to take them, a point of more general application which will be made again shortly. What cannot really be said is what will be the consequences of that decision. There has been no subsequent case directly on the point,[91] although it might be imagined that it has effectively

---

[90] See p. 237, above.
[91] But it was cited in *Commonwealth Construction* v. *Imperial Oil* (1976) 69 D.L.R. (3d) at 566. More recent English cases have "denied" subrogation on more traditional grounds; see pp. 251–253, above.

stymied the application of subrogation in the employer's liability field as a matter of practice, at least until a party is prepared to take the matter to the House of Lords. Legally, the reasoning of James L.J. and the alternative reasoning of Lord Denning, cannot stand if an insurer inserts an express term conferring subrogation rights in its policy, although a solution might be found in a doctrine which requires the insurer to exercise its rights under the policy in good faith in the interests of itself and the insured.[92] When and whether *Morris* v. *Ford* will be relied upon simply cannot be predicted.

THE FUTURE OF SUBROGATION

It is appropriate to conclude this chapter with some general comments about the role of subrogation, although lack of space precludes any detail. There can be no doubt that to the extent that it prevents an insured from making a profit from a loss it is an eminently sound principle. However, in the context of subrogation actions, the doctrine has attracted criticism. First, it must be rare for an insurer to exercise subrogation rights except against a defendant who is also insured, simply because there is little point otherwise. If so, this can be said to be wasteful and expensive in resources; it unnecessarily promotes multiple insurance, requiring that the same risk be covered both by first party and third party policies. Secondly, if the defendant is not, in fact, insured, throwing liability on him relieves the insurer who has been paid to assume the risk in question and who is able to distribute the cost among the premium-paying public. In a sense, therefore, subrogation may work to curtail the very essence of insurance which is risk distribution. The arguments are, of course, political ones encompassing the whole question of individual responsibility for civil wrongs in the legal system. For reasons which have been merely outlined here, and have been much more cogently and more fully argued elsewhere,[93] it

---

[92] See further [1979] J.B.L. 124 at 134–136.
[93] See especially the forceful critique by Hasson, "Subrogation in Insurance Law—a critical evaluation" (1985) 5 Oxford J. Legal Stud. 416. See also Harper and James, *Tort*, para. 25–23; Fleming (1966) 54 Calif.L.R. 1478 at 1533–1542; Young, *Cases and Materials on Insurance*, p. 342. For a contrary view, see Horn, *Subrogation in Insurance Theory and Practice*.

is suggested that no harm would be done, and a great deal of resources would be saved, if we followed the Scandinavian practice[94] of permitting insurers to exercise subrogation rights only against a wrongdoer who was guilty of real misconduct.

---

[94] See Hellner, *Försäkringsgivarens regressätt* (*The Insurers Right of Subrogation*) (1953) pp. 257 *et seq.* (English summary).

Chapter 16

CONTRIBUTION AND DOUBLE INSURANCE

Like subrogation, contribution is a principle designed to prevent unjust enrichment. It too applies only to those insurance contracts that are contracts of indemnity. Unlike subrogation, however, contribution applies not as between insured and insurer but as between insurers. There is nothing wrong in an insured effecting as many policies as he wishes on the same property or against the same risk, so that he may be doubly insured. If he suffers a loss, he is, of course, by virtue of the doctrine of subrogation, entitled to no more than a full indemnity, but he can at common law choose from which insurer to claim. The insurer which pays is entitled to claim a contribution from the other insurer or insurers, as otherwise the latter would be unjustly enriched. The insurer claiming a contribution must sue in its own name.[1]

In practice contribution is most unlikely to arise in quite this way because of a standard term in all indemnity insurances. This will provide that if there is any other insurance on the property or the risk covered by the policy, the insurer will not be liable to pay or contribute more than its rateable proportion of any loss or damage. Such a rateable proportion clause does not affect the basic legal principles of double insurance, but it simply prevents the insured from recovering all his loss from one insurer. He is compelled to claim the appropriate proportion from each and the insurers are relieved of the burden of having to claim contributions *inter se*.

Whether the issue arises as a matter of general law or under such a rateable proportion clause, the same conditions must be fulfilled before it can be said that there is double insurance. Essentially these are that the same property or liability is covered against the same risk under policies which are both or all legally enforceable. A number of points require further elucidation.

---

[1] *Austin* v. *Zurich General Accident & Liability Ins. Co.* [1945] K.B. 250 at 258 *per* MacKinnon L.J.; *Sydney Turf Club* v. *Crowley* (1972) 126 C.L.R. 420.

Policies with different scopes

Whether the policies cover the same property or liability is fairly easily established. It is not required, though, that the scope of the policies as a whole be the same. There may be an overlap between a motor and an employer's liability policy that can give rise to double insurance.[2] Similarly, a household policy may cover certain property owned by the insured when it is taken outside the house. This would be regarded as a small part of the total cover. The insured under such a policy might take his watch, which is one of the items so covered, to be repaired, and while it is at the repairer's, it might be covered by a policy held by the latter. This would also be a small part of the repairer's cover. Prima facie, there would be double insurance, though it may well be that the position is affected by policy conditions.

Same risk

The requirement that the risk be the same means essentially that the same interest is covered by or on behalf of the same insured. In *North British & Mercantile Insurance Co.* v. *London, Liverpool & Globe Insurance Co.*,[3] grain which belonged to the bailor was in the possession of bailees who were wharfingers. The grain was lost in circumstances whereby in law the bailees were liable for the loss. Both parties had insured this grain, the owner under an ordinary property policy, the bailee under a floating policy. The bailees recovered from their insurers who then claimed a contribution from the bailor's insurers. The Court of Appeal held that there was no right to a contribution because the policies covered different interests. The loss in the circumstances fell on the bailees and hence their insurers; had the bailor's insurers paid their insured, they would have been subrogated to the latter's right to sue the bailees. Therefore, whenever in law the loss should be borne by only one of the insureds, there is no contribution.

---

[2] e.g. *Albion Insurance Co.* v. *Government Insurance Office of New South Wales* (1969) 121 C.L.R. 342.

[3] (1877) 5 Ch.D. 569. See also *Dawson* v. *Bankers' & Traders' Ins. Co.* [1957] V.R. 491, where it was held that there was no double insurance between a motor policy and an employer's liability policy where the former policy covered a negligent employee directly, *i.e.* he was included as one of the insured, and the latter covered only his employer's vicarious liability; see also *Zurich Insurance Co.* v. *Shield Insurance Co. Ltd.*, an unreported decision of the Irish High Court, July 29, 1985. Compare the *Albion* case (note 2), where only the employer's vicarious liability was covered under both policies and there was therefore double insurance.

It should be noted, however, that in practice this legal rule is often ignored. The most notable instance is by virtue of one of the rules of the Fire Offices' Committee[4] whereby contribution is applied by agreement between insurers wherever real property[5] is, in fact, doubly insured by different people with different interests, regardless of questions of legal liability.[6]

Same insured?

The judgments in the *North British* case appear at times to imply not just that the same interest must be doubly insured, but that the insured actually be the same. It must be the law, though, that this is not required. Contribution must apply wherever an insured is in fact entitled to recovery under another policy, even if he is not the insured under that policy and hence not legally entitled to sue upon it, if, in fact, he recovers from that insurer. If, in what is likely to be the most common practical application, the bailor and bailee of goods both insure and a loss occurs in circumstances which attach no legal liability to either party, as in *Hepburn* v. *Tomlinson*,[7] and on the construction of the bailee's policy, he is entitled to claim for the benefit of the bailor, as also was the position in that case, there must be double insurance. Otherwise, the problem would be insoluble, neither party having rights against the other and thus neither party's insurer having rights to which they could succeed by virtue of subrogation to throw the loss on the other. If the bailee is entitled to recover only in respect of his own loss or only when he is legally liable to the bailor, then the position is quite different. The bailor has no claim against the bailee and hence against his insurer, and there is no double insurance.

As far as land is concerned, there are problems in law[8] when insurance is effected by two people having interests therein, if the Life Assurance Act 1774 applies.[9] Even if that Act does not apply, double insurance might arise by virtue of one party having the right to call upon the other's insurer to reinstate the property under section 83 of the Fires Prevention (Metropolis)

---

[4] See *MacGillivray and Parkington*, para. 1870.

[5] There is no agreement regarding goods, but in practice contribution may be applied ad hoc.

[6] For consideration of all the relevant insurers' agreements, including one which has the effect of making the *Albion* case (notes 2 and 3) inapplicable in Britain, see Lewis (1985) 48 M.L.R. 275 at 286–289.

[7] [1966] A.C. 451; see pp. 46–48, above.

[8] Though not in practice because of the rule of the Fire Offices' Committee mentioned above.

[9] As to this, see pp. 36–39, above.

Act 1774.[10] In one case involving a landlord and tenant who were both insured,[11] it was argued by the tenant's insurer that because the tenant had the right to require reinstatement under the Act by the landlord's insurer, the tenant was therefore doubly insured and the landlord's insurer was liable for a contribution. This argument was easily rejected. It was clear that the tenant had not exercised his statutory right and hence there could be no question on the facts of the case of his having a right under the two policies. The judgment implies that the result would have been the same even if he had made a demand for reinstatement but, with respect, this may be doubted. Following a proper demand, the landlord's insurer would have had to comply, thus indemnifying the tenant. As contribution is an equitable principle to prevent unjust enrichment, it must be flexible enough to allow that the tenant's insurer is liable for its share, otherwise the insurer with the primary liability might escape quite unjustifiably. The same would apply if the position of the parties was reversed or if their relationship was that of mortgagor and mortgagee or vendor and purchaser.

THE RATIO OF CONTRIBUTION

Whether the question of contribution arises generally or as the result of a rateable proportion clause, it remains to be considered how the contributions of the different insurers are worked out. This can be a very complex question,[12] but for present purposes the basic principles only will be examined and it will be assumed that there are only two insurers involved. There has been a noticeable lack of case-law on this question, and the ratios to be applied may depend as much on the practices of insurers as much as on binding legal authority.

The real problems arise when the sums insured by each insurer are not the same or where the policies in question have different ranges so that it is difficult properly to compare the sums insured. It may be necessary here to distinguish between property and liability insurances, the reason being that in property insurance, the premium is calculated with reference to the sum insured, whereas there is not necessarily the same relationship in liability insurance. In property insurance where the

---

[10] See Chapter 14 at pp. 232–234.
[11] *Portavon Cinema Co. v. Price* [1939] 4 All E.R. 601.
[12] For more detail, see *MacGillivray and Parkington,* paras. 1850–1867.

cover provided under both policies is more or less the same, the contribution of each insurer can most fairly be assessed simply by reference to the sum insured. The proper result, therefore, should be that each insurer pays that proportion of a loss which his sum insured bears to the total of the sums insured. For example, if property is insured for £10,000 with insurer A and for £20,000 with insurer B, A will bear one-third and B two-thirds of any loss.

This approach is termed the "maximum liability" approach, because it always takes account of the maximum of the two insurers' liabilities. The alternative standard approach is that based on "independent liability." Here, following a loss, it is asked what each insurer would independently have been liable for and the contributions are assessed according to the proportions that each such figure bears to the total of the figures. For example, X suffers a loss of £5,000. His policy with A insurer has a sum insured of £10,000; his policy with B a limit of £50,000. Each insurer would independently have been liable for the full amount of the loss. Their contribution is therefore equal because £5,000 plus £5,000 divided by $\frac{£5,000}{£10,000}$ is £5,000. If X's loss were £11,000, A would be liable independently for £10,000, B for £11,000. Therefore, A bears $\frac{10,000}{10,000+11,000}$, that is $\frac{10}{21}$, of the loss and B $\frac{11}{21}$. On this basis, wherever the loss is smaller than the lesser of the sums insured, the insurers will bear it equally. A loss falling between the sums insured will attract a ratio whereby the insurer with the larger sum insured will gradually attract more liability. Only when the loss is the same as, or greater than, the total of the sums insured will the calculation be the same as under the maximum liability approach.

Liability insurances

It has been conclusively settled in *Commercial Union Assurance Co. v. Hayden*[13] that the independent liability approach is the legal basis in liability insurance. The principal reasons for this were first that liability insurance premiums are not calculated pro rata according to the sum insured; in the case itself the plaintiff had charged £6 for cover of £100,000, whereas the defendant had charged £5 for only £10,000 of identical cover. Secondly, the bulk of claims in liability insurance fall within a low limit. "Each limit of liability and each premium may be taken to be fixed without knowledge of the limit under any other policy . . . it is difficult to suppose that when a limit of

[13] [1977] Q.B. 804.

£10,000 was fixed by the defendant, it could have been intended that if there happened to be another policy with a limit of £100,000, the defendant should be liable for only one-eleventh of the claim, however small. The independent liability basis is much more realistic in its results.... The obvious purpose of having a limit of liability under an insurance policy[14] is to protect the insurer from the effect of exceptionally large claims: it seems to me artificial to use the limits under two policies to adjust liability in respect of claims which are within the limits of either policy."[15] Finally, some stress was laid upon the fact that certain liability policies are unlimited; in these cases the maximum liability approach would simply be impossible to apply.

Policies with different ranges

There remains the question of which method of assessment applies where the policies have different ranges.[16] The example which was used earlier of the watch can be used again here. Imagine that the owner's household policy has a sum insured of £10,000, but there is no specific sum for the watch which is worth £20. The repairer has a floating policy covering all goods in his possession from time to time which is a goods policy and not a liability policy. His sum insured is £3,000. The watch is stolen, neither party being responsible, so that both insurers are prima facie liable. It could hardly be right here, albeit it is a case of property insurance, to apply the maximum liability ratio, so that the owner's insurer should bear $\frac{10}{13}$ and the repairer's insurer $\frac{3}{13}$ of £20. That would ignore the fact that both policies cover many other items and are essentially quite different. In this case the independent liability approach is the only realistic one so that each insurer is liable for half the loss up to the lesser of the sums insured. This was the method adopted in *American Surety Co. of New York* v. *Wrightson*[17] in relation to fidelity insurance effected by an employer against the dishonesty of his employees, where one of the policies also had a much wider scope, and it is submitted that it is the only workable approach.[18]

---

[14] This must mean in respect of liability policies only.
[15] Cairns L.J. at 815–816.
[16] "Non-concurrent policies" is the usual jargon.
[17] (1910) 103 L.T. 663.
[18] *MacGillivray and Parkington*, para. 1867, suggest that the independent liability basis might be adopted in all cases.

Conditions Regarding Double Insurance

Apart from the rateable proportion clauses already discussed, most policies of indemnity also contain other conditions relevant to double insurance which are of importance. These fall into two categories. The first sort purports to oust the liability of the insurer if the liability is covered elsewhere. The second requires notification of double insurance.

Conditions ousting liability

Modern examples of this sort of condition are as follows:

> "There shall be no liability under this insurance in respect of any claim where the insured is entitled to indemnity under any other insurance except in respect of any excess beyond the amount which would have been covered under such other insurance had this insurance not been effected."
>
> "There shall be no liability hereunder in respect of any claim for which the assured are entitled to any indemnity under any other policy."

Problems will arise if one or both of the insurers covering the same risk have this sort of clause. If one insurer does have, but the other does not, then the latter should be solely and wholly liable. The first insurer's liability is excluded and so far as the second is concerned, there is, therefore, no double insurance. If both insurers have such a clause, the position is more complex. It has arisen in a number of cases.

In *Gale v. Motor Union Insurance Co.*,[19] L was driving G's car when he caused an accident. Prima facie L was insured both by his own motor policy, because that had an extension covering the driving of cars other than his own with the owner's consent, and by G's policy on G's car, because that had a standard permitted driver extension. However, both extensions had qualifications which in effect provided that they were not applicable if the person concerned was otherwise insured. Both policies also had rateable proportion conditions. Roche J. held that the conditions purporting to oust liability were not clear, and that the only way to read them was as referring to cases where the other cover gave complete and full indemnity. Here, because of the rateable proportion clauses, neither policy, when looked at from the point of view of the other one, gave complete cover. There-

---

[19] [1928] 1 K.B. 359.

fore, neither clause applied and the insurers were both liable rateably. According to this reasoning, the presence of rateable proportion clauses in both policies was vital.

Weddell v. *Road Transport & General Insurance Co.*[20] involved similar facts in that a negligent driver was prima facie covered by both his own and the relevant car owner's policies. His own policy had a rateable proportion clause and a clause excluding liability if there was other insurance. The owner's policy was more subtly worded; under the extension, liability was excluded if there was other insurance. There was a rateable proportion clause but this had a proviso whereby it was declared not to impose on the insurer any liability from which, but for it, the insurer would have been excluded under the extension. In other words, the rateable proportion clause was not to apply to a situation of double insurance, and, as has been seen, the presence of a rateable proportion clause was crucial to the *ratio* in *Gale*. In fact, the driver's own insurer repudiated liability for breach of condition, so the question was whether the driver was entitled to half or all of his loss under the owner's policy. The owner's insurer did not seek to argue that it was not liable at all. Rowlatt J. went somewhat further than the judge in *Gale* had gone and held that it would be unreasonable to suppose that these extensions would cancel each other out. "The reasonable construction is to exclude from the category of co-existing cover any cover which is expressed to be itself cancelled by such co-existence, and to hold in such cases that both companies are liable, subject of course in both cases to any rateable proportion clause which there may be."[21] Thus, on the facts, the owner's insurers, because they had a rateable proportion clause, were liable for half the loss.

The judgment seems to admit that logically, if neither policy had a rateable proportion clause, neither insurer would be liable, and, further, that this ought to have been the result on the facts because of the proviso in the owner's policy whereby the rateable proportion clause should not have operated. There was "other insurance," namely, the driver's own, albeit not enforceable in respect of this loss, and therefore this should have excluded liability under the owner's policy. However, the insurer did not argue this and the *ratio* of the case appears wide enough to exclude this sort of possibility. Indeed, this must be the legal position because *Weddell* has recently been approved

[20] [1932] 2 K.B. 563.
[21] *Ibid.* at 567.

by the Court of Appeal[22] where it was said: "The court should invoke the equitable principle of contribution between co-insurers to avoid the absurdity and injustice of holding that a person who has paid premiums for cover by two insurers should be left without insurance cover because each insurer has excluded liability for the risk against which the other has indemnified him."[23]

It is clear, therefore, that the courts have not taken kindly to these clauses and it is probably safe to assume that, whatever forms of wording are adopted, they will be construed in such a manner that where there is genuine double insurance they will cancel each other out.

Conditions requiring notification

The other standard condition, found particularly in fire and other property policies, requires the insured to notify the insurer if he effects double insurance during the currency of the policy. Generally the sanction for non-disclosure will be forfeiture or repudiation of the policy, so that in law such conditions will usually be promissory or continuing warranties.[24] Obviously, such conditions are inserted by insurers to protect themselves against the possibility of fraud.

A mere accidental overlap between policies does not bring such a condition into operation. In *Australian Agricultural Co.* v. *Saunders*,[25] the insured effected a fire policy on some wool while it was in storage, in transit by land to Sydney, Australia, or in storage in Sydney until shipped. The policy contained the relevant condition. Subsequently, some wool was carried by ship to Sydney and a marine policy was effected to cover this. When this wool was in store in Sydney, it was destroyed by fire. It was held that the fire insurer was liable. The court rejected the argument of the insurers that they should have been notified of the marine policy, as the risks covered were not the same and there was no double insurance. Even if the policies had overlapped in their coverage for a brief period, it was made clear that such accidental overlap would not have required notification, though presumably if the loss had taken place during the overlap, there would have been double insurance.

---

[22] *National Employers' Mutual* v. *Hayden* [1980] 2 Lloyd's Rep. 149; see also *Austin* v. *Zurich General Accident & Liability Ins. Co.* [1945] K.B. 250.
[23] *Ibid.* at 152, *per* Stephenson L.J. See also Bridge L.J. at 154 and Templeman L.J. at 156.
[24] See Chapters 5 and 7.
[25] (1875) L.R. 10 C.P. 668.

An insured can only really be prejudiced by this sort of condition if it appears in both of the policies. If it is in only one, that one will be voidable but the other will stand, unless, of course, the latter is voidable for some other reason. Even if it is in both policies, it will be only rarely, it seems, that the insured will lose out completely. In *Equitable Fire & Accident Insurance Co. v. Ching Wo Hong*,[26] a fire policy contained the relevant condition. The insured effected a second policy, about which it did not inform the first insurer, but this policy provided that it was not effective until the first premium was paid. No premium was ever paid on it. It was held by the Privy Council that the second policy never, therefore, came into existence and the obligation to disclose it to the first insurer never arose, so that the first insurer could not avoid its policy. The same result must apply if the second policy is void, for example, for lack of insurable interest.

In an Australian case, *Steadfast Insurance Co. v. F. & B. Trading Co.*,[27] both policies contained the same condition requiring notification of existing or subsequent double insurance. Upon effecting the second policy, which was, in fact, a cover note, the insured failed to notify the first insurer and did not tell the second insurer of the first policy. The High Court held that the second policy was never effective because the second insurer had not been notified of the first policy. Therefore, there was no other insurance which the insured should have notified to the first insurer and the latter could not claim a breach of the relevant condition. In *Steadfast*, the court laid great stress on the fact that the condition in the second policy provided that non-notification forfeited all benefit under the policy, thus implying that the second policy as automatically void *ab initio*. Clearly, if the second insurer does treat its policy as avoided, that follows logically. But, with respect, it may be doubted whether the second policy was automatically void. As suggested earlier, the standard notification condition is legally a warranty, on breach of which a policy is voidable,[28] not void, at the insurer's option, as it is clear that an insurer can waive such a breach. If, in fact,

---

[26] [1907] A.C. 96.
[27] (1972) 46 A.L.J.R. 10.
[28] Even this may not be strictly correct. Voidability is a common explanation of the result of a breach of warranty, and in this context it is not surprising, given that the standard terms often say that failure to notify other insurance renders the contract void or voidable. However, as has been argued earlier (see p. 74 footnote 9 and p. 100 footnote 5), a breach of warranty should give the insurer the right to repudiate, but should not destroy the entire contract.

the second insurer avoids, then the result in *Steadfast* may be correct.[29] But if it does not, then the second insurance stands and the first is voidable for breach of warranty. Even here, of course, the insured is not really prejudiced.

However, the second policy may be valid but the insurer entitled to avoid liability under it for the particular loss by virtue of a breach of condition *stricto sensu*, such as the failure to give notice in time. Here non-notification of the second policy to the first insurer will entitle it to avoid its policy and the second insurer will not be liable for the reason stated.[30] The same would apply if the second policy were repudiated but not *ab initio*, that is for breach of a continuing warranty. In this case, therefore, the insured will be prejudiced by a failure to comply with a notification condition.

---

[29] But see note 28. Clearly the result in *Steadfast* is fair on the facts.
[30] See Walsh J. in the *Steadfast* case at 14.

Chapter 17

LIFE INSURANCE

Life insurance is chosen as the first area for consideration of principles peculiar to particular types of insurance rather than of general application. Here there are two such broad areas of principle, the assignment of life policies and the law relating to trusts of life policies. These will be discussed because of their particular practical importance and because they have thrown up problems for life insurance, even though questions of assignment and trusts are, of course, of much more general application. Detail on questions such as mortgages of life policies, the law of succession or the bankruptcy of the life insured is felt to be unnecessary here, as there are no principles peculiar to life insurance or problems raised by these in this area. Furthermore, there are certain technical questions, no doubt of great importance, which are more than adequately dealt with elsewhere.[1] Examples of these would be the law relating to proof of death and proving title to a life policy.

The modern forms of life policies are numerous, ranging from the traditional whole life policy and the term policy through endowment policies to annuities and policies linked to investment in securities or property. In addition to regulation under the Insurance Companies Act 1982,[2] many life policies of the latter sort fall within the definition of "investments" in Schedule 1 of the Financial Services Act 1986,[3] and are thus subject to the scheme of investor protection provided for under that Act.[4]

Assignment of Life Policies

Life insurance policies are undoubtedly a valuable piece of property, normally attracting a surrender value after the payment of a number of premiums. They can be sold or otherwise

---

[1] See especially, *MacGillivray and Parkington*, Chapter 21.
[2] See chapter 2.
[3] See para. 10 to Part I of that Schedule.
[4] Detailed consideration of this is outside the scope of this book; for one particular aspect, see pp. 59–60, above.

disposed of or used as security, features which are assisted by the fact that the requirement of insurable interest exists only at the date the policy is effected.[5] Many dealings of this sort with life policies will in law be assignments, regarding which there are a number of special rules. The description "assignment" covers any case where the insured disposes entirely of his interest in the policy, whether by way of sale, gift or mortgage. If a policy is used as security, some of the statutory formalities as to assignment may be used even where the insured does not dispose entirely of his interest. The use of a life policy in such circumstances may very well attract some of the provisions of the Consumer Credit Act 1974, that is, if it is used in connection with a regulated consumer credit agreement.[6]

Assignment as mortgage

If a dealing with a life policy appears to be an absolute assignment, but in reality is a mortgage as security for a debt, the mortgagee, the insured, is entitled to redeem the mortgage on repayment of the debt and recover his policy, notwithstanding any provision to the contrary. In deciding whether or not a dealing with a life policy is an outright assignment or a mortgage, the court will look at the surrounding circumstances and parol evidence is admissible. For example, in the Irish case of *Murphy v. Taylor*,[7] a policy for £999 was assigned for a consideration of £144. The evidence showed that the assignor in fact borrowed the latter sum from the assignee. The latter later recovered £600 from the insurer. It was held that the substance of the transaction was that of a mortgage to secure a debt. Therefore, after allowing for the debt of £144, the assignor was entitled to redeem the mortgage and recover from the assignee the remainder of the £600 that he had recovered from the insurer.

The rule allowing the insured to redeem what is in substance a mortgage of a life policy is part of the general law relating to mortgages whereby clogs or fetters on the equity of redemption or equitable right to redeem are void. Details on these should be sought elsewhere,[8] but one interesting example in the insurance context is the decision in *Salt v. Marquess of Northampton*.[9]

---

[5] Chapter 3.
[6] For the detail, see Part VIII of the 1974 Act and Hill-Smith, *Consumer Credit: Law and Practice*, Chapter 8.
[7] (1850) 1 Ir.Ch.R. 92.
[8] *e.g.* Megarry and Wade, *Law of Real Property* (5th ed.), pp. 964–971.
[9] [1892] A.C. 1.

X borrowed £10,000 from an insurer and secured this by a charge on his reversionary interest in certain property. In addition, he agreed to pay the premiums on a policy for £34,000 taken out by the insurers against the possibility of the interest not vesting. It was agreed that if X paid off the loan before the interest vested, the policy would be assigned to him, but if he died before repayment and vesting, the policy would belong to the insurers. The latter event occurred. It was held that, despite the agreement, the transaction was in substance a mortgage, and the personal representatives of X were entitled to redeem and recover the proceeds of the policy, after deducting the loan and interest.

Statutory assignment

Prior to the Policies of Assurance Act 1867, a life policy was not assignable at law. Although equity always permitted such assignments, the assignee could only sue to enforce the policy if he joined the assignor in the action, and an insurer could not obtain a good discharge against payment from the assignee alone. The 1867 Act permits legal assignments so that the assignee of a life policy can, if the requirements of the Act are complied with, enforce it in his own name (s.1). Furthermore, a life policy is itself a chose in action,[10] one of the forms of intangible personal property, so that an alternative procedure for assignment lies under section 136 of the Law of Property Act 1925. In addition, an assignment which is incomplete according to statutory requirements may well still be valid as an equitable assignment.

There is one essential difference between the two statutory procedures. Under the 1867 Act, an assignment is valid if it is of the assignor's whole interest in the policy or of merely a part of it, by way of mortgage. Under section 136, an assignment must be absolute, that is it must be of the assignor's whole interest. Therefore, a mortgage whereby the whole interest in a life policy is charged can be effected under section 136, but not one whereby only part is charged.

An assignment under the 1867 Act must be in the form prescribed in the Schedule to the Act or in words with a similar effect and it must be endorsed on the policy or contained in a separate instrument (s.5). Written notice of the assignment must be given to the insurer at its principal place of business

---

[10] *Re Moore* (1878) 8 Ch.D. 519.

(s.3). An assignment under section 136 must simply be in writing but again notice must be given to the debtor, that is the insurer. In neither case is the consent of the insurers necessary, but a condition in the policy making it non-assignable is effective to prevent a legal assignment, although it cannot prevent an effective equitable assignment.[11]

In most cases, therefore, the statutory procedures are alternative devices for achieving the same result, and which one is used must simply be a matter of preference.[12] Even if one of the statutory procedures is not complied with, an assignment may be effective in equity as has been noted. This may be because there was a failure to give notice to the insurer,[13] because there was merely an agreement to assign, or because the policy was simply delivered to the assignee, for example, as security. If there have been more than one purported assignments of the same policy, the well-established rules as to priority apply.[14] Briefly, a legal assignee has priority over anyone except an earlier equitable assignment of which he has notice or an earlier legal assignment. Equitable assignments generally rank in order of creation, except that the first such assignee to give notice to the insurers will take priority over any prior assignments of which he had no notice. If there is any doubt as to who is entitled to the policy monies, in this or any other context, the insurer may pay them into court under the Life Assurance Companies (Payment into Court) Act 1896.[15]

Trusts of Life Policies

It may frequently be alleged that the insured under a life policy established a trust of the policy for the benefit of another. This will normally arise only on an own-life policy. If such a trust can be shown to exist, it has two distinct advantages. The first is that on the death of the life insured, the monies will belong to and go directly to the beneficiary, thus avoiding and not being counted as a part of the insured's estate. Secondly, if the insured becomes bankrupt, the beneficiary can claim the policy

---

[11] *Re Turcan* (1888) 40 Ch.D. 5.
[12] But see *MacGillivray and Parkington*, para. 1478.
[13] *e.g. Williams* v. *Thorp* (1828) 2 Sim. 257.
[14] See, further, *MacGillivray and Parkington*, paras. 1494 to 1503.
[15] See *MacGillivray and Parkington*, paras. 1466 to 1470.

without its being subject to the claims of the insured's creditors, provided that the trust itself was not created in order to defraud creditors.[16]

Section 11 trusts

The easiest way to establish such a trust is under the provisions of section 11 of the Married Women's Property Act 1882, although this section is limited in its application. Under it, a policy effected on his or her own life by a married man or woman, and expressed to be for the benefit of his or her spouse and/or children,[17] creates a trust in favour of the spouse and/or children, and the money payable under the policy does not form part of the insured's estate.

It should be noted first that section 11 applies only to policies effected by a married man or woman on his or her own life. Thus, for example, a policy by a father on the life of his son, even if legal, which must be doubtful,[18] cannot fall within section 11.[19] If the section does apply, the insured is a trustee and must therefore act with respect to the policy in the best interests of the beneficiaries. For example, if he has an option to surrender the policy, that may properly be exercised only in the interests of the beneficiaries; it is not exercisable in order to defeat the trust, and if the policy is surrendered, the money received will probably be held for the ultimate benefit of the beneficiaries.[20]

Section 11 applies to any policies securing benefits payable on the death of the life insured, including an accident policy covering only death by accident[21] and an endowment policy which provides for payment if the insured dies before the expiry of the stated period.[22] If the policy names the beneficiary or beneficiaries, then the latter acquire an immediate vested interest in it. In *Cousins* v. *Sun Life Assurance Society*,[23] a wife was the named beneficiary of a policy effected by her husband whom she predeceased. It was held that the policy monies

---

[16] Insolvency Act 1986, ss.423–425; proviso to Married Women's Property Act 1882, s.11.
[17] "Children" includes adopted and illegitimate children; Adoption Act 1976, s.39; Family Law Reform Act 1969, s.19.
[18] See below p. 275 and Chapter 3.
[19] *Re Engelbach* [1924] 2 Ch. 348.
[20] *Re Fleetwood's Policy* [1926] Ch. 48.
[21] *Re Gladitz* [1937] Ch. 588.
[22] *Re Ioakimidis' Policy Trusts* [1925] Ch. 403.
[23] [1933] Ch. 126.

belonged to the wife's estate, even though the husband had remarried. It should be noted that divorce does not of itself change any rights under a section 11 policy, but that these can be varied as part of a general settlement of property rights under section 24 of the Matrimonial Causes Act 1973.

If the policy does not name the beneficiaries but is merely expressed to be for the benefit of the insured's wife and children, for example, the beneficiaries have only a contingent interest, and only those people who fit the description on the death of the life insured will be entitled to benefit.

Other trusts

If section 11 is inapplicable, then establishing a trust of a life policy necessitates proving an exception to the doctrine of privity of contract, whereby a third party to a contract cannot enforce it even if it was made for his benefit.[24] In addition, it is a well-established principle of trusts law that a person will not be regarded as having declared himself a trustee of property in the absence of words showing a clear intention to do so.[25] Quite apart from these points, many of the cases dealing with trusts of life policies reveal other deficiencies in the law relating to life insurance. If A effects a policy on his own life for the benefit of B, there are no problems if a trust is created, the point to which we shall shortly return, and provided that B's name is inserted in the policy.[26] But often the point arises because it appears that A has effected a policy on B's life for the benefit of B. The law is clear that A must therefore have an insurable interest in the life of B,[27] quite apart from whether or not there is a trust in B's favour. Many of the policies in the relevant cases took a form which it appears is quite common, whereby a parent insures the life of his child for the latter's benefit. It may well be an endowment policy perhaps effected for the purposes of paying school fees. Whether or not such a policy is lawful must be open to great doubt, as a parent does not usually have an insurable interest in the life of his child.[28] The question is rarely raised in this context, usually because the insurer will have already handed over the money, so that the sole question is whether A or B is entitled to it, and insurers who did raise it would attract

---

[24] *Beswick v. Beswick* [1968] A.C. 58.
[25] e.g. *Jones v. Lock* (1865) 1 Ch.App. 25.
[26] Life Assurance Act 1774, s.2; see Chapter 3, pp. 33–35.
[27] Life Assurance Act 1774, s.1; see Chapter 3, pp. 26–33.
[28] *Halford v. Kymer* (1830) 10 B. & C. 724.

unfavourable publicity. Nevertheless, the point should be recognised as a consequence of the narrowness of the law governing insurable interest, and perhaps also as a factor which should encourage the court to find a trust. If this is so, the position is not so much A insuring B's life for the benefit of B as A acting for B in insuring B's life, perhaps because, as an infant, B is unable to do so himself.

The cases appear to reveal more willingness latterly to find that a trust has been created, but two things are clear.[29] First, the mere fact that A takes out a policy which is expressed to be for the benefit of B or on behalf of B does not constitute a trust for B. Secondly, the mere fact that the policy provides that the policy monies are to be payable to B does not create a trust in favour of B. For example, in *Re Engelbach*,[30] a father proposed "for his daughter" an endowment policy whereby she was to receive £3,000 if she should reach the age of 21. If she died before then, her father was entitled to recover the premiums paid. It was held that the father's estate, on his death, was entitled to the £3,000 when the daughter became 21. Simply, there was no sufficient evidence to create a trust. Similarly, in *Re Sinclair*,[31] the insured was godfather to a baby of six months. He effected an endowment policy wherein the baby was referred to as "the nominee" and the monies were payable to the child at 21. Again no trust arose because there was insufficient evidence. In both these cases, and indeed in the other ones to the same effect,[32] the policies must strictly have been illegal for want of insurable interest.

It should be noted though that if on similar facts, the "beneficiary" is, in fact, paid the insurance money, he will normally be entitled to keep it, even if there was no trust in his favour. The only situation where this would not be the case is if the policy compels the conclusion that he was to receive it merely as nominee or agent for the insured.[33] A court is most unlikely to conclude this nowdays, unless the wording of the policy compels it, so that if in fact the insurer pays the "beneficiary," the result is a useful way around the decisions just discussed.

---

[29] Plowman J. in *Re Foster* [1966] 1 W.L.R. 222 at 227.
[30] [1924] 2 Ch. 348.
[31] [1938] Ch. 799.
[32] *e.g. Cleaver* v. *Mutual Reserve Fund Life Ass.* [1892] 1 Q.B. 147; *Re Foster* [1938] 3 All E.R. 357.
[33] *Re Schebsman* [1944] 1 Ch. 83, approved in *Beswick* v. *Beswick*, above, where the House of Lords disapproved of *Re Engelbach*, above, in so far as it held to the contrary.

Modern Cases

Modern policy wordings and more modern cases evince in any event a greater willingness to find a trust. In *Re Webb*,[34] a father took out policies on the lives of his two children. He was described as "the grantee" and in the proposal form as wishing to effect insurance "on behalf of and for the benefit of the person . . . named as the life assured." Each policy provided (1) that on the child's death at or after the age of 21, the money would be paid to his representatives, and, on his 21st birthday, all the father's interest in the policy would cease; until then the father had power to surrender, assign and otherwise deal with the policy, and the father would recover the premiums paid if the child died before the age of 21; (2) that if the father, having paid all the premiums due, died before the child reached 21, the policies would remain in force until the child's 21st birthday. The father did die before the children were 21, and the question was whether the policies which survived by reason of the term mentioned belonged to his estate or to the children. It was held that they belonged to the children, having been effected by the father on trust for them. According to Farwell J. there was more than a mere taking out of a policy for the benefit of another as in the earlier cases. The terms of the policies were sufficient to establish a trust, especially that providing that the father's interest in them would cease completely when the children were 21 and that providing that the policy monies themselves were never payable until the children reached the specified age, thus making it clear that the father had no interest in these. This is logically sound, since such provisions are inconsistent with the father or nominal insured having the whole beneficial interest in the policy. A beneficial interest must lie elsewhere, that is with the children, and hence there must be a trust.

Re Webb was followed in *Re Foster*,[35] where the policy was not quite in the same form. It provided that upon the child becoming 21, the rights vested in the father (the grantee) to surrender or charge the policy until the child reached that age were to be vested in the child. Plowman J. held that the fact that these rights were vested absolutely in the child at 21 was inconsistent with the father thereafter retaining any beneficial interest, so that although this latter point was not expressly spelt out, as in *Re Webb*, it was necessarily impliedly provided, and the same result followed.

---

[34] [1941] Ch. 225.
[35] [1966] 1 W.L.R. 222.

As a result of these cases, it appears likely nowadays that the court will strive to find a trust where policies are taken out for children, not least because it avoids any insurable interest problems. In effect, therefore, the children in these cases were insuring their own lives through a trustee. At all times, the trustee must act in accordance with the responsibilities surrounding that position. For example, although he will probably until a stated age have the right to surrender or assign the policy, he can properly do so only if it is in the best interests of the child. When the latter reaches the specified age, he has full powers over the policy and, if the trust still exists, will be able to terminate it.[36] He will also, if necessary, be able to enforce it through the trustee, but he will be able to enforce it directly only if he becomes legal owner or if there is a new agreement arising by virtue of his paying and the insurer accepting from him the premiums due. It must be stressed though that all cases must turn on their particular facts and on the provisions in the policies, and it is by no means impossible that a case will occur when these are not sufficient to establish a trust. It has sensibly been suggested that section 11 of the Married Women's Property Act be extended to cover these child policies.[37]

Group insurance

The trust question has hitherto been considered solely in the context of family arrangements. The other equally common area where the same problems can arise is that of group insurance policies, for example, taken out by an employer on the lives of his employees or a group of them for the benefit of the latter. The circumstances may make it clear that the employees are beneficiaries under a trust, as in *Bowskill* v. *Dawson (No. 2)*,[38] where the employer entered into a trust deed with the trustee company which effected the policy for the employees. There were clear references to the fact that, *inter alia*, any sums received by the trust company were to be held on trust for the employees and the court had no difficulty in holding that the latter were therefore beneficiaries under the trusts of the deed.

By contrast, there were no such references in *Green* v. *Russell*,[39] where an employer, called the insured, effected a group accident policy for the benefit of his employees named in a schedule to the policy. The policy expressly provided that the

---

[36] *Saunders* v. *Vautier* (1841) Cr. & Ph. 240.
[37] Law Revision Committee, 6th Interim Report, p. 32.
[38] [1955] 1 Q.B. 13.
[39] [1959] 2 Q.B. 226.

insurer was entitled to treat the insured as absolute owner and was not bound to recognise any equitable or other claim or interest in the policy. In the light of this, it was held that the employees had no legal or equitable claim to the policy, in spite of the fact that one of the employees covered, or rather his widow, had received a sum of money paid under the policy.[40] There was clearly no basis for implying a trust on the authorities already mentioned. It must therefore be doubtful whether the policy was strictly legally enforceable, as the employer may not have had an insurable interest in the lives of his employees, or at least not to the extent of the amount each employee was insured for.[41] It seems likely in practice that group policies of this nature are not effected always with terms that would enable the court to find a trust.

---

[40] The case arose under the Fatal Accidents Acts, the question being whether the third party who caused the death of the employee in question could deduct the insurance money from the damages he was liable to pay to the widow.

[41] See also the comments in Chapter 3, at pp. 32–33.

Chapter 18

LIABILITY INSURANCE IN GENERAL

Insurance against the insured's potential legal liability to a third party, whether in contract or tort, is of course commonplace. In a number of instances, such insurance is required to be effected by statute, most notably in the fields of motor vehicle and employer's liability insurance. The additional requirements and restrictions imposed in these fields will be considered in Chapters 19 and 20. This chapter will concentrate upon aspects common to all liability insurances, which range from those effected by householders to public liability and professional indemnity policies. The intention is to consider those matters which appear genuinely to be common to all such insurances, rather than matters arising as the result of detailed policy wordings concerning the risks covered and excepted. For the latter, reference must be made elsewhere.

There are four headings: first, the statutory protection given to a third party in the event of the insured's bankruptcy or liquidation; second, the important questions that arise from standard conditions to be found in all liability insurance policies; third, some questions which can arise concerning the sums insured and costs; and fourth, the insurers' duty to the victim of the insured.

Bankruptcy of the Insured

At common law, if an insured went bankrupt, or, if a company, went into liquidation, after a claim arose against him by a third party, any money paid by his insurers to indemnify the insured against the claim after the commencement of the bankruptcy or liquidation went towards the general assets of the bankrupt or insolvent company, and were not entitled to be claimed by the third party.[1] The latter had merely the right to prove in the bankruptcy or liquidation as an ordinary creditor along with all the other ordinary creditors of the insured, because he had no rights in respect of the contract between insured and insurer.

---

[1] *Re Harrington Motor Co.* [1928] Ch. 105.

This was clearly unjust and in 1930, the Third Parties (Rights Against Insurers) Act was passed to remedy the situation. In essence, the Act statutorily subrogates the third party to the position of the insured. Section 1(1) provides:

> "Where under any contract of insurance a person (hereinafter referred to as the insured) is insured against liabilities to third parties which he may incur, then
>
> (a) in the event of the insured becoming bankrupt . . . , or
>
> (b) in the case of the insured being a company, [being wound up[2] or subject to receivership][3];
>
> if, either before or after that event, any such liability as aforesaid is incurred by the insured, his rights against the insurer under the contract in respect of the liability shall, notwithstanding anything in any Act or rule of law to the contrary, be transferred to and vest in the third party to whom the liability was so incurred."

By section 1(2), the same applies where the insured dies insolvent, and by section 1(3), it is impossible to contract out of the section's provisions. This probably includes a provision in the insurance contract whereby the insurer's liability arises only when the insured himself has paid the third party.[4] Obviously, in effect this is an exclusion since the Act is relevant only where the insured is insolvent and hence unable to pay the third party.

Section 2 casts upon the insured who becomes bankrupt the duty to inform the third party who has a claim of any relevant insurance, and section 3 provides that settlements made between the insurer and the bankrupt or liquidated insured are of no effect as regards the third party.

Deficiencies in the Act

The intervening years have seen a number of reported decisions which in varying degrees tend to restrict the effectiveness of the Act so far as third parties are concerned. It is clear first of all that the insured's rights are transferred to the third party only when a liability is incurred by the insured, and a

---

[2] Other than a voluntary winding up merely for the purpose of a reconstruction or amalgamation: s.1(6).

[3] By amendments made by the Insolvency Acts 1985 and 1986, this case is extended to the situations where a company is made the subject of an administration order or adopts a voluntary arrangement under the 1986 Act.

[4] *Re Allobrogia Steamship Corp.* [1978] 3 All E.R. 423 at 432.

liability is not incurred for these purposes[5] until the third party obtains judgment against or an admission of liability from the insured. In *Post Office* v. *Norwich Union Fire Insurance Co.*,[6] the insureds were contractors engaged in road works. In the course of their excavations they damaged a cable belonging to the Post Office. The latter claimed that this was the fault of the contractors, though this was denied, the contractors claiming that it was the fault of a Post Office engineer. The contractors having gone into liquidation, the Post Office sued their insurers under the 1930 Act before the insured's liability was established. It was held that the action was premature. The third party gets no better rights than the insured, and the latter's rights arise only when his liability to the third party has been determined or agreed.[7] The correct procedure in this sort of case is for the third party to obtain the leave of the court to bring proceedings against the bankrupt insured. Only when these proceedings have been determined can the insurer be liable under the 1930 Act. While the decision in *Norwich Union* cannot logically be faulted, it is nonetheless somewhat artificial as almost inevitably in such cases the insurers will in practice be the real defendant and once the insured's liability is established, immediately satisfy it. However, insurers have their own good reasons for not wishing to appear as the defendants in civil actions, principally the fear that it would gain them bad publicity,[8] and these are clearly legitimate reasons within the context of the tort/liability insurance system.

One of the reasons for the decision in the *Norwich Union* case was that the plaintiff obtains his rights under the 1930 Act subject to the conditions of the policy.[9] There a condition forbad the insured making any admission of liability without the insurer's consent, and the third party was subject also to this term. This point is of general application, so that, except in

---

[5] For other purposes, *e.g.* regarding the limitation period for an action on a liability policy, the liability may be incurred when the event causing the loss takes place: *Chandris* v. *Argo Ins.* [1963] 2 Lloyd's Rep. 65. Contrast, however, *Green & Silley Weir Ltd.* v. *British Railways Board* [1985] 1 All E.R. 237, especially at 242.

[6] [1967] 2 Q.B. 363.

[7] This was the *ratio* of Lord Denning M.R. and the principal *ratio* of Salmon L.J. However, the latter also relied upon the fact that the third party takes subject to any conditions in the policy, one of which forbad the insured from admitting liability in any way without the insurer's consent (as to this, see below). Harman L.J. relied on this latter reason only.

[8] See Salmon L.J. [1967] 2 Q.B. at 378.

[9] See note 7.

compulsory motor insurance and, to a lesser extent in employer's liability insurance, where insurers' rights are more circumscribed by statute,[10] any defence which the insurers have against the insured under the insurance contract is available against the third party. This might be the right to avoid the policy for non-disclosure or breach of warranty,[11] the right to avoid liability for breach of condition, or the right to insist upon arbitration. In *Freshwater* v. *Western Australian Assurance Co.*[12] and *Smith* v. *Pearl Assurance Co.*,[13] the insurers' right in motor policies to insist upon arbitration as a condition precedent to liability was upheld against the injured third party. In fact these decisions have probably been overruled by statute so far as motor insurance is concerned,[14] but the principle holds good for other liability insurances.[15] In *Farrell* v. *Federated Employers' Insurance Association Ltd.*,[16] a breach of condition by an employer insured against liability to his employees was held effective against an injured employee,[17] and in *Pioneer Concrete (U.K.) Ltd.* v. *National Employers Mutual General Insurance Association Ltd.*,[18] a breach of condition requiring immediate notification by the insured of legal proceedings instituted against it could be relied upon against the innocent third party.

However, insurers cannot simply claim to set off against the amount due to the third party any premiums due but unpaid by the insured. In *Murray* v. *Legal & General Assurance Society*,[19] it was held that the rights and liabilities of the insured transferred to the third party are only those rights and liabilities in respect of the liability incurred by the insured to the third party. The right to claim premiums was a general right, not dependant on any term of the policy. It would appear that the effect of this decision would be reversed if there were an express term in a

---

[10] See Chapters 19 and 20.
[11] See, *e.g. McCormick* v. *National Motor and Accident Ins. Union Ltd.* (1934) 43 Ll.L.R. 361.
[12] [1933] 1 K.B. 515.
[13] [1939] 1 All E.R. 95.
[14] By section 148(2) Road Traffic Act 1972; see *Jones* v. *Birch Bros.* [1933] 2 K.B. 597 and p. 308, below.
[15] See *Socony Mobil Oil Co. Inc.* v. *West of England Ship Owners Mutual Ins. Ass.* [1984] 2 Lloyd's Rep. 408, noted [1985] J.B.L. 403.
[16] [1970] 1 W.L.R. 1400.
[17] The actual decision in the context of employers' liability insurance is overruled by the Employers' Liability (Compulsory Insurance) Regulations: see pp. 324–325, below.
[18] [1985] 1 Lloyd's Rep. 274; see [1985] J.B.L. 333.
[19] [1969] 3 All E.R. 794.

liability policy that it was a condition precedent to the liability of the insurer for any particular claim that all premiums owing under the policy before the claim arose were duly paid.

CONTRACTUAL PROVISIONS

There are basically two common form conditions of relevance for present purposes. They concern admissions of liability and the conduct of proceedings and the obligation of the insured to take reasonable care.

Admissions of liability and the conduct of proceedings
The standard term reads something like the following:

> "No admission of liability or offer or promise of payment, whether expressed or implied, shall be made without the written consent of the insurer, which shall be entitled at its own discretion to take over and conduct in the name of the insured the defence or settlement of any claim."

Professional indemnity policies may have in addition a clause providing that proceedings by the third party are not to be contested unless a Queen's Counsel so advises (the "Q.C. clause").[20]

Control of proceedings—duty of insurer
The clause cited contains two elements, that prohibiting unauthorised admissions of liability and that giving the insurer the right to control proceedings against the insured. In respect of the latter, it would seem from the standard wording that the insurer has an absolute discretion as to what is done, but it is clear that this discretion is controlled. The insurers have "the right to decide upon the proper tactics to pursue in the conduct of the action,[21] provided that they do so in what they bona fide consider to be the common interest of themselves and their assured."[22]

A blatant ignoring of the interests of the insured occurred in *Groom* v. *Crocker*[23] where, quite without foundation and know-

---

[20] As to this, see *West Wake Price and Co.* v. *Ching* [1957] 1 W.L.R. 45.
[21] Including the appointment of solicitors to represent the insured. However, the insurers cannot compel the insured to accept legal representation: *Barrett Bros.* v. *Davies* [1966] 1 W.L.R. 1334.
[22] Lord Greene M.R. in *Groom* v. *Crocker* [1939] 1 K.B. 194 at 203.
[23] Note 22.

ing of its inaccuracy, the solicitors acting for the insurers admitted to the third party claimant that the insured had been negligent. It was held that this was a clear breach of duty and the insured was entitled to damages for breach of contract and to damages in tort for libel. The contract damages, however, were only nominal, as the insurers had paid the third party the sum he claimed, and the court declined to award damages for injury to reputation or feelings.[24] That *Groom* v. *Crocker* did not, however, establish a very strict limit on the insurer's discretion is evident from the later case of *Beacon Insurance Co.* v. *Langdale*.[25] Here the insurers did not admit that their motor insured was negligent, but without his knowledge they settled the third party's claim with a strict denial of liability. They then sued the insured for the £5 excess which the policy provided for and it was held that they were entitled to succeed. They had acted quite properly, had made an advantageous settlement and denied liability. With respect, the niceties of paying up but with a denial of liability may be lost on some insureds. The defendant in the case continued to deny that he was liable and would not therefore see why he should have to pay anything until the contrary were proved. Furthermore, such evidence as there is from the report suggests that the third party recovered sufficient to cover him only for his out of pocket expenses and not for the fairly severe injuries he recovered, implying that it was by no means certain that the insured was liable.

Despite any sympathy that might be felt for such an insured, it can safely be said that in law the insurer can settle with the third party so long as they do not unjustifiably admit liability, and, possibly, so long as they do not unjustifiably settle beyond the policy limits or refuse a settlement offer by the third party within these limits. There is no English authority on this latter point, but the question has been much litigated in the United States of America where there are decisions holding that if a liability insurer refuses an offer of settlement by the third party within the policy limits, and the latter subsequently recovers more than the sum insured in a civil action against the insured, the insurer is liable for the whole amount.[26] It is suggested that such conduct on the part of an insurer here should also entail civil liability as a breach of the duty to act in good faith laid

---

[24] But see now, *e.g. Heywood* v. *Wellers* [1976] 1 All E.R. 300.
[25] [1939] 4 All E.R. 209.
[26] See especially, *Crisci* v. *Security Ins. Co.* 66 Cal. (2d) 425, 426 P. (2d) 173 (1967). The action was categorised as tortious. It has been followed on numerous occasions in the U.S.A.

down by *Groom* v. *Crocker*. The American cases have often also awarded the insured punitive damages, but it is not suggested that the English courts would, or should, do so.

On the other hand, it is clear that the standard condition in English policies does not oblige the insurers to take over the insured's defence,[27] so that there can be no basis for any liability on the insurer if it chooses not to do so, other than to indemnify the insured within the limits of the policy if the latter is in fact adjudged legally liable to the third party. In practice, a refusal by the insurer to conduct the defence is unlikely, since it would hardly wish to be without a say in negotiations.[28]

No estoppel

If an insurer does take control of proceedings under the standard condition, it is not necessarily thereby prevented from subsequently denying liability to indemnify the insured. This may arise because of a non-disclosure or breach of warranty or condition by the insured discovered only at a later date. If, however, the insurer does discover such a right to avoid liability, it will be deemed to have waived its right if it continues to act for the insured.[29] Another situation where the insurer might seek to avoid liability is on the grounds that the event that occurred was not in fact within the cover provided by the policy. Provided that the insurer does not clearly admit to liability, the question arises whether the mere fact that it conducted the defence is sufficient ground for holding that it cannot subsequently deny liability. The only conceivable legal basis for such a conclusion would be by application of the doctrine of estoppel. That such an estoppel could operate in this context has been denied by an English court in the case of *Soole* v. *Royal Insurance Co.*.[30] The insured effected a policy to indemnity himself against the possible successful enforcement by his neighbours of a restrictive covenant on his property. His defence against the action by his neighbours, which action was in fact successful, was conducted by the insurers, but they subsequently denied that they were liable to indemnify him. In fact they were held liable, but the court also held that, if they had

---

[27] As American policies often do; see the discussion by Stephen J. in *Distillers Co.* v. *Ajax Ins. Co.* (1974) 48 A.L.J.R. 136, esp. at 147.

[28] But compare the attitude of the insurers in *Distillers* v. *Ajax*, above, discussed below.

[29] *Evans* v. *Employers' Mutual* [1936] 1 K.B. 505.

[30] [1971] 2 Lloyd's Rep. 332. Compare *Hansen* v. *Marco Engineering (Aust.) Pty. Ltd.* [1948] V.L.R. 198, where it was held that the insurer was estopped.

not been, their conduct in defending the insured would not have estopped them from denying liability. That conduct did not amount to an unequivocal representation that they would indemnify the insured regardless, because no insurer when it takes over the defence of its insured can be sure that it will be liable in the long run. For example, the third party's claim might fail. The insurer's conduct of the defence is merely an indication that the proceedings may give rise to a liability to indemnify the insured.

Admissions of liability

The part of the standard condition which prohibits admissions of liability etc. without the insurer's consent is obviously very important, and is no doubt regarded by insurers as essential for the protection of their interests. There can be no doubt as to the validity of such a condition,[31] and it should not matter on principle whether or not the insurer has in fact been prejudiced by an admission by its insured, for example if there can be no doubt whatsoever as to the latter's legal liability.[32] What is perhaps slightly disturbing about this standard condition is its width and the fact that an insurer could rely on a fairly casual "it's my fault" said or written to the third party by the insured to avoid liability, despite the lack of any real prejudice to their position. It must be admitted though that a case with no prejudice at all might not be so likely, as the insurer could always argue that it might well have persuaded the third party to accept a smaller settlement.

Insurer's refusal to defend

The question may arise whether an insurer is still entitled to rely upon this condition if in fact it elects not to have anything to do with the insured's defence against the third party. The essence of the condition is that it prohibits the insured from settling without consent. If the insurer refuses to consent, the insured will be compelled to let the matter go to litigation unless he can argue that by refusing to have anything to do with his defence the insurer has forfeited its right to rely upon the condition. This question, which appears never to have been considered in the English courts, produced a difference of opinion in the High Court of Australia in *Distillers Co. Ltd.* v. *Ajax Insurance Co. Ltd..*[33] The dispute arose out of the manufac-

---

[31] See, *e.g. Terry* v. *Trafalgar Ins. Co.* [1970] 1 Lloyd's Rep. 524.
[32] *Ibid.*
[33] (1974) 48 A.L.J.R. 136.

ture of drugs containing thalidomide which the insured, a subsidiary of the United Kingdom company, had distributed in Australia. These drugs were of course taken by pregnant women and, allegedly owing to the negligence of Distillers, caused severe damage to their unborn foetuses. Distillers had public liability cover with Ajax, the policy containing the relevant condition. Upon being sued for negligence, Distillers wished to consider compromising with the third parties, but Ajax refused to consent to this, at the same time refusing to conduct Distillers' defence. By a majority, it was held that the insurers were entitled to refuse consent without incurring any liability. Gibbs J., dissenting, preferred to follow an Irish case[34] and held that the two aspects of the standard condition were linked, so that the right to rely upon no admissions without consent applied only where the insurer in fact conducted the insured's defence. The decision of the majority appears correct in principle, but Stephen J., one of the majority, in an important judgment which it is suggested should be followed, made it clear that the decision would not confer upon an insurer an arbitrary power to refuse consent. He referred in particular to the sort of case where a conflict between insured and insurer might arise, where the claim against the insured is above the sum insured under the policy and the insured is anxious to settle below that figure whereas the insurer would gain little from a settlement close to the limit and might prefer to fight the case. He said that in such a case, the insurer must exercise its powers under the policy with due regard to the interests of the insured, following *Groom* v. *Crocker*[35] on the analogous point already discussed. The position must depend on a reasonable estimate of the third party's claim. If that has every chance of succeeding, it would be improper for the insurer to refuse to consent to a settlement substantially within the policy limits. If, on the other hand, the third party's claim is doubtful, and the only reason or a principal reason why the insured wishes to settle is to avoid the bad publicity attendant on being sued, the insurer would be justified in refusing its consent. The result is that if the insurer refuses its consent and leaves the insured to act alone, but the latter enters into a quite reasonable settlement, the insurer will be liable to indemnify him regardless of the breach of condition.

---

[34] *General Omnibus Co. Ltd.* v. *London General Ins. Co. Ltd.* [1936] I.R. 596.
[35] See p. 284, above.

The obligation to take reasonable precautions

The second standard condition requires the insured to take reasonable precautions or care to avoid loss. Such a clause construed literally would negative a large part of the cover intended to be effected, since one of the major purposes of a liability policy is to insure the insured against liability in negligence, and negligence is a failure to take reasonable care when a duty of care is owed. So the courts have adopted a common sense construction of this condition. In *Woolfall & Rimmer* v. *Moyle*,[36] an employer, the insured, was vicariously liable for the acts of a foreman who had failed to ensure that certain scaffolding was safe. The court rejected the insurer's argument that the insured had therefore failed to take reasonable precautions. The insured had complied with that condition by selecting a competent foreman and reasonably delegating to him certain tasks. The insured was not personally negligent, which was the circumstance when the condition might apply.

The Court of Appeal went further than this in the later case of *Fraser* v. *Furman*,[37] so that only recklessness or worse on the part of the insured will now amount to a breach of this condition. Reasonable care does not mean reasonable as between the insured and third party, but as between insured and insurer having regard to the commercial purpose of the contract which includes indemnity against the insured's own negligence. The insured's omission or act "must be at least reckless, that is to say, made with actual recognition by the insured himself that a danger exists, and not caring whether or not it is averted. The purpose of the condition is to ensure that the insured will not, because he is covered against loss by the policy, refrain from taking precautions which he knows ought to be taken."[38]

SUMS INSURED AND COSTS

It has already been noted how the sum insured in a liability policy may be of great importance in the context of an admission of liability condition. More generally, while the sum

---

[36] [1942] 1 K.B. 66.
[37] [1967] 1 W.L.R. 898.
[38] [1967] 1 W.L.R. at 906, *per* Diplock L.J. See also *Aluminium Wire and Cable Co. Ltd.* v. *Allstate Insurance Co. Ltd.* [1985] 2 Lloyd's Rep. 280. A similar condition in a non-liability insurance policy is unlikely to receive such a generous construction; see p. 162 above.

insured obviously puts the limit of the insurer's liability, and is commonplace except in relation to personal injury aspects of motor insurance where statute does not allow it, it may be expressed in different ways. For example, the policy may have a limit applying to any one contractual period, regardless of the number of claims made, or the limit may apply to each accident or each occurrence or each claim, with no global maximum. The first sort of limit causes no problems, and it has been held that where the limit is per accident, each separate claim by a third party arises out of a separate accident. For example, in *South Staffordshire Tramways Co.* v. *Sickness and Accident Assurance Association*,[39] a policy indemnifying the insured against liability for accidents caused by vehicles had a limit of "£250 in respect of any one accident." One of the insured's trams overturned injuring forty passengers. It was held that each passenger had an accident and therefore the insurer was potentially liable for 40 × £250.

If, however, the limit is expressed to be per occurrence, then it seems that the number of occurrences is the number of times the insured is negligent. If there is only one negligent act, there is only one occurrence and the policy limit will apply regardless of how many individual claims may be made by third parties as a result. In *Forney* v. *Dominion Insurance Co. Ltd.*,[40] a solicitor's professional indemnity policy had a limit of £3,000 per occurrence. His assistant was negligent in advising a client about a cause of action in tort. The matter involved a motor accident when a man driving negligently injured some of his family and caused the death of himself and his father in law. The survivors, including the driver's widow, were advised to sue the driver's estate, which was quite proper, but the assistant failed to issue the writs in time. In addition, she advised the widow to act as the driver's administratrix which was also negligent, because it meant that the widow would effectively lose her damages, not being able in her personal capacity to sue herself as representing the driver's estate. It was held that the two acts of negligence were two occurrences, and the insurer's maximum liability was therefore £6,000. It would seem that the same construction would apply where the limit applies per claim, that is, that claim means claim by the insured against the insurer rather than claim by each third party against the insured. This was

---

[39] [1891] 1 Q.B. 402.
[40] [1969] 1 W.L.R. 928.

certainly the construction adopted in a case where the relevant limit was contained in an excess clause in a liability policy.[41]

Liability policies invariably include in their cover any costs incurred by the insured, in addition to the damages he is liable to pay. This would not usually include the costs of the insured in successfully defending a claim as the provision as to costs normally applies only where the insurer is liable to indemnify the insured,[42] but the insured will in general recover these from the plaintiff third party. Costs though will normally be limited, for example, by being included together with damages in the sum insured, or by being limited to the same proportion which the indemnity provided bears to the insured's loss where the latter exceeds the former because it is greater than the sum insured by the policy.

INSURER'S DUTY TO THE VICTIM

Frequently in practice liability insurers will negotiate directly on their insured's behalf with the latter's victim. For obvious reasons, but to the potential detriment of the victim, they will seek to keep their liability as low as possible and may well induce the victim to agree to a settlement for an amount below his legal entitlement. Where the victim so relies on the insurers, it is likely that a fiduciary relationship will arise and that the settlement will be voidable on the ground of undue influence unless the insurers either inform the victim of the desirability of seeking independent advice or make an offer which is realistic in respect of the victim's loss.[43]

---

[41] *Trollope & Colls Ltd.* v. *Haydon* [1977] 1 Lloyd's Rep. 244.
[42] *Cross* v. *British Oak Ins. Co.* [1938] 2 K.B. 167 at 174.
[43] *Horry* v. *Tate & Lyle Refineries Ltd.* [1982] 2 Lloyd's Rep. 416, applying *Lloyds Bank Ltd.* v. *Bundy* [1975] Q.B. 326; see Merkin (1983) 46 M.L.R. 91. The contract of settlement may also be voidable for misrepresentation: see *Saunders* v. *Ford Motor Co. Ltd.* [1970] 1 Lloyd's Rep. 379.

Chapter 19

MOTOR INSURANCE

Motor insurance must be the type of insurance which most people have most dealings with and knowledge of, primarily, of course, because some cover for anyone who drives a car or other motor vehicle is compulsory. What the law requires at present is that anyone who uses or causes or permits another to use a motor vehicle on a road must be insured against liability to pay damages for death or bodily injury caused by or arising out of the use of the vehicle.[1] The exact scope of this requirement will be considered shortly. From the end of 1988, pursuant to the Second E.E.C. Directive on Motor Insurance,[2] it will also be compulsory to insure against liability in respect of damage to a third party's property. The changes that this will involve are considered at the end of this chapter.

It should be noted that in practice most motor policies have long covered third party property damage. A "comprehensive" policy will generally also cover first party property damage, that is insurance of the vehicle as goods against loss, and first party injury, that is in effect a personal accident insurance under which the insured who is killed or injured when involved in an accident in his vehicle will receive a stated sum. A comprehensive policy often also covers personal effects in the vehicle. The other common form of motor policy which does not just cover third party liability is the third party, fire and theft policy; in addition to third party liability, this covers insurance of the vehicle itself but limited to those losses evident from the description.

It should also be noted that in practice a policy may not just cover the insured himself. Cover may extend either to named others or possibly to anyone driving the car with the insured's permission, and also often the insured driving other vehicles.[3] In addition, there are various categories of use, for example "social, domestic and pleasure purposes" and "business pur-

---

[1] Road Traffic Act 1972, ss.143 and 145.
[2] Directive 84/5, O.J. L8/17.
[3] For the double insurance problems that can arise as a result of these extensions, see pp. 265–267, above.

poses," adopted by insurers, which will obviously determine the uses to which the vehicle can be put while remaining covered.[4]

Competition between insurers since the ending of the motor tariff in 1968, as well as affecting premium rates, has seen the introduction of added varieties in cover in comprehensive policies. For example, there are usually special provisions regarding windscreen damage whereby the insured may be able to have a broken windscreen replaced and only claim later, and without prejudice to his no claims bonus. Some policies now provide for the insured to be entitled to claim the cost of hiring an alternative vehicle while his is being repaired, and there are special policies available to people over particular ages.

Also of special importance in the field of motor insurance are excesses,[5] no claims and loyalty bonuses, and the "knock for knock" agreements. No claims bonuses provide for specified reductions in premiums if no claim, or no relevant claim, is made during the previous year.[6] The legal effect of "knock for knock" agreements has been examined in an earlier chapter.[7]

The Scope of Compulsory Cover

Part VI of the Road Traffic Act 1972, which governs the compulsory aspects of motor insurance, defines these obligations and also provides special protection to the injured third party from the strict contractual rights of the insurer as against the insured. The basic obligations will be examined here and the latter aspect will be considered later. As noted above, these obligations will shortly be extended; the detail is considered at the end of the chapter.

Subject to the exceptions in section 144,[8] section 143 provides that "it is not lawful for a person to use, or to cause or permit to use, or to cause or permit any other person to use, a motor vehicle on a road" unless there is in force a policy covering the

---

[4] See pp. 301–303, below.

[5] See p. 227, above.

[6] Loyalty bonuses tend to allow for an unlimited number of claims over a longer period without their being lost. Technically there may be difficulties in showing a legal entitlement to such bonuses; see p. 70, above.

[7] See pp. 253–255, above.

[8] Particularly vehicles owned by public bodies and vehicles owned by a person who has deposited £15,000 (a ludicrously small sum nowadays, but one which the Government intends to increase) in court.

required third party risks or a security in relation to those risks.[9] The required risks are listed in section 145 (as amended) and are: (1) insurance against liability in respect of death or bodily injury to any person caused by or arising out of, the use of the vehicle on a road in Great Britain[10]; (2) insurance against any liability in the other member states of the EEC which those states require; and (3) insurance against liabilities in respect of emergency treatment.[11] Heading (1) does not include two liabilities however, namely, the liability of an employer to an employee in respect of death or bodily injury arising out of and in the course of his employment, and any contractual liability.[12] The former is now covered by compulsory employer's liability insurance.[13] The latter exclusion makes it clear that only tortious liability is required to be covered.

The basic obligation arising from the words of section 143 cited above has been the subject of considerable case law. One problem has been the meaning of the word "road," defined in section 196(1) of the 1972 Act as "any highway and any other road to which the public has access." It is a question of fact whether any other road is a road for these purposes, so that, for example, a hotel forecourt habitually used by the public as a road has been held to be a road,[14] whereas a car park has been held not to be.[15] When part of a vehicle is on a public road after being driven from private property, insurance is required, it seems.[16]

Use of a vehicle

The major problem has been the meanings of "use" and to "cause" or "permit" use. Use includes the leaving of a car on a road, even though it is incapable at present of being mechanically propelled.[17] On the other hand, it is not so wide as to include, for example, the case of someone being a passenger in

---

[9] For securities, see Road Traffic Act 1972, s.146.
[10] This does not mean that the user has to be insured against his potential liability to the driver, *e.g.* because he has negligently let him drive an unsafe vehicle; the driver is not within the words "any person": *Cooper* v. *Motor Insurers' Bureau* [1985] Q.B. 575.
[11] As to this, see, ss.155–156.
[12] s.145(4).
[13] See Chapter 20.
[14] *Bugge* v. *Taylor* [1941] 1 K.B. 198; compare *Thomas* v. *Dando* [1951] 2 K.B. 620.
[15] *Griffin* v. *Squire* [1958] 1 W.L.R. 1106.
[16] *Randall* v. *M.I.B.* [1968] 2 Lloyd's Rep. 553.
[17] *Elliott* v. *Grey* [1960] 1 Q.B. 367.

a car[18] or asking another to transport some goods in his car, even though it could perhaps be said colloquially that that person was using the other's car. In the context of the Road Traffic Act, use implies an element of controlling, managing or operating the vehicle at the relevant time.[19] In *Brown* v. *Roberts*,[20] the passenger in a car was negligent in opening her door and thereby injured a pedestrian. It was held that she was not using the car in the statutory sense, so that the driver was not therefore causing or permitting her to use it and thus not liable in damages for breach of statutory duty in not insuring her against her potential liability. Simply, the passenger had no control over the vehicle. It was admitted in that case though, that there could be more than one person using a vehicle at any given time within the statutory meaning, and in *Leathley* v. *Tatton*,[21] it was held that a passenger involved in a criminal adventure with others to steal and take away a car was using the car for the purposes of section 143.

Causing or permitting use

Whether someone causes or permits another to use a vehicle is a question of fact. Clearly it is so if, for example, X allows Y to drive his car. "Cause" involves an express or positive mandate to use a car in a particular way, whereas "permit" is looser, and merely denotes express or implied allowance to use a vehicle.[22] In *McLeod* v. *Buchanan*,[23] a man appointed his brother as manager of his farm and bought him a car which was insured for business and private use. The car having proved unsatisfactory, the man authorised his brother to buy a van instead; this was insured for business use only, but was in fact used for private purposes. It was held that the man had permitted his brother to use the van while uninsured. The van was given to him for the same purposes as the car, and the brother was not told not to use it for private purposes. In *Lyons* v. *May*,[24] a garage owner was driving a car back from the garage after repair, at the request of the car's owner. It was held that the latter had caused or permitted the use of the car. In contrast, in

---

[18] e.g. *B. (A Minor)* v. *Knight* [1981] R.T.R. 136.
[19] *Brown* v. *Roberts* [1965] 1 Q.B. 1 at 15, *per* Megaw J.
[20] See note 19.
[21] [1980] R.T.R. 21. See also *Cobb* v. *Williams* [1973] R.T.R. 113. Compare *B (A Minor)* v. *Knight*, above.
[22] Lord Wright in *McLeod* v. *Buchanan* [1940] 2 All E.R. 179 at 187.
[23] See note 22.
[24] [1948] 2 All E.R. 1062.

Watkins v. *O'Shaughnessy*,[25] an auctioneer sold a car which the purchaser drove away immediately without, to the auctioneer's knowledge, being insured. It was held that the auctioneer had not caused or permitted the use of the car because, having sold it, he no longer had any control over it.

Policy required

Section 143 requires that there be in force a "policy" of insurance (or a security). A policy exists for these purposes even though it is voidable for non-disclosure, misrepresentation or breach of warranty,[26] and it has been held that avoidance for one of these reasons does not amount to avoidance *ab initio* for criminal law purposes.[27] Policy includes a cover note (s.158).[28] There is rather curious authority to the effect that the existence of a mere contract of insurance is not enough to satisfy the statute. In *Roberts* v. *Warne*,[29] the policy in question did not cover the particular driver who was using the car. However, a cover note had been arranged to effect this and when this expired, the insurers clearly regarded the driver as covered. The problems arose largely because of communication difficulties during a postal strike. The conviction of the driver for using the car without insurance and of the owner for causing or permitting this were upheld by the Divisional Court. Even if the insurers were contractually bound to cover the driver, which may well have been the case, the *policy* did not cover him and hence there was no policy as section 143 requires. With respect, this must be incorrect.[30] There is no magic in the word "policy" in general and no reason to read it in section 143 as meaning other than a legally enforceable contract of insurance. Even an enforceable oral contract should suffice.

Certificate of insurance

In addition to the requirement under section 143 to have a policy, whatever that may mean, section 147 provides that the policy is of no effect unless and until the insurer delivers to the insured a certificate of insurance.[31] There are various other pro-

---

[25] [1939] 1 All E.R. 384.
[26] *Adams* v. *Dunne* [1978] R.T.R. 281.
[27] *Goodbarne* v. *Buck* [1940] 1 K.B. 771.
[28] But it must be contractually binding; see *Taylor* v. *Allon* [1966] 1 Q.B. 304, discussed at p. 64, above.
[29] [1973] R.T.R. 217.
[30] See (1973) Crim.L.R. 244.
[31] See s.147(2) for the certificate of security when the obligation is satisfied by a security rather than by insurance.

visions governing certificates, mainly concerned with the fact that they constitute the easily checkable evidence of compliance with the insurance obligation[32] and that they must be produced in order to obtain a road fund licence for a vehicle.[33] While the certificate or parts of it may be incorporated into the contract of insurance or policy, for example, concerning the permitted user of the vehicle, if there is any conflict between the two, the policy prevails, and the certificate itself is not a contract of insurance.[34]

Sanctions for failure to insure

The consequences of a failure to comply with the obligation to insure under section 143 are potentially two-fold. First, it is a criminal offence of strict liability.[35] Secondly, commission of the offence is a breach of statutory duty and anyone who suffers loss as a result can sue in tort for damages. The importance of this is not against the negligent driver, who would be liable in negligence anyway, but against someone who used the car with him or caused or permitted him to use it. The meanings of these expressions, as already discussed, may therefore be of importance in this context as well as in the criminal context. In *Monk* v. *Warbey*,[36] the defendant owner of a car lent it to a friend who permitted another to drive. Neither of the latter was insured. It was held that the plaintiff who had been injured by the negligence of the driver could sue the owner. It would appear that the owner's insurer would be liable in such circumstances to indemnify him against this liability, as the standard policy wordings do not require the insured to be driving, but indemnify him against "legal liability . . . arising from an accident caused by, through or in connection with the insured car." Since 1946, the Motor Insurers' Bureau (M.I.B.), as will be seen, indemnifies such uninsured drivers, but it has been held that this does not remove the action for breach of statutory duty. In the case in question, *Corfield* v. *Groves*,[37–38] judgment was awarded against the owner subject to the proviso that if the M.I.B. did satisfy the judgment, it could not be enforced against

---

[32] See Road Traffic Act 1972, s.162, which gives the police power to require the production of a certificate, backed by a criminal penalty.
[33] *Ibid.* s.153.
[34] *Biddle* v. *Johnston* [1965] 2 Lloyd's Rep. 121.
[35] Subject to the exception in s.143(2).
[36] [1935] 1 K.B. 75.
[37–38] [1950] 1 All E.R. 488.

the owner. In practice, therefore, this action is really only relevant if for some reason the M.I.B. is not liable.

COMMON TERMS AND EXCEPTIONS

It is now appropriate to consider the most important of the standard terms and conditions that are found in motor policies. These are important to compulsory and non-compulsory insurance alike, because, even though, as will be seen, some of them may not be enforceable against a third party victim where insurance was compulsory, they may remain of effect between insurer and insured so that the insurer who has had to pay the third party may be entitled to recover this sum of money from the insured. Three headings will be considered here: standard extensions; limitations on use; and common-form conditions relating to the condition of the insured vehicle.

Standard extensions

It is common for motor policies to cover more than just the insured's driving of the car or vehicle in question. For example, cover may extend to the spouse of the insured, to particular named drivers or drivers identified by a class, or, most widely, to anyone driving the vehicle on the insured's order or with the insured's permission. Only the last sort of extension can give rise to relevant legal problems, but before examining these, one important point of general interest relates to the status of the other driver in terms of the contract between insured and insurer.

At common law, the insured can enforce the contract in so far as it confers a benefit on a third party, there being in effect a waiver of any requirement of insurable interest.[39] Presumably the insured holds any money recovered on trust for the third party. The latter though cannot enforce the contract himself.[40] The common law may now, however, be redundant in this context, for section 148(4) of the 1972 Act provides:

> "Notwithstanding anything in any enactment, a person issuing a policy of insurance under section 145 of this Act shall be liable to indemnify the persons or classes of persons specified in the policy in respect of any liability which

---

[39] *Williams v. Baltic Ins. Ass. of London* [1924] 2 K.B. 282; see pp. 48–49, above.
[40] *Vandepitte v. Preferred Accident Ins. Corp. of New York* [1933] A.C. 70; see pp. 49–50 above, but see note 19a on p. 49.

Common Terms and Exceptions

the policy purports to cover in the case of those persons or classes of persons."

Thus, the third party can enforce the contract directly, subject, of course, to any right in the insurer to avoid liability,[41] and he is not dependant on the owner insuring as his trustee or agent.[42] In effect, he is by statute a party to the contract. It is as yet undecided whether section 148(4) covers only the compulsory aspects of a motor policy, and thus, whether to recover in respect of liability for third party damage would necessitate the *Williams* v. *Baltic*[43] type of procedure or a ratification, if that is permissible, by the third party.[44] The subsection refers to "a person issuing a policy under section 145" which, of course, concerns only compulsory insurance, but it does say that the insurer must indemnify the third party "in respect of *any liability* which the policy purports to cover." Assuming therefore that the policy satisfies section 145, it is suggested that the third party will be covered by it in respect of any third party liability within the policy's terms, unless there is anything to the contrary in the policy.

Permitted drivers

The question of whether someone is driving with the insured's permission, other than in obvious cases, has occasioned some difficulties. One problem is whether a permitted driver can himself give permission to another so that the other is covered, in the absence of the insured's direct consent. It would appear that this is not possible. In the Canadian case of *Minister of Transport* v. *Canadian General Insurance*,[45] a son of the insured was permitted to drive the car in question. He purported to give permission to a friend. It was held that the friend was not insured. It seems likely that an English court would reach the same conclusions.[46] In *Morgans* v. *Launchberry*,[47] the permitted driver, the husband of the insured, gave permission to another to drive the car. The latter was negligent and injured or killed the passengers in the car. The case strictly involved

---

[41] *Guardian Assurance* v. *Sutherland* [1939] 2 All E.R. 246.
[42] *Tattersall* v. *Drysdale* [1935] 2 K.B. 174.
[43] See note 39.
[44] See p. 49, above. Of course shortly, when such liability is compulsorily insurable, as described on pp. 318–320, below, the point will be largely academic.
[45] (1971) 18 D.L.R. (3d) 617.
[46] See *Sands* v. *O'Connell* [1981] R.T.R. 42.
[47] [1973] A.C. 127.

only the point of tort law as to whether the insured as owner of the car was vicariously liable for the acts of the driver and the House of Lords held that she was not. However, a passage in Lord Denning's judgment in the Court of Appeal[48] indicates that if the insured were not liable, her insurers would not be because the driver did not have her permission. This is why the issue was fought as one of vicarious liability.[49]

That the insured can become the third party and recover as such if injured by the negligence of someone whom he permitted to drive the car is well established. In *Digby* v. *General Accident*,[50] the insured's policy covered anyone driving with her permission. She gave such permission to her chauffeur and was then, as a passenger, injured by his negligent driving. It was held that the insurers were liable to indemnify the chauffeur in respect of his liability to the insured.

Permission once given can obviously be revoked. In the absence of such revocation, it appears that permission continues even when the insured dies. In *Kelly* v. *Cornhill Insurance Co.*,[51] the insured gave permission to his son to drive the insured car and soon afterwards died. Some eight months later the son was involved in an accident, the policy period not having expired. By a bare majority, the House of Lords held that the son was entitled to sue under the policy, the permission of his father not having been revoked by his death. It should be noted that there was little merit in the insurers' defence, as under the policy the father was expressly precluded from driving; it had been effected solely for the son's benefit. While there are obvious difficulties in saying that permission continues in such a case in the absence of its renewal by the insured's personal representatives in whom the ownership of the car and policy will have vested, the result is sensible, since otherwise a permitted driver could automatically and without his knowledge become uninsured, even for example in the course of a particular journey. The decision in *Kelly* implies that the insured's personal representatives in such a case would have the power to revoke the permission. Otherwise it must continue until the expiry of the policy. Presumably in this and any other case,

---

[48] [1971] 2 Q.B. 245 at 253.
[49] At the time of the case, liability to passengers did not have to be insured against; now the injured parties in such a situation would recover compensation from the M.I.B. if all else failed.
[50] [1943] A.C. 121.
[51] [1964] 1 All E.R. 321.

revocation of permission is effective only when actually communicated to the permittee.

However, a purchaser of a car cannot be claiming to drive with the former owner, the insured's, permission, unless the insurers expressly consent. Here the insured ceases to have any insurable interest in the car, his policy lapses and is not assignable.[52]

Limitations on use

As was mentioned earlier, insurers have well established categories of permitted user of an insured vehicle which are enforceable even against an injured third party. These vary from, for example, use covering only social, domestic and pleasure purposes and use by the insured for travel to and from his place of business to use by the insured in person or use by others in connection with the insured's or his employer's business. Few legal difficulties can arise over some of the distinctions adopted, but in one respect there is a body of case law. If an insured is covered for social, domestic and pleasure purposes and not for business use, or at least only for travelling to and from work, the distinctions become important and not always easy to apply. As Roskill L.J. has pointed out,[53] there will be cases falling each side of the line when a phrase such as social, domestic and pleasure purposes is used, and it is impossible to state any firm principle under which it can be predicted on which side of the line a particular case will fall. It must depend on the facts of the particular case. In *Jones* v. *Welsh Insurance Corporation*,[54] the policy covered social etc. purposes and use in connection with the insured's business as stated in the schedule. The latter stated the insured's business as that of motor mechanic. In addition, the insured farmed a few sheep, really as a hobby but with the aim of making a small profit. He was carrying some sheep when the relevant accident occurred. It was held that the insurers were not liable. The insured was carrying on the business of sheep farming; this was not stated in the schedule and thus the cover did not apply.

In *Wood* v. *General Accident*,[55] a garage proprietor was being driven in his own car by one of his drivers to a firm with which he intended to negotiate a business contract when an accident

---

[52] *Peters* v. *General Fire & Accident Ins.* [1938] 2 All E.R. 267; see p. 135, above.
[53] *Seddon* v. *Binnions* [1978] 1 Lloyd's Rep. 381 at 384–385.
[54] [1937] 4 All E.R. 149.
[55] (1948) 65 T.L.R. 53.

happened. It was held that though it was convenient and comfortable for him to make the journey like this, the car was not being used for social, etc., purposes. Travelling to work, therefore, is seemingly not a social, domestic or pleasure purpose; it must be separately covered. In *Seddon* v. *Binions*,[56] a father who helped his son occasionally on Sundays in the latter's business of carpet layer was driving home in his son's car his son's only employee who had toothache. Having delivered the latter, the father intended to go home for his lunch. The father's own policy covered his driving of other cars but only for social, etc., purposes. The son's insurers had paid in respect of the accident that occurred and were claiming a contribution from the father's insurers. It was held that the latter were not liable, the essential purpose of the journey being a business one, namely the father transporting his son's employee back from work.

Use or driving for purposes connected with the motor trade may be excluded, as in *Browning* v. *Phoenix Assurance Co. Ltd.*,[57] where a garage employee was authorised by the insured to drive his car in order to warm the engine oil before it was drained at the garage. It was held that the insurers were not liable in respect of an accident which occurred when the employee was driving the car for pleasure the day after the oil had been drained.[58] It was also clear that the car would not have been insured while the oil was being warmed. The exclusion may though be qualified so that cover is provided while the vehicle is merely in the custody or control of a motor trader for the purposes of repair, that is so long as it is not being driven by someone other than the insured or a permitted driver.[59]

A case may arise when the purposes of a journey are mixed. For example, an insured covered for social, etc., purposes but not for business purposes might be travelling to a business

---

[56] See note 53.

[57] [1960] 2 Lloyd's Rep. 360.

[58] The principal ground for the decision was that the employee was not a permitted driver in this respect.

[59] See the Court of Appeal's construction of somewhat difficult terms to this effect in *Samuelson* v. *National Insurance and Guarantee Corp. Ltd.* [1985] 2 Lloyd's Rep. 541. The actual decision was concerned with whether or not the insured vehicle was being driven by or in the charge of a person other than an authorised driver. It was made clear that once someone has completed his present journey, he is no longer in charge of the vehicle for insurance purposes. Thus, although the car had not been insured while being driven by a repairer on his way to collect spare parts, cover reattached once his journey was completed and the insured could recover for the theft of the car from where the repairer had parked it.

meeting followed by a social dinner. In *Seddon* v. *Binions*,[60] the view of the trial judge was that there was a mixed purpose; the father was driving for social, etc., purposes in going home for lunch, not being an employee of his son and hence not strictly travelling from work, and for business purposes in taking his son's employee home. It was held, and the Court of Appeal confirmed this, that in this event the policy would not apply since the car was partly being used for an unauthorised purpose.

Conditions regarding the condition of the insured vehicle

Motor policies universally provide that the insurers are not to be liable when the insured vehicle is being driven in an unsafe or unroadworthy condition and/or if the insured fails to maintain the vehicle in an efficient or roadworthy condition. Such provisions may be drafted as exceptions to the risk or found under the heading "conditions" and framed as conditions precedent or possibly promissory warranties. The latter is, it appears, the more common usage now. The importance of this lies in the fact that as conditions or warranties, there is no requirement in law[61] that there be any causal connection between the breach and a loss, and, although the insurer will not be able to rely upon a breach as against an injured third party, as will be seen later, he may well be able to recover from the insured as damages for breach of condition the money he has to pay to the third party.

A marine analogy?

The standard exception or condition has occasioned some difficulty. In *Barrett* v. *London General Insurance*,[62] Goddard J. held that, because of the verbal similarities, roadworthiness was to be interpreted in an analogous way to seaworthiness in a marine policy. In the latter context, seaworthiness is required only at the commencement of a voyage. The learned judge applied the same reasoning to a car journey in holding that a car whose foot brake failed at the time of the relevant accident was not unroadworthy in the absence of proof that it was not working when the insured set out on his journey. He may have been influenced by the fact that had the injured third party's claim arisen slightly later, the insurer would not have been able to take the point because of the imminent introduction of the

[60] See notes 53 and 56.
[61] But note the effects of the *Statement of General Insurance Practice*; see p. 120, above.
[62] [1935] 1 K.B. 238.

statutory provisons[63] which are now section 148 of the Road Traffic Act 1972. His reasoning was expressly disapproved by the Privy Council in *Trickett* v. *Queensland Insurance Co.*,[64] though the exception in question there did not concern roadworthiness as such but applied if the car was being driven in "a damaged or unsafe condition." The insured was involved in an accident at night at a time when the lights on his car were not working. It was held that this was sufficient to render the car damaged or unsafe. The knowledge of the insured was irrelevant, as was the question whether or not the lights were working at the beginning of the journey. The question was simply one of fact to be judged objectively.

More recently it has been suggested that the marine analogy may be useful, but it appears unlikely that the decision in *Barrett* would be followed. The usual wording of this sort of an exception is "while the car is being driven," and this must include anything that happens during a journey and not just at the start of it.[65] In *Clarke* v. *National Insurance Corporation*,[66] a four-seater car was driven with nine people in it. The Court of Appeal held that it was thereby rendered unroadworthy, although, with the normal number of people in it, it would have been quite safe. Unroadworthiness does not relate to just the mechanical condition of a vehicle, but can include any other relevant factors. In marine cases, overloading can render a ship unseaworthy, and the analogy was apt to this extent.

The term as a condition or warranty

In all these cases, the term was an exception and phrased in such a way that, fairly clearly, it should be properly read in a continuing objective sense. As noted above, modern policies may well have replaced this exception by a condition or warranty requiring the insured to maintain the vehicle in a roadworthy or efficient condition. It has been suggested that these alternatives mean the same,[67] but it would seem that the term is both narrower and wider if phrased as a condition or warranty. It is narrower because as a condition or warranty, it cannot be read wholly objectively. If a car's lights or brakes, for example, fail quite unexpectedly in the course of a journey, it may not be

---

[63] Road Traffic Act 1934, referred to at [1935] 1 K.B. at 240.
[64] [1936] A.C. 159.
[65] *Clarke* v. *National Ins. Corp.* [1963] 3 All E.R. 375 at 377.
[66] See note 65.
[67] Sellers J. in *Brown* v. *Zurich General Accident and Liability Ins. Co.* [1954] 2 Lloyd's Rep. 243 at 246.

possible to say that the insured has failed to maintain the car in a roadworthy or efficient condition, whereas it can be said that the car is being driven in an unroadworthy condition. An insured's failure to maintain imports the notion of his knowing or being in a position where he ought to know that something is wrong, which requires the insurer to show more than a simple fact. This view is supported by the decision in *Conn v. Westminster Motor Insurance Association Ltd.*,[68] discussed below, where the insured should have known that his taxi's tyres were no good, as this was easily visible, but the same did not apply in relation to his braking system.

On the other hand, a condition or warranty as to roadworthiness is wider than an exception because there need be no connection between the breach of the condition or warranty and an accident which subsequently occurs. In *Conn's* case, as mentioned above, the insured's tyres on his taxi-cab were so badly worn that there was no tread on them and they were illegal. It was held that this amounted to a breach of a condition to maintain his vehicle in an efficient condition upon which the insurers could rely, even though the state of the tyres did not cause or contribute to the relevant accident.[69]

Insured's liability in damages

One question remains in this context. If a condition or warranty as to roadworthiness or maintaining a vehicle in a reasonable or efficient condition is broken, the insurers cannot rely upon the breach as against an injured third party, but, if they have to compensate such a person, they have a statutory right to recover this money from the insured.[70] It may be, however, that they do not have to rely on this right, and that they have a remedy in a case of non-compulsory insurance where they pay a third party for property damage where not legally obliged to because of the breach. There is authority that breach of this sort of condition gives the insurers the right to claim damages from the insured. In *National Farmers' Union Mutual Insurance Society v. Dawson*,[71] the breach was not of the condition in the insured's policy requiring him to keep his car in an efficient state of repair, but of a part of the same condition requiring the

---

[68] [1966] 1 Lloyd's Rep. 407.
[69] Note though that there are cases requiring a causal connection in respect of a mere "condition" (see p. 105, above) and that in practice this is required where the *Statement of General Insurance Practice* applies (see p. 120, above).
[70] Proviso to Road Traffic Act 1972, s.148(1) discussed at p. 307, below.
[71] [1941] 2 K.B. 424.

insured to use all care and diligence to avoid accidents and prevent loss. This is a not uncommon additional condition. Compliance with it was precedent to the insurers' liability, so that it was certainly a condition precedent and may have been a warranty. The insured was unfit to drive through drink and caused an accident. This was clearly a breach of the condition cited. The insurers paid the injured third party and then sought to recover this sum from the insured. They relied first on the statutory right but failed because it was held that they could have relied upon the breach as against the third party albeit they did not. Their second point was, however, upheld, namely the right to recover the money as damages for breach of contract by the insured. With respect, this result is highly suspect. First, it could be argued that the insurers suffered no loss because they need not, and therefore should not, have paid the third party. Secondly, the effect of conditions precedent and warranties is to relieve the insurers of liability if they are broken. That is their purpose. They are not the same as conditions in other contracts. Either insurers can rely upon a breach to avoid liability or else they can choose or be compelled not to do so. If they are compelled, statute provides a remedy. If they choose not to avoid liability, there is no merit or logic in allowing them to recover from the insured.

Third Parties' Rights under the Road Traffic Act

As has been seen already, as well as rendering some insurance compulsory, the Road Traffic Act 1972 also interferes with the contractual rights of insurers for the benefit of injured or killed third parties to whom the insured is legally liable.[72]

First, section 148(1) provides that so much of the policy as purports to restrict the insurance of the persons insured by reference to any of a list of specified matters is of no effect as regards insurance compulsorily required. This is a neat way of invalidating certain terms in policies regardless of their exact legal status. They may be framed as warranties, conditions or

---

[72] Changes to and extensions of these provisions as respects the existing compulsory insurance requirements as well as the new ones will come into force in 1988 when the Second EEC Directive is implemented; see the end of this chapter.

exceptions, but if they relate to a matter within the list, they will be of no effect regardless. The list is as follows:
- (a) the age or physical or mental condition of persons driving the vehicle;
- (b) the condition of the vehicle;
- (c) the number of persons that the vehicle carries;
- (d) the weight or physical characteristics of the goods that the vehicle carries;
- (e) the times at which or the areas within which the vehicle is used;
- (f) the horse power or cylinder capacity or value of the vehicle;
- (g) the carrying on the vehicle of any particular apparatus;
- (h) the carrying on the vehicle of any particular means of identification other than any means of identification required to be carried by or under the Vehicles (Excise) Act 1971.

In most respects the sorts of warranties, conditions or exceptions avoided by section 148(1) are clear. For example, conditions or exceptions relating to roadworthiness, etc., will be of no effect; they fall within (b) above. A breach of warranty in a proposal form as to the value or size of engine of a vehicle will fall within (f). The condition in *National Farmers' Union Mutual* v. *Dawson*, however, to which reference has been made,[73] was held not to fall within (c), and a limitation as to use is always effective as against third parties.[74] What is not clear is why the list has never been amended since its introduction in the Road Traffic Act 1934. Why should an insurer be liable to a third party even if, say, the insured has failed in the most deliberate and dangerous way to keep his vehicle roadworthy, whereas it could avoid liability for the slightest infringement of a limitation as to use? Since in all cases where the insurers can rely upon an exception or breach of warranty or condition, despite section 148(1), the Motor Insurers' Bureau will have to satisfy the third party's judgment, as will be seen later, the logic of retaining an incomplete list as against a complete list or even no list at all is not easy to follow. As has already been seen, the proviso to the subsection entitles the insurer compelled to pay the third party but who would otherwise have avoided liability to recoup this money from the insured.

---

[73] See text at note 71.
[74] *Jones* v. *Welsh Ins. Corp.*, above, note 54; the limitation did not fall within para. (d).

Breaches of condition

Section 148(2) invalidates other breaches of condition by an insured so far as the injured third party is concerned. The conditions covered are those providing that no liability shall arise under the policy, or that any liability so arising shall cease, in the event of some specified thing being done or omitted to be done after the happening of the event giving rise to the claim. This clearly covers a breach by the insured of a condition regarding notice or particulars of loss, and it must also cover an admission of liability in breach of the standard conditions.[75] Whether an arbitration clause is caught by section 148(2) is an open question if it has the *Scott* v. *Avery* addition making it a condition precedent to the insurer's liability. The majority of the Court of Appeal in *Jones* v. *Birch Bros.*[76] inclined to the view that such a clause would be caught, but it was held that one without the *Scott* v. *Avery* addition was valid. In view of the unlikelihood of arbitration ever being used in motor vehicle disputes,[77] the question seems totally academic now.

The proviso to section 148(2) in effect allows insurers to insert in their policies provisions allowing them to recover back from the insured money which they have had to pay to a third party only by virtue of the subsection. There is no automatic right given to insurers as there is under section 148(1), although it must be arguable that insurers would have that right in quasi-contract, as there is a general principle that a plaintiff compelled by law to make a payment discharging the defendant's liability to a third party can recover that sum from the defendant.[78]

Insurer's duty to satisfy judgments

The key provision so far as third parties are concerned is section 149. This provides that, provided that a certificate of insurance has been delivered to the insured, a judgment against him obtained in respect of liabilities compulsorily insurable must be satisfied by the insurer, whether or not the latter may have the right to avoid or cancel the policy. The award that must be satisfied includes costs and interest awarded. Thus, the third party in this field has a direct right against the insurer analogous to that provided under the Third Parties (Rights against Insurers)

---

[75] See pp. 284–288, above.
[76] [1933] 2 K.B. 597.
[77] See p. 204, above.
[78] See Goff and Jones, *The Law of Restitution*, (3rd ed.), Chap. 14.

Third Parties' Rights under the Road Traffic Act

Act 1930,[79] but much more extensive, in particular because of the provisions of section 148. This right is qualified, however, in four respects:

(1) It arises only where the insurer was given notice, formally,[80] of the proceedings against the insured before or within seven days of their commencement (s.149(2)(*a*)). This includes a counter claim by an injured defendant against an insured plaintiff, where appropriate.[81]

(2) It is not exercisable where execution of a judgment has been stayed pending an appeal (s.149(2)(*b*)).

(3) It does not apply if the insured's policy was cancelled before the relevant accident, either by mutual consent or under a term in the policy, and the certificate of insurance was surrendered or the insured made a statutory declaration that it was lost or destroyed within 14 days of the cancellation, or within the same period the insurer commenced proceedings in respect of the failure to surrender the certificate (s.149(2)(*c*)).

(4) It does not apply if the policy was obtained by non-disclosure or misrepresentation of a material fact and the insurer, within three months of the commencement of the proceedings against the insured obtains a declaration of the court to this effect, and the third party receives notice of the action for a declaration and the particulars of the non-disclosure or misrepresentation within seven days of its being commenced (s.149(3)).[82]

This last qualification raises some interesting points. Obviously it does not remove the insurer's right to avoid for non-disclosure or misrepresentation, but it limits the effectiveness of that right. However, it appears strictly not to include avoidance for breach of warranty, for example by virtue of a misstatement on a proposal form warranted to be true. Section 149(3) refers expressly to the insurer's right to avoid *apart from* any provisions contained in the policy, meaning only the general right to avoid given by the common law or equity.[83] Warranties arise from express provisions.[84] Thus, an insurer can avoid liability for breach of warranty as against the injured third party, without using the section 149(3) procedure, unless,

---

[79] See Chapter 18.
[80] *Herbert* v. *Railway Passengers Ass. Co.* [1938] 1 All E.R. 650.
[81] *Cross* v. *British Oak Ins. Co.* [1938] 2 K.B. 167.
[82] The third party has the right to be a party to this action.
[83] *Merchants' & Manufacturers' Ins. Co.* v. *Hunt* [1941] 1 K.B. 295.
[84] See generally, Chapters 5 and 7.

of course, the warranty relates to one of the matters in section 148(1), in which case the breach cannot be relied on at all. However, as was seen in an earlier chapter,[85] the cases have not always been too accurate in distinguishing non-disclosures, misrepresentation and warranties, and what appears strictly to be a breach of warranty has been treated as a misrepresentation or non-disclosure.[86]

Materiality is defined for the purposes of section 149(3) in the usual way, in subsection 5, namely, "of such a nature as to influence the judgment of a prudent insurer in determining whether he will take the risk and, if so, at what premium and on what conditions." However, it is not enough to show non-disclosure or misrepresentation of such a material fact. The insurer in this context must also show that he himself was induced by the non-disclosure or misrepresentation to issue the policy as section 149(3) requires that the insurer show that the policy was *obtained* by non-disclosure or misrepresentation.[87]

If insurers are liable under section 149 to satisfy judgment awarded to a third party, but could have avoided liability as between themselves and the insured, but chose not to do so, they can recover from the insured the amount paid to the third party (s.149(4)).

By section 150,[88] the fact that the insured goes bankrupt or dies insolvent or, if a company, goes into liquidation, administration or receivership, does not affect the liability of the insured in respect of compulsory insurance, notwithstanding anything in the Third Parties (Rights against Insurers) Act 1930. In other words, the sections in the Road Traffic Act regarding the third parties' rights continue to apply, but otherwise section 150 incorporates the statutory assignment of the 1930 Act.[89]

Information regarding insurance

Finally, under section 151, the driver against whom a claim is made in respect of damage compulsorily insurable is under a duty, enforceable by criminal penalties, on the demand of the third party, to give him information as to whether or not he was

---

[85] See Chapter 5.
[86] *Merchants' & Manufacturers' Ins. Co. v. Hunt*, above; compare *Zurich General Accident v. Morrison* [1942] 2 K.B. 53 which did concern a pure non-disclosure.
[87] *Zurich v. Morrison*, above.
[88] As amended by the Insolvency Acts 1985 and 1986.
[89] See Chapter 18.

insured and, if so, such details of his insurance as are specified in his certificate of insurance.

Third Parties' Rights against the Motor Insurers' Bureau

The lack of reported cases in recent years concerning the sections in the Road Traffic Act which have just been examined probably illustrates the relative unimportance of those sections since the M.I.B. was established. In 1937, the Cassel Committee[90] recommended that a central fund be established to protect the victims of road accidents who received no compensation despite the protection afforded by the Road Traffic Act. Obviously the Act could not cover the situation of the driver who did not, in fact, have insurance cover nor was it really relevant when 5¾5¾'99t" llvrer went into liquidation. Furthermore, as has been seen, there are occasions when an insurer can rely on terms in the policy to avoid liability to the third party despite sections 148 and 149 of the 1972 Act. Finally, the victim of an untraced or "hit and run" driver can of necessity not be protected by the statute. In this last respect, the Cassel Committee did not consider it practicable to give such victims rights against the fund and this remained the position until 1969, although they did have a discretionary entitlement before then.

It was probably fears of possible nationalisation of motor insurance business that led the motor insurers to conclude, on December 31, 1945, the first agreement between their creation, the M.I.B., and the Minister of Transport. It is now a condition of authorisation to transact motor insurance business that the insurer be a member of M.I.B. Ltd.[91] The important of the M.I.B. can be judged simply from the fact that, between 1946 and 1970, it paid out £5,263,893 to 12,861 applicants. There are now three agreements between M.I.B. and the Secretary of State for the Environment. What will be hereafter referred to as the first one is now dated November 22, 1972 and is in substance the original 1945 agreement with amendments, and is entitled "Compensation of Victims of Uninsured Drivers." The second agreement, bearing the same date, but being an amended version of one first agreed in 1969, is entitled "Compensation of Victims of Untraced Drivers." The third agreement dates from

---
[90] Cmnd. 5528, paras. 151–168.
[91] Road Traffic Act 1974, s.20.

1977, bears the same title as the second and provides for an accelerated procedure for claims in respect of the victim of hit and run drivers.[92]

The first M.I.B. agreement

This applies in respect of accidents occurring on or after December 1, 1972. It provides in essence that if a person injured or killed in a road accident obtains a judgment in respect of any liability required to be insured against and if that judgment is not satisfied in full within seven days, the M.I.B. will satisfy it. Thus, the first three categories of the uninsured driver, the driver without effective insurance and the driver whose insurer goes bankrupt are covered. However, the last case is now covered by the Policyholders Protection Act 1975,[93] under sections 6 and 7 of which the Policyholders Protection Board has a duty fully to satisfy the claims of the insured whose insurer becomes insolvent when the insurance was compulsory.

Different procedures operate depending upon whether or not the driver was insured, but his insurer was able to avoid liability. If this is so, that insurer normally acts as agent for the M.I.B., although the latter pays the claim. Only where there is no insurance or the insurer is not known is the claim made directly to the M.I.B.

There are a number of conditions precedent to M.I.B.'s liability and a number of exceptions. The conditions are

> (i) that notice is given before or within seven days of the commencement of the relevant proceedings to the M.I.B. or to the insurer concerned, depending on the procedure applicable; (ii) that M.I.B. is supplied with any information it reasonably requires; (iii) that if required, the applicant obtains judgment against all the tortfeasors involved; and (iv) that any judgment obtained is assigned to M.I.B.

Exceptions

The exceptions cover principally vehicles owned by the Crown, the cases where insurance is not compulsory under section 144 of the Road Traffic Act, unless, in fact, there is insurance in such a case, and cases where the victim was a passenger and party to some scheme to steal the vehicle or, being the owner of or using

---

[92] All the agreements are published by H.M.S.O. The first will be amended and possibly reissued because of the extension of M.I.B.'s liability under the Second Directive; see the end of this chapter.
[93] See Chapter 2.

the vehicle, he knew or had reason to believe that there was no insurance in force as required by the Road Traffic Act.

This last exception was the subject of *Porter* v. *M.I.B.*[94] The plaintiff had brought a car into the country from Holland but was not insured to drive it. She asked an acquaintance to do so, knowing that he drove a car and assuming that he was insured. In fact, he was not. He negligently caused an accident and injured the plaintiff. The M.I.B. argued that they were not bound to satisfy the judgment awarded against the friend by virtue of the exception, but it was held that they were liable. The exception was to be construed from the point of view of the victim. She assumed that the acquaintance was insured and there was nothing which should have caused her to have reason to believe otherwise.

It is as well to stress that the M.I.B. agreements apply only when insurance was compulsorily required so that if, for example, the accident in question did not happen on a road, the M.I.B. can, and does, take the point in defence.[95]

The first agreement covered hit and run victims only on an *ex gratia* basis, a most unsatisfactory state of affairs highlighted by the decision in *Adams* v. *Andrews*[96] and its sequel.[97] This was remedied in 1969.

The second M.I.B. agreement

This agreement is necessarily much more complex than the first, because there will of course be no judgment against a tortfeasor for the M.I.B. to satisfy. A number of conditions must be satisfied by an applicant for an award:

(1) The applicant must be unable to trace the person responsible for the death or injury or a person partly so responsible.

(2) The death or injury must have been caused in circumstances such that on the balance of probabilities the untraced person would have been liable to the applicant in damages.

(3) That liability must have been one required to be insured against under the 1972 Act; this is assumed in the absence of evidence to the contrary.

(4) The death or injury must not have been caused deliberately; this is presumably because such a victim would have a

---

[94] [1978] 2 Lloyd's Rep. 463.
[95] See, *e.g. Buchanan* v. *M.I.B.* [1955] 1 W.L.R. 488; *Randall* v. *M.I.B.* [1968] 1 W.L.R. 1900.
[96] [1964] 2 Lloyd's Rep. 349.
[97] A full account is given in Williams, *The Motor Insurers' Bureau*.

statutory claim from the Criminal Injuries Compensation Board.

(5) The application must be made in writing within three years of the accident.

Paragraph 2 of clause 1 contains exceptions which are much the same as the exceptions to the first agreement already mentioned.

The amount of compensation awarded to the applicant is assessed on the same basis as a court would assess damages in a tort action (clause 3) except that the M.I.B. does not award damages for pain and suffering or loss of expectation of life or loss of earnings in so far as they have been paid by the applicant's employer (clause 4).

Clause 5 contains the special provisions dealing with the cases where an untraced driver was only partly to blame for the accident. Here the applicant may be required to obtain judgment against the known driver or the known principal of an unidentified driver, or the applicant may have obtained such judgment without being required to do so. If this judgment is not satisfied at all within three months, M.I.B. awards an amount equal to the untraced person's contribution to a full award, namely, that proportion which a court would have awarded if proceedings had been taken against all the tortfeasors. If this judgment is only partly satisfied within three months, M.I.B. awards an amount equal to either the unsatisfied part of the judgment or the untraced person's contribution, whichever is the greater. If the applicant has not obtained, and is not required by M.I.B. to obtain, judgment against the known driver, and has not received any payment as compensation from any such person, the amount the M.I.B. awards is an amount equal to the untraced person's contribution to a full award.

Conditions precedent

Clause 6 specifies three conditions precedent to the liability of M.I.B., namely:

(1) The applicant must give all such assistance as M.I.B. reasonably requires to enable any necessary investigation to be carried out.

(2) If required, the applicant must take all reasonable steps to obtain judgment against any person or persons in respect of their liability to the applicant; this is subject to his being indemnified against costs by M.I.B.

(3) If required, the applicant must assign to M.I.B., or their

nominee, any judgment obtained by him; if this produces a surplus over what the M.I.B. paid the applicant, the M.I.B. is accountable for this after deducting the reasonable expenses of the recovery of the sum for which the judgment was given.

By virtue of clause 8, if required to do so, the applicant must furnish a statutory declaration concerning the facts and circumstances upon which his claim is based.

Investigation and report

M.I.B. must, by clause 7, investigate any claim made to them. They may decide that the case is not one covered by the agreement and thus reject it giving these reasons (clause 9(1)). Otherwise they must cause a report to be made on the basis of which they must decide whether to make an award and the amount of the award. The meaning of clause 7 and of other clauses in the agreement was considered in *Persson* v. *London Country Buses*.[98] P, a bus conductor employed by the first defendants, was injured when the bus he was on stopped suddenly. The first defendants rejected his claim against them on the ground that the accident was caused not by the bus driver but by another motorist. This motorist was untraced and so P made a claim against the M.I.B. This was rejected on the ground that M.I.B. were not satisfied that in the circumstances the untraced driver would have been liable. P then claimed to sue M.I.B. without pursuing his rights of appeal under the agreement. This point will be considered later, but in the course of the case the court considered the basic nature of M.I.B.'s obligations under clauses 3 and 7. Clause 3 states that M.I.B. "shall award" such damages as a court would, which, P argued, put them under an obligation to do so. It was held, however, that clause 3 was expressly subject to the later provisions in the agreement, including clause 7. Under clause 7 M.I.B. has a duty to make a decision in respect of an award, but not actually to make an award if they consider that the facts do not warrant it.

Decision and appeals

Clause 9 provides that when M.I.B. has decided whether or not to make a payment, they must notify the applicant of their decision, setting out the circumstances and evidence of the death or injury, and, if they refuse to make an award, the reasons for that refusal. Clauses 11 onwards deal with appeals. The applicant may appeal against any decision unfavourable to him, including on the *quantum* of the award, within six weeks,

[98] [1974] 1 All E.R. 1251.

to an arbitrator. The latter must be a Queen's Counsel selected by the Secretary of State from a panel. He may also or alternatively make comments to the M.I.B. which may result in further consideration. If there is further communication from M.I.B. following such comments, the applicant has six weeks from the date of this communication to consider his appeal. Clause 12 provides that when appealing, the applicant must undertake to abide by the decision of the arbitrator.

Where the appeal is only on *quantum*, the M.I.B. may ask the arbitrator to consider also the issue of liability (cl. 14). M.I.B. sends all the relevant documents to the arbitrator, who can ask for further investigation (cl. 15). The applicant must be allowed to comment on such further investigation (cl. 17). If the arbitrator considers the appeal to be unreasonable, he may award that the applicant pay his fees. Otherwise, these are born by the M.I.B. and each party to the appeal bears its own costs (cl. 21 and 22).

The result of the provisions regarding appeals, in particular the undertaking required under clause 12, is that on questions of fact, the applicant has no recourse to the courts. *Persson's* case[99] decided that the applicant's action against the M.I.B. disclosed no cause of action, since P had not complied with the provisions for appeal in the agreement, in accordance with the general principle that where the parties to a contract have agreed in language which clearly shows who is to decide certain facts, then no right of action in the courts is vested in the parties until the facts have been decided according to the contract.[1] The arbitrator's decision will thus be final unless he or M.I.B. have misapplied the law. Legal problems for decision by the court may arise on, for example, the construction of the agreement itself, on whether or not a case is within the Road Traffic Act requirements, or if the arbitrator has placed the burden of proof on the wrong person.[2]

The third M.I.B. agreement

As was seen earlier, the third agreement dating from 1977 also deals with the victims of untraced drivers. It provides for a quicker procedure for settling such claims where no known motorist was involved. After a preliminary investigation, M.I.B. may instead of making a report simply offer a sum in compensation to the applicant, assessed as under the second agree-

---

[99] See note 98.
[1] *Cipriani* v. *Barnett* [1933] A.C. 83.
[2] See, *e.g. Elizabeth* v. *M.I.B.* [1981] R.T.R. 405.

ment. If that offer is accepted, in the form specified in the schedule to the third agreement, that concludes the matter and there is no right of appeal to an arbitrator. If the offer is not accepted, the matter will be determined in accordance with the procedure under the principal agreement.

Procedural questions

A number of procedural questions have arisen in the context of the M.I.B. agreements. The first relates to their enforcement. It is clear that, if necessary, the Secretary of State could sue M.I.B. as a party to the agreements which in law are binding contracts as given under seal. On the other hand, strictly speaking, an injured person has no right to enforce any of the agreements, not being a party to them, though it may be that he could enforce them indirectly by joining the Secretary of State as a party to an action brought against M.I.B.,[3] and he could enforce a judgment awarded against M.I.B. in favour of the Secretary of State.[4] In practice this is all rather academic. M.I.B. has been sued on a number of occasions by injured third parties and has said that it will never take the point of privity.[5] Should it ever be so minded, there can be little doubt that legislation would follow.

Joinder of M.I.B.

Another more important point concerns the right of M.I.B. to be joined as a defendant in an action brought by an injured third party. Order 15, rule 6(2)(b) of the Rules of the Supreme Court now authorises the joinder as a party of "any person between whom and any party to the cause or matter there may exist a question or issue arising out of or relating to or connected with any relief or remedy claimed in the cause or matter which in the opinion of the court it would be just and convenient to determine as between him and that party as well as between the parties to the cause or matter." Even before the wider wording of this rule was introduced, it was held that M.I.B. could be joined in an action against an uninsured driver.[6] There can be no doubt now that the court will allow

---

[3] See Lord Denning M.R. in *Gurtner* v. *Circuit* [1968] 1 All E.R. 328.
[4] Ibid.
[5] See, *e.g. Albert* v. *M.I.B.* [1972] A.C. 301; *Coward* v. *M.I.B.* [1963] 1 Q.B. 259 at 265.
[6] *Gurtner* v. *Circuit*, above, overruling *Fire, Auto & Marine Ins. Co.* v. *Greene* [1964] 2 Q.B. 687.

M.I.B. to be joined as a defendant when liability may arise on them under the first agreement.

The second and third agreements raise different issues. In the normal event, of course, there will be no action, the defendant being untraced. But, as has been seen, under the second agreement, the M.I.B. can require the applicant to take action against identified persons who may have been partly responsible. In this sort of case, it was held in *White* v. *London Transport Executive*,[7] under the former wording of R.S.C. Ord. 15, rule 6(2)(*b*), that M.I.B. could not claim to be joined as it was not necessary to do so. Under the terms of the second agreement, M.I.B. will in practice be "behind" the plaintiff because of the considerable powers of control the agreement gives them. No doubt the same view would be taken even though the court has a broader discretion under the amended rule.

Substituted service

Finally, the question has arisen as to the right of an injured plaintiff to obtain an order for substituted service of his writ claiming damages on M.I.B., under R.S.C. Ord. 65, rule 4, when it is not possible to serve the writ on the tortfeasor. In *Clarke* v. *Vedel*,[8] the plaintiff was run down by a motor cyclist who gave his name as David Vedel. In fact there was no record of the birth of a David Vedel at the date of birth the driver gave and no such person at the address he gave. Nonetheless the plaintiff sued "David Vedel" and, being unable to serve the writ, successfully obtained an order for substituted service on the M.I.B. The Court of Appeal confirmed that the order should be set aside. In effect, the negligent driver was untraceable, so that the M.I.B. agreement applicable was the second one under which there is no right to sue M.I.B. unless and until they have refused to consider an application. Only if the plaintiff's cause of action is truly against an uninsured driver can such an order be obtained.

Extension of Compulsory Requirements

As mentioned earlier in this chapter, implementation of the Second E.E.C. Directive on Motor Insurance will extend and

---

[7] [1971] 3 All E.R. 1.
[8] [1979] R.T.R. 26.

modify the requirements of the Road Traffic Act 1972.[9] The Motor Vehicles (Compulsory Insurance) Regulations 1987[10] implement the Directive as from December 31, 1988. They do so simply by amending sections of the 1972 Act.

Extended obligation to insure

First, section 145(3)(*a*)[11] will be replaced by a requirement to insure against liability for damage to property as well as liability for death or bodily injury.[12] Second, the exceptions in section 145(4) are replaced by a more comprehensive list.[13] This includes the existing cases of employment and contractual liabilities[14] and what will be the new section 145(4)(*b*) allows for a limit of £250,000 in respect of "damage to property caused by or arising out of any one accident involving the vehicle."[15] It will be expressly provided that it is not compulsory to insure against liability in respect of damage to the vehicle, liability in respect of damage to goods carried for hire or reward in or on the vehicle and liability of a person in respect of damage to property in his custody or under his control, for example the belongings of passengers.

Third parties' rights

The other amendment is of section 149 by regulation 3.[16] The substantial change will be the replacement of section 149(1) by new subsections (1) to (1E). In part these new subsections merely reflect the new compulsory requirements by extending the insurer's duty to satisfy judgments in respect of property damage up to the £250,000 limit of compulsory insurance.[17] However, they also effect more fundamental changes.

First, as against the third party injured or killed or whose

[9] There will also be amendments to the M.I.B. agreement on uninsured drivers, as described below. There will not be any extension of the untraced drivers' agreement to cases of property damage.

[10] This account is based on the draft regulations; at the time of writing the statutory instrument had not been laid before Parliament.

[11] See p. 294, above.

[12] Reg. 2(2).

[13] Reg. 2(3).

[14] See p. 294, above.

[15] This limit is much higher than that required by the Directive. Most policies on private vehicles do not have a limit though commercial policies often do. A limit has been adopted in order to limit the effect on the M.I.B. in cases of uninsured drivers. Note the broad construction of "accident" in this sort of context; see p. 290, above.

[16] Note that there is no change to the terms of s.148; see p. 306, above and note 22 below.

[17] There are some complicated qualifications here.

property is damaged, an insurer will not be able to rely upon the driver of the vehicle who caused the accident not being a permitted driver under the terms of the insured's insurance,[18] unless the third party was allowing himself to be carried in or upon the vehicle and knew or had reason to believe that the vehicle had been stolen or unlawfully taken.[19] The effect of this must be, for example, that if a car thief, driving the stolen car, injures or kills someone or damages someone's property, the insurer of the car's owner must satisfy the plaintiff's judgment against the thief.[20] However, the insurer can recover what it has to pay from the driver.[21]

Second, any condition in a policy which purports to restrict its operation by requiring a driver to hold a licence to drive is invalid as respects the insurer's duty to satisfy judgments.[22] Again, an insurer can recover the amount it has to pay out from the unlicensed driver.[23]

Changes to the M.I.B. agreements

The uninsured drivers' agreement, the first agreement described earlier,[24] will be amended to cover cases of property damage, although the detail is not known at the time of writing. It appears likely from the Department of Transport's consultative document on the Directive that there will probably be an excess in operation, *i.e.* claims below a certain figure will not be recoverable from the M.I.B., and it may be that the victim in the case of property damage will have no recourse against the M.I.B. when he has recovered under his own insurance, *e.g.* under his comprehensive motor policy in respect of damage to his car and under his buildings policy in respect of damage to his house. As the consultative document recognised, in respect of motor policies this might will have an adverse effect on motor insured's no claims discounts. There may also be a strict time-limit on applications to the M.I.B. regarding property damage claims.

---

[18] The new s.149(1A)(b).

[19] The new s.149(1C), unless he did not realise this until after the journey commenced and could not reasonably be expected to have alighted from the vehicle.

[20] As opposed to the present situation in respect of personal injury claims when the M.I.B. is liable.

[21] The new s.149(4B).

[22] *Quaere* why this was not introduced by amending the list in s.148(1).

[23] The new s.149(4A).

[24] See pp. 312–313.

Chapter 20

EMPLOYERS' LIABILITY AND OTHER COMPULSORY INSURANCES

In this chapter will be examined the heads of and the rules peculiar to those liability insurances other than motor insurance which are compulsory. Foremost among these is employers' liability insurance.

EMPLOYERS' LIABILITY INSURANCE

An employee injured at work has, broadly speaking, the right to claim compensation from the State, regardless of questions of fault, under the social security legislation.[1] This replaced workmen's compensation which was an important class of insurance business for many years. The employee who can show that his employer, or someone for whom the latter is responsible, was at fault in some way will also have the right to claim damages in tort from him. This may be in negligence or it may be for breach of statutory duty. Statistically, work accidents rank with road accidents as the most common source of tort actions. Against an employer who is not insured or not effectively insured this tort action may be worthless. Some notorious instances of employers being without cover led to the enactment of the Employers' Liability (Compulsory Insurance) Act 1969.

Section 1(1) provides that, subject to some exceptions which will be considered later, every employer carrying on any business in Great Britain shall insure and maintain insurance under one or more approved policies with an authorised insurer against liability for bodily injury or disease sustained by his employees, and arising out of and in the course of their employment in Great Britain in that business, but except in so far as regulations otherwise provide, not including injury or disease suffered or contracted outside Great Britain.[2]

---

[1] Strictly this legislation covers "employed earners" which is wider than "employees." See generally Ogus and Barendt, *Law of Social Security* (2nd ed.), Chapter 8.

[2] The Act was brought into force on January 1, 1972 by the Employers' Liability (Compulsory Insurance) Regulations (S.I. 1971 No. 117), hereafter referred to as the "Regulations."

As with motor insurance, a policy effected by an employer can be wider than the statute prescribes. For example, it might not be limited to liability "arising out of and in the course of employment." In practice, though, this phrase does appear as the standard limit in employer's liability policies. Its meaning is thus important both for this reason and because it defines the scope of the statutory requirement. The phrase also appears in the Road Traffic Act 1972,[3] and it was the classic formula in the workmen's compensation legislation. It is clear that it has the same meaning in any of these contexts where it survives unchanged, but the fact that its meaning has been enlarged in the social security context[4] must be ignored.[5]

Out of and in the course of employment

On the other hand, the formula is still the basic one for industrial injury benefit purposes, and it must be the case that decisions on its interpretation in the statutory context which are not concerned with the statutory extensions are of relevance to its meaning in an employer's liability policy and section 1 of the 1969 Act. There is an incredible number of decisions on its meaning in social security legislation, but this is not the place where those decisions can be considered in any detail.[6] One or two will, however, be referred to. Broadly, the formula covers two different principles. "In the course of employment" means that "the accident must arise when the employee is doing what a man so employed might reasonably do during a time during which he was employed and at a place where he may reasonably be during that time to do that thing."[7] Therefore, employees travelling to and from work are not in the course of their employment, even if travelling in vehicles provided by their employers, unless their terms of employment oblige them so to travel.[8] In *Vandyke* v. *Fender*,[9] V and F were employees of R

---

[3] s.145; see p. 294, above.
[4] See, *e.g.* Social Security Act 1975, s.53.
[5] *Vandyke* v. *Fender* [1970] 2 Q.B. 292.
[6] See, *e.g.* Ogus and Barendt, *op. cit.*, pp. 271–287.
[7] Lord Loreburn in *Moore* v. *Manchester Liners Ltd.* [1910] A.C. 498 at 500–501.
[8] Note, however, that in an industrial injury benefit case, the test of obligation to travel has been held inapplicable: *Nancollas* v. *Insurance Officer* [1985] 1 All E.R. 833. Doubt was raised by Donaldson M.R. on the interpretation of old workmen's compensation cases put forward in *Vandyke* v. *Fender* (see below). It may be therefore that when the opportunity arises in a dispute on an employers' liability policy, the courts will adopt the view of the *Nancollas* case that there is no overriding principle concerning whether or not travel is in the course of employment.
[9] [1970] 2 Q.B. 292.

Ltd. They worked some distance from home and R Ltd. agreed to provide a car in which F would drive himself and V to work. R Ltd. also paid an amount towards petrol costs. While they were driving to work one day, V was injured owing to F's negligence. One of the questions for decision was whether R Ltd.'s employer's liability insurers were liable to pick up the bill or whether the relevant motor insurer[10] was liable. It was held that the employer's liability insurer was not liable as the accident did not arise in the course of employment, V not being obliged to travel in the car. In contrast, in *Paterson v. Costain & Press (Overseas) Ltd.*,[11] the plaintiff employee was injured due to the negligence of his employer's driver while being taken from the office to the construction site where the plaintiff had been told that he was required. It was the defendant employer's practice to transport their employees to the site. It was held that the accident did arise in the course of the plaintiff's employment as he was in the vehicle under an obligation to go to the site in obedience to what he had been told. The defendant's employers' liability insurers were therefore liable to indemnify them against their liability to the plaintiff.

Even an accident at work is not necessarily in the course of employment. A policeman playing football for his force in a match against another force at the force sports ground was held not to be covered for state compensation when he was injured during the match even though participation was expected of him.[12] The Court of Appeal rejected the argument that "in the course of employment" includes matters reasonably incidental to employment, except where the accident occurs at the place of work during an interruption, for example, for a tea break.

If an employee is injured outside his strict hours of work, this will not necessarily not be in the course of employment. A reasonable period at the beginning and end of work will usually be included.[13]

The other limb of the formula, namely, "out of employment," is somewhat looser. Essentially it requires a causal connection between the employment and the accident. It seems unlikely that it can give rise to any problems in the employers' liability insurance field. If an employer has been adjudged or has agreed to be legally liable in tort to an employee, a necessary precondi-

---

[10] In fact, the M.I.B., as the motor insurer had failed.
[11] [1979] 2 Lloyd's Rep. 204.
[12] *R. v. National Insurance Commissioner, ex parte Michael* [1977] 1 W.L.R. 109.
[13] See, *e.g. R. v. National Insurance Commissioner, ex parte East* [1976] I.C.R. 206.

tion of the insurers' liability, it must follow that the liability of the employer arose out of the employee's employment.

Employees covered

Section 2 of the 1969 Act defines "employee" for the purposes of the obligation to insure under section 1. It means anyone who works under a contract of service or apprenticeship, express or implied, written or oral, thus excluding any obligation to insure against liability to the self-employed, those who work under a contract for services. The distinction between a contract of service and a contract for services can be a fine one. It has caused problems in many areas of the law and reference should be made elsewhere for details.[14] Section 2(2) also excludes the obligation to insure in respect of employees who are close relatives within the list specified and employees not ordinarily resident in Great Britain except in so far as regulations provide otherwise.[15]

Prohibited conditions

There is one further point in connection with section 1(1) of the Act. This requires that insurance be by "approved policies," defined as policies of insurance "not subject to any conditions or exceptions prohibited for these purposes by regulations" (s.1(3)). The regulations which brought the Act into effect duly list four prohibited conditions "in whatever terms" which will be examined shortly. It is clear that the prohibited conditions may not be conditions in the strict sense; they may be warranties. However, they are only prohibited if they are conditions precedent to liability under the policy, either generally (*i.e.* as warranties) or in respect of a particular claim (*i.e.* as conditions precedent). Thus it is perfectly permissible to have conditions which are not precedent to liability, but merely give the insurer the right to claim damages for breach. This is confirmed by regulation 2(2), whereby a policy can expressly provide for the insured to pay the insurer any sums which the insurer is liable to pay and which have been paid to employees.

The conditions prohibited are those "providing that no liability shall arise or liability shall cease":

(*a*) "in the event of some specified thing being done or omit-

---

[14] See, *e.g.* Smith & Wood, *Industrial Law*, 3rd ed., chapter 1.
[15] Note Regulation 4.

ted to be done after the happening of the event giving rise to a claim under the policy."

This is analogous to section 148(2) of the Road Traffic Act 1972,[16] and covers such matters as failure to give notice or particulars of loss in time and unauthorised admissions of liability. Thus, it reverses *Farrell* v. *Federated Employers Insurance Co.*,[17] but it may be doubted whether it prohibits a condition making the prior payment of due premiums by the insured precedent to liability, as it only covers things "after the happening of the event. . . . "[18]

> (b) "unless the policyholder takes reasonable care to protect his employees against the risk of bodily injury or disease in the course of employment"

As has been seen earlier,[19] the courts have interpreted conditions in liability policies generally requiring the insured to take reasonable care as applicable only if an employer is more than merely negligent, so in this sense the prohibition changes nothing. Even recklessness would not entitle an insurer to avoid liability, it is suggested, if it relies merely upon a condition to take reasonable care, for such a condition is prohibited.[20] However, a condition expressly providing that recklessness debars liability would arguably be enforceable.

> (c) "unless the policyholder complies with the requirements of any enactment for the protection of employees against the risk of bodily injury or disease in the course of their employment."

The meaning of this is evident.

> (d) "unless the policyholder keeps specified records or provides the insurer with or makes available to him information therefrom."

It is not uncommon for premiums for employers' liability policies to be adjusted by reference to wages and salaries actually

---

[16] See p. 308, above.
[17] [1970] 1 W.L.R. 1400; see p. 283, above.
[18] See *Murray* v. *Legal & General Ass. Co.* [1969] 3 All E.R. 794, discussed at p. 283, above.
[19] Chapter 18, p. 289.
[20] *Contra* Hasson, "The Employers' Liability (Compulsory Insurance) Act—A Broken Reed" [1974] I.L.J. 79 at 84, esp. note 32.

paid by the employer, and for the policy to provide for the keeping of records for this purpose. Failure to comply cannot now defeat an employee's claim.[21]

Sums insured

Employers are not required to maintain policies with no limit on the maximum liability of the insurer, but policies must have a sum insured of £2 million in respect of claims relating to any one or more of their employees arising out of any one occurrence.[22]

Exceptions

Section 3 of the 1969 Act exempts certain employers altogether from the requirement to insure. Basically these are certain local government councils, nationalised industries and any employer specifically exempted by regulations. The latter[23] list a number of other public bodies which are exempt.

Enforcement

Enforcement of the 1969 Act is effected by first ensuring the display of certificates of insurance, secondly permitting inspections of certificates and policies, and thirdly by criminal penalties.[24]

Section 4(1) requires insurers to issue certificates in the form prescribed in the Regulations, and regulation 6 requires these to be displayed at any place of business where an employer employs any person whose claims may be the subject of indemnity under the insurance. Employers must produce their certificates, or copies, to an officer of the Health and Safety Executive on being served with notice to do so.[25] In addition, any inspector authorised by the Secretary of State can demand to inspect any policy of employers' liability insurance on reasonable notice.[26]

---

[21] With respect, Hasson, *op. cit.* at 85, is wrong to suggest that this "merely restates the common law rule." Although such a condition was held not to be precedent to liability in *Re Bradley and Essex and Suffolk Accident Indemnity Soc.* [1912] 1 K.B. 415 (see p. 118, above), this was on the construction of the policy in question, not as a general rule.

[22] s.1(2) and Regulation 3. As to "occurrence," see p. 290, above.

[23] S.I. 1971, No. 1933, S.I. 1974, No. 208 and S.I. 1981, No. 1489.

[24] As to the penalty, see s.5.

[25] s.4(2) and Reg. 7 (as substituted by S.I. 1975 No. 194).

[26] s.4(2) and Reg. 8.

Comment[27]

When compared with the Road Traffic Act provisions relating to third party motor insurance, the 1969 Act and the regulations made thereunder appear paltry and maybe even inadequate. There is no mechanism whereby the injured employee can recover directly from the insurer, save where his employer goes bankrupt and he can use the provisions of the Third Parties (Rights against Insurers) Act 1930.[28] There are no restrictions on the right of the insurer to avoid the policy for non-disclosure, misrepresentation or breach of warranty, and it is conceivable, though perhaps unlikely in practice, that policies could contain quite wide-ranging exceptions not falling foul of the prohibitions in regulation 2. Perhaps most importantly, if an employer is not insured or not effectively insured, there is no equivalent of the Motor Insurers' Bureau. These deficiencies seem all the stranger when it is considered that the event which gave the final impetus to the enactment of the Act was a fire in Glasgow when the employer's insurers successfully avoided liability for non-disclosure and injured employees were uncompensated. It can hardly be denied that the compulsory insurance scheme for employers is a half-hearted system.

OTHER COMPULSORY INSURANCES

There are a number of other instances where third party insurance is in effect compulsory although in none of these are there any provisions affecting the contractual position between insurer and insured. The most important of these are the following. Professional indemnity insurance may be required, not by statute, but by the rules of the profession. If, as for example is the case with the Law Society, one has to be a member of the body concerned in order to practice, insurance is effectively compulsory. In this particular instance, the Law Society now operates a self-insurance scheme to which all solicitors must subscribe. Insurance is required by statute or by rules made under statutory authority in an increasing number of similar cases.[29]

Riding Establishments are required to insure against their

---

[27] See also Hasson, *op. cit.* and Simpson (1972) 35 M.L.R. 63.
[28] Chapter 18.
[29] For example, under the Insurance Brokers Registration Act 1977, the Estate Agents Act 1979 and rules made under the auspices of the Financial Services Act 1986.

liability to those who hire and use their horses and against the liability of the latter for injury to third parties.[30] The operator of a nuclear establishment is required to effect insurance under the Nuclear Installations Act 1965–1969, though this is done in a rather special way with a committee of insurers. Although statute does not in terms require it, aircraft operators are in practice required to insure against third party liabilities because an applicant for an air service licence must state what provision he has or proposes to have in respect of such insurance,[31] and an applicant providing an unsatisfactory answer is hardly likely to be granted a licence.

---

[30] Riding Establishments Act 1964, s.1.
[31] Civil Aviation (Licensing) Regulations 1964 (S.I. 1964 No. 1116) made under Civil Aviation (Licensing) Act 1960, s.2.

INDEX

ACCIDENT. *See also* ACCIDENT
    INSURANCE.
  as limit in liability policies, 290
  as limit in motor insurance, 319
  meaning, 171–179
ACCIDENT INSURANCE,
  causation, 186–188
  meaning of accident, 171–179
  measurement of loss, 215
  subrogation and, 236
  whether contract of indemnity, 236–237
ADVERTISEMENT, 58
AGENT. *See also* BROKER.
  actual authority, 141–142
  apparent authority, 142–143
  cover-notes, 62–63
  duty of care and skill, 146–151
  fiduciary duties, 145–146
  imputation of knowledge to principal, 85–86, 112–114, 144–145
  ostensible authority, 142–143
  proposal forms, 111–116
  ratification, 48, 49–50, 143
  regulation of, 4, 151–156
  types of, 137–138
  whether insured's or insurer's, 138–140
ALL RISKS, 169
ARBITRATION, 204–206
  Personal Insurances Arbitration Service, 4, 204
ARBITRATION CLAUSE,
  independent validity, 205–206
  motor policies, 308
  non-enforcement, 204–205
ASSIGNMENT,
  benefit of insurance policy, 132–135
  cause of action, 249
  life policies, 270–273
  non-life policies, 135–136
  subject matter of policy, 128–132
AVERAGE, 227

BAILEE. *See* BAILMENT.

BAILMENT,
  double insurance, 260–261
  insurance by bailee, 46–48
  subrogation, 251–253
BASIS OF THE CONTRACT CLAUSE, 106–108
BROKER. *See also* AGENT.
  duties, 145–151
  Lloyd's, 137, 138
  regulation, 153–155
  types, 137–138

CAUSATION. *See* PROXIMATE CAUSE.
CANCELLATION CLAUSES, 68–69
CANCELLATION OF LIFE POLICIES, 59–60
CLAIMS PROCEDURE,
  arbitration, 204–206
  conditions regarding, 116–117
  fraudulent claims, 209–211
  notice of loss, 199–201
  particulars of loss, 201–204
  settlement of claims, 211–214
  waiver and estoppel, 206–209
CLAUSES DESCRIPTIVE OF THE RISK, 109–111
COMPREHENSIVE, 160, 168, 292
COMPULSORY INSURANCE. *See also* MOTOR INSURANCE, EMPLOYERS' LIABILITY INSURANCE.
  public policy, 194–195
  types of, 327–328
CONDITIONS,
  distinction from warranties, 75, 104–105
  double insurance, 265–269
  employers' liability insurance, 324–326
  liability insurance, 284–289
  mere, 117–119
  motor insurance, 303–306
  nature of, 116–119
  practice, 120
  precedent, 75, 104–105, 117–119
  proof of breach, 119
  subrogation, 249–251
  suspensive, 75
  types of, 116–117

Index

CONDITIONS PRECEDENT. *See* CONDITIONS.
CONSEQUENTIAL LOSSES, 44, 182
CONSTRUCTION,
  accident, 171–179
  context, 165–166
  contra proferentem, 166–168
  fire, 169–171
  general, 157–158
  legibility, 158–159
  loss, 179–181
  ordinary meaning, 164
  principles, 163–164
  reasonable expectations, 159–161
  specific descriptions, 168–169
  technical meaning, 164–165
CONSUMER CREDIT ACT 1974,
  life policies, 271
  premiums, 122
CONTINGENCY INSURANCE. *See* LIFE INSURANCE.
CONTRA PROFERENTEM, 166–168
CONTRACT OF INSURANCE,
  contract of adhesion, 160
  cover-note. *See* COVER-NOTES.
  definition, 7–14
  duration and renewal, 67–71
  formalities. *See* FORMALITIES.
  formation. *See* FORMATION OF INSURANCE CONTRACT.
  history, 1–3
  meaning, 7–14
  parties, 15–22
  reform and practice, 3–5
CONTRACTORS' INSURANCE,
  subrogation, 253
  third parties interests, 47–48
CONTRIBUTION. *See also* DOUBLE INSURANCE.
  nature, 259
  rateable proportion clauses, 259
  ratio, 262–264
  requirements, 259–262
  subrogation compared, 259
COVER-NOTES,
  authority of agent, 62–63
  contract, 63–64
  motor insurance, 296
  relationship with policy, 67
  termination, 67
  terms, 64–67
CRIME,
  public policy rules, 191–198
  word in insurance policy, 164–165

CRIMINAL CONVICTIONS,
  duty to disclose, 91–94

DAYS OF GRACE, 70–71
DISCLOSURE, DUTY OF. *See* NON-DISCLOSURE.
  insurers, 80–81
DOUBLE INSURANCE. *See also* CONTRIBUTION.
  conditions ousting liability, 265–267
  conditions requiring notification, 267–269
  nature of, 259–262

EEC,
  draft directive on insurance contract law, 96
  freedom of establishment, 16–17
  freedom of services, 17, 96
  motor insurance, 318–320
EIUSDEM GENERIS, 163
EMPLOYERS' LIABILITY INSURANCE,
  conditions prohibited, 324–326
  deficiencies, 327
  enforcement, 326
  exceptions, 326
  obligation, 321–324
  public policy, 194–195
  sums insured, 326
ESTOPPEL,
  regarding claims, 206–209
  regarding liability cover, 286–287
EX TURPI CAUSA NON ORITUR ACTIO, 190
EXCESS CLAUSES, 227, 254

FIRE, 169–171
FIRE INSURANCE. *See also* REAL PROPERTY.
  history, 3
  meaning, 169–171
  reinstatement. *See* REINSTATEMENT.
FLOOD, 166
FORFEITURE ACT 1982, 192
FORMALITIES, 58–60
FORMATION OF CONTRACT,
  acceptance, 56–57
  advertisements, 58
  changes in risk, 56
  counter-offer, 55–56
  inducements, 58
  Lloyd's, 60–61
  offer, 53–54
  proposal form. *See* PROPOSAL FORM.
FRANCHISE CLAUSES, 227–228

Index

FRAUD,
    claims, 209–211
    pre-contractual, 78
FRAUDULENT CLAIMS, 209–211

GOODS,
    insurable interest, 44–50
    loss, 179–181
    meaning, 45
    "new for old", 219
    partial loss, 221–223
    sale, 42, 130–132, 134–135
    third parties' interest, 46–50
    total loss, 217–219

HIRE-PURCHASE CONTRACT,
    insurable interest, 42
    measure of indemnity, 224
    reinstatement, 235
    subrogation, 253

ILLEGALITY,
    contract, 72–73
    insurable interest, 35
    performance. *See* PUBLIC POLICY.
    recovery of premiums. *See*
        PREMIUMS.
    statutory, 73
    unauthorised insurer, 73
    use of insured property, 73
INCREASE OF RISK, 94–96
INDEMNITY, PRINCIPLE OF, 7, 25, 38, 39, 43, 44, 215, 236, *and see* MEASUREMENT OF LOSS.
INHERENT VICE, 169
INSURABLE INTEREST. *See also* INSURABLE INTEREST IN LIFE INSURANCE, INSURABLE INTEREST IN PROPERTY INSURANCE.
    common law requirements, 24–25
    history, 24–25
    statutory requirements, 25
    wagers, 24, 25, 36
INSURABLE INTEREST IN LIFE INSURANCE,
    business relationships, 31–33
    failure to show, 35
    family relationships, 29–31
    husband and wife, 29
    insertion of names, 33–35
    law reform, 35–36
    parent and child, 29–31
    pecuniary interest, 28–29
    premiums, 125–127

INSURABLE INTEREST IN LIFE INSURANCE—*cont*.
    trusts of life policies, 275–276
    time, 26–28
INSURABLE INTEREST IN PROPERTY INSURANCE,
    common law, 25, 37
    creditor, 41
    factual expectation of loss, 40
    hire-purchase, 42
    landlord and tenant, 43
    meaning, 39–44
    possession, 42
    proprietary right, 40–41
    relationship with indemnity, 215
    sale of goods, 42
    shareholder, 41
    spouses, 42–43
    statutory requirements, 36–39
    third parties' interests, 46–52
    time, 36–39
    waiver, 44–45
INSURANCE,
    classifications, 5–7
    definition, 7–14
    history, 1–3
    nature, 8–9, 161–163
    practice, 3–5
    terminology, 7
INSURANCE OMBUDSMAN BUREAU, 4–5, 162
INSURED, 15, *and see* INSURABLE INTEREST.
INSURER. *See* REGULATION OF INSURERS.
INTERMEDIARIES. *See* AGENT, BROKER.
INTEREST, RECOVERY OF,
    insured's claim, 228
    subrogation, 248–249

JOINT INSURANCES, 211, 252

LAND. *See* REAL PROPERTY.
LANDLORD AND TENANT,
    contribution, 262
    indemnity, 224–225
    insurable interest, 36–37, 43, 50–52
    reinstatement, 234
    subrogation, 251–252
LAW COMMISSION, 4, 96–98, 119–120
LIABILITY INSURANCE. *See also* COMPULSORY INSURANCE, EMPLOYERS' LIABILITY INSURANCE *and* MOTOR INSURANCE.
    accident, 174–179

LIABILITY INSURANCE—*cont.*
  admissions of liability, 287–288
  contribution, 263–264
  control of proceedings, 284–286
  duty of insured, 289
  duty of insurer to insured, 284–286
  duty of insurer to victim, 291
  nature, 5–6
  public policy, 192–197
  Q.C. clause, 284
  sums insured, 289–291
  third parties' rights, 280–284
LIBEL, 191
LIFE INSURANCE,
  assignment, 270–273
  cancellation, 59–60
  contingency contract, 6–7, 163, 215
  cooling-off, 59–60
  days of grace, 70–71
  forms, 6–7, 270
  group policies, 278–279
  indemnity aspects, 27–28, 32, 237
  insurable interest. *See* INSURABLE INTEREST IN LIFE INSURANCE.
  investment nature, 6, 59, 270
  Married Women's Property Act policies, 274–275
  mortgages, 271–272
  public policy, 190–192
  subrogation, 237
  suicide, 191–192
  surrender, 69
  surrender values, 69, 270
  terminology, 7
  trusts, 273–279
LLOYD'S. *See also* BROKER.
  authorisation, 17–18
  formation of contract, 60–61
  nature of, 2
  reinstatement, 232
LOSS,
  deliberate act, 161–162, 190–191
  cause. *See* PROXIMATE CAUSE.
  consequential, 182
  constructive total, 179
  costs of prevention, 183–184
  general, 179–181
  insured peril imminent, 183
  measure. *See* MEASUREMENT OF LOSS.
  negligent act, 162, 289
  notice, 199–201
  partial, 216–217
  particulars, 201–203
  total, 216–217

MARINE INSURANCE, 1–3, 24–25, 58, 73, 79, 88, 136, 179, 184, 210, 242, 303–304
MATERIAL FACTS. *See* NON-DISCLOSURE.
MEASUREMENT OF LOSS,
  betterment, 221, 223
  damages, 216
  excess clauses, 227
  franchise clauses, 227–228
  general, 215–235
  insured with limited interest, 224–225
  interest, 228
  partial loss, 221–223
  replacement value, 219
  reinstatement cost, 222–223
  sum insured, 215–216
  total loss of goods, 217–219
  total loss of land, 219–221
  under-insurance, 226–227
  valued policy, 225–226
MISREPRESENTATION,
  general, 74, 78–80
  motor insurance, 309–310
  practice, 96–98
MISTAKE,
  contract of insurance, 72
  contract of settlement, 212–214
MORAL HAZARD, 90–94
MORTGAGES,
  contribution, 262
  insurable interest, 43–44, 52
  measure of indemnity, 224
  life policies, 271–272
  reinstatement, 234, 235
  subrogation, 251
MOTOR INSURANCE. *See also* MOTOR INSURERS' BUREAU.
  certificate, 296–297
  comprehensive, 292
  compulsory requirements, 293–296, 319
  conditions, 303–306
  extension of compulsory insurance, 318–320
  general, 292–320
  knock for knock agreements, 253–255
  limitation on use, 301–303
  no claims bonus, 70, 254, 293
  permitted drivers, 298–301
  policy, 296

Index

MOTOR INSURANCE—*cont.*
  public policy, 193–194
  statutory duty, 297–298
  third parties' rights, 306–311
  third party, 292
  use, 294–296
MOTOR INSURERS' BUREAU,
  enforcement, 317
  generally, 311–318, 320
  joinder, 317–318
  substituted service, 318
  uninsured drivers, 312–313, 320
  untraced drivers, 313–317

NON-DISCLOSURE,
  during contract, 94–96
  facts not needing to be disclosed, 85–87
  generally, 80–98
  insurer's duty, 80–81
  knowledge of proposer, 83–84
  material facts, 89–94
  materiality, evidence, 89
  materiality, test, 87–89
  moral hazard, 90–94
  motor insurance, 309–310
  opinion, 83–84
  physical hazard, 90
  rationale, 82–83
  renewal, 68, 82
  reform and practice, 96–98
  statement of fact, 83
  waiver, 86–87

PERSONAL INSURANCES ARBITRATION SERVICE, 4–5
POLICY,
  definition of insurance, 11–14
  motor insurance, 296
POLICYHOLDER, 7. *See also* POLICYHOLDERS' PROTECTION ACT.
POLICYHOLDERS' PROTECTION ACT, 22–23, 312
PREMIUMS,
  calculation, 121, 262–264
  need for, 121
  payment, 121–123
  payment as precondition, 55–56
  return of, illegality, 125–127
  return of, total failure of consideration, 124–125
PREVENTION COSTS, 182–184

PROPERTY INSURANCE. *See* BAILMENT, FIRE INSURANCE, GOODS, INSURABLE INTEREST IN PROPERTY INSURANCE, LANDLORD AND TENANT, MORTGAGES, REAL PROPERTY, VENDOR AND PURCHASER.
PROPOSAL FORMS,
  agent's completion, 111–116
  clauses descriptive of risk, 109–111
  incorporation by basis clause, 106–108
  offer, 53–54
  statements of practice, 53, 90, 98, 120
  waiver of duty of disclosure, 86–87
PROXIMATE CAUSE,
  accident cases, 186–188
  competing causes, 188–189
  generally, 185–189
  meaning, 185
  no excepted peril, 185, 189
PUBLIC POLICY,
  comments, 197–198
  compulsory insurances, 193–195
  first party insurances, 190–192
  motor insurance, 193–194
  third party insurances, 192–197

RATEABLE PROPORTION, 259
REAL PROPERTY,
  contribution, 261–262
  insurable interest. *See* INSURABLE INTEREST IN PROPERTY INSURANCE.
  Life Assurance Act, 36–39
  partial loss, 221–223
  sale of, 128–130, 132–134
  third parties' interests, 50–52
  total loss, 219–221
REGULATION OF INSURANCE,
  insurers, 15–22
  intermediaries, 151–156
  policy terms, 4, 159
  premiums, 121
  self-regulation, 4–5 *and see* INSURANCE OMBUDSMAN, *Statements of Insurance, Practice.*
REHABILITATION OF OFFENDERS ACT, 93–94
REINSTATEMENT,
  contractual, 229–232
  double insurance, 261–262
  insurable interest, 38–39, 51

REINSTATEMENT—*cont.*
  statutory, 232–234
  third party's right, 235
RENEWAL, 67–68, 70–71
RIOT, 165
RISK, 8, 161–163

SALE OF GOODS,
  assignment, 130–132, 134–135
  insurable interest, 42
SETTLEMENT OF CLAIMS,
  generally, 211–214
  liability insurance, 284–288, 291
STATEMENTS OF INSURANCE PRACTICE, 4,
    53–54, 78, 87, 90, 97–98, 103, 106,
    120, 159, 199, 303, 305
SUBROGATION,
  application, 236–237
  assignment compared, 249
  contractual, 237–238, 245, 246,
    249–251, 257
  contribution compared, 259
  control of proceedings, 245–246
  denial of, 255–257
  full indemnity, 240–241, 244–245
  future of, 257–258
  gifts, 241–242
  insured may not profit, 239–243
  insured must have right to sue, 248
  insured's duty, 246–247
  insured's right to take action,
    243–257
  interest, 248–249
  meaning, 238–239
  origins, 237–238
  surplus, 242–243
  two or more persons interested,
    251–253
  waiver, 253–255
SUICIDE, 161, 191–192
SUM INSURED,
  contribution, 262–264
  employers' liability insurance,
    326
  generally, 215–216
  liability insurance, 288, 289–291
  motor insurance, 319
SURRENDER, 69
SURRENDER VALUE, 69, 270

TEMPORARY COVER. *See* COVER-NOTES.
TERMS. *See* CONDITIONS, CLAUSES
    DESCRIPTIVE OF THE RISK,
    CONSTRUCTION, WARRANTIES.

THIRD PARTY INSURANCE. *See* LIABILITY
    INSURANCE.
TOTAL LOSS, 216–217
TRUST. *See* LIFE INSURANCE.

UBERRIMA FIDES. *See also* NON-
    DISCLOSURE.
  duty of disclosure on insured, 80,
    81–82
  duty of disclosure on insurer, 80–81
  generally, 8, 14, 80
  throughout policy, 210
UNDER-INSURANCE,
  average, 227
  effect, 226–227
UNFAIR CONTRACT TERMS ACT, 8,
    13–14, 159
UTMOST GOOD FAITH. *See* NON-
    DISCLOSURE, UBERRIMA FIDES.

VALUED POLICIES, 225–226
VENDOR AND PURCHASER,
  contribution, 262
  insurable interest, 43–44, 50–52
  real property, 128–130, 132–134
  reinstatement, 234
  sale of goods, 42, 130–132, 134–135
  subrogation, 239, 252
VOID CONTRACTS AND POLICIES, 72–73
VOIDABLE CONTRACTS AND POLICIES.
    See also FRAUD,
    MISREPRESENTATION, MISTAKE,
    NON-DISCLOSURE, WARRANTIES.
  generally, 74–75
  loss of right to avoid, 76–77

WAGER, 24, 25, 36
WAIVER,
  claims, 206–209
  disclosure, 86–87
  insurable interest, 44–45
  liability insurance, 286
  subrogation, 253–255
WARRANTIES,
  basis of the contract clause, 79,
    106–108
  clauses descriptive of the risk
    distinguished, 109–111
  conditions distinguished, 74,
    104–105
  creation, 103–108
  effect of breach, 100
  employers' liability insurance,
    324–326

WARRANTIES—*cont.*
  interpretation, 108
  meaning, 74, 101
  motor insurance, 303–306, 307, 310
  nature, 74, 101
  opinion, 103

WARRANTIES—*cont.*
  prefect or past, 101
  promissory, 101–103
  reform and practice, 119–120
  strict compliance, 99–100
WEAR AND TEAR, 162–163